Plato's Sun-Like Good

Plato's Sun-Like Good is a revolutionary discussion of the *Republic*'s philosopher-rulers, their dialectic, and their relation to the form of the good. With detailed arguments Sarah Broadie explains how, if we think of the form of the good as 'interrogative', we can re-conceive those central reference-points of Platonism in down-to-earth terms without loss to our sense of Plato's philosophical greatness. The book's main aims are, first, to show how for Plato the form of the good is of practical value in a way that we can understand; secondly, to make sense of the connection he draws between dialectic and the form of the good; and thirdly, to make sense of the relationship between the form of the good and other forms while respecting the contours of the sun-good analogy and remaining faithful to the text of the *Republic* itself.

SARAH BROADIE is Bishop Wardlaw Professor of Philosophy at the University of St Andrews. She is author of *Aristotle and Beyond: Essays on Metaphysics and Ethics* (Cambridge University Press, 2007) and *Nature and Divinity in Plato's 'Timaeus'* (Cambridge University Press, 2011), and editor of *Aristotle's Nicomachean Ethics: A Philosophical Introduction and Commentary* (2002). She has published dozens of book chapters and articles on Plato and Aristotle, and was awarded an OBE in 2019 for services to classical philosophy.

T0370732

Plato's Sun-Like Good

Dialectic in the Republic

Sarah Broadie

University of St Andrews

CAMBRIDGE
UNIVERSITY PRESS

Shaftesbury Road, Cambridge CB2 8EA, United Kingdom

One Liberty Plaza, 20th Floor, New York, NY 10006, USA

477 Williamstown Road, Port Melbourne, VIC 3207, Australia

314–321, 3rd Floor, Plot 3, Splendor Forum, Jasola District Centre, New Delhi – 110025, India

103 Penang Road, #05–06/07, Visioncrest Commercial, Singapore 238467

Cambridge University Press is part of Cambridge University Press & Assessment, a department of the University of Cambridge.

We share the University's mission to contribute to society through the pursuit of education, learning and research at the highest international levels of excellence.

www.cambridge.org
Information on this title: www.cambridge.org/9781009016407

DOI: 10.1017/9781009025379

© Sarah Broadie 2021

This publication is in copyright. Subject to statutory exception and to the provisions of relevant collective licensing agreements, no reproduction of any part may take place without the written permission of Cambridge University Press & Assessment.

First published 2021
First paperback edition 2023

A catalogue record for this publication is available from the British Library

Library of Congress Cataloging-in-Publication data
Names: Broadie, Sarah, author.
Title: Plato's sun-like good : dialectic in the Republic / Sarah Broadie.
Description: First edition. | Cambridge, United Kingdom ; New York, NY, USA: Cambridge University Press, 2021. | Includes bibliographical references and index.
Identifiers: LCCN 2021019444 (print) | LCCN 2021019445 (ebook) | ISBN 9781316516874 (hardback) | ISBN 9781009016407 (paperback) | ISBN 9781009025379 (epub)
Subjects: LCSH: Plato. Republic. | Good and evil.
Classification: LCC B398.G65 B76 2021 (print) | LCC B398.G65 (ebook) | DDC 321/ .07–dc23
LC record available at https://lccn.loc.gov/2021019444
LC ebook record available at https://lccn.loc.gov/2021019445

ISBN   978-1-316-51687-4   Hardback
ISBN   978-1-009-01640-7   Paperback

Cambridge University Press & Assessment has no responsibility for the persistence or accuracy of URLs for external or third-party internet websites referred to in this publication and does not guarantee that any content on such websites is, or will remain, accurate or appropriate.

The philosophers' motto: *illuminatio dominus meus*

Contents

Acknowledgements

I have had the opportunity to present a few parts of this book to many audiences, provoking much helpful discussion. The work has also benefited from probing comments on earlier drafts by Rachel Barney, Sean Kelsey, Tony Long, Mitchell Miller, Richard Patterson, and Christopher Rowe. The most recent version owes significant improvements to Alex Long and Barbara Sattler, and to an anonymous reader for Cambridge University Press. I warmly thank all these scholars for their generosity.

Parts of Sections 2.3 and 4.3 were delivered as the 2020 Aquinas Lecture at Marquette University. I am grateful to Dr James South, Director of Marquette University Press, for the Press's permission to reproduce that material here.

Part 1 Approaching the Sun-Good Analogy

1.1 Introductory

'In the case of things that are seen, I think you'll say that the sun is cause not only of their being able to be seen, but also of their coming-into-being, their growth and their sustenance – even while not itself *being* coming-into-being.'

'Yes, of course.'
'Just so, in the case of things that are known, you need to say not only that being known belongs to them because of the good, but also that being and reality [or: essence] accrue to them because of it, even while the good itself is not reality [or: essence], but is even beyond reality [or: essence], superior to it in dignity and power.'

(Republic 509b1–9)[1]

These words round off the great parallel by which Plato illustrates the good, or the form of the good,[2] through analogy with the sun.[3] This book is an attempt to understand the epistemology and ontology of that superlative form. According to the *Republic*, the form of the good is somehow central to the intellectual method that characterizes truly excellent rulers. So, the book is equally about this method, which Plato calls 'dialectic'.

Dialectic is the kind of thinking practised by philosophers, so dialectical rulers are rulers who are philosophers. Rather than turning straight to Plato's analogy between the form of the good and the sun, it makes sense to approach from an earlier point, the point where philosophical rule is introduced as a requirement of the truly good human society. Socrates puts forward this thesis expecting it to drench him with a

[1] Throughout I follow S. R. Slings's Oxford Classical Text of the *Republic* (2003). I mainly use Christopher Rowe's 2012 translation of that edition with occasional modifications.
[2] These expressions are close to being intersubstitutable in the part of the *Republic* that concerns us. Crombie 1962, 111 n. 2; Delcomminette 2006, 2: 'qu'est-ce que l'Idée du bien sinon le bien considéré come *objet de connaissance*?'; also Penner 2007a, 118–20; Rowe 2007a, 138–45; 2007c, 244. In contexts such as 'X knows/does not know –', 'X inquires about –', it seems indifferent whether one completes them with 'the good', 'what the good is', 'the form of the good', 'the good as such', or 'the good abstractly conceived'. Also, although the *form* of the good is not of or for anyone, it does not follow that there is no such thing as my good or yours. I use 'form' for both *idea* and *eidos* in the text.
[3] For a very clear exposition of the analogy see Ferrari 2013, 158–62.

1

huge wave of scornful laughter (473c–d). This is the last and, he thinks, the most absurd-seeming of his three subversive proposals concerning the truly good city-state; the others were education for leadership of girls and women on the same terms as boys and men, and elimination of individual families within the guardian sector (451c–464d). The third proposal is distinctive in being said to represent not only a feature of the truly good city-state but the single least change (presumably, the single least disruptive change) needed to bring such an entity into existence (473b). If and only if supreme power is joined with philosophy, whether by philosophers becoming rulers or rulers becoming philosophers, can the truly good city come into being.[4] And the truly good city is not mere fantasy, a unicorn somewhere over the rainbow. It is a real possibility, Socrates emphasizes, even though its likelihood is remote (499b–d; cf. 502a–c)[5]. Hence combining philosophy with power is a real possibility too.

But before entering into any detail about philosophy's intellectual contribution to the task of ruling, Socrates must dispel false assumptions about philosophy. One stumbling block is that the word 'philosophy' suggests an unbounded, even omnivorous passion for wisdom and learning (474c8–475c): but then there is a question of what to mean by 'learning'. Those people who run about Athens and Attica attending each and every spectacle and show with indiscriminate passion – aren't they in some sense learning things at each encounter, so that the experiences they love so insatiably could be called experiences of 'learning'? Whereas true philosophers love to learn *truth* and to acquire *knowledge*, and truth and the objects of knowledge are not mere 'sights and sounds' but changeless intelligible forms, which to the lovers of sights and sounds are unreal and meaningless (475d–476d). Still, the lovers of sights and sounds cannot be expected simply to concede that what they pursue is something other than real knowledge (since then they would be admitting that what they so keenly do is inferior). So, Socrates offers an argument to persuade them that at best they acquire opinion (*doxa*), not knowledge (476d–484a).[6]

Next, Socrates argues that the true philosopher's passion for truth brings with it a train of moral and intellectual virtues such as moderation, liberality, courage, justice, gentleness, good memory, quickness to learn (485c–487a). He then addresses a series of popular misunderstandings and bad images of philosophy: philosophers are useless; some of the most obvious examples are morally corrupt

---

[4] On 'if and only if' see D. Morrison 2007, 236 with n. 8.

[5] I follow, e.g., Burnyeat 1992, D. Morrison 2007, and Vegetti 2013a, in taking the claim of real possibility to be sincere. Whether it is realistic is another question. On the problem of feasibility see Annas 2017, 23–30. Socrates is careful not to set the standard unrealistically high: he says that the main question of the *Republic*, whether justice is good for the just person, does not depend on assuming that a perfectly just person is possible, and then he interprets his claim about the good city's possibility as a claim about *approximating* the Callipolis portrayed in words (472b–473b). For an interesting complex discussion see Schofield 2006, ch. 5.

[6] The argument is discussed in Section 2.19.

and sell their souls to public opinion; certain low-grade small-souled intellectual dabblers have usurped the honorific description 'philosopher'; philosophy is not a serious occupation for mature people but a brief stage of youthful education to be left behind or dipped into as an occasional pastime (487c–498a).[7] But none of these impressions, Socrates contends, is the fault of philosophy itself as distinct from its contingent social and cultural circumstances. If the misconceptions were cleared away, ordinary people, initially hostile, could be persuaded that philosophers should be their rulers (499d–500b; 501c–502a).[8]

1.2   The Philosopher-Rulers' Intellectual Task

Next, after a reflection on the fact that all-round excellence, moral and intellectual, depends on a combination of characteristics not easily found together (503b–d), Socrates makes the *Republic*'s first allusion to the *topics* which philosopher-rulers must be capable of handling. He begins by speaking of them simply as 'the most important things to learn' (*ta megista mathēmata*, 503e3). 'But what exactly are these?' asks Adeimantus. Socrates' response, which refers Adeimantus back to an earlier moment in the dialogue, is a pointer rather than a direct clarification:

'You probably remember', I said, 'that after distinguishing three kinds of element in the soul we tried to reach conclusions about justice, moderation, courage and wisdom, and say what each of them is.'
    'If I didn't remember that', he said, 'I'd deserve not to hear the rest.' (504a)

This refers back to Book IV, 441e–442d, thereby suggesting that the 'things most important to learn' are the natures of the four main virtues; and this impression is not cancelled by anything that comes later. But instead of now going on to say more about the virtues, as one might expect, Socrates refers Adeimantus back yet again to some still earlier remarks about method. He says:

'So do you also remember what we said before that?'

'What was that?'

'I think what we were trying to say was that in order to get the finest view possible of the things in question,[9] we'd need to take another and longer way round, and then

---

[7] See Vegetti 2001, 269–74 on a range of cultural reasons why rule by philosophers must have seemed 'un scandaleux paradoxe'.

[8] Roslyn Weiss has proposed the daring thesis that the central books of the *Republic* feature two 'distinct and irreconcilable portraits of the philosopher', 'the philosopher by nature' and 'the philosopher by design' (Weiss, 2012). Weiss's arguments, even if convincing, are mostly orthogonal to the concerns of this book, which are the metaphysics and epistemology of *Republic* V–VII. It seems that her two philosophers differ not in metaphysics and epistemology but in moral character.

[9] 'The things in question' may refer to the virtues or the elements in the soul, or both. There is the same ambiguity in 'this matter' at Book IV, 435d1–3, on which passage see below in the main text. The interpreter must decide whether the main topic of the 'longer and more exact way' will be the soul, mentioned explicitly just before, at 435c5, or the virtues. If the latter, 435c5 ff. must

they'd become clearly visible to us, but that meanwhile it would be possible to apply proofs that were on the same level as the things we'd been saying up to that point. You people said that that was enough for you, and it was on this understanding that we said what we said then – to me, it seemed to lack exactness (*tēs men akribeias ... ellipē*); whether you were happy with it is for you to say.'

'It seemed to me to deal with the subject in due measure,' he said, 'and so it did to the others too.' (504a9–b)

This interchange refers to Book IV, 435c9–d7, a moment in the run-up to the proof that the soul has three elements analogous to the three classes in the city. Justice and the other three main virtues have already been defined for the city in terms of its three classes. Socrates then pointed out that these definitions can be transferred to the virtues in the individual provided it can be shown that the individual soul is made up of factors sufficiently analogous to the classes in the city. Soon will come the proof that the soul does have the right kind of tripartite structure and that its virtues correspond to those of the city; and the resulting definition of justice in the individual will supposedly make it impossible to deny the main theorem of the *Republic*: that justice is a better condition for the individual than injustice. But, before initiating those important arguments, Socrates emphasized that the style of approach he and his companions are using, while adequate for the current purpose, is incapable of giving them 'an *exact* hold on this matter' (*akribōs men touto ... ou mē pote labōmen*): attaining an exact hold would require going by a different road, one that would be longer and more challenging (435d3).

When in Book IV we worked towards those major conclusions about the anatomy of the soul, the associated definitions of the virtues, and the goodness of justice for the just soul itself, we may not have paid much attention to Plato's warning that we were following an intellectually inferior path for understanding the virtues. But now in Book VI, after the concept of the philosopher-ruler has been defended at length, we are told in effect that what the *Republic* has taught us so far concerning the things most important to learn

---

be read on the spot as referring to the tripartite psychology about to be presented on the shorter way; but it must also, when we get to the back-reference at VI, 504a–b, be read retrospectively as pointing to the topic of the virtues as studied by the trainee rulers (but not by the characters of the *Republic* nor by us) on the longer way. This discrepancy is certainly a bit awkward, but not deeply surprising given that composition of the huge *Republic* was probably intermittent. Penner 2007b, 26–30, argues convincingly that the discrepancy is minor given the close relationship between the tripartite psychology and the virtues as defined in Book IV, and that the longer way will say more about the virtues (although now involving the form of the good); see also Sedley 2013, 76; Scott 2015, 44–5; Rowett 2018, 143. I follow this general interpretation, but without sharing Penner's view that the longer road is entered by Socrates and his interlocutors, hence by the reader. Rowe thinks that the longer way treats of the soul and includes the argument in Book X about the soul's simplicity and immortality (Rowe 2007c, ch. 5; see also Scott 2015, 53; for objections Szlezák 2015, 247–50).

about, namely the virtues, falls decidedly short of what learning about them would be if it were conducted with full exactness.

So, what have we, along with the interlocutors of Socrates, been missing? Well, nothing that we needed in order to get this far in the argument of the *Republic*. For in calling the approach 'inexact' Socrates does not say it was wrong to adopt it. After all, it was he who ushered his interlocutors and us along that path. It was good enough for them and us. What he does now say is that the inexact approach would be unacceptable for the guardian of the ideal city and its laws. The inexact approach is lazy (at least for anyone able to follow the exact one) and laziness 'is the last thing we want to find in someone guarding the city and its laws' (504c5–7). The ruler-guardian's task, even if not ours, is 'to go round by the longer route and work just as hard at his studies as he does in the gymnasium, or else . . . he'll never get to the end of the most important thing to learn (*to megiston mathēma*), and the one that is most appropriate to him' (504c9–d3).

Let us postpone the question of Socrates' shift here, unexplained, from plural to singular: from speaking, as before (503e3), of the *things* most important to learn to speaking now of the *thing* most important to learn. Let us first try to get a grip on the charge of inexactness.

The Book IV definitions of the virtues in both city and individual soul were given in terms of the different parts and their distinct functions. The entity is wise just in case the part that ought to rule, reason, rules the others and does so from knowledge of what is in the interest of the whole and each part; it is courageous iff the part that ought to execute the ruler's prescriptions can be counted on to do so despite distracting pains and pleasures; it is moderate iff all three parts share the belief that reason should rule; and it is just iff every part performs its proper function (428d–433d; 441e–443d). The just individual, and presumably also the just city, will call 'just' or 'unjust' whatever action preserves or disrupts the correct internal arrangement, and will call the attitude that issues in such action 'wisdom' or 'ignorance' as the case may be (443e–444a).[10] All this says very little about what exactly wisdom knows or how it gets to know it. How does wisdom determine what would be in the interest of the whole and each part, and what it would be just and harmony-preserving to do? Granted, the Book IV account of wisdom and justice is enough to answer the main question of the *Republic*, whether justice is to the just person's advantage or benefit; but as an account of what specific sorts of conduct justice demands and how wisdom determines answers to such specific questions, it is unsatisfactorily sketchy and thin.

---

[10] On what this 'calling' amounts to, see Section 2.20.

At least, that is how it seems if we think that for us, even though we are not the rulers but are looking at them from the outside, there has to be more to say about their wisdom and its method for understanding justice and the other virtues. But one might not think that. On a first reading of the *Republic*, having reached the end of Book IV, one might have the impression that the rulers' upbringing as described in Books II–IV is enough to qualify them for rule; and we might find this conclusion satisfactory, and not expect further specification of what the wisdom and justice *are* that especially qualify them to rule. After all, many people seem to think that there is no great story to be told about how a well brought-up person, one who has absorbed good values through training and practice and the right encouragement, in obedience to good authorities and presented with none but good examples, ends up knowing what specific conduct is demanded by justice and the other virtues. We know already that Plato's guardians have had that sort of upbringing, so what more needs to be said? They are thoroughly decent people, and because it is a properly ordered city they do not have to battle to stay decent while living closely with people whose values are opposed to theirs:[11] so we can take it for granted that they will know what is just and what is not, what to enjoin and what to forbid. They will surely often have to think their way to an answer, weighing up considerations for and against, so it is certainly true that they *reason* (*logizesthai* and cognates occur at 439d–d5; 440b1–5; cf. *bouleuesthai* 353d5). But they don't have a distinct identifiable *method* for reaching their judgements. But why should that matter, given that they are reliable? What is important is that those in positions of responsibility come out with the right judgements in situations as they arise, and this is what well brought-up people, like the rulers in the *Republic*, can be trusted to do.

To Plato, at least in this dialogue, this common-sense picture of moral wisdom and moral authority is dangerously lazy if taken as the last word.[12] Good rulers are not equipped to rule simply by being decent sensible people (even if they could be relied on to remain so), and a philosophical account of the ideal ruler has to say something about what more is needed.[13] Of course,

---

[11] The guardian class lives segregated from ordinary citizens.

[12] Cf. the myth of Er on the soul lucky enough to draw first pick for its next life. It makes an appalling choice; its level of luck is matched by the depth of its stupidity. This soul, we are told, had lived its previous life under a well-ordered constitution, *partaking of virtue through habit without philosophy* (619b6–d1). The same danger presumably awaits non-philosophical citizens even of Callipolis.

[13] Cf. Shorey 1895, 219–20. The present discussion assumes that the options are rule by common sense unbolstered by any special intellectual training versus rule by philosophy understood as Plato understands it. (His conception of *philosophia* was not uncontested when he wrote the *Republic*, as we know from the works of his contemporary, Isocrates.) But in the actual culture a third option might have suggested itself: rule by something like the supposed expertise in management and politics offered in the fifth century by Protagoras (cf. 600c–d and *Protagoras*

philosophy as exemplified by Socrates cannot give a complete *a priori* catalogue of things that it would be just for ideal rulers to prescribe (to expect *that* level of exactness would be unreasonable), but philosophy can say something definite, even if general and abstract, about the ideal rulers' kind of *method* for deciding what to prescribe. For, according to Plato, there is, in the area in which they have to operate, a rational method, not just hunches and intuitions and semi-articulated inferences of a well-nurtured moral sensibility; and applying the method sure-footedly is not easy. Applying it (and passing it on to future rulers) involves reflective, articulate, understanding of what one is doing. Hence, access to the method and practising it well requires one to be a philosopher with special intellectual training. The rulers' exercise of their special method, and the special training they need for this end, is what Socrates means by 'the longer route'.

We and Socrates' interlocutors, and even Socrates himself, cannot explore the philosopher-rulers' specific practical decisions or their rationales.[14] The philosopher-rulers develop and exercise the wisdom for ruling by following the longer way, but Socrates and his interlocutors do not take that path and are not going to acquire that wisdom, at least so far as it concerns rulers.[15] Even so, Socrates must not conclude the philosophical defence of justice (or for that matter the defence of philosophy) before saying something *about* the longer way and the special method on which the rulers depend. He must at least say enough to explain why the best rulers have to be philosophers. Everyone would agree that wisdom should rule: this is a banal truism. But with 'wisdom' interpreted as some sort of *philosophical expertise* it becomes a surprising,

---

318d–319a); see A. G. Long 2013b. Plato ignores this because, as emerged in the *Protagoras*, Protagorean political wisdom apart from its rhetorical element turns out to be, at best, much the same as common-sense decency (*Protagoras* 327e–328b). In the *Republic* the sophists, presumably including Protagoras, are more darkly represented as knowing only the opinions and feelings of the mob, along with tricks for manipulating them (493a–d).

[14] On 'practical decisions': this is as good a place as any to confront the well-known problem posed by the *Republic* doctrine that particular objects of sense cannot be objects of knowledge (*epistēmē*) or intelligence (*noēsis*); see especially the argument against the sight-lovers (476d–480a). The problem seems to threaten the very notion of philosopher-rulers: as philosophers they must have knowledge of values, but as rulers ('returned to the cave') they must be intelligent about concrete particulars. But the main point is that because of their commerce with the forms, the returners have a more expert grasp of particulars than anyone else (*muriōi beltion ... gnōsesthe hekasta ta eidola hatta esti kai hōn*, 520c4); whether this is called *epistēmē* may seem unimportant. There is room to say that while they see each particular *as* an instance of some form which they have explored when beyond the cave, their cognitive contact with the particular as such is informed perception, not 'intelligence' or 'knowledge'; see Moss 2021, ch. 4, section 5. Another possibility is that the cognitive demotion of sense experience is restricted to when a sensible object is presented in response to a question like 'What is beauty?' (Penner 1987, 109–13). Philosophers back in the cave no longer seek answers to such questions but apply answers they have discovered in the upper world.

[15] Cf. Rowett 2018, 143–5.

even paradoxical, claim. To show that the claim is nonetheless a truth, Plato must remove false images of philosophy, as we have seen, but he must also explain or at least sketch what philosophy actually offers that rulers need. This is what he tries to do in Books V–VII of the *Republic*. He has to make it clear that (a) there is much more to be known about justice and the other virtues than we needed to know in order to follow the main argument that justice is good in itself for the agent, even though (b) *we* cannot know this 'great deal more' so far as it concerns the rulers; and he has to make it clear that (c) the knowledge of this 'great deal more' in anyone who does possess such knowledge is not a miraculous gift or the sturdy natural offshoot of non-intellectual good upbringing, but is to be attained through use of an identifiable rational method, a method whose general nature can be explained to us even if only in abstract outline. (This method is going to be called 'dialectic' or 'dialectical'.)[16] For us to be rationally convinced that rulers must be philosophers, we don't need to know or be able to find out everything that philosopher-rulers would know; but if their method could not even be delineated to us, then we would have from Plato a mere dogmatic assertion (however dressed up) that rulers need something called 'philosophy'.[17] We might accept this, but our acceptance would be mindless, not based on understanding.[18]

---

[16] Why does Socrates call the longer way 'another, longer, way *round*' (*allē makrotera ... periodos ... perielthonti*, 504b2)? Perhaps because it involves the dialectician-rulers in the same task, in a sense, as the one he himself undertook at 368c6–7, namely the pinning down of what justice is (along with the other three cardinal virtues, all four being mentioned at 504a4–6). Socrates and his imagined rulers pose and answer the same question, but at different levels, as we shall see. A longer way to the (in a sense) same destination is naturally called 'circuitous'; see LSJ *perierchomai* I.1. (I am not convinced that *makrotera periodos* implies that the 'shorter way' is also a circuit, *pace* Scott 2015, 84.)

[17] Giving us a sense of their method might be unnecessary if it doesn't matter what their philosophizing consists of as long as they philosophize; for instance, if 'The best rulers are reluctant rulers' (519c–521b; 540b2–5; cf. 347b–d) were a sufficient reason for installing *philosopher*-rulers, who (it is assumed) would readily relinquish power on account of their love affair with philosophy. In such a scenario there need be no connection between the content of their philosophizing and their wise government: any consuming hobby, e.g. horsemanship (cf. Antiphon, *Parmenides* 126c), would provide suitably reluctant rulers. It hardly needs saying that for Plato there is more to the value of rule by philosophers than their willingness to *retire* from ruling; see e.g. the sea-captain simile, 488a–489c.

[18] The fact that rule by philosophers in the good city corresponds to rule by wise *reason* in the individual explains why the other two soul-parts are not topics of Books VI–VII. The silence is not evidence that Socrates now explains the human soul in terms of intellect alone, thereby reverting to the monistic psychology of earlier dialogues, as has been suggested by Sedley 2013. In fact, as Sedley himself notes, 490b3–4, 518c4–d1, 527d8, and 532c6 imply that there is more to the soul than intellect. The claim that the true philosopher will not be a lover of bodily pleasures or of money because all his passions (*epithumiai*) are channelled towards learning (485d6–e2) is hardly evidence that the tripartite psychology has been suspended (thus Sedley 2013, 79). It is common sense, regardless of one's psychological theory, that strong interest in one thing distracts from others (cf. Aristotle, *Nicomachean Ethics* 1175b3–15, on pleasure). Again, the central books' statement (505e1–2) that the good is what every soul pursues, doing

1.3   'The Most Important Thing to Learn': Between Plural and Singular

Let us return to Socrates' slide from the plural to the singular, from 'the most important *things* to learn' (503e3; cf. 504e1–2) to 'the most important *thing* to learn' (504d2–3; cf. 504e3–4). Adeimantus is puzzled by the singular. Is Socrates still making the same point that was agreed to a moment ago, the point that the rulers must have an exact understanding (not just a sketch, *hupographē*, 504d6) of the virtues, or is he now referring to some different most important thing to learn – something more important even than the virtues (504d4–5)? Of course, the latter is the case, and, as we are about to be told, this even more important thing is the form of the good (505a2). But Socrates' teasing and confusing turn from plural to singular is designed, I take it, to convey that the topic of the virtues and the topic of the form of the good are closely intertwined without being identical. Just how we shall think they are related will depend on how we interpret the sun-analogy.

Another telling ambivalence shows up in a slightly later passage:

'At any rate,' I said, 'I imagine that [1] if it's not known exactly in what way just things and beautiful things are good these won't have acquired a guard for themselves who's worth anything very much, that is, if he lacks that knowledge; and it's my guess that [2] no one will properly know just and beautiful things before [i.e. before he knows in what way they are good].'

'That's a fair guess,' he said.

'So will the arrangements for our city be completely in order if it's a guard like this who oversees it – one who is a knower of these things[19] (*ho toutōn epistēmōn*)?'

'Surely,' he said. (506a4–b2)

In his first speech here, Socrates says that [1] good guardianship of just things and beautiful things depends on 'knowing in exactly what way they are good', and then he immediately adds that [2] not knowing in what way they are good

---

everything for its sake, etc., is not 'in *manifest* tension' (Sedley's phrase, my emphasis) with the case of wretched Leontius at 439e5–440a5. To Leontius, arguably (see Lesses 1987; Moss 2008; Ferber 2013), indulging his somewhat twisted longing *was* the good thing to do even though he also felt it as shameful. The good on that occasion appeared to him as an indecent kind of pleasure; the alternative behaviour appeared to him seemly but not good; but this is a familiar phenomenon: cf. Polus, *Gorgias* 474c–d; 475b. Still, even if the longer way does not imply revision of the tripartite psychology of Book IV, it does raise a question uncatered for by that psychology: is reason, in Aristotelian terms, fundamentally theoretical or practical – and, if both, how are these functions related? Reason in Book IV was practical (428b–d; 441e; 442c); in Books V–VII it seems much more theoretical – not least, of course, because of the rulers' special mathematical education.

[19] This phrase sits on the fence between 'knower of these things' *simpliciter* and 'knower of the way in which these things, etc. are good'.

amounts to not knowing just things and beautiful things themselves. But on the face of it this is a contradiction. Knowing in what way just things, etc. are good surely presupposes first recognizing them *as* just things; but the next sentence says that the very recognition of just things *as* just things depends on first knowing in what way they are good. This last occurrence of 'they' must refer to things that are candidates for being counted as just, etc.: then the point in [2] would be that recognizing that they really are just, etc. involves recognizing their goodness. Plato must mean us to be wondering whether the goodness that in some way belongs to just things is internal to them or somehow additional and external.

The notion of externality seemed to be in the ascendant when, slightly earlier in the text, Socrates finally named the most important thing to learn: it is the form (*idea*) of the good.

'. . . it is the form of the good that is the most important thing to learn, since it is what brings about the goodness and usefulness (*chrēsima kai ōphelima*) both of just things and of the rest.' (505a2–4)[20]

(I take 'the rest' to mean things picked out by terms for the other virtues.) The above translation has smoothed out a knotty expression. More literally, this is what Plato says:

'. . . it is the form of the good that is the most important thing to learn, <since> it is by making additional use of it [sc. the form] (*hēi proschrēsamena*) that both just things and the rest come to be good and useful.'[21]

It is as though just things, etc. come to their full fruition, whatever that amounts to, through appropriating for themselves the distinct form of the good. Whatever the full meaning of this, it shows the good as somehow added to the just things, etc., or brought to bear on them, as if it is not an intrinsic part of them. Here we are given a pre-echo of the sun-analogy: for whatever the exact relation of the literal sun to the objects it illuminates and nurtures, this sun is clearly external to them.

1.4   What Further Knowledge Does the Longer Way Achieve?

Socrates goes on to assert as common ground between himself and his current interlocutor, Adeimantus, that we do not properly know the form of the good,

---

[20] See Section 3.3 for close discussion of this passage with other translation options.

[21] A. A. Long 2020 is exceptional in commenting on *proschrēsamena*; the word is indeed, as he says, 'rather surprising'. Adam 1907, 51, glosses it with 'by *koinōnia* with the Idea of the Good'. The translations of Jowett, Shorey, Lindsay, Cornford, Grube/Reeve, Waterfield, Griffith, Leroux, Rowe, and Emlyn-Jones and Preddy play down or ignore the *pros-* prefix. Chambry, Bloom, and Rufener take some account of it; so do Lee and Vegetti in notes to their translations.

and that unless we know it all the rest of our knowledge and possessions are worthless (505a5–b4). He reminds Adeimantus that some people define the good as pleasure, and others as wisdom, and points out flaws in both definitions (505b5–d1). But one thing, he asserts, is clear about the good: everyone wants only *real* good, not specious good, whereas when it comes to just things and beautiful things many people are content to have the appearance without the reality. And *every* soul wants the good, doing everything for the sake of it even while being in the dark about what it is (505d5–506a2). It is at this point that Socrates comes out with the ambivalent declaration we examined in the previous section: a good city's guardians of just things and beautiful things must (1) know in what way just things and beautiful things are good, and (2) without knowing this, they will not properly know the just and beautiful things themselves (506a4–8).[22]

So, what is that knowledge which the guardians must have and which they can acquire only by going a longer way than that travelled by Socrates and his interlocutors, and by readers of the *Republic*? Two alternative answers suggest themselves, corresponding to whether we highlight (1) or (2) just above. One answer says that the guardians need to know in what way things correctly identified as just and beautiful are, as such, indeed also good – i.e. useful and beneficial to just agents – so that agents will never have reason to choose semblances of justice rather than the real thing. The other answer says that the guardians need to know which things are really just and beautiful, and that they attain this knowledge by getting to know in what way these things have goodness. Both answers hark back to the Book II theme of the appearance versus reality of justice (361a–362b; 363a; 365b–d; 367b6–e4). It is natural to take the first answer with the following emphasis: there is no great problem about knowing which things are really just and morally beautiful; the problem is getting people who do know this to value justice itself as a good – their own good – rather than valuing only what they can win by cheating from behind a façade of justice. In the second answer the emphasis is that the problem is in discerning which things really are just rather than merely seeming so, and the form of the good somehow helps with this.

Many scholars have endorsed the first answer understood according to the stated emphasis. But this in my view is less plausible because the knowledge it says the guardians must have – that justice is good in itself – is the conclusion which Socrates and we already possess from the argument about parts and virtues of city and individual towards the end of Book IV. Surely the guardians, since they are to be philosophers, will have imbibed that argument. For that, however, they would have not needed any longer and more exact way

---

[22] See also 534c4–5, which couples knowing the form of the good with knowing other good things, but without the ambivalence discussed.

than has already been successfully travelled by Socrates and his friends.[23] Surely, though, the philosopher-rulers' trumpeted and to us enigmatic longer way must accomplish more than the disparaged shorter way, which had already been expounded and traversed before Socrates even started to construct the philosopher-side of the philosopher-ruler identified with the third wave in Book V.

So, we are thrown on to the second answer: the guardians, through some sort of reference to the good, must be able to recognize which specific things are really just and beautiful.[24] This, in my view, is the main thing required of the guardians according to Books VI and VII. Explaining this will be the agenda in much of what lies ahead in this book.

Finally, in Part 1: when we come to grips with the sun-analogy and its close sequent the image of the divided line, we shall have to make a decision about the import of Socrates' rejection of those two definitions of the good, as wisdom and as pleasure. Is the message that these attempts to state the nature of the good were naïve and misguided, but some other attempt, perhaps more sophisticated and *recherché*, open only to specially trained philosophers, would in principle be successful? Or is the message that 'wisdom' and 'pleasure' between them exhaust the range of possible definitions of the good, or at any rate, are so typical that others would fare no better? In the latter case, the good or the form of the good does not contribute to the philosopher's dialectical journey as a nature grasped in correct definition.[25] So it must contribute in some other way.

---

[23] In any case they would not have needed the shorter way's *argument* to convince them since their strict moral upbringing will have taught them to value justice for its own sake. It may seem that 445b5–7, referring to what immediately precedes, supports the first answer about what is learnt on the longer way of Books V – VII. But the passage does not address the longer way. It points ahead to VIII and IX: specifically, to what we learn about the internal benefit of justice by considering the types of unjust souls and cities.

[24] Just as Socrates and his companions must be able to recognize the virtues of potential rulers and friends. 'And there's a need to be particularly on the watch', I said, 'when it comes to moderation, and courage, and high-mindedness, and all the other parts of virtue, to ensure that spurious examples don't pass themselves off as genuine. If ever there is less than a complete understanding of how to look for things like this, whether on the part of an individual or a city, then without knowing it people start employing cripples and pretenders for whatever they happen to get from them, whether <they employ them> as friends or as rulers' (536a). For the translation see Adam 1907, 146. The thought is already present in Book III, 402b9–c8.

[25] Cf. Rowett 2018, 148–50.

Part 2 The Form of the Good and Knowledge

2.1 Sun, Cave, and Sun Again

What is the purpose of the sun-image?[1] The question may seem misplaced. We virtually identify Plato as the philosopher who created this mega-famous emblem of the good, so isn't it strange to ask *why* he did, as if there needs to be a middle term, an explanation? Yet, if we think of Plato in the midst of writing rather than as author of the finished work by which his name would be known forever after, it makes sense to wonder why he chose to fashion this simile rather than get straight to the point in plain words. The point in plain words is that the good is what causes the intelligibles to be known and even to be (509b5–9). In the hypothetical scenario of Plato's having Socrates just state this straight out, surely Glaucon or Adeimantus, the main interlocutors, (given their profile so far) would have had to be made to ask: 'But what is that supposed to mean, Socrates?' or 'Huh?' And even Plato might have been at a loss to imagine how Socrates could have answered them in yet plainer words. As it is, they are given the sun-image, which stuns them into acquiescence. And no doubt Plato would be hoping to stun his readers too, if not into acceptance at least into willingness to grant the idea, whatever it amounts to, a chance – let it sink in so that we wait to see if what follows helps make it more intelligible. I assume that Plato aims to get us on to a ledge, albeit a narrow one, between dismissive bafflement and blind acceptance. The state between would be a state, not yet of understanding, but of receptivity to whatever clues to understanding might lurk in whatever comes next.

So here is imagery doing its familiar job of going proxy for plain argument or explanation. In this case Plato's purpose (I think) is to gain time for something a bit more like explanation by throwing the sun-image out to us first. But this is very far from being the only or most interesting effect of the sun-image. Let us now think about it first by itself, and then along with its fellow, that of the cave.

---

[1] It is, of course, because of this image and the surrounding analogy that 'sun-like good' is in the title of this volume. But Plato uses the word 'sun-like', *hēlioeidēs* (apparently coined by him for this context), not of the form of the good but of the eye, 'the most sun-like of the organs of sense' (508b3–4), and of vision and light (508e5–509a2).

The Sun on first encounter seems to be a straightforwardly happy picture, whereas the Cave will be anything but straightforwardly happy. It will not merely *say* that the primitive human condition is one of being seriously out of touch with real values: it means to plunge us into deep anxiety for *ourselves* on this score (514a2; 515a5). For making us aware that our hitherto comfortable unreflective life is repulsive and humiliating is a step towards the concrete practicability of a city ruled by reason (see Section 1.1): such a city can only begin to be built when enough of us become conscious of our deficiency and start to find it hateful. At any rate, what is at stake for the cave-prisoners – what they lack but might attain – gains its meaning from the already presented epistemology of the Sun. But the two similes are also connected retroactively. The Sun undergoes a gestalt shift between when we first encounter it, on its own, and when we look back at it after encountering the Cave. On the first occasion the Sun is simply majestic and beneficent. The picture is of a serene set of relationships in which all is as it should be. 'Vision' (i.e. the activity of seeing) is in the eyes, and they see clearly (*saphōs*), because the sun carries out its appointed task of shedding its light on the visible objects. The imagery is set up so that the sun as source of light stands out as crucial in the causation of seeing. Seeing requires eyes with the power to see and coloured objects to be seen, but these two factors are presented as preconditions. Their presence is necessary but insufficient because they are unable to work unless they work together, and for that they need something additional to yoke them, namely light from the sun (507c–508a). Then and only then is there actual vision of the objects. It is taken for granted that the eyes themselves are in good working order: given the objects, *all* that eyes need is that third, yoking, factor, the sunlight, so that, given it, they immediately see, and see well. The analogy, then, on first encounter invites the deceptively simple conclusion that the intellect too just knows the intelligible objects when and only when the form of the good is present as source of intellectual illumination. We may certainly wonder what this last condition amounts to, but what the image plainly says is that there *is* an intellect, and there *are* intelligible objects, and that all they need so as to be joined as actual knowers and known is the intellectual light that comes from the presence of the form of the good. It is this last part that is puzzling and absorbs our attention: *how* exactly does the form of the good provide the illumination that tips the previously disjunct partners over from the potentiality to the actuality of being knower and known? (Or: what exactly *is* the form of the good that it does this?) In this perspective, just as we take it for granted that the intelligible objects are there, so we take it for granted that the intellect is ready to do its work, passing straight into actual knowing and understanding given the presence of the good. It is as if its ability to do this is as unremarkable as the eye's ability to pass from not seeing things to seeing them given the presence of the sun.

But at this point one might get a sense of suddenly being in very elevated territory. Since the form of the good is eternal, it is always and necessarily present, and the same is true for the other intelligibles. But what about the intellect? Is Socrates talking about a similarly elevated intellect – an intellect that is always actively knowing and understanding the forms because it is always in a situation in which all the conditions are present? But if so, how can he still be talking about what seemed to be the topic of his discussion so far, namely the wisdom of *human* rulers and *their* 'greatest thing to learn'? For human is what rulers even of Callipolis are; yet it is typical of the human intellect often to be almost unaware of its own existence and power, and to exercise itself not in knowledge but in false or baseless opinion. And even the most highly educated human intellects are sometimes asleep or distracted. Has Socrates skipped out of the groove of the main conversation into something theological?

This particular puzzlement is an effect of a first-time encounter with the sun-analogy. It is dispelled once we experience the allegory of the cave. In putting them together we follow the instruction at 517a–b6 where Socrates, having just presented the Cave, says that this image 'as a whole should be connected with (*proshapteon*) what was being said before', and then reprises the sun-analogy, interpreting the cave-world as the visible realm and the fire in the cave as the sun.[2] The Cave shows that the intellectual condition presupposed in the sun-analogy is one that humans can attain but only with great difficulty. We are born far short of it and it develops in us only if we go out of our way and struggle for it ourselves. The reader now sees how much the Sun left unsaid when it showed, as if this were the most natural thing in the world, the intellect getting the benefit of intellectual vision as smoothly as healthy eyes enjoy the benefit of sensory vision in sunlight. We were absurdly naïve, we are now in a position to realize, if at first we took the sun-analogy to apply to us straight-forwardly just like that. The naïveté was not in our lacking a clear grasp of exactly *how* the form of the good does for the intellect what the sun does for the eyes (this is indeed still mysterious and it is hardly naïve to be baffled by it at this stage), but in our taking it for granted that there is no problem about how the human intellect itself comes to be in the condition it needs to be in if the form of the good is to bring it cognitive benefit. If, on the other hand, we were wary here instead of naïve, we might have been drawn to the perplexing conclusion that Socrates, unaccountably, must have strayed into talking just about a divine intellect.

From the Cave we infer that the Sun was showing not (or certainly not only) divine intellection but what the human intellect ought to be and can with

---

[2] Although the divided line is not mentioned at 517a8–b6, many scholars see the passage as a directive also to connect Cave with Line.

difficulty become. But now we might start to wonder why this shortfall from what ought to be is not replicated on the physical, sensory, side of things. We also never stopped to ask, 'How come the eyes even *have* their ability to see well in sunlight?' But that wasn't exactly careless of us: it was simply reasonable, since we all know that the ability to see well in the sun is native to the eyes. The power of good literal vision is plainly not developed through an arduous education instigated, if at all, by ourselves, but is innate to our species. It is part of the natural order which is present independently of human efforts. Plato speaks of the craftsman, the demiurge, of our sense faculties (507c5–7), and presumably here as elsewhere he sees the arrangements of the cosmos as due to divine intelligence. This theme is mostly out of sight in the *Republic*, but it briefly surfaces when, taking Sun and Cave together, we contrast the original deficiency of human intellect not only with its perfectibility through human education,[3] but also with the purely natural god-given perfection of our literal vision. And since the sun-analogy surely applies to intellect in general, the present study will also have to try to make sense of it in relation also to divine, world-making, intellect, even though the human intellect, in particular the development of wisdom in human rulers, is far and away Plato's greatest concern in these central books of the *Republic*.

2.2   Connecting Sun and Line

Since in the text the Divided Line comes between the Cave and the Sun, we might think of the Line as mapping the stages on the Cave's path from initial imprisonment to full enjoyment of sunlit vision. While this may be correct, I shall not (anywhere in this book) engage in the thorny enterprise of matching segments of the Line with stages in the cognitive progress that starts from the depths of the cave.[4] After all, the first time we encounter the Line we cannot, of course, be aware of that question since we do not yet know of the cave and the journey out of it. So, what does the Line impart on first encounter? This is the question of this section.

After Socrates puts forward the sun-analogy, Glaucon begs for an exhaustive account of the form of the good. Socrates says there is much about it that he

---

[3] The Cave is the story of 'our nature in relation to education and lack of education' (514a1–2).
[4] Socrates' assertion at 517a8–b4 that the whole image of the cave must be applied to 'what was said before' is sometimes understood as a directive to fit the stages of the journey up through and out of the cave to the sections of the line. However, less fine-grained interpretations are also plausible. Certainly Plato means to relate Cave and Line: the characterization at 533d6 of the liberating mathematical disciplines as *dianoia* refers back to the Line (511d8; cf. d3), and the line sections are reprised at 533e3–534a1. But the fact that mathematics is viewed as essential to the cognitive progress does not automatically legitimate reading a 'dynamic' perspective back into the Line itself. See Benson forthcoming for a vigorous defence of the view that the line sections are not meant to correspond to stages of the journey.

has to leave out, but what he *can* say for now, he will (509c5–10, esp. 9–10). This gives the impression that what is about to follow will still be about the good. But Socrates now moves rather abruptly to something apparently very different, and quite dry and academic by comparison with the Sun. He lays out a theory of cognitive levels and their objects via the Divided Line (509d–511e; cf. 533e–534a), and he discusses differences between the highest cognitive level – where 'dialectic' is located – and the next one down, typified by mathematics. It is striking and perplexing that the good, or the form of the good, is never as such mentioned in the Divided Line discussion. It reappears by name only at 517b8 near the end of the Cave narrative, altogether eight Stephanus pages after the last clear reference to it (509b6).[5]

It is not hard to see the Cave as a natural correlate of the Sun. The Sun stands for the heights and the Cave for the depths and the journey upwards. But what is the austere Divided Line doing in the middle of this feast of imagery of light and darkness? What is the connection between the Line and the sun-like good? If there is a connection (as the Socratic response at 509e9–10 certainly seems to imply), why is the good never mentioned in so many words in the Divided Line's discussion of cognitive levels?

These questions can be answered together, although the explanation will take some time. First of all, if one thing is clear about the form of the good in *Republic* VI–VII, it is that direct words would not be very effective for explaining it, anyway not to Socrates' interlocutors and not to readers of the *Republic*. Now, one way of presenting it indirectly is analogy, hence the Sun; but another would be to characterize it by reference to a method or discipline in which it importantly figures – in particular by reference to the role it plays in that method. The method in question is sketched in the Divided Line under the title of 'the power of dialectic' (*tēi tou dialegesthai dunamei*, 511b3); it corresponds to the highest portion of the line, which Socrates will label '*noēsis*' ('intelligence', 511d8) and *epistēmē* ('knowledge', 533e4; 534a5). The sketch gives a purely *formal*, in the sense of contentless, schema of what dialectic does, how it works, and what it needs in order to function. One of its formal elements, he says, is a 'non-hypothetical principle (or beginning, *archē*; 510b6–7; 511b5–6; cf. 511a6). Having specified this requirement of dialectic, he wants us (I suggest), without being told, to look and see whether any item recently discussed would measure up to it, i.e. be a fitting candidate for that formal role of non-hypothetical principle. The expected answer, of course, is 'Yes! The good or the form of the good is a perfect candidate!'

In what way the good fits the role of non-hypothetical principle we shall consider later (Section 2.6).[6] Meanwhile, the point to take in is this: we have

---

[5] But its image, the sun, does put in an appearance at 516a–b.
[6] See note 43 for some different views on the identity of the non-hypothetical principle.

been led to *characterize* the good (the form of the good) in terms of its fitness for a certain role in an independently (because schematically) characterized intellectual discipline. This explains why (a) the Divided Line with its embedded discussion of the nature of dialectic is juxtaposed to the sun-analogy's explicit presentation of the good; in other words, it explains why Socrates offers the Line as if in response to Glaucon's begging to hear more about the good. It is also now clear why (b) within the Divided Line the good never appears by name. The reason for (a), namely the juxtaposition, is that the sun-analogy and the sketch of the cognitively most excellent section of the line, namely dialectic, are both telling us, albeit in very different fashions, about the good. And the reason for (b), namely the Line's not naming the good as such, is that if Plato had spoken here explicitly about the latter and its role in dialectic, he would have given the impression that the method he is calling dialectic is to be understood and characterized in terms of some sort of relation it has to the good considered as the good. After all, it is not as if the nature of dialectic itself is already crystal clear: we would naturally clutch at anything that might tell us more about it. So, if we were told outright that dialectic involves a principle which is nothing other than the form of the good, we would almost certainly think that we were being shown something of an answer to the question 'What is this method called "dialectic"?' We would think it parallel to the situation in which someone mentions 'health' as the first step in explaining the nature of medical science. We already know something of what health is. A comparable answer for someone curious about the nature of dialectic could only work if the questioner already had some sort of adequate grasp of the good (the form of the good). Yet, in actuality what prompted Socrates to present the Divided Line in the first place was Glaucon's continuing to press him to explain the good. And 'What *is* the good?' is surely also still the reader's question at this point of the dialogue.

This great question has not in any very obvious way been answered by the sun-analogy, which I suggested in Section 2.1 was offered as a holding operation. The Divided Line – that is, the characterization of dialectic given in the Line – moves us a bit closer to an answer. It does so by bringing to the fore a certain formal role within dialectic, the role of the non-hypothetical principle. We are then meant to realize for ourselves that nothing fits that role as well as the form of the good, and in realizing this, we learn something (presumably something uniquely distinguishing[7]) about the form of the good.

---

[7] There could be, and logically Plato could recognize, more than one non-hypothetical principle, either different ones common to all arguments and subject-matters, such as the principle of non-contradiction in Aristotle, or different ones occurring in different arguments and subject-matters. But there is no sign that Plato is interested in this in *Republic* VI–VII. I am assuming that while he distinguishes the role of non-hypothetical principle from its conspicuous bearer, the form of the good, he is not concerned with the possibility of other bearers. Bailey 2006 discusses the

But we gain this result because dialectic, and within it the role of the non-hypothetical principle, have been characterized independently of any reference to the good.[8] It is in order to creep up on the good indirectly, via its formal role, that Plato, I suggest, presents the Divided Line without at any point mentioning the good as such.[9]

But the Divided Line's sketch of dialectic does something else for him too, which I shall now try to explain. The sketch proceeds without mentioning the good as such, but even so, by means of the sketch he manages to give an inkling of *how* the good fulfils its great function of causing the objects of intellect to be known, just as the sun causes the objects of vision to be seen. Exactly what is shown will become more apparent in later sections. For now I focus solely on Plato's concern that there should *be* some sort of showing of how the good produces knowledge. This concern is an important indicator of Plato's intellectual seriousness, as we are about to see.

There is something which holds of the sun, the actual sun, that does not carry over to its analogue, the good. Consider how it is a total platitude that we see by the light of the sun. The fact is obvious from everyday experience. Because it is such a platitude, we don't need or feel we need an explanation of *how* we see by the light of the sun in order to be assured *that* we do. It may well be that on the everyday level, although obviously not on today's scientific level, we in effect treat the platitude as an immediate essential truth: as if it belongs to the nature of the sun – and may even be part of what people colloquially mean by 'the sun' – that it enables sighted creatures like us to see visible things. But it is not at all like this with the analogous statement about the good, namely that it causes intelligibles to be known. This is cryptic. The grandeur of the sun-analogy might excite us into wanting that assertion to be true, but why should we be expected to accept that it *is* true, just like that? My view is that Plato does not expect unreasoned acceptance here any more than anywhere else, and that he provides rational support for the analogy.

---

possibility of a plurality, and the relation between Plato's *anhupothetos archē* and the principle of non-contradiction in Aristotle. See also Baltzly 1996, 156–7; Repellini 2013, 189.

[8] I am not claiming that Plato presents the good in terms of its role in a method *already established and recognized* in the real world outside the dialogue. On the contrary, he here lays down, possibly for the first time, the formal nature of what he here designates 'dialectic'. (Whether it is the same as or goes beyond the method sketched at *Phaedo* 100a and 101d–e is a matter of scholarly debate.) In the *Republic* he simultaneously tailors the nature of the method, and his notion of the good as the perfect candidate for a certain role in that method, precisely so that they fit together. My contention is not that *in his own thinking* the method had occurred to him earlier than the place in it of the good. It is, rather, that he wants us, or Socrates wants his interlocutors, first to get the sense of having a grip on the formalities of the method, and then come to see that we thereby have an indirect fix on the good – specifically, on how it contributes to the dialectical reasoning that distinguishes the philosopher-ruler.

[9] Although most scholars identify the form of the good with the non-hypothetical principle, none, as far as I know, has explained why Plato leaves the identity unstated.

The support consists in an outline (via the sketch of dialectic) of *how* the good causes objects of intellect to be known. For in this case only by acquiring a sense of *how* it is so can we be expected to accept *that* it is so. Plato is writing for the philosophically minded, and these are people who would not or should not accept the sun–good analogy simply because it is beautiful and is backed by the authority of Plato or the Socrates-figure.

Everyday experience assures us that the sun illuminates visible objects, whether or not we have the slightest idea of how this manages to be so; but when we (including Glaucon and Adeimantus) are first confronted with the sun–good analogy we lack any comparable basis for accepting that the good does stand to intelligibles as the sun stands to visibles. We have at this stage no basis for accepting the analogy as conveying philosophical truth rather than simply enjoying it as a splendid image. But next we are presented with the Divided Line, in particular its sketch of the dialectical method and the role in this of the non-hypothetical principle. That is: we are given a sketch (no more) of *how* the thing which fills that role (we are bound to think that what fills it is the good since nothing else in the vicinity is a plausible candidate) makes it the case that intelligibles get to be known. So, the Divided Line gives us what we didn't have before: something of a *reason* for accepting the sun-analogy in the first place, or at any rate for not just bracketing it as wonderful poetry or dismissing it as hot air. By being shown (even if with no detail) something of the dialectical method, and tacitly reading the good into the role of dialectic's non-hypothetical principle, we do succeed in learning something, even though something very schematic, of *how* the good sheds light on the other forms: it does so by acting as the non-hypothetical principle of dialectic.[10] We now have at least a modicum of understanding of the *how*, and this gives us some assurance of the *that*.

To reap this benefit we don't need an intricate explanation of how the good 'works' in making things known (analogous to a modern theory, invoking photons, reflectances, the optic nerve, etc., of how things get to be seen in sunlight); an outline of an explanation is enough to convince us, provided it conveys a sense of there being plenty of relevant in-depth detail in the background, even though we ourselves may not be the people, or now may not be the time, for a fine-grained exposition.

At any rate, this, I suggest, is what Plato provides in the Divided Line's discussion of dialectic: not only (1) (as argued above) an indirect characterization of the good in terms of the role it will assume (the good being not yet named as such in this connection) in the independently characterized discipline of dialectic, but also (2) an indication of how, once the good or the form of the

---

[10] Section 2.8 suggests how to flesh this out.

good takes on its role in that discipline, it does then cause the objects of intellect to be known. By giving us something of a sense of *the way in which* the form of the good enables things to be known, the sketch of dialectic in the Divided Line helps assure us *that* this is so, or, in other words, that the good has earned its right to be illustrated by the sun considered as cause of vision. Hence, we don't have to accept the sun–good analogy just because it is beautiful, or because it has Plato's authority. The analogy, as we said, was meant as a holding operation, fending off both knee-jerk acceptance and knee-jerk dismissal of the claim about the good and knowledge, thus making a space of rational receptivity. It made space for that claim's plausibility to emerge via the thumbnail sketch of dialectic. But exactly what this sketch is meant to convey will become clearer only in subsequent sections.

I have emphasized the sketchiness of Plato's account of dialectic in the Divided Line. This account is not supplemented by much more elaboration in the few subsequent passages about dialectic (for a summary and references see Section 2.4). What we are mainly told is that dialectic is radically different from mathematics in two ways (on which more later). The thinness of what Plato says on this topic in the *Republic* is a puzzle in itself. If, as I have suggested, his account of the method of dialectic is meant to characterize the all-important form of the good in terms of its occupancy of a certain formal role in the method, why are we not given a richer and clearer picture of dialectic itself? If we are meant to get a grip on the form of the good via a grip on dialectic, why isn't the grip we are offered on dialectic more generous with detail?

We shall see as we go on that this absence of detail has two main causes. First, Socrates, or Plato, for a reason to be discussed later (Section 2.18), is not in a position to display the workings of dialectic by giving fleshed-out examples. Secondly, apart from the word 'hypothesis' Plato has virtually no technical terminology for labelling or describing the structures and moves of dialectic in the *Republic*, and for comparing them with structures and moves of other disciplines.[11] For these two reasons he can provide no more than an outline in logically impoverished language of what he means by 'dialectic' in this dialogue; and it may be thought that he has only a shaky conception of what he is trying to mean. But this outline, I have argued, is our sole clue to

---

[11] Robinson 1953, 1–2, 27–8, 45–6; Annas, 1981, 288–9. Cf. Lloyd 1990, 82: 'Both mathematics and philosophy ... provide excellent examples of rigorous demonstrations from the fifth century BC, though in neither field is there, at any stage, any formal analysis of the concept, and indeed the vocabulary available for describing the elements and procedures of a proof is very limited.' See Lloyd's illustration from the fifth-century mathematician Hippocrates of Chios, 1990. 81. Plato has no terms or no clear terms for 'premiss', 'implication/entailment', 'deduction', 'conditional proposition'; or for 'defeasible' or '*ceteris paribus*' (Aristotle's 'for the most part'). We also miss in Plato Aristotle's 'F-*simpliciter*' (*haplōs*) paired and contrasted with some qualified form of 'F'. There is also Plato's assumption that *saphēneia* is a single property; see Section 2.5.

how it can be that the good is the source of knowledge of other intelligibles; and without this clue, I have argued, we should have no reason to accept the sun-analogy as saying something true as well as beautiful.

2.3   Higher and Lower Intellectual Levels

The line is first presented at 509e6–510b8, summarized at 511d6–e4, and reprised at 533e3–534a8. It has two main segments, S and I, unequal to each other. These represent sense and its objects, and intellection and *its* objects. Segments S and I are each divided into two sub-segments, S_1 and S_2, I_1 and I_2, such that S_1 stands to S_2, and I_1 to I_2, in the same proportion as S to I. These proportional differences represent degrees of cognitive excellence (509d6 ff.; 511d6–e4). The positive quality is *clearness* (*saphēneia*) and its opposite is obscurity (*asapheia*).[12] Thus within the whole region of things seen (also said to be the realm of *doxa*, opinion, as opposed to knowledge, 534a2–4),[13] there is a division between shadows and reflected images (the objects of what is here called *eikasia*, 'operating with semblances') and what the images are of – such things as ourselves, other animals, plants, and artefacts (the objects of what is here called *pistis*, 'conviction'). Directly looked at, animals, etc. are present to us with more 'clearness' than when reflected through images and shadows. This is so whether we know that the shadows are only shadows and look at them so as to find out via them about the three-dimensional objects, or whether we take the shadows to be the ultimate objects themselves.

SENSE (S)   **INTELLECT (I)**

eikasia (S_1)   *pistis* (S_2)   *dianoia* (I_1)   *noesis* (I_2)
'use of semblances'   'conviction'   'thoughtfulness'   'intelligence'

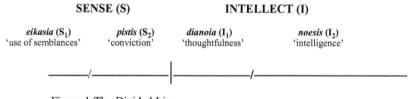

Figure 1 The Divided Line

Socrates is mainly going to focus on the difference between I_2, which is the place of dialectic, and I_1, typified by mathematics.[14] He will identify two

---

[12] These terms are applied both to the cognitive states and to their objects: 509e9–10; 511c4–6; 511e3. The ascending order of superiority goes from left to right in Figure 1.

[13] 'Things seen', a reminder of the Sun, stands for objects of sense in general. The further generalization to things opined relates the Divided Line to the Book V distinction between opinion and knowledge (479d–480a).

[14] Let me locate the position taken in this book within a range of options. (1) Mathematics exemplifies segment I_1; it and dialectic follow the same method but differ in subject-matter and, according to some, in the ontology of their objects. (2) Mathematics exemplifies segment

distinguishing features, one in the respective disciplines' use of hypotheses, the other in their use or non-use of physical models or diagrams (510b511d).[15] But before laying out and discussing these important differences, let us absorb the big message which the Divided Line already sends loud and clear. This is that mathematics (the main example of *dianoia*, 'thoughtfulness') is not merely cognitively inferior to dialectic (entitled *noēsis*, 'intelligence') *but stands as far below it as vision or sense in general stands below intellect in general* – and this latter difference, we are also told, is on a par with the difference between looking at mere shadows and looking at the things whose shadows they are.[16]

Commentators have, of course, been struck by the fact that here for the first time Plato divides intellect into higher and lower levels or kinds. They have often treated this as an invitation to investigate whether Plato postulates two correspondingly different levels of intelligible reality, the forms proper and a distinct category of 'intermediates' or mathematicals which we know from Aristotle came to be posited in Plato's school. In the *Republic* Socrates decides to pass over a detailed division of the cognized objects, so we never hear whether there are two classes of intelligibles (534a5–8). Perhaps at this point in time no one had even thought of postulating special metaphysical intermediates between forms proper and sensibles. In any case, as far as the two higher sections of the line are concerned, the ontology of the objects is unscrutinized and all the attention is on the difference between the modes or methods of cognition.[17] Plato uses the Divided Line to announce at peak volume that anyone who admires mathematics as queen of the sciences is as deeply mistaken as someone who ranks the whole of sense perception, and beliefs based on it, as cognitively superior to the whole of intellection. These mistakes

I_1; it and dialectic have different methods and different subject-matters; the question of ontology is debatable. (3) Mathematics and dialectic have the same method and different subject-matters (whatever is the case about ontology), and mathematics as such does *not* exemplify I_1: rather, I_1 (called 'dianoetic') represents certain *mathematicians* who misapply the mathematical method. There is a considerable literature clustering round each of (1) and (2). For option (3) see Benson 2012. My own view falls under option (2); reasons for regarding the methods as different will emerge in Section 2.14.

[15] There seems to be no consensus on whether or how these differentiae are connected. Plato does not say. It is quite often suggested that diagrams make the ungrounded hypotheses of mathematics seem more certain or more perspicuous than they are (e.g. Robinson 1953, 155–6; Denyer 2007, 300–2). Repellini 2013, 183–4, suggests the reverse relationship: the hypotheses help determine what a diagrammatic image is a representation of. Netz 2003 argues that what the mathematicians 'hypothesize' (= put on the table as a starting point) is the diagram itself. See Yang 2005 for a detailed discussion of connections, if any, between the use of hypotheses and the use of diagrams in mathematics.

[16] It seems that modern commentators tend not to register the full magnitude by which dialectic outranks mathematics. E.g. Denyer 2007, 303, describes the message of the Divided Line as: 'mathematical thought does not have *quite* the clarity of intellect' (emphasis added).

[17] Cf. Lafrance 1980, 84; Benson 2015, 239–40.

are shown up as equal enormities by the fact that in both cases the real cognitive values stand to each other in the same proportion. It is a kind of blindness and mistaking of dream for reality to regard sense rather than intellect as the ultimate arbiter of truth (476c–d), and it is also a kind of blindness and dream-like illusion, an analogous and equally aberrant kind, when mathematicians equate their science with the highest cognitive achievement (533b5–c6; 534b8–d1). In fact, the branches of mathematics do not really deserve to be called 'sciences', although we label them thus out of habit (533d). The basic set-up of proportions in the Line makes this general message perfectly plain at the outset, even before Socrates has begun to explain what dialectic is.[18] (In fact his explanation of what dialectic is consists almost entirely in laying down how it differs from mathematics in respect of those two features, the use of hypotheses and the use of diagrams.) Plato, I just said, *uses* the Divided Line to proclaim that assigning the highest cognitive rank to mathematics is as misguided as any philistinic refusal to look beyond sense experience; but we should not ignore the more extreme possibility that proclaiming this was his whole reason for setting up the Line at all. However that may be, Socrates, I suggest, is not finding fault with the mathematical method as such;[19] he is finding fault with claims to the effect that it, rather than dialectic, represents the very best that cognition can offer.[20]

---

[18] This message is just as plain when Socrates re-formulates the proportions at 533e3–534a8, saying that as 'knowledge' (= 'intelligence' in the first formulation) is to 'conviction' (sense-based grasp of solid physical objects), so 'thoughtfulness' (which includes mathematics) is to 'use of semblances'. In other words, 'thoughtfulness' in the general sphere of intellection is *as inferior as* 'use of semblances' in the sense-based sphere.

[19] Thus Burnyeat 1987, 219; 2000, 37.

[20] Some interpreters see the divided line as ranking all four cognitive states (and perhaps also their objects) in relation to each other. If so, one would expect the two intermediate states, conviction (or *pistis* = sense-based beliefs about solid physical objects) and thoughtfulness (or *dianoia* = mainly mathematics), to be assigned different levels of 'clearness', the latter higher than the former. Such a ranking seems assured by the fact that (i) conviction is part of the sense-realm and thoughtfulness part of the intellection-realm, and (ii) the whole of the latter is superior to the whole of the former. It is a difficulty for this interpretation that, by mathematical necessity, segments S_2 and I_1 are equal, and that (almost certainly) Plato knows this. See Foley 2008 for a survey of responses to the equality of S_2 and I_1. (This famous difficulty arises only if differences in level of 'clearness' are supposed to be represented by differences in length of the sections of the line, but there seems to be nothing else about the line-sections that could represent different levels of 'clearness'. If *greater* length stands for greater 'clearness' – a common assumption but not shared by all commentators; see Denyer 2007, 292–3 – there is the further problem, noted by Smith 2018, that the whole I-portion turns out to have more clearness than its most exalted part, and similarly for the S-portion as a whole in relation to its better part, S_2.) However, the equality of S_2 and I_1 becomes insignificant if we read the line not as a rank-ordering of all four cognitive states, but as showing that the identical proportion holds (a) between the state corresponding to section S of the line and that corresponding to I, and (b) between that corresponding to S_1 and that corresponding to S_2, and (c) between that corresponding to I_1 and that corresponding to I_2. Cf. Stocks 1911, 76–7; J. Morrison 1977, 221, 225–7; Austin 1979, 290: 'we have on our hands six segments, grouped in pairs, in every pair a longer and a

The message is a stupendous, even shocking, put-down for mathematics. Even in those early days before Euclid's systematization,[21] mathematical reasoning was surely regarded as uniquely exact, rigorous, perspicuous, and fertile in delivering assured results.[22] Also, the mathematics of the day already embodied a considerable history of widely recognized development, whereas the Socratic technique associated with the name 'dialectic', whatever exactly it is supposed to consist in, was an idiosyncratic upstart by comparison. The *Republic*'s claim that another discipline is cognitively far more excellent than mathematics is hardly less audacious than the famous three waves: no private families for guardians, equal opportunity for women to enter higher education and government, and rule by philosophers. The claim may even strike us as downright impertinent, given that it is not yet clear what so-called dialectic is even supposed to be. Yet the claim is certainly not based on any intrinsic contempt on Plato's part for mathematics, for he is going to make mathematics, in its fullest development across all its known branches, the basis of the future rulers' training in dialectic. Mathematics, although subservient, will be recognized in all its magnificence. But this simply brings out the surpassing importance of dialectic, since only the very great is properly subserved by the great.[23]

In apportioning the two intellectual segments of the line in the way he does, Plato must be responding to a felt need, whether purely self-generated or triggered by contemporary comments, to explain the relationship between dialectical inquiry, associated with his Socrates-character, and mathematical reasoning. The Socrates of certain pre-*Republic* dialogues was shown at moments operating or trying to operate mathematically. His main subject-matter was not mathematical but ethical, but he had bouts of applying a mathematical approach to his own questions and of giving sometimes quite

shorter in the same ratio'; Karasmanis 1988, 157; also Scott 2015, 96–7, although he is coming from the different problematic of mapping stages in the journey from the cave on to the segments of the Line. Given this emphasis, the states corresponding to S_2 and I_1 are mentioned only for comparison with, respectively, those corresponding to S_1 and I_2, and not for comparison with each other. The fact that S_2 and I_1 turn out equal says nothing about the relation between the corresponding cognitive states, because the latter are simply not up for comparison, even if we cannot help noting the equality of the corresponding line-segments. (The problem, such as it is, arises even if we abstract from length and rewrite the proportions simply in terms of greater and lesser as such.)

[21] There had already been some systematization by the fifth-century Hippocrates of Chios.

[22] On 'regarded', see 528b5–6 for the idea that the prestige of a discipline encourages its development.

[23] Burnyeat 2000, 42: 'mathematics is not criticised but *placed*. Its intermediate placing in the larger epistemological and ontological scheme of the *Republic* will enable it to play a pivotal, and highly positive, role in the education of future rulers.'

technical mathematical illustrations.[24] At some point, so I assume, Plato must have asked himself how far he should go with borrowing the mathematical kind of reasoning for his own philosophical purposes – or how much weight to place on the assumption that mathematics is the model for what philosophical reasoning ought to be. After all, the epistemic quality of mathematical thinking is impressive to anyone who can understand it, and it is clear that at some stage Plato made himself familiar with some quite advanced mathematics. It seems highly probable that at some point he found it necessary to face the question whether the *mos geometricus* is the right way for philosophy (or for philosophy typified, as in the *Republic*, by the philosopher-ruler). Whether or not he was ever deeply tempted by this approach, by the time we get to the Divided Line he has turned sharply away from it.[25]

For he now insists on those two deep differences between mathematics and dialectic (the latter being the philosopher's discipline *par excellence*): the one that turns on the role of hypotheses, and the one that turns on the use or not of diagrams. We shall first look at the question of hypotheses, which also involves considering the non-hypothetical principle of dialectic.

2.4   Mathematical versus Dialectical Hypotheses

Socrates gives this outline of mathematical reasoning:

I think you do know that when people occupy themselves with things like geometry, or arithmetic, or anything else like that, they start by hypothesizing the odd, the even, the

---

[24] At *Meno* 86e–87c, discussing whether virtue is teachable, Socrates resorts to what he says is a typical move in geometry: investigate the truth of *p* by first identifying an equivalent proposition *q* and investigating *q*. He gives a geometrical illustration before applying the tactic to the question about virtue. He has already (*Meno* 74e–76a) used a geometrical example to explain what he wants from Meno by way of a definition of virtue. At 82b–85e he demonstrates the possibility of successful inquiry with a step-by-step geometrical example, using a diagram. This, via the associated theory of knowledge through recollection (81a–e; 85b–86d), is supposed to show the way forward for successful inquiry into ethical matters such as virtue. *Phaedo* adduces the recollection theory, referring to *Meno*-style episodes with diagrams (*Phaedo* 72e–73a) and using the example of the form of equality, but making the general claim that recollection gives access to all forms, including the beautiful, the good, the just, and the holy (75c–d). The Socrates of *Meno* and *Phaedo* assumes that the method and epistemology of mathematical discovery can be extended to ethical discovery. If the doctrine of recollection had come to be associated with the phenomenon of mathematical proof, the *Republic*'s concern to drive a wedge between mathematics and the ideal ruler's type of inquiry may explain its marked silence on the idea that inquiry is recollection. However, recollection of ethical forms appears in the *Phaedrus* (249b–c; 249e–250a; cf. 254b6–7) which may be later than the *Republic*. See Vlastos 1988, 388–9 on the attraction of the mathematical model for Plato, and Mueller 1992 for a valuable discussion of mathematics in relation to dialectic in *Meno*, *Phaedo*, and *Republic*.

[25] For more on this see the end of Section 2.17. On the *Republic*'s often unnoticed ambivalence towards mathematics see Dixsaut 2005, 229–30. Also Schofield 1997, 227: 'Having in earlier dialogues exploited with enthusiasm the procedures of mathematics, he now introduces some criticism too.' The criticism, Schofield indicates, is not aimed at mathematics as such but at using it as a model for 'true dialectical thinking'.

various figures, the three kinds of angles, and so on, and parallel things in other disciplines, depending on which one they're in; and then they go on to behave as if they know about them, having introduced them as hypotheses, and they don't think it necessary to give any further account of them, either to themselves or to anyone else, on the grounds that they're obvious to anyone. Proceeding from these beginnings through the rest of their argument consistently (*homologoumenōs*[26]), they finish whatever investigation it is they're embarked on. (510c2 –d3; cf. 511a4–7)

Dialectical reasoning is very different, and what Plato says about it is some-what scattered. Putting several passages together, we get the following mosaic-picture.

1 Dialectic too starts from suppositions or hypotheses, but far from using them as fixed principles (*archas*, 511b4) it uses them as provisional stepping-off points 511b2–5).

2 In treating its hypotheses in this way dialectic goes towards 'the principle of everything' (*epi tēn tou pantos archēn*), not stopping short of that which is non-hypothetical (*mechri tou anhupothetou*, 511b5–6). (For as long as it is dealing with something merely hypothetical, it has not yet reached the principle of everything.)

3 It moves towards the principle itself, 'dislodging' (*anairousa*) its own hypotheses (533c8–9). This is by contrast with mathematics, which leaves its hypotheses 'undisturbed' (*akinētous*) and cannot 'give an account of them' (533b5–c3).

4 Dialectic makes its way towards the essence of each thing (towards 'each thing as it really is in itself') and does not desist before it takes hold of the form of the good in thought (532a5–b2).

5 It takes hold of the principle of everything so as to give itself a firm purchase (*hina bebaiōsētai*, 533d1).

6 Hanging on to those things that hang from the principle, dialectic moves downwards towards its conclusion (511b6–c1).

7 Since mathematics, by contrast, has a starting point (*archē*) which it doesn't know and an end point and intermediate steps woven out of what it doesn't know, it cannot amount to real knowledge (*epistēmē*, 533c3–6). The impli-cation is that dialectic, because of its non-hypothetical principle, does yield real knowledge.

While much here begs for interpretation, let me start by raising the question whether the propositions that feature in dialectic are or include the very same initial hypotheses which mathematics uses but fails to account for. If so, the thought then is that dialectic somehow completes what mathematics leaves

---

[26] For the translation see Adam 1907, 68; Robinson 1953, 148, 150; disputed by Burnyeat 2000, 23, n. 33 and defended in recent work by Lesley Brown.

unfinished, providing a ground for the mathematical hypotheses. The alternative is that dialectic's material is typically different and special to dialectic. Scholars are divided on this. Here I state summarily my view that the hypotheses handled by dialectic are typically different, and have a different subject-matter, from the ones used but left unaccounted for by mathematics. Thus, it is not the central task of dialectic to put basic hypotheses of mathematics on some more secure footing than they enjoy in mathematics itself.[27]

So, dialectic does not merely treat its hypotheses as provisional assumptions: it 'dislodges' them. This is by contrast with mathematics, which leaves its hypotheses 'in place' or 'undisturbed' and gives no account of them. The word just translated as 'dislodges' carries several shades of meaning here: 'lifts up', 'does away with', and 'removes'. These correspond to what I take to be stages of the dialectical process. (i) Dialecticians refuse to treat a proposed hypothesis about the nature of, e.g., justice as a fixed point or limit on their investigation: on the contrary, they *lift it up* so as to examine and test it for truth in the open; this involves seeing what follows from supposing it true.[28] (ii) After the testing (whatever this consists in) they may discard or *do away with* it because it fails the test. Perhaps there would be stages or degrees of testing, but let us for a moment assume that every tested formula is fully tested, i.e. tested to the point where no further testing would make any difference. Thus, (iii) dialectical testing *removes* the formula from its original position as hypothesis or ungrounded assumption, since now it has either been grounded through its relation to the non-hypothetical superior principle or it has been discarded: either way, it is no longer an ungrounded assumption.[29] The superior principle (the non-hypothetical 'principle of everything') is presumably invoked in the testing: it provides the test or perhaps the final one of a series of tests. Thus, items that survive full testing are thereby secured a firm purchase by the principle of everything. They hang on to the support they get from it, and other things in turn are supported by (hang on to) them: these represent the steps in which dialectic now travels 'downwards', which perhaps means towards more determinate or more fully analysed answers to the question that launched the whole dialectical inquiry.

A lot here remains quite obscure, but we can glean at least one important point of difference between the mathematical and dialectical procedures. In both disciplines the reasoning starts from 'hypotheses' – assumptions, postulates, or suppositions – but then operates with them in opposite ways. In mathematics what starts from hypotheses is a process of proof. The proof is from them in the sense of being based on them as premises. They act as a control on what else will be allowed into the system or line of reasoning. Since

[27] More on this in Section 4.3.   [28] Cf. Bailey 2006, 124–5.
[29] Robinson 1953, 161; Ross 1953, 57.

this is the function of the mathematical assumptions – namely, to be the basis of mathematical proof – they are necessarily and rightly unquestioned in that context.[30] They remain as fixed points at every subsequent stage of the proceedings since the proceedings are legitimized by being based on them. But Plato now looks at these mathematical assumptions, and the conclusions based on them, not just in their home context of mathematical reasoning, and not just in terms of their power to generate results impossible to achieve through sense experience,[31] but in terms of a contrast with dialectic. In dialectic, the hypotheses or suppositional starting points are propositions or definitions to be tested and possibly discarded. So, the assumptions from which dialectic gets going are hypotheses in an overtly 'provisional' sense. They start their career as only provisional, but this status of theirs is itself only provisional, because as a result of testing they will be either dropped or adopted as better than merely provisional.

Of course, any criterion or basis for testing them, whatever it might be, necessarily goes unquestioned in the context of its use as a test. In this respect the dialectical test, whatever it consists in, would be a fixed point for dialectic in the same way, and for the same reason, as the basic mathematical premises are for mathematics. But we have also been told that dialectic has, distinctively, a non-hypothetical principle. As a principle this controls which items are to be discarded from the investigation and which to be retained. But *its* status as an unquestioned fixture is not a mere function of the fact that we are using it as a test for rejection or admittance (the point here being that, when testing, one, of course, has to take for granted the testing instrument by which one operates), but instead springs from its own unconditional, non-context-relative, authority as a criterion which by its very nature refuses to be disregarded or superseded or side-lined as irrelevant.[32]

Now that we have been told about this new piece of dialectical apparatus, the unconditionally non-hypothetical principle, suppose we look back again at the starting points of mathematical reasoning: the latter by comparison begin to appear as '*mere* hypotheses', assumed and held on to for the sake of argument – for the sake of seeing what follows from them. They come across as unsupported, so that unless they are somehow self-supported, whatever that would mean, they and the items derived from them seem to hang in the air. This impression of simply hanging in the air rests on two contrasts. On the one hand, there is the contrast with the non-hypothetical principle of dialectic, and on the other hand, there is the contrast with the initial hypotheses of a dialectical argument, which, as the argument proceeds, will be definitely established or definitely ruled out. Looked at initially, in the context of

---

[30] Cf. Burnyeat 1987, 218–19; 2000, 37–8; Wolfsdorf 2008, 37–41.
[31] Such as the incommensurability of the diagonal.   [32] More on this in Section 2.6.

mathematics by itself, the mathematical starting points may have felt obvious and foundational; but looked at in terms of the contrast with dialectic they feel baseless and untested, and their status as basic comes to seem merely relative, i.e. to the theorems deducible from them.[33] This, at any rate, is the impression that Plato wants to insinuate.

He has Socrates say that the mathematicians, having introduced the odd and even, etc. as hypotheses, behave as if they *know* these things,[34] and don't think it necessary to give an account of them, taking them to be obvious to everyone (*hōs panti phanerōn*, 510c7–8). Now, Plato obviously recognizes that if mathematicians by their reasoning aim not merely to produce previously unknown results for themselves but also to prove them to the world, they must start from what is familiar and apparent to everyone.[35] They would have no use for obscure or contestable or blatantly arbitrary starting points. Many have found it fascinating that the diagonal of a square is incommensurable with its side, but the fascination depends on understanding that this is not a fiction but follows from starting points which they themselves take to be obviously true. Also, the fascination is not simply with the result by itself but with the fact that this exotic truth emerges with logical inevitability from what seem truistic starting points. So, Plato must grant that in mathematics there is an epistemic disparity between starting points and results to the extent that, before any proof is given, the former are plain and the latter are hidden. But this seems to be compatible with the thought that in the end the former are no more absolutely uncontestable or indubitable than the latter. It cannot be ruled out, Plato may have thought, that some obviously absurd result will turn out to follow from seemingly obvious mathematical starting points, in which case one would have to abandon or revise one or another of them. (The parallel situation often arises in what we may call the dialectic of Plato's earlier dialogues; so why not in

---

[33] Could Plato have realized that the only mathematical certainties are true conditionals connecting axioms with theorems, or meta-statements to the effect that something follows from something? He lacks terminology for this point, so would have had to convey it through examples contrasting asserted *p* with 'If *p* . . .'. This would have considerably extended the relevant part of the Divided Line passage, which in actuality allots about equal space to the use of hypotheses and the use of diagrams, the two differentiae of mathematics. See also note 36.

[34] Here he is talking about the working mathematicians of his day, rather than *Republic* VII's imagined trainee rulers undergoing their mathematical education.

[35] Plato, anyway here, seems to show no interest in the non-deductive inquiry (analysis) whereby mathematicians work back to their accepted starting points, looking for ways to solve questions such as the ratio of diagonal to side in the square. He also ignores the fact that actually identifying the odd and the even *as a starting point* at all for scientific knowledge of the natural numbers was some ancient thinker's stroke of genius, comparable to the mythical Theuth's original division of the phonemes (*Philebus* 18b6–d2). Perhaps anyone can see that odd and even are exhaustive contraries, but to see the pair as *a starting point of number theory* is surely an achievement not to be taken for granted. Plato seems to focus entirely on the subsequent stage in which it is already mathematical practice that odd and even are starting points.

mathematics?) By contrast, an absolutely non-provisional starting point would be such that we simply refuse to entertain the possibility that, even when used and reasoned with correctly, it might generate a false result. So, if this kind of starting point ever does seem to generate an unpalatable result, either we must learn to live with it, as Parmenides must have expected of his audience when the Way of Truth led him to abandon anything implying negative states of affairs, or we must blame ourselves for faulty reasoning whether or not we can identify any error.

As for the mathematicians whose discipline has now been shown to be epistemically inferior to dialectic: under pressure of Socrates' contrast with dialectic they can surely admit that their starting points have no claim to being never negotiable; but they are still going to go on doing mathematics! They will still go on laying down starting points, moving forward from them to draw conclusions.[36] Even if they concede that the starting points are not absolutely and in principle beyond all challenge (including challenges currently inconceivable), these are what they currently have to depend on, and they are not going to shut up shop. They cannot any longer (if they ever did) think of their discipline as exemplifying perfect knowledge and perfectly unclouded *saphēneia* ('clearness'). But believing this about mathematics is surely not essential to doing mathematics.[37]

Before ending the present section, let me briefly note some unfinished business in the mosaic presentation of dialectic given above. I discussed the mathematician's and the dialectician's different and opposed ways with hypotheses. But I did not discuss proposition (4) of the mosaic. Proposition (4) says: 'Dialectic makes its way towards the essence of each thing (towards "each thing as it really is in itself") and does not desist before it takes hold of the form of the good in thought' (532a5–b1). Questions: (a) How does dialectic's approach towards the essences of things relate to its way with hypotheses? (b) How does dialectic's taking hold of the form of the good relate to its approach towards the essences? Are these two separate operations, or does the first include the second, or is one for the sake of the other? If the latter, which way round? And (c) which essences are in question? Our answers to the questions under (b) must be constrained by what has already been

---

[36] It is logically open to them, after carrying out a proof, to substitute a conditional proposition at each step and by transitivity of implication wind up with a conditional whose antecedent conjoins the starting points of the proof and whose consequent is the conclusion. They could claim that this conditional has a perfect right to be embraced as unquestionably true while conceding that its antecedent does not; cf. Netz 2003, 311. But perhaps in Plato's day such conditionalization was not a feature of mathematical practice; the result 'The diagonal is incommensurate with the side *iff* certain things are true (and we're not saying whether they are or not)' is a lot less arresting than the categorical result.

[37] Cf. Burnyeat 2000, 41.

declared in the sun-analogy: the form of the good makes it the case that the other forms are known. This point has already been laid down, although we have yet to discuss what exactly it amounts to (see Section 2.8). The answer to question (c), which essences are in play, will be discussed in Section 2.7 under that section's question (8).[38] As for question (a) here, I shall assume with many scholars that the dialectical hypotheses that are tested and then either discarded altogether or accepted non-hypothetically are proposed accounts of the relevant essences; dialectic's attack on these hypotheses is its way of approaching the essences.

2.5   Saphēneia

What exactly is *saphēneia*, here translated as 'clearness' simply to give it a label in English? It is the quality of cognitive excellence by which Plato ranks both the states represented by the sections of the divided line and the objects of those states considered as objects of cognition; but what exactly is it? This is itself quite a cloudy issue.[39] *Saphēneia* seems, in fact, to be the absence or opposite of a number of epistemic defects which we tend to regard as distinct: ambiguity of meaning, vagueness or lack of precision, incoherence, inaccuracy, failure to be illuminating, superficiality as distinct from profundity, indirectness, uncertainty, or lack of evidence. Today philosophers draw sharp distinctions between the question of the meaning of a proposition, the question of its truth, the question of its evidence, and the question whether it is more or less illuminating; and they tend to assume that the question of meaning must be settled before the others can be sensibly raised. By contrast, Plato uses *saphēneia* and *saphēs/saphes* (the adjective) for many, to us, distinct scientifically desirable qualities. So, the same item might be more *saphes* than another by being less ambiguous or vague, but also less so by being less certain. 'My passport is in the third drawer of the filing cabinet' though more precise may be less certain than 'My passport is in the filing cabinet.' 'The United Kingdom will rejoin the European Union by 2050' lacks *saphēneia* because 'rejoin' can be interpreted in many ways, because one or both parties may no longer exist, and because however we take it the prediction is deeply uncertain. Quite possibly no one had explicitly recognized even the difference between meaning or meaningfulness and truth before Plato himself took some steps in that direction in his dialogue *Sophist*, which all agree was written later than the

---

[38] To anticipate briefly: near the beginning of the discussion of the form of the good it becomes clear that what the philosopher-ruler needs above all to know are forms of the virtues or things falling under them, and how they relate to the good (506a–b).

[39] An invaluable article is Lesher 2010, on *saphēs* and *saphēneia* in Plato and authors going back to Homer. He says that a *logos* is said to have *saphēneia* if it gives a 'full, accurate, and sure awareness of the realities', 181.

Republic. Therefore, we should use a fairly light touch in interpreting the *Republic*'s comparison of mathematics and dialectic in respect of greater and lesser *saphēneia*.

Even if Plato is naïve in treating cognitive excellence as all one thing, the Divided Line teaches an enduring lesson by the way it foregrounds the difference between reasoned and unreasoned judgements. In both subdivisions of the intellectual segment, what is grasped is grasped on the basis of grounds or reasons or an argument, whereas this is not so in the subdivisions of the sensory part. This is not to say that judgements about physical objects (and shadows, etc.) presented to the senses are irrational. But typically they are a-rational. The sun-analogy assumes that we can depend on our faculty of vision to see well in sunlight, and Plato must think that the same holds for the other senses: in the right conditions they can be relied on to give correct information about sensible objects – just like that. This is information to which we have non-rational access. This suggests that for Plato the fundamental difference between intellect in general and sense in general is the difference between cognition whose success depends on adducing grounds and reasons, and cognition whose success depends on the functioning of various non-rational faculties. Although he himself speaks of intellect as the eye of the soul and of intellectual grasp as vision (e.g. 517a–d; 519a–b; 533d), this is misleading if taken to mean that he simply thinks of intellect as a spiritual eye trained on incorporeal objects. For this leaves the activity of reaso*ning* completely out of the picture. The Divided Line tells us that the radical cognitive difference is between what is and what is not rationally grounded. Then, within the realm of the grounded it sets up a contrast between what is grounded absolutely (dialectical conclusions) and what is grounded only conditionally (mathematical ones).[40]

Returning to 'the' quality of *saphēneia*, let us try to capture it compendiously as follows: one item (proposal, claim, statement, presentation of a thing, message, etc., or even entire science) has less *saphēneia* than another if it is less effective in making the truth present to the mind of a properly attuned recipient, or comes with features that make it doubtful whether things really are as it purports to present them as being. An item comes with such features if (as we would say) its content is ambiguous, or vague, or imprecise or rough or

---

[40] Plato allows himself, however, to overlay these distinctions with the very different theme of original versus image. As three-dimensional physical objects stand to their shadows and reflections, so the intelligibles studied by mathematics stand to the physical objects (models and diagrams) used in that study (510b4–5; 510d–511a2). This suggests, although Plato does not state it, either that the objects studied by dialectic are originals of which the objects studied by mathematics are images, or that dialectical discourse is the authentic original of which mathematical discourse is a mere image or imitation. Such notions unfortunately distract from the distinctions drawn in terms of rational grounding.

enigmatic; but also if its meaning is indistinct because not completely spelled out, or if it goes beyond the evidence, or if it is too superficial to be of much cognitive value;[41] and also if it falls short of being a full or downright assertion, for example if it is presented or received in a provisional or ironic manner, or any manner uncommitted to excluding rivals or alternatives.

The whole discipline of mathematics is what Plato compares for *saphēneia* against dialectic, but it is easier to focus on mathematical moves and statements. Mathematics has less 'clearness' because its moves and statements are not perfectly grounded in one or more unassailable principles. The results depend on the starting points, and we are not in a position to assert *a priori* and wholesale that our reliance on these could never be reasonably challenged. Conceivably, Plato divined that the starting points of mathematics are not, or not all, irreplaceable. Conceivably, he glimpsed the possibility of, e.g., alternative geometrical systems with different axiom-sets. From this point of view a truly non-hypothetical principle would be not only unchallengeable but not conceivably replaceable by anything else. Hence the system in which it operates would not be just one alternative among possible others. Perhaps, too, any such irreplaceable something will be such that even before human beings introduce it into articulate disciplined reasoning, they cannot fail to engage with it on some level in just about all their waking activities. More on this in the next section.[42]

2.6   The Form of the Good as Non-Hypothetical Principle

Most of what Socrates says about the non-hypothetical principle of dialectic remains on the formal or purely logical level, without specific reference to the good. I suggested in Section 2.2 that this is because Plato is trying to present dialectic in a way that will help us get a grip on the good as something

---

[41] To take offhand two very different examples: 'The finger is both large and small' is true but not *saphes* because indeterminate (we would say that it is a conjunction of incomplete sentences). 'We should act in accordance with the *orthos logos*' is true but not *saphes* because it is unrevealing (Aristotle, *Nicomachean Ethics* 1138b25–26).

[42] My discussion of the Divided Line passes over several important questions. (1) Does it make sense to rank sense against intellect on a scale of cognitive excellence, given that they make such heterogeneous contributions? (2) Does Plato include unreasoned strong impressions about good and evil under the umbrella of 'sense'? If so, this makes for a discontinuity between Line and Sun, but a continuity between Line and Cave since it seems fairly clear that the shadows watched by the prisoners include shadows of values or shadowy valorizations. That 'sense' in the Line is not restricted to sense-perception may be indicated by the shift to 'opinion' at 534a2–4. If the answer to (2) is 'Yes', a positive answer to (1) becomes more reasonable since unreasoned opinions about good and evil are plainly of less cognitive value than reasoned judgements about the same. Such mere opinions might be said to usurp the function of reasoned judgement, whereas my perception under good conditions that there is a tomato in front of me is more trustworthy than someone else's inference to the same fact.

pre-eminently suited to play a role in dialectic, this role being the formally specified one of non-hypothetical principle. To avoid circularity Plato must present this formal role without mentioning that the good is the obvious candidate. Even so, we, and presumably Glaucon and Adeimantus and the others, not to speak of Socrates himself, probably have a pretty good suspicion of what the non-hypothetical principle will turn out to be. It will turn out to be the very thing which the sun-analogy and this whole discussion of dialectic in the Divided Line are meant to help us understand, namely the good or the form of the good.[43] This form was first introduced by Socrates as 'the supremely important thing to learn' (*to megiston mathēma*, 504d2–505a3). It, i.e. the good, is that without which nothing else is worthwhile (505a1–4). It is that which we fail to know properly despite its being the one thing that matters to us most to know – or even that matters to us *at all* to know (505a6–b3). None of us wants to possess mere semblances of good things: some people are content with empty appearances of the beautiful and just, but with the good everyone wants only the real thing (505d5–9). The good is what every soul pursues and does everything it does for the sake of, 'divining that there is such a thing, but puzzled and unable to get an adequate grasp on what exactly it is, or come to any stable conviction about it as it can about everything else, and so missing any benefit there might have been in anything else' (505e1–5).[44] Socrates, conversing at this point with Adeimantus, delivers this string of insights without argument or clarification, as if they are or should be

---

[43] This is the understanding of most scholars. *Per contra* Bedu-Addo 1978 argues that the philosophers do not grasp the form of the good until the moment at the end of their fifteen years of practical training when they are about to start governing (540a4–b1, on which see Section 2.10). Their study of dialectic (which preceded the practical training) involved cognition of a non-hypothetical principle that is not the form of the good. Sayre 1995, 173–81, has detailed arguments for the same conclusion. See also Delcomminette 2006, 7–10, 605–6: he separates the non-hypothetical dialectical principle from the sun-like good on the ground that the latter is the form of the ideality of all forms as such, whereas dialectic seeks knowledge of specific forms. See also Nails 2013, 88–100, with response by Franklin 2013. Nails's argument is that the non-hypothetical principle is said to be the principle of everything, whereas the form of the good is cause only of good things. This depends on taking 'everything' in a very strong sense, but see note 55. Against these interpretations: it seems unlikely that the sun-like form of the good is completely absent from the Line, given that the Line immediately succeeds the Sun and is offered by Socrates in response to Glaucon's plea to hear more about the good (509c5–11). See Robinson 1953, 159–60. Also, if the non-hypothetical principle is not the form of the good, we are left in the dark over what the latter contributes to dialectic. If it contributes nothing there seems to be no connection between Sun and Divided Line. Boyle 1974 argues that the non-hypothetical principle is not the form of the good itself but a propositional definition of it. This depends on assuming that Plato has, in the *Republic*, a clear sense of the difference between a proposition and an object, or between a sentence and a complex name: I would not bet on this, given that the examples of mathematical hypotheses, the odd and the even, etc., are what we would call objects, not propositions (510c3–5).

[44] It is a paradox that we are so ignorant about what we ourselves know matters to us most. This paradox is why humankind needs governance by philosophy.

unsurprising and uncontroversial to the assembled company.[45] They are a bunch of *endoxa* pointing towards the pre-eminence of the good, which excels over other values such as justice and even beauty through its uniquely inescapable hold on all of us.[46] Plugging the good thus characterized into the somewhat technical role of dialectical non-hypothetical principle is a leap which, Plato assumes, listeners and readers can make for themselves.

In speaking of the non-hypothetical, he must mean, minimally, that when an item *H* is hypothetical we can reason from or with the help of *H* while leaving it open whether *H* is real or true, whereas in reasoning that depends on a non-hypothetical item *N-H* we are committed to the reality or truth of *N-H*. He probably, however, also thinks that the highest mission and achievement of reason and reasoning is to seek and find the truth, so that if we reason from what we know are only hypothetical starting points and have no concern at any stage to verify them, our reasoning is *ipso facto* inferior to truth-seeking reasoning. He probably also thinks that if mathematicians and their admirers regard mathematics as queen of the sciences, this can only be because they assume that their starting points (and therefore their conclusions) are indubitably true, although they have no ground for assuming this and ought to treat the starting points as only hypothetical. He may also think that once we are clear that the starting points of mathematics are only hypothetical, we see that mathematics falls short of being the highest use of reason: for now we see that mathematicians have no assurance that their assertions latch on to or reflect some sort of independent reality, which implies that the success, if any, of their assertions is at the mercy of accident – accidental coincidence with independent reality – and not therefore a pure achievement of mathematical intellect all by itself. Plato might even think that while we can admire trains of mathematical thought as exquisite mentifacts fascinating in themselves, it is simply a mistake to treat them as having or needing the validation of gripping on to, or presenting, a supposed independent reality: this (he may think) is what becomes clear once we take full stock of the merely hypothetical nature of mathematical starting points.[47] Internal coherence cannot be sufficient for any truth worth the name (cf. *homologoumenōs*, 510d2; *homologian*, 533c5).

---

[45] Cf. 504e6–505a7: Socrates says what Adeimantus already knows.

[46] Lines 505d5–9 are not telling us (as El Murr 2014, 56–7 seems to suggest) that the form of the good uniquely brings it home to us that there is a difference between appearance and reality. They are telling us that the good is unique in that no one would knowingly accept the appearance of it without the reality. This attitude presupposes awareness that appearance may not coincide with reality.

[47] This line of thought raises a difficult question about the ontology of whatever it is that mathematics investigates: without truth, need there be an ontology at all, and can there be one? Perhaps it is not surprising that Socrates winds up saying that he will leave aside the question of what the *objects* are that correspond to the levels of cognition on the Divided Line

What if mathematicians or their admirers stuck to their guns and declared that the starting points of mathematics are self-evidently true, so that they have every right to treat them as non-hypothetical? Plato could reasonably question their right to be so confident that their starting points could never yield an unacceptable result. If so challenged, they ought to admit that although their starting points seem to be utterly plausible and blameless, they cannot swear that from these beginnings nothing untoward could ever emerge. (Probably at some stage people had been sure that all lines are commensurable.) So, for this reason, and not because they do not care about truth, the mathematicians must concede that their starting points are provisional in that it cannot be ruled out that one or more might one day have to be given up. If they do care about truth and not just internal coherence, then the most they can do is hope to arrive at truth while allowing that even the very best mathematical skill might miss it.

If this is why Plato regards mathematics as inferior, he may be committing himself to an impossible task when it comes to dialectic. This would be the task of successfully defending the allegedly non-hypothetical principle against a similar sceptical attack: if this principle, like the starting points of mathematics, is a premiss entailing the conclusions in which dialecticians are interested, then how can one be sure that a false conclusion would never be found to follow? And if one cannot, the allegedly non-hypothetical item is revealed as just a hypothesis, and dialectic as no better than mathematics in this respect.

I think, however, that Plato is not just comparing the groundedness of one intellectual method, dialectic, with the ungroundedness of another, mathematics. He is also tracking a contrast based on the notion of a non-hypothetical item as one that we are not free to ignore or set aside at *any* juncture of life: it is a sort of fixed point that unavoidably accompanies us whatever we are doing. We ignore mathematical starting points and the whole question of their truth or reality when we turn to something other than mathematics. What is more, we would do this even if mathematical starting points were somehow perfectly and transparently self-authenticating. It is different with the good. The endoxic remarks suggest that if we are awake at all, whether deliberately reasoning or not, we cannot but care about the goodness of what we are doing or what is happening to us, whether or not we determine its goodness correctly. On this view, even if the good is not itself a mathematical principle, it is inevitably an underlying concern when we *do* mathematics as it is when we voluntarily do anything. We do mathematics, or anything else, because we think doing it is in some way good.[48] The idea that the good (uniquely, let us assume) has an

---

(534a5–8): such discussion would involve difficult and perhaps inconclusive forays into the ontology of mathematics.

[48] Cf. Rose 1966, 195–6. Arguably even the acratic agent, voluntarily going against reason, follows what she takes to be good (see e.g. Moss 2008). Even on the older view that in ignoring

unreflective hold on everyone in every corner of life may also suggest that a kind of reasoning, namely dialectic, that refers reflectively to the good that is inescapably desired, has a sort of primacy over all other types of reasoning. The thought would be that dialectic is more important and worthwhile because potentially more life-transforming than any other sort of reasoning. It might also be held that no human life fully deserves to be called a *life of reason* if its reflective reasonings never relate to the thing that no one can ever fail to care about.

But it is quite unclear in what way dealing with what everyone inescapably desires makes dialectic superior in respect of *saphēneia* or cognitive excellence. For *saphēneia* is not the same as importance or worthwhileness. Mathematics may be less important but still excel over dialectic in *saphēneia* (cf. *Philebus* 58a–d where Socrates seems to admit a divergence between *saphēneia* and usefulness). It is true that the odd and the even, the three kinds of angles, etc., are not at the heart of all our endeavours in the way Plato claims for the good. Let us grant that from the point of view of life in general those mathematical elements can often be side-lined whereas the good never can. But if we return to the narrower context of a comparison between two kinds of reasoning, mathematical and dialectical, it is doubtful that Plato is entitled to valorize dialectic at the expense of mathematics. Why should one kind be intellectually superior to another simply because, unlike the other, it explicitly employs a principle that is also an implicit concern of ours in all our activities?

Plato might have a reply something like this: 'Granted, mathematicians start from suppositions that are less questionable than their derived results; they could not otherwise play the game of proof. But once you admit that mathematics has only the ability to reason *from* its starting points and not the ability to ground the starting points themselves, then you must admit that the coherence of a mathematical demonstration is no guarantee that its derived assertions are true of an independent reality. Not only that, but mathematics cannot even guarantee coherence, since, as you have admitted, no sensible mathematician would swear that her starting points, however indubitable they seem *now*, could never lead to an unacceptable result; and if that were seen to happen there might well be doubt about which of the starting points ought to be rejected, and about whether other results still stand once a given starting point has been removed. Compare mathematics now with a discipline that (a) relies on a truly non-hypothetical principle, one that cannot be doubted and cannot be brushed aside, and (b) starts like mathematics from suppositions ("hypotheses") but gets rid of them all through critical examination: some are refuted

reason the acratic altogether fails to *aim at* the good, one can still attribute to her an underlying *concern* about it although she is on holiday from putting this into practice. The concern is obviously there if she is ashamed while yielding to temptation and feels remorse afterwards.

and cease to figure at all in the ensuing reasoning, and the others win through, ceasing to be mere suppositions and becoming trusty assertions on which further things may be built. Mathematics, by contrast, is never weaned from its diet of suppositions. So, isn't it obvious that this other discipline, whether or not it is more *important*, has more *saphēneia* than mathematics? Given what you tell me about future developments in philosophy, I, Plato, accept that *saphēneia* is a vague and elastic notion: but it is still not meaningless, and it does not just mean "importance". What it connotes is not a single quality but a cluster of qualities *desirable for the seeker of truth and understanding*. They are disparate, I concede, but they have that in common. And isn't it obvious from what I have just said that the kind of reasoning, dialectic, that systematically banishes its hypotheses or else turns them into trusted results, exceeds supposition-dependent mathematics in respect of qualities prized by the truth-seeker?'

This might be a good reply if one could find reasons to become convinced (i) that dialectic really can avail itself of a truly non-hypothetical principle, one that cannot be doubted and cannot be brushed aside, so that use of such a principle really does yield results that are more cognitively admirable than those of mathematics. And one would also like to understand (ii) just how the alleged non-hypothetical principle contributes to the business of 'getting rid of the hypotheses through critical examination'; for if it does not contribute to that it would seem to be completely useless. Plato's imagined reply does not answer these questions, but we return to them in several of the following sections.

2.7   Dialectic and the Good: Some Questions

We shall return to the comparison between dialectic and mathematics in Section 2.14 on diagrams, and also in Section 2.17. Meanwhile let us try to get clear, or clearer, about the way in which the discipline called 'dialectic' engages with the good. Here are some questions:

1 Is dialectic in the *Republic* a science that studies the good as its subject-matter? Geology is the science that studies the earth: analogously, is dialectic agathology?
2 Does dialectic study a certain metaphysical being or substance called 'the good' or 'the form of the good'?
3 Does dialectic try to define or explain the nature of something labelled 'the good', concerning which it makes sense to ask 'Is the good pleasure? Is it wisdom?' even if these particular answers are unsatisfactory? (This question was raised at the end of Part 1.)
4 Do phrases such as '*the* good', 'the form of the good', pick out a property which all good things as such have in common, a universal corresponding to

the adjective 'good'? Or do they pick out one special kind of good from among the various kinds of good things, a kind that is somehow pre-eminent over the others in that their value somehow depends on it?

5 Does dialectic study the good in the sense of trying to determine in a systematic way which things are good, and whether there are general criteria for being good, such as harmony, balance, fittingness, etc.?

6 Does dialectic study what we might call 'the logic of goodness', exploring such principles as that if A is a greater good than B, and B than C in the same respect, then A is a greater good than C – the kind of work Aristotle does in *Topics* III, 1–5? (In fact, there is nothing like this in the *Republic*.)

7 Contrary to what was raised in (1)–(3), does the good relate to dialectic not as an object or topic or subject to be studied and investigated or even contemplated, but as a resource mobilized – without itself being an object of attention – in the process of exploring or contemplating something else? If so, then the good, or the concept or notion of it, would be more like a tool than an object or focus of dialectical inquiry. It would be part of the dialectical apparatus for finding things out rather than something that the method finds out about. It would be intelligently and effectively managed, without itself being looked at or attended to, in the course of examining something else.[49] (If, however, we engage in the study, investigation, or contemplation of basic dialectical inquiry itself, then any tools it uses themselves become objects of this meta-level study. The line between these levels may in practice be easy to miss if dialectic, like many other disciplines, is expected to police itself, reflecting critically on its own ways and elements.[50])

8 If, as *per* (7), dialectic invokes the good as a tool *by which to investigate* rather than as an object *to be investigated*, then what are the objects which dialectic investigates?

I shall not attempt to face all these questions now. I hope that in each case an answer will emerge before too long. But I shall now pre-emptively endorse the suggestion of Question (7), namely that the good or the form of the good is primarily a tool or resource for use in dialectical inquiry, rather than an object (or topic or subject) to be investigated in such inquiry.[51] The sun, the analogue of the good, is above all presented as the cause whereby other things, ordinary visible things, come to be seen by creatures with vision (508a; 509b). It is, of

---

[49] This distinction is not captured by the contrast between looking at X for its own sake and looking at X in order to look at something else, Y, for its own sake. The distinction needed for the present discussion is between looking *at* X for whatever reason, and using X to look at Y without looking at X.

[50] This distinction of levels will come up again in Section 2.10.

[51] For more on this see Section 2.8.

course, true that we can also see the sun itself, and Plato mentions this at 508b9–10 (cf. 516b); but on the whole his wording suggests that in seeing the sun we see it as source of light by which we also see other things. At no point does he clearly announce that people do or should engage in a visual examination of the sun in order to find out about its own intrinsic nature. In fact, it is not clear that he thinks it even has an intrinsic nature, i.e. a nature other than being the ultimate source of the highest grade of visibility (508b5; 508c4–d1).[52] If we adhere to the analogy, the form of the good, although it is itself known (508e3[53]), is known as essentially a resource whereby certain other things are known. In Section 2.2 I suggested that one reason Plato places the Divided Line, with its sketch of dialectic, immediately after the sun-analogy is in order to clarify the good by presenting the setting in which the good, in accordance with the sun-analogy, causes the being-known of other things (this setting being dialectic).

It may be as well to mark an unclarity in the penultimate sentence above: 'the form of the good . . . is known as essentially a resource whereby certain other things are known'. These words may be taken to mean that Socrates and his companions, and Plato's readers, to the extent that they do get to know the form of the good, get to know it as that by which certain other things are known. And indeed this is exactly what Socrates teaches about the form, and what we others learn about it through the sun-analogy. What we learn is something *about* the form of the good, namely that it has, or is, a power of making certain other things known. But the words might also be taken to mean that Socrates, and we, to the extent that we can get a fix on the form of the good as that by which other things are known, can get to know those other things. This would be a mistake if applied indiscriminately. We have come to focus on dialectic in the context of the *Republic* where dialectic is billed as the intellectual method of ideal rulers. The dialectical knowledge salient in this context is knowledge reached by them: it is the knowledge *they* get of 'other things' thanks somehow to the form of the good. In studying what Plato says about the rulers' method we are not ourselves practising the method; it is being described to us. So, what Plato says about the rulers' method does not *eo ipso* put *us* in a position to take advantage of the form of the good's power to illuminate those 'other things' which it illuminates for them. As far as their knowledge is concerned, we are on the outside, and so are Glaucon and Adeimantus and even (as it will turn out) Socrates. The rulers are at the primary level of contact with the form of the good, and at this level their contact consists in their expert use of it so as to find out about the other things. It is tool, not object, of their primary interest, even if it is the object of ours.

---

[52] By contrast with the moon or a fire deep in a cave.
[53] Reading *gignōskomenēs*; on the construction see Slings 2005, 111–12.

I am labouring this because unless we are clear about the difference between the two levels – the primary one and the meta-level at which one looks at what is done at the primary level (a difference for which Plato has no dedicated label) – we can fall into the confusion of thinking that the dialecticians' primary activity consists not precisely in operating with the form of the good in such a way as *to get the benefit* of its 'epistemico-veritative effects',[54] but also in studying it *as* the cause of those epistemico-veritative effects. This is like saying that looking at things in sunlight must include scrutinizing or theorizing about the sun as cause of our seeing, or that taking an aspirin for a headache includes a study of what it is about aspirin that relieves pain. If that were correct, the rulers' dialectic of *Republic* VI–VII would be, at the primary level, an exercise on their part in theoretical epistemology and, of course, ontology or metaphysics. One would then have to solve (or evade) the question of how their engaging first and foremost in *these* disciplines enhances their skill as rulers.

I turn now to Question (8) above: what are those objects, things other than the form of the good, which the dialectician gets to know? We have already in Part 1, when discussing the philosopher-rulers, traced Plato's answer to this question: the things which they get to know, by a long and difficult path presumably involving dialectic, are the forms of the qualities which back in Book IV Socrates approached by a shorter, easier, but less exact, route, defining them by reference to aspects of the soul. These qualities were justice, moderation, courage, and wisdom (cf. VI 504a). For, according to the text, the paramount task of rulers is to 'guard' these virtues, i.e. to uphold and preserve uncorrupted the norms of action which these virtues represent. This is why the ruler must be a philosopher, trained to bring dialectical exactness to bear on investigating what these ethical and political norms amount to, what they

---

[54] This is the phrase of Vegetti, 2013b, 208–10. Vegetti is an immensely helpful exponent of the *Republic*, but here he risks falling into the described confusion. His account of dialectic as sketched at 534b3 ff. divides the method into three stages, the second of which (534b8–c1) he says consists in giving, of the form of the good, 'an analysis of its causal *dynamis*'. (In the 2013 English translation, the paragraph running across 208–9 has two incorrect references: 534b8 ff. instead of 534b3 ff., repeated from Vegetti's original, p. 422, and 532b9 ff. instead of 534b9 ff.) Vegetti then puts 534b3 ff. alongside 508e1–3 in the sun-analogy. But in this he seems to overlook the difference between the form of the good *qua* analogically presented to Glaucon and the reader, and the form of the good *qua* playing its role in the ruler-dialecticians' primary activity, which is *doing* dialectic. Nothing in the text tells us to envisage that their *doing* dialectic includes being introduced to the form of the good by means of the sun-analogy! In doing dialectic they do not 'give an analysis' of that form 'in terms of its causal power': rather, they *use* its power of illumination. The analogy is for the dialogue's interlocutors and readers. A similar misreading is apparent in Penner 2008, 250–1, where 'the longer road' is equated with Socrates' survey of topics (epistemological, metaphysical, and educational) in *Republic* VI–VII. Glaucon and Adeimantus, and we readers, are just given the survey. We do not ourselves take the longer road (435d1–7; 504b–c). Taking it is the business of the dialectician-rulers which *Republic* VI–VII is about.

demand in practice. The previous set of definitions was only a 'sketch' (504d6).

Like the claim that the form of the good is a tool or resource for, as opposed to an object of, the rulers' investigation, the claim that their object of inquiry (what the sun-analogy anonymously calls 'the things that are known', 508c1; 509b5) is, or is first and foremost, the *virtue*-forms has major exegetical consequences. If 'the things that are known' does refer to the forms of the virtues along with any other forms that need to be investigated in order to investigate the forms of the virtues, then we lack evidence for holding, as has often been held, that the sun-analogy points towards an investigation by the ruler-dialecticians into the first principle of absolutely everything there is – the first principle of the entire domain of intelligible forms presided over by the form of the good and finally debouching into the world of sensible particulars. In fact, the sun-analogy in itself leaves us in the dark on whether Plato when composing the *Republic* recognized or was even interested in some kind of system *of all things*.[55]

We know from the Divided Line that dialectic is not expertise about every branch of the intelligible world, because the Line makes it clear that dialectic is

---

[55] In fact, *Republic* 379b3–16 argues that the good is *not* the cause of all things as it is not the cause of evils. At 517b9–c1 the form of the good is 'the cause for everything of everything right and beautiful'. At 511b6 the dialectical method is said not to stop short of that which is non-hypothetical 'as it goes towards the principle of all (*epi tēn tou pantos archēn iōn*)'. Given the context, *tou pantos* is more likely to mean the first principle of all the dialectician's reasonings rather than the ontological first cause of all reality. To get from the former meaning to the latter, one has to make the additional assumption that the task of dialectic as Plato envisages it here is to investigate the first cause of all reality. Still more weakly, *tou pantos archēn* may mean 'nothing else than the synthetic starting point relative to each question under examination' (Vegetti 2013b, 211). As for the idea that there is a system of all forms, Plato gestures towards this at *Meno* 81c9–d3, but does not develop it. In the post-*Republic Parmenides* the indecisiveness of youthful Socrates over which things have forms suggests that the 'classic' theory of forms, there under attack, had no clear criterion; but without some criterion for membership one could hardly postulate a comprehensive system of forms (as distinct from an unorganized diversity of form-types postulated piecemeal for inquiries in various contexts). Aristotle's *De Ideis* is evidence that in the early Academy there was no stable view among Platonists about the population of the form-realm. It might seem that the *Timaeus* postulates a comprehensive system of forms in arguing that the demiurge follows an intelligible model in constructing the cosmos. But this intelligible model, although itself a system of many parts, is never said to be a system of *all* forms, and the argument does not require it to be. On the contrary, Plato's express reason for postulating an intelligible model for the cosmos strongly suggests that implicitly in the *Timaeus* (as well as explicitly at *Cratylus* 389a–e and *Republic* 596b2 and 597b4–5), he recognizes forms for human artefacts. He argues that since artificers produce a finer product by following an intelligible model rather than a sensible one, and since the cosmos is beautiful and its cause good, this cause must have worked from an intelligible model (*Timaeus* 28a6–b2; 28c3–29b1). This argument's first premise is a generalization obviously based on cases of excellent human artifice – what else could it be based on? But the intelligible models used by human artificers to make things like shuttles and couches cannot be parts of the *world-maker's* paradigm, since shuttles and couches would then be natural objects, 'growing on trees'. There is

not mathematics. It may be tempting to conclude that dialectic in the *Republic* has no special subject-matter, and that it therefore studies intelligible being as such, leading reality back to the first principle or principles of absolutely everything.[56] It may also be that the form of the good has a role in the formation of the cosmos (see Section 4.4). But such metaphysical and cosmological projects are not Plato's main preoccupation in Books V–VII of the *Republic* if we read them in the ethical-political context of the whole dialogue. By contrast, the human task of safeguarding basic ethical norms in a good human society is very much his main preoccupation.[57]

2.8   The Role of the Form of the Good in Dialectic

It is very strange, at least from our point of view, that Plato never says exactly how the form of the good enters into his rulers' dialectic, or in just what way the non-hypothetical principle does its job as principle. Conceivably, he thinks that detail about this would be pedantic, or unnecessary because the matter is obvious, or that it makes no important difference how exactly the principle does its work. At any rate, his silence on this is a major part of what makes the discussion of dialectic in the *Republic* peculiarly baffling. A common interpretation takes the form of the good to be the content of some kind of ultimate premiss from which consequences are somehow derived. The premiss model and its difficulties will be discussed in Section 2.11. But the premiss model is not the only possibility. An alternative which I consider much more promising is the interrogative model, as I call it. Explaining this is the task of the present section.

Let us begin by thinking about what the future rulers' dialectical education is likely to involve. First, the chronological plan of their whole special curriculum. This curriculum is restricted to twenty-year-olds who have been

---

no way of directly integrating the form of couch into the complex form that guided the construction of the world (cf. Broadie 2012, 81–2). Postulating (along with the divine demiurge) a single fully integrated system of forms risks denying that there are forms of human artefacts, which some members of the early Academy duly did (see Broadie 2007; Ferrari 2007).

[56] See Krämer 1990; a more recent exponent is Szlezák; for a compendious formulation see Szlezák 2001. The issue is not whether Plato ever had views on the first principles of everything – it seems clear that at some point he did, from Aristotle's testimony on the 'unwritten theories' – but whether such theorizing helps determine what he is doing in the *Republic*.

[57] For a strong statement of the view that the form of the good is the apex of a comprehensive system see Gerson 2020, 120–3. For scepticism on Plato's systematicity about forms see Press 2002. The notion that the sun-analogy signifies a comprehensive hierarchy of Platonic forms has led some scholars to conclude that the Socrates-character in the *Republic* represents something sharply discontinuous with the non-metaphysical Socrates of many earlier dialogues.

found to excel not only in intellectual potential but also in moral virtue, music, and physical training (503c–d; 521d–522a; 535a–536b; 537a–b). First they enter a ten-year course of mathematical study (period 1). Then the best ones (537d; 539d) proceed to five years of dialectic (period 2). But this brings them only to the halfway point of their total preparation. For they then embark on a further fifteen years of work in the public arena, not yet as rulers but in positions of responsibility as military commanders, administrators, public relations officers, etc. (period 3; 539d–540a; cf. 484d5).

As I understand it, when the trainees move into the dialectical part of their education (into period 2), what happens is something like this: they start by developing skills of logic and conceptual analysis such as we see practised by Socrates in earlier dialogues and in the *Republic* itself. Thus they practise checking for and identifying equivocations, circularities in reasoning, and other fallacies such as those of composition and division. They learn to extract more precise meanings from ordinary words that are vague or indeterminate. They strengthen and perhaps become more reflective about argumentative techniques which they will already have practised in studying mathematics, e.g. the use of inference-patterns such as *modus ponens*, disjunctive syllogism, *reductio ad absurdum*. They learn how to reason by analogy and induction from cases – operations where there are no neat diagrams as in mathematics to reassure them that they are making sense or are on the right track. They learn that some terms indicate priority and posteriority, e.g. good *per se* and instrumental good, and they learn to look for the correct ordering in specific cases. They learn the difference between *explanandum* and *explanans*. They learn that inter-entailment between two formulae is no guarantee that either gives the essence or definition of the other; and that even if one side is more fundamental, inter-entailment does not show which. They become familiar with the idea of a genus and its species or 'parts'. They learn to distinguish between the plurality of kinds and the plurality of particular instances. They learn to be aware of the direction in which an argument is travelling: is it seeking to prove Y from some already established X, or is it inferring to the reality of X as the best explanation for Y? They learn to judge relevance, and to make distinctions reflecting the real structures of things rather than generated by accidents of language. They check to see whether a proposed definition of something has consequences that conflict with what they take to be some fact. So far their subject-matter could be anything, but at some point they are set to work on producing accounts or definitions of the virtues or patterns of virtuous action. They propose accounts and test them with the analytic skills just mentioned, and they discard or refine accordingly. First they work on definitions of individual virtues, and then, probably, they examine a set of several definitions for overall coherence and harmony.

Suppose now that on the basis just sketched, they have reached formulae which neither they nor their teacher can fault by analytic skills. Then, as

I understand or imagine it, the teacher gets them to start asking a new kind of question. Suppose an analytically faultless formula for, say, justice is given by 'EFG'. The new question is: 'But is it the case that whatever conforms to "EFG" is, in fact, without qualification *good*?' How are they to determine the answer? An attractive-seeming kind of response that relies on work they have done so far would be: 'Of course whatever conforms to "EFG" is an unqualified good, because we have found that "EFG" says what justice is (it has survived all our criticisms so far) and justice is essentially one sort or species of intrinsic and unconditional good.'[58] But this is the wrong kind of answer. In making them ask themselves whether whatever is EFG is good, the teacher is getting them to test further whether 'EFG' *does* define justice adequately. The new query, correctly understood as introducing an *additional test*, gets them to treat it as an open question – even at this stage – whether whatever is EFG is an unqualified good, and hence as an open question whether 'EFG' is a satisfactory account of the essence of justice.[59] Plato gives an important clue when he says at 534b9 that the good dialectician 'separates' or 'removes' or 'sets apart' (*aphelōn*) the form (*idea*) of the good 'from all other things'. I take this to mean (in part) that they must ask concerning each object they scrutinize whether it really is good, not just assume that the good is present in it. They must not predicate 'good' of it without first, so to speak, trying to withhold the predicate ('setting it apart') and finding that this is impossible or unreasonable. So, let us suppose, they first ask: 'Is justice good?', i.e. they try to 'separate' good from justice. They are unable to, and without a shadow of doubt they answer 'Yes'. Then they must query the proposed formula: 'Is EFG good?' If on consideration the answer is negative or uncertain, they know that 'EFG' fails as a definition of justice. The proof is that good cannot be absent from justice, and it can be absent from EFG.[60] Whenever they think they have found

[58] I assume that their moral formation in Callipolis leaves them in no doubt about this. Possibly, too, their dialectical training has included something like the Book IV argument that justice consists in the good order of our core nature, the soul.

[59] This resembles Moore's open question argument, except that the latter targets proposed definitions of 'good', whereas this one targets proposed definitions of specific virtues.

[60] It will become clear later (Section 2.14) that good sometimes is and sometimes is not absent from EFG depending on context. Does the 'can' in 'can be absent from EFG' mean metaphysical possibility of some kind, or epistemic possibility? I do not think we should expect Plato to have an answer to this question. I believe, however, that (given a trained inquirer) the epistemic possibility of absence is enough to ditch 'EFG' as adequate for *saying what justice is*. An adequate formula for a value such as justice must enable decision-makers to identify just actions, just arrangements, etc., with maximal rational assurance on any given occasion. (For simplicity I am leaving aside degrees of likelihood.) The case is not like that of defining water as H_2O. If we are not sure that this is the correct definition, we can take samples identified in terms of H_2O (we know them to have been constituted from the correct amounts of hydrogen and oxygen) and test whether they boil at 100 °C at sea level, etc., or we can start with samples of what boils at 100 °C, etc. and analyse them physically into elements in the correct amounts for H_2O. This is possible because we have knowledgeable access to water without going via the

a formula for justice that might work, they apply the same procedure, and again may receive a negative or unsure answer.[61] And so on, until they find a formula such that 'Is what this formula presents in fact good?' elicits a confident affirmative answer.[62] Some such procedure for sifting out inadequate formulae for such things as justice is, I think, what Socrates is talking about at 506a, shortly before introducing the sun-analogy, when he says:

At any rate, I imagine that if it's not known exactly how just things and beautiful things are good, these [sc. just things, etc.] won't have acquired a guard for themselves who's worth anything very much, that is, if he lacks that knowledge . . .[63]

That is to say: 'just things and beautiful [i.e. morally admirable] things' does duty for proposed specifications of the just and admirable such as 'each citizen does the task for which he or she is fitted'. One can take 'just things and beautiful things' as meaning 'things which are *prima facie* just and beautiful' (there being an implicit contrast with things that are obviously unjust and shameful or indifferent). If it is not known whether, and indeed in what way, it is good that each does that for which each is fitted, then it is not known whether this formula captures arrangements that are truly just.[64] Thus, even if what is specified *is* just, unless there is someone who *knows* that it is and in what way (as distinct from, e.g., uncritically accepting the specification

chemical definition. Hence even an expert on the macro-properties of substances can sensibly say 'I know this is water, but it may or may not be H_2O.' Plato holds that we do not have knowledgeable access to justice except via methodical discussion of what it is: this is why the concepts of justice and the other virtues are the special province of dialecticians, 'who are able to exact an account of the what-it-is (*ousia*) of each thing' (534b3–6).

[61] I am assuming that even failed formulae count as genuine intelligibles and are included when Plato speaks of the dialectician as proceeding with, by means of, and concluding in, sheer forms (*eidesin autois di'autōn eis auta*, 511b–c; cf. 510b, *autois eidesi di'autōn tēn methodon poioumenē*). The context shows that the emphasis is on a method dealing only with objects of intellection, here called 'forms' (*eidē*), as distinct from objects of sense perception: this is by contrast with the mathematicians' use of sensible diagrams and models (510d–511c). In the same way, refuted mathematical propositions still count as mathematical propositions.

[62] For most people, and certainly for anyone brought up in Callipolis, 'Justice is good' is a truism. One might lazily think 'EFG is good' is another truism, thus paving the way to equating EFG with justice. What shows 'EFG is good' to be a non-truism is the fact that, even if true, it is false in some cases, as we shall see. The dialectician has been trained to distinguish real from apparent truisms.

[63] Here Socrates is talking about full-fledged rulers, not trainees, but the main point is the same.

[64] This analysis is opposite to that of Sedley 2007, 268–9. He holds that even when we knowingly attain a correct definition of, e.g., justice, we do not understand it fully until we have worked out what makes justice or just things good, and for this we need an understanding of 'the Good itself'; likewise Blössner 2007, 381; A. G. Long 2013b, 25–6. See also the classic statement of Joseph: 'the goodness of Justice cannot be securely established, till we can see that the being of Justice, as one element in the whole scheme of things [i.e. forms], is necessary to the being of that full goodness which only the whole scheme contains' (Joseph 1948, 21). My view is that (for the dialectician-rulers) knowing whether something is good is a pre-condition for knowing whether it counts as justice.

because others accept it), there will be no one who can adequately defend ('guard') the true specification of justice if it comes under attack.

Something should be said about the meaning of 'how' or 'in what way'. This, I suggest, covers any qualification that would have to be added before it could be affirmed that 'EFG' is indeed an account of the just. For example, if the value of EFG consisted solely in its usefulness for obtaining further goods, then 'EFG' would not specify just and admirable things since nothing is just and admirable without being good in itself. The good guardian of values will only accept a given specification of justice if it is clear that what is specified is good in an intrinsic rather than instrumental 'way' (this distinction has been laid out at the beginning of Book II, 357b–d). Again, EFG might be good under one interpretation and not under another; then the guardian must know in which of these ways or senses 'EFG' captures something good, since only when taken in that way can it be accepted as an account of the just.[65] Further, EFG might be good under one kind of circumstance but not another, so the guardian must take this into account in determining whether EFG is good, e.g. returning the weapon to an insane person (cf. 331c–d).

With an eye to the wider context in the *Republic*, it is interesting to note that the two roads, shorter and longer, have the travellers moving in opposite directions between justice and the good. On the shorter road, travelled in Book IV by Socrates and his companions and by Plato's readers, the aim was to identify justice so as to discover whether (for the just person) it is good. On the longer road, travelled only by the dialecticians-in-training and the dialectician-rulers, the project (as we shall see, it has to be repeated again and again) is to discover whether something is justice (or moderation or courage or wisdom) by discovering whether it is good. Both projects have the task of determining what justice is (or what is justice), but 'justice' in the first stands for a virtue, a single quality or disposition of the person, while in the second it stands for the multiple outputs of that disposition – outputs such as actions and policies. The projects are linked through the soul's rational element. The first one establishes the rational element as ruler in the just soul,

---

[65] For example, correctly interpreting the principle of justice as each doing what he/she is fitted for depends on correctly identifying the characteristics relevant to a task. When the task is ruling, the principle yields the unorthodox result that citizens with the same talents should have the same access to higher education and high office irrespective of gender. What proves the interpretation correct is the fact that the resulting policy is *best* for the city (456e4–457a4). Dixsaut 2001, 63–8, highlights the interesting point that for Socrates it is *bad dialectic* (verbal antilogic, eristic, 454a–b) to discriminate between male and female when the task at issue is the non-biological one of governing. It is *faulty reasoning, fallacious*, to treat the irrelevant as relevant even if there is an underlying moral cause such as androcentric bias. It follows that good dialectic cannot be pinned down by a set of rules, since there can hardly be a general rule telling us which things are relevant. A. G. Long 2013b, 26–7 shows how the passage illustrates the political relevance of dialectic.

and in the second project that same rational element is actively at work on specific problems.

Let us return to the trainees and their 'Is it good?' question. When at some point they reach a confident affirmative answer, what is their situation now? Have they finally reached the best formula for, say, justice? Are they entitled to trust it or should they withhold complete assent because in some future passage of dialectic it, like previous attempts at definition, might be overthrown by an objection not yet thought of? And what prompts them to give one answer rather than another?

These are important questions, but before pursuing them we should pin down the relevant meaning of 'good'. There are, of course, at least two uses of this adjective, predicative and attributive. We use it attributively when speaking of a good car, a good day for going to the beach, a good method of exterminating rats, a good liar (Ross's example). We use it predicatively when we say that something is good, or a good, period: e.g. 'Harmless pleasure is good [or: a good thing].' In the question that we and the dialecticians are concerned with, 'good' occurs predicatively, and for them as for us it means (so I claim) nothing more complicated than 'desirable, to be pursued'.[66]

[66] Here are some points to bear in mind. (a) The attributive use does not entail the predicative. A good method of exterminating my enemies is a good thing, to be pursued, protected, etc., only if it is good or a good thing that my enemies be exterminated. (b) In the way I shall use 'predicative use', it is not assumed that the object referred to is a final or intrinsic good. It makes sense to say 'A scalpel is a good thing' if one has an end to be implemented by means of a scalpel, although the statement is true only if this end is a good thing – but, again, it need not be a final good. (c) Recognizing the predicative use of 'good' leaves it open whether all goods are *of*, or *for*, or *in relation to* some sentient being. That is, it allows for, without entailing, the view that some things are what some philosophers call 'goods *simpliciter*' or 'absolute goods'. Against 'absolutism' see Thomson 2008 and Kraut 2011; in favour e.g. Arneson 2010 and Crisp 2013 with a helpful discussion by Stroud 2013. Note that in applying 'good' predicatively to Z, I say *simpliciter* that Z is good, i.e. I neither add a qualification nor exclude adding one, so I am not committed to 'Z is good *simpliciter*'. Some interpreters (e.g. Cooper 1977) hold that Plato's form of the good is (or is the form of) what is good absolutely, i.e. not for or in relation to anything. I do not think that Plato's text bears this out, at least when the form of the good is taken in the context of the rulers' dialectical reasoning; see the beginning of Section 2.20. (d) Reasons why X is (predicatively) good are automatically *pro tanto* reasons for pursuing it, preserving it, etc. (given that X is a practicable thing). Arguably, judging that X is good just is judging that there are reasons for pursuing it, etc. Certainly, that X is good is not an additional reason for pursuing it over and above the reasons why it is good. So, one might think that 'good' adds nothing and ought to drop out of the picture. Plato, however, is obviously not about to dispense with the form of the good. But he is not on that account committed to the unnecessary idea that a thing's goodness is a reason to pursue it over and above the reasons why it is good. I do not see why, if we leave aside the 'wrong kind of reasons' problem (on which see e.g. Gertken and Kiesewetter 2017), he could not have identified X's being good with X's being such that there is reason to pursue it. Such a move highlights the fact that correct predicative use of 'good' essentially involves giving reasons. In principle Plato could have asserted the identity in a non-reductionist spirit, i.e. without claiming that either side is more fundamental; but 'good' is the handier expression because his Greek lacks a precise synonym for 'reason' in the sense relevant here.

This all seems fairly pedestrian. It is, however, perfectly natural to say that the dialectical students test their formulae or definitions *in the light* of their 'Is it good?' question. The question 'sheds light' in that asking it directs attention to the crucial criterion for whether something counts as justice. Thus, the term (or in the Platonic context, the form) introduced by unqualified predicative use of 'good' is the ultimate key to value in virtue of its power, when handled by properly trained dialecticians for interrogating their definitions, to ensure that something other than, e.g., justice does not pass for justice. Only when predicative 'good' plays this interrogating role do the forms, essences, or natures of the virtues come to be securely recognized as such,[67] with the result (for the ideal city) that they are not just 'there' in the landscape of forms but pass to fuller actualization in impact on human life, becoming 'useful and beneficial' (505a2–4). So, in this interrogating role, the ordinary predicative use of 'good' – or rather the intelligible[68] form which such use conveys – is like the sun which gives visible things their visibility and their being. In a slightly more technical idiom, the form of the good is the ontological counterpart of an interrogative propositional function or open sentence. It is the ontological counterpart of 'good(–)?' understood as taking proposed virtue-formulae as its arguments, yielding a set of determinate questions which further inquiry can then turn into answers, i.e. declarative sentences having truth-value. The Platonic form of the good, according to the present proposal, is not itself a question; it is interrogative because it is (in a non-Platonistic sense of 'form') the *form* common to a certain class of questions.

   Understood in this way, Plato's form of the good is a non-hypothetical principle of dialectic. It is (a) *non-hypothetical* because in general we cannot but care about whether something in our lives or the lives of whoever we are responsible for is good or not – we cannot (unless we are abysmally depressed) ignore this concern, and we cannot just *decide* to take account of it as if we might have decided not to. The form of the good is (b) a *principle* of dialectic because taken interrogatively, i.e. as demanding a 'Yes' or 'No' answer, it acts as a control on, or governs, what is or is not to count as a correct dialectical result. Furthermore, in rightly conducted dialectic it is non-negotiable that the human virtues, which the rulers' dialectic is concerned to identify, are *good* qualities:[69] this is not just a stipulation from which practitioners of the method might release themselves.

[67] Several scholars have seen this, although without mentioning interrogation, e.g. Adam 1907, 53 commenting on 506a3 ff.; Rowe 2007a, 148–51; 2007c, 246–7.
[68] 'Intelligible' in general in this book does not imply 'definable by analysis'. In this sense Plato's good is as indefinable as G. E. Moore's. 'Intelligible' means 'to be accessed intellectually' as opposed to sensually. Plato's good is an intelligible because reasons must be given for claiming that something is good.
[69] Even Thrasymachus recognized this, and hence refused to agree that justice is a virtue (348c–d).

A signal advantage of the interrogative interpretation is its concinnity with the *separateness* of the sun, the analogue of the good. The sun is not merely notionally or conceptually distinguishable from the objects it makes visible and sustains: it is outside them, separate from them, in the heavens above them ('in its own place', 516b5–6). Some interpreters identify Plato's good with the generic aspect of intelligible justice, temperance, etc., and some with the entire harmonious system of forms, and some even with the shared substance or, as it were, metaphysical fabric of forms as such, namely their common attributes of intelligibility, eternity, and separateness from sensible things.[70] But if any of these had been Plato's meaning, why would he have chosen the *sun* as analogue of the good? The sun neither is nor becomes some sort of constituent of the illuminated objects; nor is it a system of which they are the members; the illuminated objects neither are nor become specific versions or vessels of the sun; nor is the sun a sort of general nature running through all of them that renders them possible objects of vision.[71] But consider the dialecticians' question with the simple intelligible good at its heart – let's call it 'the G-question'. The G-question is *brought to bear* on the targeted formulae; it is *reached for* as a distinct tool *brought in*. Or, to change the metaphor slightly, the targets are the true forms of justice, etc., obscured for the moment by imperfect definitions, and we *hold the formulae up to* the G-question, treating it as a distinct source of illumination, one that clears the way for true formulations by exposing imposters. What is more, the G-question remains distinct from the objects on which it is brought to bear even when a particular bout of interrogation has resulted in every feasible definitional correction: for on other occasions the very same G-question – on the same topic of justice or whatever – may always be asked again. (We shall see more about this in Section 2.15.)

There is no possibility of interrogating the value of the method of the G-question by some further standard of value, for there is no further standard; and we cannot use the question to interrogate itself since if we distrust it enough to interrogate it, we cannot trust any answer it elicits, whether about other intelligibles or about itself. The sun-analogy cleverly implies this. We can't see the sun as we do other objects, i.e. only because and when they are illuminated. Nothing, not even itself, illuminates the sun, as if we could see it only if it turned its rays back on to itself – in which case those rays would fail to illuminate anything else.

An advantage of the present interpretation is that it immunizes the form of the good against an objection which goes back to Aristotle (*Nicomachean Ethics* 1096a23–29; *Eudemian Ethics* 1217b26–36). The term 'good' is not in

---

[70] For discussion see Sections 3.5 and 3.6.   [71] Cf. Vegetti 2013c, 149.

any one of the Aristotelian categories but occurs across all of them: the good in the category of substance is a substance (god or intelligence), in the category of quality it is a quality (virtue), in the category of quantity, a quantity (the right amount), and so on. From this Aristotle infers that 'good' does not stand for or mean some unique entity such as a Platonic form is supposed to be. However, Aristotle's theory of categories is a way of dividing up types of *declarative* predication. But if the sun-like form of the good is interrogative, and is properly expressed by an interrogative propositional function or open sentence 'good(–)?' (or 'Is – good?'), then the term 'good' can be regarded as categorially indeterminate. A single formula (the open sentence) expresses the sun-like form, so the uniqueness of that form is not impugned. When we fill the blank with the name or designation of a determinate entity, we get a determinate question. In this question (and in the associated declarative answers, positive and negative), 'good' takes on the category of the determinate entity whose name was substituted for the blank.[72] For example, if we substitute 'EFG', then, depending on whether 'EFG' names a person or a quality or a quantity, etc., we have a determinate question about a categorially determinate item. The sun-like form of the good corresponds to what all such determinate questions have in common. Aristotle may object: 'But what they have in common is *just an abstraction derived from the determinate questions and answers: it is not anything in itself.*' But this begs the question against what I take to be the distinctively Platonic position, which is that the form of the good is metaphysically prior to the determinate items to which it accommodates itself in the formation of determinate kinds of good thing. We can, after all, ask whether *this* – something that just presents itself to thought or sense experience – is good ('Should we pursue *this*, value it, take it on board?') even before we have determined which Aristotelian category *this* belongs to. If, as I think, the sun-like form of the good is essentially interrogative, and if the interrogation using categorially indeterminate '*this*' is not out of order (arguments claiming it *is* out of order must be careful not to beg the question), then the Aristotelian objection fails.[73]

2.9   Some Objections and Replies

(1) The proposed interpretation may seem intolerably artificial in claiming that Plato's transcendent sun-like good is the form of the good *in interrogative mode*. Surely, one might think, the form as such is not in interrogative mode:

---

[72] I am assuming that the question is asked of one item at a time.

[73] On the form's essential interrogativity see (1) in the next section. On the priority of its interrogative function see Sections 4.2 and 4.4 ('any responsible judgement *that* X is good ... rides on the back of the corresponding question *whether*', p. 201).

we humans sometimes bring the form to bear in questions we ask, but this is an incidental or external and superficial fact about the form. The Platonic form is a separate reality, not a human attitude – not even a human attitude to a form – and only such things as human attitudes can be interrogative. In response: I do not think it absurd to suppose that for Plato the form of the good is such that for us to apprehend it correctly in itself *is* for us to apprehend it as triggering critical interrogation of the real value of *something else*. (Inquiry is a mental attitude, but a principle of inquiry is not a mental attitude.) The thought is that getting used to trigger the determination of value is not something that just happens to the form of the good: what this form in itself essentially is, is the stimulus or signal that sets the intellect on the path of determining value. So, we do *not* harness it to an extraneous purpose – instead we apprehend it precisely as what it really is – when we grasp it generally as that in the light of which the positive or negative value of other things becomes known. It might even be said that the good is such that the intellect would simply be failing to grasp this form, would clutch at it uncomprehendingly, if it failed to treat it as that in the interrogating light of which we discover the value of other things.[74] The thought is that judging X to be good is not primarily the upshot of, as it were, stumbling upon, or being handed, the information that X is good, but concludes interrogation *whether* it is good. Excellence in operating with the form of the good in this way is what the dialecticians of the *Republic* are

---

[74] Compare the familiar point that for Plato, as for a number of philosophers, some things, e.g. beauty, are such that the attitude of love or admiration is built into any adequate grasp of them in objects. Consider also that in Aristotle and sometimes in Plato the terms for definable essence are nominalizations of 'What is it?' or some closely related question. These convenient labels may have the deeper rationale that the items so labelled are by nature such that they can only become better known to non-omniscient beings if such potential knowers *inquire into what they are*. (By contrast, most of what we are sensually aware of at any given moment comes to us without prior interrogative interest on our part.) A related point arises from the fact that Plato often explains (ordinary) forms as paradigms for sensible particulars: are the forms essentially paradigms? Is it built into their nature that they are there to be imitated or implemented in a sensible medium (we might want to add 'unless something prevents'), or is implementation merely incidental to them? It is unclear where Plato himself stands on this. According to Proclus, Plato's forms are essentially and in themselves paradigms; for his opponent Philoponus, a Christian who accepted the creation story of Genesis, they only became so through God's decision to create (Philoponus 2004, ch. 2). Given these parallels, it does not seem far-fetched to hold that for Plato a certain item, the form of the good, is such that a condition of being in the correct primary or first-order cognitive relation to it is that one brings it to bear *in inquiring* what other things are good (for the reason for 'primary or first-order' see Section 2.10). While working on the present material I was heartened to come across the following by David Wiggins: 'What the historical lexicographer recapitulates under "good", we might say, is the history of our constant interrogation of the life that we lead and the place where we lead it, our constant interrogation of things that concern us or might concern us or ought to concern us' (Wiggins 2009, 198). In a footnote to this passage Wiggins says: 'In their several ways, Ayer, Stevenson, Hare, Ziff and Scanlon all see this. Of course.' I take him to mean (at least) that the point would be common ground between meta-ethical realists and anti-realists.

trained for, and it is intrinsic to their dialectical activity to operate with it in this way. Conversely (so I am suggesting Plato would assume), the use of ordinary predicative 'good' by well-trained dialecticians to interrogate definitions of major *per se* goods is what the term itself is above all *for*: i.e. predicative 'good' comes fully into its own only when wielded by competent questioners in relation to that sort of subject-matter; and all other uses, whether with objects less grand or questioners less intellectually demanding, or in declarative utterances, would be imitations or in some other way dependents of that primary one. (For more on declarative predications of 'good' and their dependence on interrogative ones see Section 4.2.)

The idea that the good in its interrogative function is our test of the value of other things is not to be misconstrued as the notion that the good is a standard in the sense of a template or paradigm to which other things should conform or strive to conform. After all, the sun is not in *this* sense the standard that distinguishes well-grown from defective plants and animals: to be well-grown is not to be a good approximation to the sun. Instead, the essentially interrogative good is the source of the *objectivity* of judgements of value made in its light: for being genuinely interrogative means being discerning or critical, not merely demanding a correct answer but presupposing that correctness may diverge from apparent truth and correctness.[75] We discern things *by* the light-shedding sun and, intellectually, *by* the interrogative good, and we also evaluate some things *by*, in the sense of 'by reference to' or 'by comparison with', a standard against which we check them as measuring up to it or not (e.g. a portrait to the original) – but the relations behind these two uses of 'by' are very different.

(2) One may wonder why, if the interrogative interpretation is correct, Plato omits to *say* that the good functions as a question. The answer surely is that he does not need to say this: it is well known that the dialectician's typical activity proceeds by questions and answers.[76] If the good essentially comes into play in dialectic, it is hardly surprising that the good is essentially interrogative. 'Is it

---

[75] We can conceive of an omniscient god saying about his creation: 'Now, let's see – is it good?' not because he is uncertain or must take steps to find out (so it is a sort of rhetorical question), but because the very posing of the question encapsulates the *objectivity* of the already known by him true answer. He has said, 'Let there be X', and consequently there was, and is, X; but it is not the case that he then said, 'Let X be good', and consequently X *was* good: rather, having made X he saw that it was good, and, perhaps we can add, this 'seeing' represents his knowledge that it would have still have been good even if *per impossibile* he had not known that it would be (Genesis 1.4, 10, 12, 18, 21, 25, 31).

[76] *Republic* 336c2–6; 487b3–5; 531e3–4; 534d9–10; *Protagoras* 336c; 338c–e; 348a; *Phaedo* 75d1–3; 78d1–2; *Cratylus* 390c5–7 (cf. 398d4–6). See Robinson 1953, 75–84; and A. G. Long 2013a for a thorough study of internal questioning in Plato. 'The question is the prevalent mode of speech in dialectic,' Fink 2012, 5.

good?' will be one of a standard series of questions clarifying and testing a proposed virtue-definition. And since written Greek in Plato's time had no question mark, he could not help us by writing the Greek equivalent of 'The sun-like form of the good is expressed by "Good?"'

(3) Another objection is that the sun-like form of the good must surely be something richer and more philosophically interesting than what is conveyed by the colourless predicative use of the word. This will be discussed below in Section 2.11, 'The non-hypothetical principle as first premiss'. For now it is enough to say that a main reason for thinking that the form must be rich and interesting is the assumption that its place in dialectical reasoning is that of a premiss from which the dialecticians derive answers to their questions. Since the interrogative interpretation dispenses with that assumption, it is to that extent uncommitted to theorizing the form as rich and interesting.

(4) Even so, the present proposal seems to be in serious conflict with the text at several points. The proposal assumes that Plato's form of the good is not an object for study or investigation by the dialectical method, but a 'seen through' instrument or resource of that method itself, its objects for investigation being forms other than the good. (For this reason I translate *to megiston mathēma* as 'the most important thing to learn', rather than 'the most important object of study' or 'the most important subject-matter' as is more usual. We learn methods by getting practice in using them, but using them is not yet studying them: that is the task of a second-level activity, methodology.) However, the proposal seemingly flies in the face of a number of passages where the dialectician is said to behold, contemplate, view, apprehend, the good – language suggesting that the good is the central and even cognitively final object of the dialectician's interest as distinct from a sort of tool for learning about something else. I shall discuss these passages in the next section.

2.10   Textual Counter-evidence

There seems to be clear textual evidence against the interrogative interpretation of the form of the good in dialectic. Certain passages show or seem to show the dialectician looking at, focusing on, attending to, or studying the form of the good itself, hence *not* 'looking through or by means of it' as a lens or source of clarity for identifying other things such as the virtue-forms. I shall look first at the most telling of these passages. It comes at the end of Plato's long exposition of the intellectual training of his future rulers:

And when they've reached the age of fifty [i.e. straight after the fifteen years' practical training, period 3], those who have stayed the course and met the highest standards in everything they've had to do or learn must now be led to the end-point (*telos*) <of their journey>, and must be compelled to lift the ray of their soul directing it towards the very thing that sheds light on all things; and having seen (*idontas*) the good itself they must order city, citizens, and themselves, using it as their paradigm. For the rest of their lives they must take turns at this [ordering the city], devoting the greater part of their lives to philosophy but submitting themselves to political labours when their turn comes and ruling, each for the city's sake, not because it's a fine thing to do but as something that has to be done; and having educated others like themselves to take their place as city-guards they will go off to inhabit the Isles of the Blest, while the city sets up memorials and sacrifices for them at public expense – as demi-gods, if the Pythia agrees, or if not, as divinely happy individuals. (540a4–c2)

I shall mainly discuss the lines 540a4–b1 because they constitute the most conspicuous piece of counter-evidence to the interrogative interpretation of the form of the good. If it can be shown not to threaten that interpretation after all, the other passages, absent support from this one, will not seem very challenging.

Lines 540a4–b1 present a double difficulty for the interrogative interpretation: first, at the level of forms it shows the about-to-be rulers squarely focusing on the form of the good itself rather than using it as a methodic resource for investigating other forms; and secondly, it says that they are then to use the form of the good as a *paradigm or pattern* in their work of ordering the city and the soul. Why is the latter a difficulty for the interrogative interpretation? Well, it is hard to see what could be meant by using a *question* as the paradigm for ordering a city or anything else. Moreover, if, as may seem quite plausible, we take 'using it (sc. the form of the good) as a paradigm for ordering the city, citizens, and themselves' to mean 'ordering the city, etc. by using the form of the good as pattern or model *of the order to be set up in the city*, etc.', then the interrogative interpretation certainly bites the dust. This is because the interrogative interpretation assumes that the form of the good is a sort of tool for identifying the virtues. Now, in general, if an organizer seeking to realize some kind of orderly arrangement in the material world takes as guidance an ideal model of the arrangement to be realized, there must be homomorphism of some kind between the arrangement to be realized and the ideal model. But the ruler above all seeks to realize justice and the other virtues concretely in the city and in individuals. Hence, if the form of the good is *itself* the model or paradigm of the order which the ruler seeks to produce, the form of the good must be a combination or system of the forms of justice and the other virtues.[77] But in that case, in grasping the form of the good, the inquirer already grasps the forms of the virtues, hence cannot be using the former to get knowledge of the latter.

On this interpretation, 540a4–b1 echoes two much earlier passages, 484c–d and 500b–501c.[78] There, the rulers are said to look to intelligible patterns or

---

[77] More on system-theories in Section 3.6.
[78] This is the interpretation of Adam 1907, 153; Shorey 1935, vol. II, 230; N. White 2006, 362; Vegetti, 2013c, 138.

models, and these models are certainly the forms of justice, temperance, etc. (see especially 484c9 and 500e3; cf. 500c3–6; 501b2–3). But there are two differences. One is that the earlier passages are uncoloured by any reference to the form of the good, which only enters the discussion at 504e–505a. The other difference is that the earlier passages simply assume that the rulers know what the virtues are, i.e. have the correct virtue-paradigms. It is still to be explained that getting to know what the virtues are cannot at all be taken for granted – that it will be a major task for those who will rule, requiring the exacting longer way round (504a–e).

When we get to the theme of the longer way round, we find that it segues into the beginnings of the discussion of the form of the good (504e). One has the impression – not one I think we should fight against – that the theme of the good is intimately related to that of the longer way round. Socrates then assembles a number of *endoxa* about the good, including the two failed definitions, and then no more than two Stephanus pages on he introduces the 'offspring of the good' (506e), which turns out to be the sun, and we are on the brink of the sun-analogy which starts at 507c. The clear message of the sun-analogy (even if we do not understand exactly what makes the message true) is that the form of the good is what enables the other forms (forms of the virtues) to be known.

The point of this recapitulation is to cast doubt on the idea that at 540a–b the philosopher-rulers gaze at the form of the good so as to absorb it as their paradigm to be followed in *making the city and citizens virtuous*. In the two earlier passages (484c–d and 500b–501c) their paradigms for that task were indeed the forms of the virtues. If at 540a–b the form of the good is now the paradigm which the ruler follows for making the city, etc. virtuous, then the form of the good is identical with the forms of the virtues. Therefore we should not think of the form of the good as a premiss or something premiss-like from which the philosophers *derive* true definitions, and hence paradigms, of the virtues.[79] Nor should we think of it as a principle for correcting accounts of the virtues (cf. Section 3.6 on system accounts of the form of the good). For 540a–b says that they take the form of the good *itself* as their paradigm – their paradigm for ordering the city, etc., on the interpretation we are considering. Treating the form of the good as the source or principle for determining the virtue-forms as practical paradigms for shaping the city is not the same as treating *it* as a practical paradigm for shaping the city. Moreover, the supposed identity *as paradigms* between the form of the good and the complex of virtue-forms seems to me to imply a *transparent* identity such that to know either is to know the other. Thus, it makes no sense to say that the form of the good is

---

[79] On the form of the good as first premiss of dialectical reasoning see Section 2.11.

what *enables* the virtue-forms to be known: the relationship is too close. And in any case an identity relationship makes nonsense of the sun-analogy because the sun is only too obviously different from the collectivity of objects it renders visible.

So, in this identity picture the form of the good is not something *through which* or *by the aid of which* the dialectician clarifies the nature of the virtues, distinguishing true from false claimants to the name. Instead, since the form of the good is identical with the forms of the virtues or the complex of them, finding out what they are is identical with exploring the nature of the good. In terms of the now familiar distinction, the form of the good is itself an object of epistemic interest, not a tool for satisfying an interest in something else. This position may seem fine, since most scholars take the epistemic role of the form of the good to be precisely that of object of interest. But it comes at a high price, namely that we have been given no idea, not even an analogy-based idea, of how the form of the good enables the true virtue-forms and the virtue-form-pretenders to be known respectively for what they are. For the form of the good, on the line of thought we have just been tracing, is too closely related to the virtue-forms to be of any help in identifying them. The problem of identifying them now becomes the problem of identifying *it*. But how does anyone identify it? Do the philosopher-rulers just *see* what the form of the good is, and hence what the virtues are? Or do they have an argument that brings them to understand what it is? But, in that case, what does the argument start from? Does it start from another non-hypothetical principle, one we are never told about? If so, how can the form of the good itself rank as a *principle*? Or does the argument start from provisional hypotheses? If so, how can the form of the good purportedly derived from these avoid being provisional too?

The assumption leading to this impasse is that when, at the end of their training, the philosophers lift up their eyes to the form of the good as their paradigm for ordering the city, etc. (540a7–b1), they are looking to it for guidance *for making the city, etc. virtuous, i.e. for determining what measures to implement at the concrete empirical level.*[80] It was indeed guidance for that level that the philosophers received by attending to intelligible paradigms back at 484c–d and 500b–501c. There we had, on one side, forms – forms of the virtues – and, on the other side, various envisaged concrete instantiations of them in the city and in individuals. But the form of the good as presented in the sun-analogy had no place in this scenario, because the 'others' to which the

---

[80] The otherwise very different interpretation of Szlezák incorporates the same assumption. In his view, the form of the good is the One of the unwritten doctrines, and the future ruler is meant to follow this model by implementing unity (= justice as the right binding together of parts) in city and in souls (Szlezák 2003, 102–3).

analogy says it relates are not sensible instantiations of anything, but other forms. So, what can Plato mean at 540a–b when he says that the about-to-be rulers are to behold the form of the good and then use it as their paradigm in bringing order to city, citizens, and themselves?

Rather than turning straight to this problem, let us note a strange thing about this passage. It is something that should puzzle any interpreter, however one understands the form of the good. The puzzle is what to make of the *temporal position* in the lives of the trainees of that moment when they must raise their vision to behold the good which they will use as paradigm. Plato very deliberately makes this moment culminate the whole training regime, placing it not within or even at the end of the five-year period of dialectical study, but at the end of the subsequent fifteen-year period of practical experience (period 3). In other words, this moment comes just when they are on the brink of taking up sovereign control of the city.[81] And yet, the grasping of the non-hypothetical principle, which most scholars agree should be identified with the form of the good, has previously figured in the setting of dialectic (practised in period 2). So, does dialectical activity's contact with the non-hypothetical principle occur for the very first time only *after* a fifteen-year break for practical experience? This implies that what was learnt in the five previous years was only a truncated part of the dialectical exercise, a part in which the non-hypothetical principle never figured at all.[82] Then why, when dialectic along with the non-hypothetical principle was first introduced at 510b6–7, were we not told then of a truncation or separation of dialectic itself into an incomplete stage and a completing one which would follow fifteen (*fifteen*) years later?[83] Or is it that full bouts of dialectic did occur before this very long practical interval, but now the method, or its climactic moment, is brought in once again just before the trainees go down to rule, perhaps in order to reinforce what dialectic taught them all those years before? Or was the non-hypothetical principle (= the form of the good) an element of dialectic even in period 2, but the years of practical experience in period 3 have developed it from an outline-paradigm into a richly informative paradigm for moulding the lives of city and individuals? If so, why has Plato not told us? It would not have been hard to explain.

We can sidestep these questions if we suppose, as I shall, that what 540a–b says the philosophers must do at the moment of transition from trainees to

---

[81] Those of them who get the first turn to rule; cf. 540b1–2.
[82] For this view see Adam 1907, 153; Cornford 1932b, 184–5; Burnyeat 2000, 5; Gentzler 2005, 488; Scott 2015, 50 ('the final dialectical push').
[83] 'The reader has not been prepared to find the vision of Good separated in time from training in moral dialectic', Cornford 1932b, 184–5. The oddity of the separation has led some scholars to conclude that the non-hypothetical principle of dialectic is not the form of the good that figures at 540a4–b1. For a detailed argument along these lines see Delcomminette 2006, 7–10.

rulers is: commit themselves to the dialectical *method*, typified here by the role in it of the good, *in general and as such*. In other words, we are shown them not engaging with the good at the first-order level where they use dialectic in one or another particular inquiry into virtue, but as focusing on and endorsing this entire method-*type*. What they must do, according to the present text, is enter into a general commitment to reach conclusions about fundamental norms and values through dialectical inquiry bringing to bear the form of the good. I have argued that in their first-order dialectical activity that form is not what they inquire *about* but occurs interrogatively, as a means of clarifying what they do inquire about. However, when at the meta-level they focus on that form as epitomizing their method, and dedicate themselves to this method as such, they are not *using* the interrogatively inflected form: they are (in the philosophically technical sense) *mentioning* it.[84] On this meta-level the good is indeed an object of interest for them in its own right, not a tool for investigating something else. And on this level the good *qua* epitomizing the rulers' method is the paradigm they adopt: it is the general template for determining the shape of specific dialectical inquiries. It is not a paradigm consisting of the virtue-forms themselves, a paradigm whose character would be reflected in implementations of the virtues on the ground in people's lives. Nor is it a super-paradigm-form of which the virtue-forms themselves are metaphysical imitations. Rather, it is the general pattern for *inquiry* into the virtues, i.e. into what it is that the virtues demand should be done at the concrete empirical level. It is a methodological paradigm. Adopting it is the primary step in the work of 'ordering city, citizens, and themselves'.

So, at the moment of transition to supreme power the philosophers must make a second-order undertaking to carry out their first-order deliberations always in the light of the good.[85] They must commit themselves to this as their

---

[84] Plato, of course, has no device for indicating the switch of focus from the philosophers' first-order use of the form of the good to their meta-reflection about it.

[85] This interpretation helps explain the compulsion expressed by 'must be led' (*akteon*) and 'must be compelled' (*anankasteon*) at 540a6–7. If the *telos* at 540a6 ('the end-point of their journey' in Rowe's translation) is first-order contemplation of the form of the good, it is rather mysterious that the philosophers need compelling towards it ('the fully mature guardian might be expected to leap toward the Good when it is first opportune', Shields 2007, 21). On the present interpretation the *telos* is actual ruling, which has been the purpose of the education from which they are now finally graduating. We know already that they do not take on the job eagerly (519c–521b; cf. 540b4–5), so the compulsion answers to this reluctance. Lines 540a4–c2 comprise a single sentence, something which a modern translation is unlikely to reproduce. In its second clause, starting at 540a6, *anankasteon* governs the infinitives *apoblepsai* (a8), *kosmein* (b1), and *oikein* (b7), the subject in each case being the graduands. (Presumably it also governs *poiein* at c1, although the understood subject is the city.) It is certainly strange to speak of them as under compulsion to order *themselves* (b1), but even stranger to say it of their eventual passage to the Isles of the Blest (b6–7). I think that Plato wanted (a) to bundle all these episodes defining a ruler's career into one huge clause representing a single causally connected narrative, but also (b) to emphasize the reluctance-motif by making *anankasteon* the first word.

universal methodological principle, as 'that which sheds light on all things' (540a8): the universal 'all things' is part of the content of their meta-attitude. This moment of methodological commitment is dramatically placed at the very end of their training, presumably because, although they doubtless already have a general sense of their method, *commitment* to their method as such only weighs in with complete seriousness when nothing further stands between them and the full burden of political responsibility. Plato may even be hinting at a solemn inaugural act, a formal ceremony matching the *post mortem* ceremonies envisaged a few lines later, of self-identification with the method as such of the G-question.

Just as 'the good' or 'the form of the good' turns out to have a double reference, reflecting the difference between first-order use and second-order methodological reflection, so too its description 'the most important thing to learn' (*to megiston mathēma*, 504d2–505a2; recalled at 519c9–10). What is most important to learn is both the skill of applying 'good' correctly in particular bouts of dialectical reasoning and the general axiom that this is the foundation of all true values.

So, in sum, the work of the rulers is distinguished by two paradigms or sets of paradigms. (1) Having obtained correct accounts of what justice and the other virtues demand, they use these as guides or paradigms for bringing concrete order to city, citizens, and themselves. They earlier obtained those correct accounts by using a dialectical method which involved the form of the good (*not* as a paradigm or pattern by which to recognize the virtues, but nonetheless as a tool for discriminating real from spurious ones). (2) At the moment of embarking on their career as fully trained ruler-intellectuals, they undertook to follow the general pattern of this method in all their inquiries into the true nature of the virtues. Depicting them as lifting up their gaze towards the all-illuminating form of the good[86] is a way of saying that the general method to which they harnessed themselves as about-to-be bearers of supreme responsibility is that of examining (not the good itself, but) other forms in light

As a result, actions one might suppose unreluctant come within its grammatical scope (although b4–5 applies only to ruling). Also, the career as a whole might be said to be undertaken with some reluctance because one of its parts is. Cf. 519c8–d2, where apprehending the good figures as 'enforced' because it is grammatically co-ordinate with ascent from the cave, described at 515e–516a as a matter of being dragged up. On the good-ward compulsion see also 519c4–d7, where sighting the form of the good (which, we are reminded, is 'the most important thing to learn') is the final preliminary to the *practical* task which lovers of learning would refuse if they were allowed to (*hekontas einai ou praxousin*, 519c4–5). The vignette at 540a6–7 of the graduands fixating on the form of the good catches them not so much lost in blissful contemplation as screwing themselves up intellectually for their imminent plunge into the rough seas of government.

[86] Since what is depicted is an act of considering the method, not of using it, the prefix of *anaklinontas* at 540a7 is no evidence that the primary activity of dialectic includes an 'ascent' to dialectic's non-hypothetical principle; on this supposed ascent see Section 2.11.

of the good. On this interpretation the passage 540a4–b1 is not evidence that in first-order dialectical activity the form of the good occurs as an object to be discovered and studied rather than as a tool for discovery. Thus, the interrogative interpretation of the form of the good within dialectic is not in conflict with this famous passage.

The lines about lifting up their gaze towards the form of the good are only the first part of a long sentence which goes on to sketch different phases of the philosophical career ahead. One phase will be the work of 'educating others like themselves to take their place as guardians of the state' (540b5–6). The proximity of this theme confirms our interpretation of the first part as being about the method as such. For it is pedagogically natural when passing on a discipline to others to combine practice in particular exercises with shared reflection on the overall methodology.

I turn now to other passages in which the future ruler is said to see, get sight of, view, or apprehend the form of the good: 517b9 *horasthai, ophtheisa*; 517c3 *idein*; 518d1 *theōmenē*; 519c10–d2 *idein, idōsi*; 526e2–5 *katidein, idein*; 532b1 *autēi noēsei labē(i)*; 532c7 *thean*. These all occur in the context of the educational process symbolized as beginning in the cave and ending in upper-world encounters with originals of reflections, etc., and finally the sun. In each case seeing, grasping, or looking at the form of the good marks the culmination of the education that started with number theory. None of the passages occurs within anything resembling an analysis of what happens within dialectic when that method is actually being exercised. This is important because the contrast drawn earlier (Section 2.7) between looking at, attending to, focusing on, studying X, and using Y as a looked *through* resource for looking *at* (etc.) X, had its application *within* dialectical activity. The claim was that dialectic examines X, namely some proposed account of, e.g., justice or the just, and does so by means of Y, namely the form of the good functioning as an interrogative.

In the above passages Socrates certainly speaks of the trainees as adverting to the form of the good and as apprehending it or getting to be aware of it. This, I think, can be understood as depicting what we might call meta-dialectical awareness of its relevance. (Thus, the interpretation follows much the same lines as that applied to 540a4–b1.) Imagine that towards the end of their dialectical training the moment arrives when they realize that all their analytic efforts to define justice, etc. by means of a formula such as 'EFG' fall short: they have to take a new kind of step, namely asking very deliberately whether EFG is *good*. This entails first making sure that they are not already taking it for granted that EFG is good – they must not have blocked the question by already 'knowing' the answer. They then progress to the general realization that no formula for justice or any of the virtues can succeed unless it is open-mindedly made to face the G-question, and survives the confrontation.

They have learnt that the *goodness* of (say) EFG (if it *is* good) is what makes it the case that 'EFG' says *what justice is*. Generalizing, they realize that it is because of the presence of the form of the good that some formula by which they seek to define one or another of the virtues emerges as correct, i.e. as a formula that ascribes to that virtue the character or profile that really belongs to it and in terms of which it is known. This is a moment of general meta-realization about how the form of the good contributes to first-order dialectical inquiry. The meta-realization may be prompted by, but is not the same as, a particular first-order interrogative use of that form to validate or invalidate a specific virtue-formula.

Such meta-realization is pictured in this famous passage:

> Then finally, I imagine, he'd be able to catch sight of (*katidein*) the sun, not just reflected in water, or as it appears in any alien location, but the sun itself, by itself, in its own place, and look upon it (*theasasthai*) as what it is ... And then at last he would reason (*sullogizoito*) that it was *this* that not only provided the yearly cycle of the seasons and oversaw everything in the region of the seen, but was also in a certain way the cause of those other things he and the others used to see. (516b4–c1)

At last the escaped prisoner sees the sun, and thereupon realizes in a general way that this is what is responsible for the good things under the sun, and indirectly for the objects seen in the cave; but he is not yet making his own use of the sun as a resource for charting this or that specific visible thing in the upper world. The image is of the trainee receiving his final piece of dialectical equipment as it were. The parallel passage at 517b9–c3 says:

> in the sphere of the known what is seen last, and seen with difficulty (*mogis*), is the form of the good; and ... given that it *is* seen (*ophtheisa*) one is bound to reason (*sullogistea*) that it, in fact, is cause for everything of everything right and beautiful, as both progenitor of light and of the source of light in the sphere of the seen, and the source itself of truth and intelligence in the intelligible sphere.

This, as I understand it, shows the dialectician being, so to speak, introduced to the G-question or having it presented to him: not yet using it but realizing when he meets it the extent of its power – if wielded by a properly capable questioner (human or divine) – to generate excellent effects both intellectual and physical. Plato shows here how the student's causal interest and compre-hension has grown by leaps and bounds from zero at the bottom of the cave, where as a shackled prisoner he or she received the shadow-sequence as an ultimate reality dependent on nothing, and then with difficulty descried the cave-statues or puppets and realized that these were *causing* the lowest shadows, and then in the upper world advanced from effects (natural reflec-tions in water, etc.) to causes, and then to the realization that the sun is what causes the upper world's three-dimensional objects to be and be seen, as well as causing them to cause their upper-world reflections, and indirectly via other agents (manufacturers) causing the statues in the cave and so, again indirectly, via its analogue and viceroy the fire, causing the lowest shadows. A great deal here has still to be interpreted (see in particular Part 3 on the form of the good and being, and Section 4.4 on theology and cosmology), but the main point for now is this: understanding and thinking about ('contemplating') a general causal truth, e.g. that bread nourishes (Hume's example), is not the same as *using* the cause on a given occasion to feed oneself. The latter corresponds to the dialecticians' relation to the form of the good within their first-order practice of dialectic, the former to their meta-dialectical consideration of it and the practice as such. Distinguishing these levels is essential for maintaining the thesis that *within* the first-order activity the form of the good is not an object of study but is, in fact, the content of a question wielded in order to find out about other things.[87]

This section has introduced the distinction between first-order use of the G-question *in* dialectic, and meta-awareness of the dialectical method as such. The immediate reason for invoking this distinction was to explain that moment when, their fifteen years of practical training completed, the protagonists lift up their intellectual gaze to the form of the good. The timing of this event and the description of its subjects as under *necessity* suggest that it occurs not as a move within first-order dialectic, but as marking the transition from the thirty-year training as a whole to actual rulership. The moment is described by Plato with special solemnity because (I suggest) it is when the graduates take a vow to follow the method as such, with its characteristic G-question, in all the real-life decision-making that lies immediately ahead. This, then, is a pre-eminent moment of methodological reflection *about* or attention *to* the method. But it certainly does not follow that this is the first time they attend to the method as such or to the G-question as such. On the contrary, I would suppose that, being human, they have been intermittently thinking in a general way *about* the G-question, as distinct from engaging in specific uses of it, from when it was first put into their hands as the final piece in the tool-kit of dialectic.[88] Learning

---

[87] In many passages the language of vision, as applied to the form of the good, may have filtered through from its literal use in connection with the sun. It seems to be a common impression that in the *Republic* knowledge is intellectual intuition somehow parallel to literal vision. But parallelism would equally yield the result that literally catching sight of something is only ever achieved through some sort of physical to-and-fro of deliberate moves parallel to the intellectual pattern of questioning, testing hypotheses, etc.! Kahn 2012, 167–8, warns against taking Plato's language of intellectual vision too seriously: 'the nature of the forms is not to be understood from the perspective of vision but from the perspective of λόγος, where λόγος is conceived as the dialectical pursuit of definition, the pursuit of clarity and understanding by means of linguistic exchange, by means of question and answer concerning what things are and how they are'.

[88] The two levels may be hard to disentangle because in *teaching* a tool-using skill the teacher gets the apprentice to employ it in a particular application, yet both sides necessarily see this as a case of a general technique to be applied again and again. Yet the levels differ because the

to use the G-tool finalizes their five-year training in dialectic; and vowing in general to make its use the source of the knowledge by which they will govern finalizes their thirty-year education as a whole. These are two distinct finalities, each in a different way involving the form of the good.

2.11 The Non-Hypothetical Principle as First Premiss?

A certain scholarly picture is at odds with the present suggestion that the good in the context of dialectic is interrogative in relation to proposed definitions of the virtues. According to this picture, the good (the form of the good) is a non-hypothetical first principle that makes its dialectical impact as (or as presented in) the first premiss of dialectic. The first premiss is taken to be a definition displaying the intrinsic nature of the supreme good, in formally the same manner as when an ethical theory defines the highest good as pleasure, or as virtuous activity in a complete life, or as the greatest happiness of the greatest number. The *definiendum* in these examples is not the meaning of the term 'good' taken in the ordinary thin predicative sense. The *definiendum* is (or is captured by) a definite description constructed from the thin predicate together with the modifier 'highest', and its referent is the good thing (i.e. the kind of good thing), whatever it is, on which (it is assumed) the goodness of all other good things somehow depends.[89] Thus, in the context of the premiss-interpretation of the form of the good in Book VI of the *Republic*, the phrase 'the form (or: idea) of the good' means 'the form of the highest good' in the sense just explained, and the supposed premiss presents the correct answer to the question to which 'pleasure' and 'wisdom' were shown to be faulty answers (505b5–d1). The premiss specifies what the highest good is, and thereby conveys information – non-obvious and perhaps recondite information – as distinct from being a truism which everyone would get right straight off. Whether to think of Plato's form of the good as given in this way by *a premiss* is the question of this section.

When Plato differentiates mathematics and dialectic on the ground that dialectic has a non-hypothetical basis, whereas the basis of mathematics is not non-hypothetical, it seems clear that he thinks of the mathematical basis as the set of first premisses or axioms, or at any rate the set of supposedly elementary objects[90] posited or definitionally presented in what we would think of as first premisses or axioms. (I shall now simply speak of 'premisses'

---

logically basic use of a tool (as in 'the hammer is for driving in nails') is not the act of teaching how to use that same tool.

[89] This is what Kant in the Second Critique calls the *bonum supremum* as distinct from the *bonum consummatum*. For more discussion of this conception see Section 4.1.

[90] Such as the odd and the even, etc.

in this context.) The point about mathematical premisses is, of course, that results are derived from them through deduction or something like deduction.[91] It is, perhaps, easy to think that, parallel-wise, Plato sees the first principle of dialectic – namely the form of the good, or some kind of proposition presenting the nature of the good – as a premiss from which the dialectician derives results, the difference between dialectician and mathematician being that the former's basic premiss is non-hypothetical whereas the latter's is not.[92] We have seen, however, that this sort of interpretation is not inevitable. It seems clear that Plato thinks that just as the premisses of a mathematical demonstration (in their case via something like derivability) control what further items are admissible into the ensuing course of reasoning, so the good or the form of the good acts as a control (*archē*, 510b6; 511b6) on what is to count as an acceptable result for the dialectician. But it does not follow that the controlling factor operates in both cases as a *deductive* starting point. It need not be the case that the form of the good controls in the precise way in which a deductive premiss or premiss-set does. The logical nexus between a premiss-set and what is deducible from it is, of course, very different from the relation between the good in interrogative mode and the results of such interrogation, but in both cases there is control over what is and is not allowed into the discourse. We cannot know that this latter similarity was not more salient to Plato than the difference of logical relationship formally conceived.[93] If the general notion of control, as opposed to a particular mode of control, was uppermost for him, this might help to explain why he does not say just how the non-hypothetical principle of dialectic gives rise to results, and therefore why he gives no explicit evidence in favour of the interrogative interpretation.

Some may think – taking it for granted that the most rigorous method of inquiry is deductive – that since dialectic ranks higher than mathematics in cognitive excellence and mathematics is deductive, *a fortiori* dialectic operates by deduction from the form of the good. But why assume that Plato sees deduction as uniquely the acme of rigour? His comparison of the two disciplines never mentions deduction or valid derivation as the *ne plus ultra* of precise reasoning. Its focus is solely on the difference between having and not having a non-hypothetical starting point, and between dispensing and not dispensing with diagrams.

---

[91] We cannot assume that Plato had exactly our concept of deduction. For instance, we think that a deduction ought to state all its premisses, whereas Plato may have assumed that it is not a fault to leave some premisses tacit.

[92] For this view see Robinson 1953, 153, 159, 168–9, 175.

[93] Cf. Mueller 1992, 183: 'for philosophical purposes he was willing to class together deduction and less formal methods of serious argumentation'. It is relevant that Plato has no exact word for 'deduction'.

Many scholars have the impression that dialectical reasoning, according to the *Republic*, makes an 'ascent' to the non-hypothetical first principle. And many understand 'ascending' here as moving to a prior premiss from which what was initially just a hypothesis can be derived. This interpretation is inspired by *Phaedo* 101d–e, where Socrates speaks of supporting a challenged hypothesis by 'going to one of the *higher* hypotheses'. It is generally held that this is a matter of identifying a less questionable hypothesis from which the challenged one is derivable. Transferring this picture to the *Republic* yields the theory that dialectic lays hold of the non-hypothetical principle as a super-premiss from which it derives the truth or falsehood of the initial, more questionable, hypotheses.

However, there is no firm evidence in the *Republic* that Plato thinks of dialectical reasoning as 'ascending' to the non-hypothetical. If he did describe it in such terms, then in light of the somewhat technical use of 'higher' in the *Phaedo* passage we should have reason to think of the non-hypothetical principle of the *Republic* as a premiss from which the dialecticians infer answers to their questions. But the text of the *Republic* does not bear this out. That is, it does not license applying the language of ascent to some move internal to dialectic.[94] (This is by contrast with ascent from the cave, on which more presently.) Yet the notion that dialectical reasoning 'ascends' to the form of the good has spread like a catchy tune. Whether interpreters start by positioning the form of the good as (or as what is presented in) a primary premiss, and consequently speak of dialectic's approach to it in terms borrowed from the *Phaedo*'s 'higher' terminology, or whether (the other way round) they first for whatever reason picture dialectic as ascending to the form of the good and consequently (again via the *Phaedo*) interpret the latter as a deductive first premiss, is impossible to say and probably varies among scholars. Either way, the text of the *Republic* does not support the idea that dialectical reasoning 'goes up' to its non-hypothetical starting point. Hence evidence that the non-hypothetical starting point, *alias* (I assume) the form of the good, functions as dialectical first premiss is not in fact forthcoming.[95]

---

[94] That dialectic has a downward path (511b7) does not imply that there was first an upward path, *pace* Cherniss 1947, 143 and Benson forthcoming, n. 53. Socrates went down to the Piraeus with Glaucon (327a1) whether or not he had previously gone up to Athens.

[95] Scholars who speak of an 'ascent' or 'upward path' within dialectic to the non-hypothetical principle, in some cases building it into their translations, include Jowett 1892; Adam 1907, 67, 71, 86, 174–6; Cornford 1932a, 42-3; 1941; Shorey 1935, vol. II; Chambry, 1946; Cherniss 1947, 143; Joseph 1948, 53; Ross 1953, 58, 70; Robinson 1953, 160–177, 182, 187, 278–9; Crombie 1962, 129–30; 1963, 554–8; Cross and Woozley 1964, 249–51; Rose 1966, 194; Gosling 1973, 107, 118; Boyle 1974, 7; N. White 1976, 99; Lafrance 1980, 90; Santas 1980/ 1999, 247; Annas 1981, 291; Reeve 1988, 77–8; Mueller 1992, 186–7; Sayre 1995, 143–4, 148, 172; Baltzly 1996, 149; Schofield 1997; Burnyeat 2000, 5, 42 n. 59; Szlezák 2001, 347, 371;

Various passages may seem to suggest the contrary.

(1) Socrates: This [sc. mathematics] is the kind of thing I included in the intelligible but with two provisos: first, that the soul was compelled to investigate it by means of hypotheses, but because it was unable to get away from hypotheses by going higher (*ou dunamenēn tōn hupothseōn anōterō ekbainein*) it failed to go to a first principle (*ouk ep' archēn iousan*); second, that it used, as images... (511a4–7).

Here Socrates says that in *mathematics* the soul cannot escape from (*ekbainein*) mere hypotheses by going higher. Either, for some reason, mathematics cannot think of anything higher to go to, or, if it can, the higher item is still only a hypothesis, not a first principle. This does not imply that *dialectic* escapes from mere hypotheses by going higher.

Glaucon, referring to the mathematicians, replies to the above:

(2) ... because they don't investigate by going up (*anelthontes*) to a first principle, but only by using hypotheses, they seem to you not to have an intelligent grasp (*noun ouk ischein*) of the things they're looking at. (511c3–d2)

Glaucon then reprises Socrates' ranking of mathematical cognition midway between opinion (*doxa*) and genuine intelligence (*nous*). Socrates responds approvingly: 'You've grasped <what I said> very adequately' (511d6). Now, when Glaucon says that mathematicians *don't* go up to a first principle perhaps he is assuming that, according to Socrates, dialecticians by contrast *do* go up to their first principle, even though Socrates has only said that they go *to* or *towards* it (*ienai epi* + accusative, 511b5–6). In that case Socrates' endorsement includes what Glaucon has imputed to him. But a different interpretation of Glaucon's words is possible. Glaucon's assumption may simply be that the mathematical method is such that if the mathematicians did have a first principle, they could only reach it by 'going up' to it as a premiss from which the rest of mathematics can be derived. Socrates can endorse this without holding that *dialectic* ascends to *its* first principle.

(3) By the other section of the intelligible understand me to mean that which reasoning itself (*autos ho logos*) takes hold of by the power of dialectic (*tēi tou dialegesthai dunamei*), treating the hypotheses not as principles but as indeed hypotheses– like places for stepping on and being launched from (*hoion epibaseis te kai hormas*) – so that it goes to the principle of everything, all the way to that which is non-hypothetical (*mechri tou anhupothetou*), and, on laying hold of it [sc. the principle of everything], descends (*katabainēi*) hanging on to those things that hang from *it* [i.e. the principle], to the conclusion, making no additional use of any perceptible thing whatsoever, but using

Karasmanis 2004, 32; Lee 2007; Patterson 2007, 1; Rowe 2007c, 220; 2012; Repellini 2013, 175, 186; Vegetti 2013b 202–3; Benson 2015, 247–8; forthcoming; Scott 2015, 23; Gerson 2018, 46–7; 2020, 122 n. 9.

forms themselves by themselves to pass to forms themselves, thus concluding in forms. (511b–c)[96]

In this passage the figure of the dialectician 'descending' via steps that depend on the first principle may suggest deduction from that principle, but this is not the only possible interpretation. Here is another. (a) When proposed definitions of virtues have been validated by passing the test of the interrogative good, they 'hang from' the form of the good in that they now have its support and are no longer mere hypotheses. (b) The dialectician now hangs on to those items immediately supported by the first principle, using them as supports in turn for the dialectical 'descent'. (c) The descent is presumably a movement towards conclusions that are closer to concrete practice than the definitions themselves. (d) Let it be granted that the steps constituting this descent are deductive. Even with this concession we lack evidence that the relationship between the first principle and the items immediately supported by it is deductive. Again, the logical difference between this relationship (non-deductive and non-inferential, if the interrogative interpretation is right)[97] and the relation (let it be deductive) between the definitions and the lower steps, may well have seemed less important to Plato, or less worth remarking on, than the fact that in both cases items which started out as mere hypotheses, and their previously hypothetical consequences, are now banished from further consideration or else are firm fixtures.

The language halfway through passage 3 may seem to describe ascent from the hypotheses to the non-hypothetical principle, and thus to treat the latter as a premiss. But the words do not say that dialectic *ascends* to the non-hypothetical principle. In colloquial English they may be translated as 'goes right up to it' (*mechri* + genitive, 511b5), but this only means 'does not stop short of it'. As for the comparison of dialectical hypotheses to 'places for stepping on and being launched from', this may, but certainly need not, be

---

[96] My translation.
[97] If the form of the good is a question *asked* – the G-question – nothing can be deduced from it. If we focus on that question *answered*, e.g. suppose the dialectician determines that EFG *is* good, and therefore *is* justice, argument is needed to show that this result is reached by *deduction* from the form of the good as premiss. *Pace* Gerson 2020, 122 n. 9, it is not 'quite explicit that the Forms are deduced from the first principle'. How, then, *does* the dialectician determine that EFG is good? Is it supposed to be self-evident that it is or that it is not? Well, not if one focuses on EFG all by itself. The dialectician must look to relevant factors such as context for reasons for judging either way. This is discussed in Section 2.14. Is returning a thing to its owner good? Not if the object is a weapon and the owner has gone out of his mind. Then, under these circumstances, returning it is not what justice is. Asking the G-question in such a case makes salient the prohibition against harming, hence (given no countervailing circumstance or countervailing practical principle) that returning the weapon would do injustice to those who risk being harmed. This conclusion is inferred from the nature of the case; it is not inferred from, but prompted by, (consideration of) the good. *Asking* 'would it be good?' brings to light reasons why it would or wouldn't be.

taken to show the dialectician *leaping up* from them to the good or the non-hypothetical principle. The point of these similes is much more likely to be that dialectic starts from hypotheses which then (as hypotheses) *are left behind*. This is by contrast with mathematics where the assumptions from which we start not only retain their status as assumptions but are fixtures or constants which we carry along throughout subsequent investigations. The initial hypotheses of dialectic launch the investigation but then, as often as not, they are discarded, i.e. refuted and replaced by more promising ones. The discarded ones served a purpose by eliciting the criticism that replaced them with something more likely to pass the test of the G-question. 'Like places for stepping on and being launched from' does not forbid us to visualize someone climbing up a ladder or staircase, but it does not demand it. 'Pushing off from and leaving behind' is central to the simile, whereas 'ascent' is just one possible way of imagining it.

It is, of course, true that in the sun-analogy the good is metaphorically presented as above the objects it illuminates. But the sun-analogy says nothing about how the good is grasped or even whether it is grasped, and it says nothing about the internal structure of dialectical reasoning. It is also true that the Cave says that the eye of the soul, from being 'sunk in barbaric mud', is gently pulled and led *upwards* (*anagei anō*, 533d2–3) by the dialectical method 'using as its supporters and helpers in the conversion (*sunerithois kai sumperiagōgois chrōmenē*)' sciences (so called) such as mathematics (see also 532b8 and c5, *epanodos* and *epanagōgēn*). The 533d2–3 picture, I think, is an amalgamation of the entire two-stage intellectual programme, mathematics followed by dialectic, rather than a description of what the trainees do at the dialectical stage proper. Dialectic appears as the principal agent of the soul's liberation through mathematics because dialectic dominates this process in the sense of being what the liberation is ultimately all about – what it is for. Dialectic – perhaps personified – is shown *using* mathematics for its own purpose. After all, Plato does not want readers to think that the trainee rulers are prescribed mathematical study just for its own sake. So he speaks here of the mathematical disciplines being employed as supporters and helpers for drawing and leading the eye of the soul upwards. This would be a very strange, in fact absurd, way of talking about a supposed logical movement internal to dialectic itself (a movement, on the interpretation we are considering, towards a deductively prior premiss). For then Plato would be saying that the way the thinker executes this internal-to-dialectic move is by making some kind of move within mathematics! But given the differences Plato insists on between the two disciplines, he can hardly think it possible to engage in both activities within a single project. The intellect's liberation is called an ascent (515e6; 517a3–5; 517b4–5; 519d1; 521c2–3; cf. 516a5; 529b4) because of the symbolism of escaping from the subterranean cave (*katageiou*, 514a3; 532b8), and then learning to raise one's eyes from shadows and reflections in water, etc., to the three-dimensional sun-lit objects and finally to the sun itself. The whole scenario makes it natural to think of the dialectician's turn to the good as the highest, because ultimate, moment of the entire intellectual education. But the focus is on this *entire* education, which consists of mathematics leading to dialectic and culminating *as a whole* in methodological reflection on the role of the good in dialectic as such (see Section 2.10 above). In short, ascent language here refers to the whole journey from illusion via mathematical education to dialectical enlightenment. So it fails to support the notion that *within* dialectic the thinker 'ascends to' the non-hypothetical principle as if the latter were a super-premiss.[98]

I have been arguing on the assumption that getting to know X by ascent to a higher premiss would consist in identifying a premiss from which X is then inferred by deduction. However, some commentators understand dialectical ascent in the *Republic* as a matter of identifying a wider genus of which X is one species, so that X gets to be defined *per genus et differentiam*; and some understand it as a matter of identifying an item on which X is grounded (whether or not this is the genus of X), and on which it therefore depends as effect on cause but without necessarily being entailed by it.[99] These proposals have the advantage of not saddling Plato with the questionable assumption that a single non-hypothetical principle could, by itself, give rise to a multiplicity of deductive results.[100] The genus-interpretation may fit the notion, espoused by some, that Plato's form of the good generates the other forms by virtually being them.[101] But if these views aim to expound a supposed ascent, internal to dialectic, to the ultimate principle, they too lack foundation, for the text gives no firm evidence of any such ascent.

---

[98] The distinction between ascent from the cave and a supposed ascent within dialectic itself was clearly drawn by Ross 1953, 70; cf. Robinson 1953, 187. The long sentence 533c8–d4 has two parts joined by *kai*, d1, the first of which deals with the internal process of dialectical reasoning, while the second shows dialectic using mathematical skills to help draw the eye of the soul out of the cave. The references to 'up', etc. at 517a3–5, b4–5, c8, and 529b4 are clearly to the latter scenario.

[99] *Timaeus* 53d speaks of principles yet higher than (*anōthen*) the basic types of triangle. If these are the numbers, or, going further back, the One and the Dyad, the relation is surely one of being grounded on without being deducible from. The language makes clear that a move to them would not be a move *within* the discipline currently being expounded (cosmology) but beyond it to a different discipline. Hence this hardly supports the notion of an ascent within dialectic in the *Republic*.

[100] For this worry see Ross 1953, 55; N. White 1976, 100; Mueller 1992, 190; Denyer 2007, 306.

[101] See e.g. Adam 1907, 62, 'all *ousiai* are only specific determinations of the Good', and Gerson's view (1990, 61; 2002, 384, 387) that the form of the good is virtually the other forms.

2.12   The Form of the Good as Object of Definition?

If the correct definition of the intrinsic nature of the good is a super-premiss for dialectic, how do dialecticians achieve knowledge of this definition? Do they, on encountering it, understand it as self-evident, transparently beyond questioning? But how do they get to encounter it? If they did approach it by 'ascent' as discussed in the last section, how would they know when they have reached something non-hypothetical? After all, one might easily have believed posits such as 'Every [whole] number is either odd or even' to be absolutely inescapable although according to Plato they are only hypotheses; so how do the dialecticians avoid a similar mistake about a proposed definition of the good? Suppose they can't find anything wrong with some proposed definition: does this show that it is correct and stands in no need of justification? But what if they came up with, say, two genuinely distinct unfaulted definitions? Neither could be decisively embraced as a non-hypothetical truth while the other remained unrefuted. If their dialectical skill arms them against all the epistemic dangers threatening indubitable arrival at, and recognition of, their non-hypothetical definitional destination, this skill must be unlike anything we or the companions of Socrates or Socrates or probably even Plato can imagine – which neatly explains why he says rather little about the nature of dialectic.[102]

If Plato holds that the non-hypothetical principle is the true definition of the good, does he think that this definition is reached by reasoning from some ulterior *principle*? If so, the definition might be suitably non-hypothetical, but it ought to be explained in what way it itself still counts as a principle. He also ought not to think of it as a definition reached by inference to the best explanation (and so principle) of some already-known things, for this sort of procedure, anyway as used in natural science, only yields a provisional result.[103] Today's best explanation of a datum may be superseded by a better one. But, in any case, there is no hint in *Republic* VI–VII that dialectic

---

[102] Showing that the dialectician's grasp of the form of the good is not an inarticulate passive experience (McCabe 2006) does not yet show what the grasping it amounts to. If grasping it is asking the G-question about something else, this is neither inarticulate nor passive.

[103] On the dialectician's findings as non-provisional see Section 2.15. Robinson 1953, 172–4, concludes that the non-hypothetical principle corresponds to a state in which the dialectician has tested and re-tested his definition of the good and can find nothing wrong with it (cf. Berti 2002; Reeve 2012, 165–6). Adherents of this view seem to lack an adequate response to the fact that any definition might one day be overturned by an objection not yet thought of, so is in a sense provisional. Suppose we construe the non-hypothetical principle as constituted by whatever definition of the good has resisted all objections so far: how then does it differ from the mathematicians' starting points? The keenest minds of the time might have tried to fault the latter without success, but even so they are only hypothetical according to Plato. By contrast, the G-question is not merely the best question we happen to be able to envisage in our current situation, since we know it as a constant for every possible juncture of life.

establishes the nature of the good by starting from other things. The salient 'other things' mentioned in the vicinity are justice, temperance, wisdom, and courage, and it seems fairly clear that in relation to them the situation is the other way round: the dialectician gets to detect authentic versions of them with the help of the non-hypothetical principle (see 504a–b and Section 1.4).

One passage, however, can be read as saying that the dialectician manages to define the form of the good. But we shall see that it need not be read in this way.

[A] 'And will you also give the name "dialectician" to someone who gets hold of <u>an account of what each thing is</u> (*ton logon hekastou lambanonta tēs ousias*)? Correspondingly, will you assert that just insofar as someone isn't able to give such an account of it either to himself or to anyone else, to that extent he lacks intelligent understanding (*noun*) of it?'

'I could hardly say he had it', he replied.

[B] 'And <u>won't it be the same</u> (*hōsautōs*) <u>with the good</u>? If someone isn't capable of demarcating it in his formulation (or: in his reasoning; *dihorisasthai logōi*), separating (*aphelōn*) the form (*idean*) of the good from everything else, and of surviving all challenges (*elenchōn*), like some kind of fighter, eager to test (*elenchein*) what he's saying not by reference to opinion but to how things truly are, and coming through all this <u>with his account left standing</u> (*aptōti tōi logōi*) – if he can't do all this, your claim will be, won't it, that he has no knowledge (*eidenai*) either about the good itself or about any other good, and that if he manages to get hold of some kind of shadowy image,[104] he does so through opinion and not through knowledge (*doxe(i), ouk epistēmēi*)? He's dreaming and dozing away his present life, you'll agree, and will get to sleep properly in Hades before he ever wakes up here?'

'Zeus!' he exclaimed. 'I'll definitely say Yes to all that!' (534b–d)

Part B shows the skilful dialectician surviving all challenges with 'his account (i.e. definition) left standing'. There are two crucial questions. The first is: his definition of what? The Greek does not say. On one reading, the definition he successfully defends is his definition of the good. In Part A the dialectician (the person with an intelligent grasp as distinct from mere opinion) was said to give an account of (define) 'what each thing is', and 'each thing' may or may not include the form of the good. However that may be, Part B is clearly about the form of the good, and on one obvious interpretation (interpretation (1) in the next paragraph) it implies that this form, the form of the good, is what the dialectician successfully defines.[105]

---

[104] It is unclear whether the image is of the form of the good or of 'any other good'.
[105] This is the view of Berti 2002. He holds that the dialectically tested hypotheses are proposed definitions of the form of the good, and that one of these is left standing, or becomes non-hypothetical, through refutation of all others. Thus, the dialectician knows how to separate out

The second crucial question is how to understand 'And won't it be the same with the good?' at the start of Part B. First interpretation (1): the next sentence declares (by nudging Glaucon into declaring) that just as (1a) in general one is intelligent about a thing if and only if one is able to *define* it (Part A has said this), so too (1b) with the form of the good: one knows it only if one is able to *define* it. Second interpretation (2) (and in my view the preferable one): the sentence after 'And won't it be the same with the good?' declares that just as (2a) there is *a* condition to be fulfilled for being intelligent about other things, which in their case is being able to define them, so too (2b) there is *a* condition to be fulfilled for knowing (i.e. being in the intelligently correct cognitive relationship with) the form of the good. But according to interpretation (2) the conditions are different. What they have in common is that whoever fails to fulfil them is dialectically inept (explicit at 534b3–6, implied by the mention of *elenchus* at 534c1 and 3). In (2a) the condition is the ability to define 'each thing', and 'each thing' does not include the form of the good. In (2b) the condition is the ability to demarcate the form of the good, to put a border round it and separate it from everything else.

Philologically, the ability to demarcate and separate the form of the good could consist in the ability to define it, since a definition should serve to distinguish its object from everything else; but equally it could be the more negatively conceived ability to ensure that the form of the good is not confused with anything else. This is consistent with the form's having, itself, *no* definable nature.[106] If the passage assumes this, i.e. that the form of the good is not itself a candidate for definition, then in Part B the account (definition) which the dialectician successfully defends is an account of something other than the good itself. Presumably it is an account of some 'other good' (534c4–5), such as one of the virtues. Even so, the long second sentence of Part B gives the strong impression that the dialectician's success in defending his account or definition of whatever he is trying to define is bound up with his ability to keep the form of the good separate from everything else. The picture that results

(*dihoristhasthai tōi logōi*) the true definition. On any given occasion only a finite number of hypotheses is examined, but since there may always be more of them the task of dialectic is never over: a final definition of the form of the good is never reached. But this leaves it unclear why the one left standing on a given occasion is any less hypothetical or provisional than the starting points of mathematics.

[106] At 532a7–b1 the dialectician is said to move towards 'that which each thing is (*auto ho estin hekaston*), and not desist until in thought by itself he gets hold of that which good is (*auto ho estin agathon*)'. This can, but need not, be understood as a bid to grasp what the objects, including the good, are (indirect question) in the sense of getting to know their essences or correct definitions. Alternatively, it says only that dialectic tries to grasp X and Y, including the good, precisely as X and Y, and not as anything else. In the case of 'each thing' (i.e. forms other than the good), this may involve looking for their essences, while in the case of the good it is simply a matter of getting hold just of *it*, not confusing it with anything else such as pleasure.

from supposing that the form of the good here is not itself a candidate for definition accords well with the interrogative interpretation offered in Section 2.8. It is a picture in which the form of the good, unlike 'each thing' mentioned in Part A, has no definable nature of its own but contributes to the defining of other things, and contributes by being demarcated and separated from everything else, i.e. by having its own indefinability upheld and respected.[107]

2.13   Dialectic and Experience

The last two sections have defended the interrogative interpretation by arguing against the rival claim that the form of the good is a definitional super-premiss. But how, on the interrogative interpretation, do the dialecticians reach answers to the G-question? In this section I shall argue that in any given episode of dialectic their answer depends on input from experience as well as their moral character.

Let us start by considering the period of their training in dialectic, i.e. period 2 (see Section 2.8). When they entered period 1 (mathematical studies) they were already about twenty years old, and had undergone intensive moral, physical, and musical training from early childhood. Their limited experience no doubt included events which they heard about from others, allowing for simple extrapolation to easily imagined circumstances. For instance, in relation to a definition of justice as truth-telling and paying debts, raising the G-question should bring it to mind that, when madness strikes, some truths are better not told and some borrowed objects better not returned: so that definition is seen to fail (cf. 331b–d). The students surely learn at this stage that they must do all they can to bring to mind whatever may be relevant for answering the G-question; hence they must learn to judge relevance and relative importance, to note commonalities and differences between considerations which come up now, and between these and ones which came up in past uses of the question, and to marshal all this together in mental conspectus. (Socrates says that looking at things together, *sunopsis*, is a vital part of the dialectical nature; 537c.) Apart from that, their main achievement at this stage may lie in developing an inveterate habit of *asking* the G-question at each point (learning not to trust in pre-G-questioned definitions) rather than in discerning good answers and the reasons for those answers. For at this stage good answers and reasons for them might be easy to discern – once the question is asked. A definition might seem very plausible until they are forced to think about how it would be if it were adopted in practice: that is, whether, e.g., justice *as so defined* is to be a value or norm controlling the actual life of the city and its

---

[107] This interpretation builds on Vegetti 2013c, 148–9. See Section 2.16 for more on separating the form of the good.

citizens. By applying some experience and empirical imagination, it may be easy to see that there might be circumstances in which patterns of behaviour conforming to the definition turn out very badly indeed.

Then the trainees enter period 3, the fifteen years of practical experience. I would suppose that this is a time not just for getting to know the ropes and routines of management and administration, but also for noticing and reflecting on any ways in which actual current policies materially diverge from norms implied by formulae for justice, etc. that might have passed the trainees' scrutiny in period 2. If there is a notable divergence, the trainees would understand that this is because the policy-makers – the current rulers – have themselves brought the G-question to bear in response to circumstances unknown or unforeseen by the trainees in their own period 2, and have answered it negatively. The rulers would have rescinded and modified the city's previously best understanding of justice, etc. in the light of new or previously unidentified circumstances. Hence the trainees in period 3 may, amongst other things, be learning to understand in detail why perhaps initially surprising, even puzzling, departures from well-loved definitions have nevertheless been rightly adopted as *good* – under pressure from the G-question as brought to bear by the rulers themselves in response to concrete circumstances. The trainees, of course, would accept the wisdom of any such changes-on-theground because their upbringing will never let them forget that this is an authoritarian state governed by the wise. They are expected, that is, not to assess independently the wisdom or not of the modifications, but to accept that these *are* good and work out the reasons for them. Their position is like that of the cosmologist in the *Timaeus* who, starting from the axiom that the natural world was intelligently made to be as good as possible, seeks from this to explain why the world and its contents are as they are

Given the fifteen years of practical training, one would think that *if* the philosophers continue to engage in dialectical thinking once they are in office,[108] then experience plays a significant role in it. For the present I am going to assume that dialectic does continue for them when they are actual rulers, in order to ask whether and how experience comes into it. But any claim that experience makes a contribution appears to conflict with the following passage:

in the lower part [of the intelligible segment of the divided line] . . . the soul now uses as images the very things that were the originals in the visible segment, and is compelled to make its investigations on the basis of hypotheses, not moving to a first principle but to a conclusion, whereas in the upper part it moves from a hypothesis to a nonhypothetical first principle, without the images it used in the previous part, and operating with forms alone, nothing else. (510b4–8; cf. 511b3–c2)

[108] This is discussed in Section 2.15.

This passage presents the two differences marking off dialectic from mathematics: resort to a non-hypothetical principle and non-reliance on diagrams or physical models. With respect to diagrams I suggest that Plato's point rests on the fact that mathematics, at least as typified by geometry, uses diagrams as foundational for its conclusions. Diagrams are not just illustrations or aids for fixing the mind on various concepts: working with them delivers answers to the geometer's questions.[109] When Plato declares that dialectic reaches its final answers by means only of forms, without additional use of any object of sense, he is surely saying that dialectic does not *draw its answers from* particular empirical examples or representations. It does not point to an actual or possible empirical case (or depiction of one) and say: 'You can *see from this* that the answer is and has to be so and so,' thereby taking itself to have justified or proved a general conclusion about what, e.g., justice demands. A proposed definition of justice, 'Telling the truth and returning what one has borrowed,' represents a standard empirical exemplar of real justice (since usually that behaviour *is* just); but instead of simply generalizing from that, the dialectician *tests* the proposal against the G-question, and rejects it because it covers cases where the borrowed object is a weapon and the owner has become psychotic. If a new formula excluding such conditions is found not to fail the test and is accepted,[110] this verdict is based on the distinct and carefully ascertained absence of grounds for rejection. The new formula does not by itself carry the information that it is immune to grounds for rejection any more than the naïve original formula carried the information that applying it under certain conditions could lead to disaster. By contrast, the mathematician's diagram, if well-constructed and well-analysed, is sufficient by itself for answering the problem. The mathematician is in a position to say, pointing to something empirically present, namely the diagram, 'You can see simply from examining this that the answer (a general answer to a general question about mathematical relationships) must be so and so.' This is because the 'case' represented by the diagram is not permeable by additional, as yet uncatered for, conditions.

If this is the right way to contrast dialectic and mathematics, then dialectic is allowed (and should be encouraged) to take note of experienced or imagined empirical situations.[111] For they will *suggest* relevant possibilities when the

[109] More on this in the next section.   [110] More on this in Section 2.19.
[111] The view against which I am arguing, that dialectic for rulers completely turns its back on experience, does seem to follow from e.g. 'it [the dialectical argument] reaches a conclusion without using anything perceptible at all' (*aisthētō(i) pantapasin oudeni proschrōmenos*, 511c1). But the choice of words echoes the description of the mathematicians at 510d5: 'they make use of objects that belong to the visible sphere' (*tois horōmenois eidesi proschrōntai*). That is to say, 511c1 denies of dialectic exactly what 510d5 asserts of geometry. The meaning then is that the former eschews the latter's *professional argumentative* use of visible objects. This leaves room for experience to play a part in suggesting relevant possibilities to the dialectician. Without a distinction between letting experience suggest possibilities and use of

G-question is applied to a definition which at first seemed faultless precisely because it had not been considered alongside those possibilities. But a type of experience cannot on its own be the sufficient ground, reason, or justification for an answer. It can and should suggest relevant considerations, but it cannot validate a dialectical conclusion. Validation is the responsibility of reasoning that necessarily goes beyond suggestive experience. In Plato's idiom, validation is reached by going to 'forms alone, nothing else'. We may see 'straight off' in the sense of 'without lapse of time' that justice demands that we *not* return a borrowed weapon to a psychopath, but there is a *reason* why the act would be wrong (even though the reason is perfectly obvious): the wrongness does not just follow from the empirical descriptions of act and lender. The reason in this case comes under the principle of preventing serious harm,[112] and it may indeed not make sense to ask why we should prevent serious harm; in other words, this may be a basic principle. But we could not learn the wrongness of not changing course to prevent serious harm simply by studying a *diagram* of something as abstract as preventing-serious-harm, since there could be no informative diagram of something so abstract.[113] There might be depictions or illustrations portraying distinct empirically specific types of it, but each would be too specific to convey more than a narrow and therefore easily inapplicable slice of what can count as preventing-serious-harm.

When Plato insists that dialectic operates 'with forms alone, nothing else', he is talking about operating with types or universals whose import can only be properly grasped through deliberate or self-aware (hence potentially self-critical) acts of thought. This rules out not only basic sensibilia such as colours and sounds, but also 'non-raw' objects of perception such as buildings, trees, human beings, and fingers, since we can generally identify these without reflection (although input from memory is involved along with pre-internalized categories and classifications). The cognitive success of perception is *alogos*, unreasoned. Thus, the relevant contrast is not between universals and particulars (even with the proviso that there is surely not a Platonic form for each logical universal), but between intelligibles and perceptibles. 'Pushing someone out of a high window' conveys something both perceptible (except perhaps to a very young child) and logically universal. But the *wrongness or rightness* of pushing someone out of a high window (the alternative might be

---

a specific empirical object to determine the solution to a problem, it is easy to think that dialectic in the *Republic* is so devoid of empirical content that it would be hopelessly impractical; see e.g. Annas 1981, 279; 1999, 104; Schofield 1997, 234.

[112] If one can, if one is aware of the situation, if doing so does not cause yet more serious harm, etc.

[113] 'Of things that are greatest and paramount in value there is no image wrought for plainly communicating them to human beings, such that he who wishes to satisfy the inquirer's soul will adequately do so by applying it to one or other of his senses,' *Statesman* 285e–286a.

that he will be burned to death in the next two minutes) is not perceptible but intelligible because the claim must be backed by a reason or by readiness to produce a reason. Even if giving the reason refers to something else that in itself is a perceptible type, adducing this *as a reason* is an act of intellection.[114] And perhaps we may (without straying from Plato) take the further step of saying that where a consideration C has perceptible content, adducing C as a reason for something brings C itself into the sphere of intelligibles ('the space of reasons').

When we treat a purported formula for, e.g., justice as really representing justice when in fact it does not, the error is likely to be (Plato may think that it always is) due to our lapsing into deciding the case by reference to a rationally unmediated empirical example. I think that this is what Plato has in mind when he has Socrates say:

When the soul directs itself towards (*apereisētai eis*) something lit by the rays of truth, and towards what *is*, it grasps and recognizes it at once, and appears to possess intelligence; but when it directs itself at what comes into being and passes away, mingled as that is with darkness, it can manage no better than opinions (*doxazei*), its power weakening as these move up and down, this way and that, just like something of no intelligence at all. (508d3–8)[115]

Here the soul that makes the 'unintelligent' judgement has become fixated on, say, remembered cases of returning what was borrowed when this was clearly a right and good thing to do, and simple-mindedly generalizes from them. Instead of directing itself towards the unchanging form, asking 'What, after all, *is* it to behave justly?' and letting the answer be determined by 'the rays of truth' that come from the G-question, it takes the answer straight from empirical examples, events which came into being and have passed away; but the generalization is no good because it is false as well as true that returning something borrowed is the just thing to do. The soul's opinion 'moves up and down' when presented with different examples; it is unanchored (cf. *Meno* 97e2–98b5), just as the truth itself of the generalization floats free of the rationally discriminable features of situations where it does obtain, and so seems as if it ought to obtain in superficially similar situations where in fact it does not.

---

[114] Suppose the explicit reason is that the passage to the stairway is on fire: this only has force because of the background assumption that we must do our best to save lives; again, there can be no diagram of doing-our-best-to-save-lives.

[115] The language ('mingled with darkness' and 'moving up and down') recalls the earlier argument against the sight-lovers (476d–480a), on which see Section 2.19. Although 'moving up and down' at 508d refers to fluctuating opinions, these fluctuate because they track the non-temporal 'flux' of types that in some cases are, e.g., just and in some the opposite. Cf. Irwin 1977.

2.14   Diagrams, Dialectic, and Context

In this section I shall continue to discuss Plato's exclusion of such things as diagrams and models from dialectic. I shall argue that he excludes them because he labours under a confusion. He is right that mathematical diagrams used as mathematicians use them are out of place in dialectic, but he is mistaken if he puts the blame on the fact that diagrams are sense-perceptible or depict types of sense-perceptible structure. As was said in the previous section, the fully constructed diagram does answer the geometer's question without remainder: that is, he or she has no need of a reason over and above the completed construction itself for accepting the correctness of the answer conveyed. But this certainly does not mean that accepting the answer is somehow reasonless! On the contrary, the process of construction is itself a reasoned analysis, as this passage from Cornford explains:

The process of 'analysing a diagram' is described in a curious passage where Aristotle, with instructive ambiguity, uses the word *diagramma* so that commentators doubt whether he means geometrical proofs (Bonitz) or geometrical constructions (Ross).

Met., 1051a,21, 'Diagrammata are discovered by an activity. For it is by dividing (drawing lines in the given figure) that people discover them. If they had already been divided, they would have been obvious; as it is, they are present potentially. Why are the angles of the triangle equal to two right angles? Because the angles about one point are equal to two right angles. So if the line parallel to the side had already been drawn, the reason would have been immediately plain to inspection ... Clearly, then, the potentially existing <*diagrammata*> are discovered by being brought into actuality. The reason is that the activity is intuition' (or, reading ἡ νόησις ἐνέργεια with Ross, 'the intuition employed is an activity'). If they (the 'diagrams' = the given figures) had already been divided, they (the 'diagrams' = geometrical constructions or proofs) would have been obvious.

Cornford continues:

Aristotle uses the word *diagramma* to mean: (1) the given figure, in which the divisions exist potentially; (2) the figure completed by making the divisions actual and thus exhibiting the proof in a picture, so that one has only to look at it to see the reason (prior truth) actually displayed in the construction itself; and (3) the proof whose 'elements' are so made obvious to inspection. What concerns us is the process by which the reason or prior truth is discerned. The geometer contemplates the given figure, a triangle, either drawn on paper or in the mind's eye. Knowing already that the angles about a single point, are equal to two right angles (*Eucl.*, I., 13), he divines that this prior truth is latent in the given figure (δυνάμει ἐνυπάρχει). He makes it explicit by producing the base of his triangle and drawing the line parallel to the side... He thus brings this 'element' in the demonstration into actual existence, making it visible to simple inspection. He has next to demonstrate that he has solved his problem. Having laid bare the 'elements' needed to compose the proof, and ascertained that they are all theorems previously established, he will now frame his demonstration in full discursive form – a deduction starting from the hypothesis, 'Let there be a triangle ABC' (*Eucl.*, I., 32). Aristotle speaks elsewhere of the 'elements of *diagrammata* and of demonstrations in general'. (Cornford 1932a, 44–5)[116]

Plato sees clearly that geometry is not about diagrams considered as particular drawings in ink or chalk, but about 'the square itself and the diagonal itself' (510d–511a). But he seems not to see that the geometer uses a diagram in order to conduct mathematical *analysis* and mathematical *demonstration* by means of it.[117] The diagram is not just a window on to the form of the square itself by itself, but an active arena of problem-solving through construction.[118] If Plato excludes the use of diagrams from dialectic on the ground that looking at diagrams necessarily gives unreasoned answers, he is mistaken, since the answers obtained through diagrams in mathematics are not unreasoned. Even so, it was by a sound instinct that he excluded from dialectic anything analogous to what geometers do by means of diagrams, as I shall now argue.

In the *Republic* the dialectical method is linked to future or actual rule by philosophers in the city. Dialectic seeks correct accounts of the virtues so as to provide philosopher-rulers with paradigms they need by which to shape the life of the city. Thus, rulers' dialectic seeks those accounts for the sake of the practical guidance they will afford. However much Plato speaks of the philosopher-rulers as 'seeing' or 'viewing' their intelligible objects, he never suggests that they only ever contemplate them aesthetically as distinct from also aiming to implement them in concrete arrangements. By contrast, he never says that human mathematicians study their abstract subject-matter always with a view to effecting some kind of concrete reproduction of mathematical relationships.[119] So Plato cannot have failed to be aware of this important difference between the two disciplines in respect of seeking practical-political guidance here on earth, even though the word naturally translated by 'practical' does not mean exactly the same to him as it does to us who have the benefit of Aristotle's precisification.[120]

---

[116] On diagrams as proofs see also Netz 1998, Section 4.

[117] On this, Cornford 1932a. 44 has a more positive view of Plato.

[118] For a very rich discussion of the multiple contributions of the diagram in ancient Greek mathematics, see Patterson 2007.

[119] The *Republic* concedes the practical utility of parts of mathematics, but prioritizes the purely abstract study. (By contrast, the Timaean divine craftsman's mathematical interests seem to be wholly subordinate to cosmopoiesis as shown in the construction of world-body and world-soul, and in the geometry of the fundamental particles. The Timaean god is never depicted engaging with abstract mathematics for its own sake.)

[120] See *Statesman* 258d–260b, which divides expertise into 'intellectual' (*gnōstikē*) versus 'practical' (*praktikē*). The latter only covers types of skilled manual labour. The political art is therefore placed under *gnōstikē*. *Gnōstikē* is subdivided into 'prescriptive' (*epitaktikē*) versus the kind that only reaches judgements (*kritikē*) and is like a spectator. The political art falls into the class of prescriptive, and arithmetical calculation into the class of *kritikē*. Aristotle, by contrast, understands *praktikē* as including ethics and political science.

Insofar as mathematics only seeks abstract results, it can afford to base its conclusions on diagrams. It can afford to treat a diagrammatic construction, expertly created and expertly read, as decisively settling the question which the inquiry has set out to answer. A diagram, on one level, is a physical particular through which we grasp abstract entities and abstract relationships. The physical particularity of a diagram drawn in chalk and not ink, here and not there, is unimportant: another instance of precisely the same inquiry will require a numerically different diagram of the same type to be drawn somewhere else, yet the mathematical result is reliably the same. There may be places where it is physically impossible to draw that type of diagram (or any diagram), but wherever it is drawn a competent person extracts from it the same answer to the same question.

What holds for diagrams in abstract mathematics also holds for the use of numbers in counting and measuring physical objects, and for the use of geometry, e.g., to calculate the pitch of the roof for a house of given dimensions or the size of a plot of land. If the physical objects retain fairly stable, fairly definite, boundaries and remain in existence long enough, then counting a group of them yields the same number whether the group is set down in town or countryside, in Athens or Sparta, and similarly with geometry in house-building and land-measurement.

If, however, we view some empirical thing A – whether action, arrangement, or state of affairs, real or imagined – as a self-sufficient 'diagram' of, e.g., *justice*, and our attitude towards justice is (in the familiar sense) practical, we go wrong because a context in which the A-type is implemented may render the resulting A unjust. The rot enters in not because the original A is a sensible *particular* rather than a universal, since there is nothing wrong with regarding it as exemplifying a type that can occur concretely here and there in different physical tokens. The rot enters in because of two things: (1) the A-type's particular realizations will be inhabited by people living their lives, so that what affects them is not the presence of A *simpliciter* but A under their given circumstances, which cannot be guaranteed not to add up to an unjust combination; and (2) the A-type does not of itself indicate reasons for implementing it here rather than there in such a way that it never parts company with justice. An A considered all by itself could be beautiful, fine, and welcome regardless of circumstances only if it were a sort of thing that exists without circumstances – thus, only if it were like the fully formed unique physical cosmos of the *Timaeus*.

The physical lines of a geometrical diagram cannot be perfectly straight or perfectly of some given curvature. A physical tangent touches the physical would-be circle along a smear rather than at a point, and so on. Yet a diagram is an adequate basis for proof despite its fuzziness. The situation is quite different if we try to base a human practical conclusion about, say, justice, on an empirical example. The problem is not that the example falls short of being a perfectly accurate embodiment of the form: it is that any such case is liable to meet with circumstances that render it an embodiment of the most blatant *in*justice.

So Plato is surely right to ban from dialectic the mindless use, diagram-wise, of empirical cases as self-sufficient sources of practical guidance. But is he right to insist that the dialectician-ruler 'operate with forms alone, nothing else' (511c1–2)? In the previous section I argued that he can allow empirical possibilities to suggest considerations relevant to the task of framing a dialectical definition. But this is not all. For dialectician-rulers must take account of actual empirical situations directly in drawing their conclusions. The central point of the present section is that whereas the truths of mathematics are independent of context, the rulers' reasoning, because it is practical, must adapt its conclusion to the actual context in which the action will be carried out or the policy implemented. Mathematics has a different logic. It engages in deductive reasoning from elements, and in analysis of problems into elements from which the solutions follow deductively. This is why the correctness of its conclusions is not hostage to context. Its reasoning is monotonic.[121] But this is true of any sort of mathematical inquiry, *including any that do not depend on diagrams*. Perhaps Plato thought that no sort of mathematics could be carried on without diagrams. But whether he actually thought this or not, characterizing mathematics in general by reference to the diagrams which are conspicuous essentials of so much ancient Greek mathematics was surely easier for him, given his lack of logical terminology, than doing so by reference to the deductive ideal of all mathematics as such. (He has no term for 'deduction'; still less has he one for 'monotonic reasoning'.)

So he falls into the confusion of banning *diagrams* from dialectic, with the result that dialectic is said to operate 'with forms alone, nothing else'. Even though Plato is clear that mathematicians study intelligible *objects* (510d–511a; cf. 525d–526b), perhaps the standard contrast of intelligibles and sense-perceptibles leads him to imagine that the physical construction and examination of a diagram in mathematics is not really an intellectual activity but a sort of stimulus for true intellectual activity. However that may be, he should have asked himself why, given that mathematics uses the diagram as its self-sufficient source of truth about intelligibles, dialectic cannot do the same. The real reason is that the mathematical diagram operates within the bounds of monotonic reasoning whereas dialectic does not; but Plato lacks the resources for getting his mind round that distinction.

---

[121] That is, adding new premisses to a premiss-set S does not affect the legitimacy of inferences drawn from S by itself.

In sum, he fails to see clearly that the reason dialectic is not a mathematical sort of method is not that mathematicians *use diagrams*, but that they use them *in the way mathematicians* do, as tools of monotonic reasoning, which is reasoning that safely ignores context. When he maintains that dialectic operates 'with forms alone, nothing else', the truth towards which he is groping is simply, I suggest, that dialectic does not go in for diagrams *as used by mathematicians*. Actually, mathematicians reason monotonically whether they use diagrams or not, and nothing prevents the non-monotonic reasoning of rulers and practical agents in general from sometimes helping itself along with models and diagrams. Plato may have rightly sensed that the *mathematical* use of diagrams has no place in dialectic but, lacking the technical distinctions for getting a grip on the precise reason why, he slipped into thinking that the use of diagrams as such has no place in dialectic. This has had the unfortunate effect of suggesting that dialectic has no empirical content and cannot refer to empirical cases.

There will be more on the relevance of context to dialectic in the next section and in Section 2.19.

2.15   Dialectic in Government

It is clear that dialectical method in the *Republic* is meant to qualify people to be excellent rulers. This leaves it open whether practising dialectic is only a propaedeutic to government, as studying mathematics is to dialectic, or whether the philosophers also turn to dialectic in the very course of operating as rulers. The question is interesting because the alternative answers reflect major interpretative differences.

Some interpretations give the impression of assuming that by the time the philosophers take up government they have learned all that they can from their dialectical commerce with the form of the good. Once in power they operate on the basis of all that the form will ever have had to give them, or all that they will ever have been able to take from it, and the activity of dialectic itself was just part of their training.[122] No doubt they continue to look to and rely on whatever they learned through training, but its lesson for them is now fixed. Being human, they may need to refresh their contact with the form, but there is no alteration in what they grasp when they return to it. But if dialectical inquiry is not to be practised in the course of actually ruling, one might ask what the point is of assigning rulership to philosophers trained in dialectic. Why not

---

[122] On this view dialectic or some development from it may also be part of their future, when they have retired from government (540b1–2). That they do not use it for governing seems to be the view of Annas 1981, 279, commenting on the practical irrelevance of dialectic as she interprets it.

make the rulers get policy from a separate college of non-ruler-sages possessed of complete dialectical knowledge?[123]

   This notion that the work of dialectical inquiry is over before the philosophers start to rule may seem to get support from the passage where just before returning into the cave 'they lift the ray of the soul ... towards ... the good itself' (540a7–9). The writing suggests that this is a one-off episode marking the transition from training to leadership; so perhaps it is an episode of receiving some sort of final understanding of the good. But I have already argued (Section 2.10) that the passage depicts the philosopher not as engaged in dialectical reasoning involving the good, or as having arrived at a culminating point of such reasoning, but as engaged in meta-reflection on that type of reasoning as such. If this is correct, the passage provides no evidence for imagining that the philosophers turn their backs on dialectic itself as soon as, and for as long as, they occupy power. In fact, if, as I suggested, 540a7 ff. shows graduating rulers committing themselves in a general way to using that method (epitomized by the form of the good), it follows that they envisage using it when actually in power.

   If the non-hypothetical principle were a premiss showing the nature of the good from which the dialectician derives results, then perhaps in principle the dialectician could learn all that is to be learned from it while still at the training stage. But we have seen that this premiss-model runs into serious difficulties (Section 2.11). The interrogative model proposed in this book avoids those difficulties, and (I shall presently argue) makes it reasonable to allow for indefinitely many re-uses of the non-hypothetical principle. At least, this is so if we grant that responses to the G-question are informed, although not justified or validated, by the respondent's experience. We have supposed that when the trainees in period 2 learn to employ the G-question to test their definitions, the material for their answers consists in their experience, such as it is, together with their moral sensibility. What else could supply the material for the answers? But extensive further experience ensues in period 3, the fifteen years of practical training, and still more again when they finally govern as full-fledged rulers. All this new experience can hardly be assumed empty of possible unforeseen counter-examples to even the so far best-developed formulae for the virtues, etc. (There is also the fact that experience at any stage may show that formulae can be given significantly different practical interpretations or realizations. Then it is a question of which kind of realization is good, or the best.) It would be ludicrous if, on entering the empirically rich circumstances of highest office, the philosophers are precluded from re-employing the

---

[123] The sole available answer seems to be that the philosophical passion fed by doing dialectic oneself is the one motive strong enough to make rulers gladly renounce power when the time comes; but see Part 1, note 17.

G-question in face of new data – instead having to rely throughout their political career on whatever virtue-definitions last passed that test while they were still in the wings preparing for office. It would therefore be ludicrous of Plato or Plato's Socrates to constrain the rulers in this way.[124]

Plato says nothing to contradict this conclusion. At 519d he contrasts his ideal rulers' obligation to rule with the freedom of actual-world philosophers to stay out of politics. (The latter are not indebted to a city that invests in philosophers for the sake of rule by them.) But this comparison of the political busy-ness of philosophers in the ideal political environment with the apolitical leisure of, e.g., Socrates and Plato, falls well short of telling us that the former have no occasion to reach new dialectical conclusions during their rule. At 540b, speaking of their adult life as a whole, Plato says that most of it is spent in free study, even though they must take their turn 'submitting themselves to political labours ... and ruling, each for the city's sake'; but this division of their time likewise fails to imply that the ideal rulers put dialectic and the G-question on hold during their period of rule. Plato contrasts their reluctance to govern with their love of uninterrupted study ('inhabiting the Isles of the Blest'), but this is not to say that in government their only commerce with dialectic consists in applying results obtained while they were still only students. Again, when he emphasizes that the ideal city will be as stable as anything in the world of becoming can be (545c–546a), he has in mind its most fundamental features, such as the three classes, rule by philosophers, the educational curriculum. It does not follow that every ethically significant policy, practice, and institution stays frozen, as they would if the rulers are unable to modify or add to the guidance provided by their earlier dialectical studies.[125] The only constant is that if on occasion they depart from existing norms, it must be a properly reasoned departure. This kind of re-thinking would be occasioned by vicissitudes to which even the best-governed community is vulnerable simply by existing in a geographical and economic environment. Civic arrangements that are just under easy circumstances may not be so

---

[124] Thus, implicitly the *Republic* parallels Plato's reservations in the *Statesman* about government on the basis of a fixed set of laws: *Statesman* 294a–300e, esp. 294b–c; 295b–296a. For 'fixed set of laws' read 'fixed set of definitions of justice, etc.'

[125] Consider, for instance, a situation of extreme military emergency like that faced by the mythical Athens in Critias' Atlantis story sketched in the *Timaeus*. This Athens had many features of the *Republic*'s ideal city, including 'philosopher-statesmen' (19e5–6; cf. 24c4–d3 with its echo of *Republic* 525b6). Socrates, one of the *Timaeus* characters, is eager for such a story: listening to it would be for him like seeing animals in movement by contrast with seeing them (or pictures of them) in a fixed position, which is how they appear in abstraction from historical circumstances (*Timaeus* 19b–c). Wouldn't a good story showing these philosopher-animals 'in movement' – at their peak of vital action – include some dramatic moment when, under pressure of events, they debate about revising one or another of their established norms? The story as we have it in the companion dialogue, *Critias*, breaks off before the real action begins.

if there is a famine or an attack from external enemies[126] or an epidemic. Just ways of regulating economic activities, whether production or exchange or raising funds for communal projects, might cease to be just if through natural or economic changes some form of production became more successful or dangerous than it used to be.[127] The fact that Plato is mostly silent about this kind of obvious possibility is hardly evidence that he thought it non-existent or that his best city would exist in a bubble of immunity to all such changes.

The interpretation which I am proposing may seem to conflict with the form of the good's status as non-hypothetical (non-provisional, non-replaceable). If, as I have argued, the form (the transcendent form analogous to the sun) should be thought of as interrogative, and if, as I am now suggesting, there is no necessary finality to such interrogation, doesn't it follow that the form of the good fails to be or to supply a non-hypothetical basis? That is to say: if every dialectical formula for, e.g., justice can in principle be tested by the G-question and be overthrown in the light of answers suggested by new circumstances, doesn't it follow that every formula, however corrected and modified and found to be faultless at a given moment, must be held as provisional on the ground that it too in future may be overturned – in which case the non-hypothetical principle, however exactly it works, leaves dialectical results as insecure as mathematics leaves mathematical ones?

The answer, surely, is no. The transcendent good manifests its non-hypothetical, unconditional, non-provisional, categorical nature on two levels. First, there is the unalterable general prescription, constant under all circumstances, to be ready to ask the G-question. Secondly, any particular answer when given by rulers with ultimate power and responsibility will be expressed in a reasoned decision on what to do here and now. It is not open to rulers to duck out of deciding, and if they have reasoned well the decision they make is the right one to enact *now*. It is a categorical judgement of what is now to be done in the name of, e.g., justice.[128] Practical judgement on what to do now is

---

[126] When discussing their intellectual education Plato does not let us forget that the rulers' earlier training has turned them into *polemikoi*, translated by Rowe 2012 as 'war-experts': 521d; 525b. On Callipolis and external wars see Hobbs 2007; Peterson 2011, 108–12.

[127] Cf. 484d1 and 425c–e; the latter is about the rulers' on-the-job legislation about contracts, various crimes, setting up juries, exaction of tolls. See Annas 2017, 19–21. This on-the-job legislation is the subject of two contrasts: (a) with the founding legislation of Callipolis (the founders being Socrates and the brothers; foundational legislation will have to be supplemented by the rulers themselves *in mediis rebus* as circumstances suggest); and (b) with the endless legislative tinkering that goes on in badly founded cities. The 'true legislator' in a well-founded one would not have to *pragmateuesthai*, make a big to-do, over new legislation, as the requirements would be obvious given the foundational framework (425e; 427a).

[128] Adam 1907, 178–9, compares dialectic with the method of natural science. This is apt, except for the fact that theoretical science may (or should) hold its best results only provisionally. This is a luxury permitted by being theoretical. Rachel Barney has suggested that the formula the rulers reach on any occasion is still provisional although it is what must be acted on. My view

not suspended or kept provisional simply because a future situation may demand a divergent judgement. Of course, justice itself, the intelligible form, never changes, but we don't need to have explored the possibly limitless depths of this form in order to know, now, that and why such and such a kind of policy would be a bad thing now, hence *not* just – even if it conforms to our previous best definition of justice. The conclusion of a piece of mathematical reasoning is always as provisional as the premisses; the conclusion of a piece of dialectic is final for *this* occasion, although never for *all* occasions.

I am supposing, in effect, that the intelligible form of, e.g., justice is a sort of indefinitely complex or resourceful norm with different qualifications up its sleeve, so to speak, answering to the variety of empirical circumstances. The ruler, in order to make good decisions on what arrangements and practices should exist in the city, does not need at any given moment to grasp the norm in its entirety. He or she only needs to apprehend it as clarifying what to do in the current situation and why this should be done. Once the ruler has, so to speak, carved out *this* part of the norm, then he or she is in the best epistemic position that anyone short of a god could be in for saying what the form of, e.g., justice demands or permits in a situation of this sort. For we assume that the ruler has been as wide ranging and critical in ascertaining the facts of the situation, and as keenly perspicacious in analysing them and in estimating likelihoods, etc., as any human being could be. (Since this is possible only if the ruler's intellectual ability to home in on the truth throughout remains uncontaminated by excesses of fear, confidence, anger, pity, pleasure, pain, etc., the ruler must also be fully grounded in the moral virtues.) It is therefore reasonable to say that the ruler, in relation to this situation, has *knowledge* of justice. He or she certainly has something far superior to mere opinion as demarcated in Book V in the argument against the sight-lovers (to be discussed further in Section 2.19).

Thus, her or his knowledge of the form of justice is never complete knowledge if that means knowledge of the what and the why of what justice would demand in every possible situation.[129] I would also hesitate to say that the rulers *approximate to* complete knowledge, even asymptotically, or that complete knowledge is their destination (since this implies they can get nearer to it even if not reach it).[130] 'Approximation' suggests increase in proximity to

---

is that they seek a formula for, say, justice so as to act on it, not so as to approximate towards complete theoretical knowledge of the virtue. So, finding (on a given occasion) the best definition, and finding a formula to be acted on, are the same operation; there is no surplus of concern about an ideally complete definition whose as yet unknown content transcends what is to be acted on here and now.

[129] They study the form-paradigm as accurately *as they can*, 484c8; cf. Adam 1907, 2, on 484, 17.

[130] On the idea that Plato's philosopher approximates to knowledge of the ethical forms see Rowe 2005, 222–3.

complete knowledge, a stage-by-stage adding to what one found out in the past. This would be like growth of a body of law which would be handed on to the next generation of rulers. Plato does not say anything in the *Republic* that either excludes this or implies it. He would obviously be aware of the danger in present rulers being tempted to see past decisions as still authoritative (or even as having *any* weight for the present) just because they were right in their day and have been recorded. Suppose, however, that decisions along with their reasons were recorded simply because they might give useful prompts in later deliberations, with no presumption of adhering to them just because they are on the books. This would result in growth of historical knowledge about past *decisions*, but it is not obvious that accumulation of records would also count as growth in some single body of knowledge of the form of, e.g., *justice*. Do I, a current philosopher-ruler, know more of the form, or am I closer to knowing the whole form, simply because not only do I know what by rational inquiry I have just found out myself, but I also know, by means of the record, what my predecessors knew? To answer this affirmatively on Plato's behalf, one would first have to show that he would accept the implication that I, in fact, have inherited knowledge from them if my only access to the datum was via a record. He might not grant this even if there were no question of the record's trustworthiness. (Elsewhere, e.g. *Theaetetus* 200e–201c, he restricts 'knowledge' to first-hand knowledge.) So, in some cases what earlier rulers once knew might help suggest a good answer for the present circumstances, but this is not to say that what they knew then and what I know now are contributions to the development of a single knowledge-system expanding over the generations. My deliberation need not ignore what they knew then, but it does not follow that I, on adding my own answer to the record of theirs, now know more than they did about what justice is.

Given that the rulers know that their knowledge of the form is only ever partial, it is surely right to call them '*philosophoi*' or lovers of wisdom rather than *sophoi*, which in this context would mean 'in complete possession of wisdom'. Plato argues that *philosophoi* are not *sophoi* at *Lysis* 218a and *Symposium* 204a. It is pleasing to see this aphorism applying to the rulers of the *Republic*.[131]

---

[131] Cf. Rowe 2005, 222–3. For an extended discussion of Plato's ambivalence between philosophers as loving wisdom and as possessing it, see D. Morrison 2007, 236–9; also Rowe 2007c, 209–10, 215, 218–19, for the important point that the philosophers count as having knowledge or expertise just in virtue of *recognizing* the one form of beauty, etc. as distinct from the many sensibles. As will emerge in Section 2.19, this recognition amounts to their readiness to seek explanations for why beauty, etc. manifest differently under different contexts or perspectives. This does not commit Plato to holding that philosophers have, at any stage, complete knowledge of any form. See also note 177 on *pantelōs gnōston* at 477a3.

The idea that their knowledge of the form is only ever partial can also be framed in terms of interpretation. Forms such as justice, which are the starting points of their executive activity as rulers, must constantly be re-interpreted in the light of specific contexts. The form of the good, brought to bear in the G-question, is their guide to the right interpretation for a given specific context. Only under a specific interpretation does a form such as justice become an actual starting point for the move from plan to execution. If such things as the form of justice, itself by itself, are starting points for all good practical thinking, then good practical thinkers, by contrast with mathematicians, must constantly re-tune their starting points, playing the same melody of justice in different keys according to circumstances. They select the keys in accordance with what would be good given the circumstances. Since (a) a melody must combine with a key to be the starting point of actual playing, and (b) without the prospect of actual playing the melody itself by itself would be idle (let us assume) and not a starting point of anything, the principle of key selection – namely the form of the good – is that whereby the practical starting points really *are* practical starting points. It is that whereby the norms of justice and other virtues become *chrēsima kai ōphelima* (505a3–4), which I translate as 'operational and beneficial'. The benefit is not some independently specifiable consequence of implementing them, but their positive impact as lived standards as distinct from mere objects of possible contemplation.[132]

2.16   Not Rigorous Enough?

The ruler's reasoning as interpreted so far is beginning to look a lot like common-sense practical reasoning. We have values which we want to implement; in practice we generally do not treat them as setting up exceptionless norms; we interpret them as we go along; we recognize that a kind of policy that was good under one set of circumstances is not good under another; without guilt or compunction we reason non-monotonically (i.e. we live with the fact that a correct conclusion based on premisses p, q, r is not guaranteed to be correct if the premiss-set is expanded to include s and t). But if an interpretation shows Plato's philosopher-rulers reasoning like us, in this mundane messy way, surely there is something wrong with the interpretation? Doesn't it dumb down the philosopher-rulers' intellectual activity, softening it for appropriation into our own comfort zone, all because we cannot stomach

---

[132] For *chrēsimos* as = the opposite of idle, ready to operate/contribute as the thing should, see 530c1–2; 411a10–b1; *Protagoras* 326b4; cf. Vlastos 1973, 7. Barnes 1991, 91–2 unquestioningly gives both adjectives an instrumentalist meaning, treating them, like 'true', as qualifiers of sentences: his example is 'Il est utile à moi que je suis à Paris'. Monsieur Taupe can be more subtle, as I hope this book will show.

viewing Plato (anyway in the *Republic*) as one who characteristically just does make vertiginously 'strange and high' demands on anything that truly deserves to count as philosophical reason – demands 'begotten by Despair upon Impossibility', as perhaps even he himself suspected?[133]

This romantic take may be thrilling for a moment, but if we think that Plato is serious about human life being redeemable through philosophy, then we must also think him deeply misguided if we saddle him with the notion that true philosopher-rulers' reasoning is completely contoured, definite, and untainted by the features just mentioned; for this attributes to him a fantastical notion of practical thought. It makes little sense to keep Plato un-dumbed-down if saving the sublimity of his flight means reading the philosopher-ruler as a blinkered monomaniac. What the *Republic* says about the rulers' dialectic is frustratingly sketchy, but this is not a licence to infer that Plato incoherently identified it with a mode of intellectual activity too perfect to be the practical thought of human beings.[134] We may, however, feel drawn towards the notion that any thinking that is *not* too perfect to be the practical thought of human beings fails to be solidly accurate reasoning. But in my view this would be a mistake.

We have already (Section 2.12) examined a passage where Plato depicts the dialectician thinker as succeeding at a very demanding complex task. This picture may give a better perspective on the question of rigour.

'If someone isn't capable of demarcating it [sc. the form of the good] in his formulation (or: in his reasoning; *dihorisasthai logōi*), separating (*aphelōn*) the form (*idean*) of the good from everything else, and of surviving all challenges (*elenchōn*), like some kind of fighter, eager to test (*elenchein*) what he's saying not by reference to opinion but to how things truly are, and coming through all of this with his account left standing – if he can't do all of this, your claim will be, won't it, that he has no knowledge either about the good itself or about any other good, and that if he manages to get a hold on some kind of shadowy image, he does so through opinion (*doxa*) and not through knowledge? He's dreaming and dozing away his present life, you'll agree, and will get to sleep properly in Hades before he ever wakes up here?'

'Zeus!' he exclaimed. 'I'll definitely say Yes to all that!' (534b–d)

I argued in Section 2.12 that the language of 'demarcating and separating' need not be taken as saying that the knowledgeable person, the true dialectician, gives a definition of the form of the good, the upshot being that this passage does not contradict the interrogative interpretation. (The account that passes all the tests is a formula for, e.g., justice, not of the good.) But what,

---

[133] 'Philosophically, one of the strongest objections to the possibility of Plato's Callipolis is that the wisdom required of its rulers is inhumanly great', D. Morrison 2007, 241. 'Perhaps one should re-read *Don Quixote* before approaching the *Republic*', Rosen 2005, 284.

[134] If he sees Callipolis as possible, he ought to see its rulers as possible.

more positively, *is* meant by 'demarcating and separating' the form of the good? It certainly means that the dialectician does not confuse the good with anything else. But 'separation' also suggests that he or she recognizes it as having a status different from that of whatever forms are referred to as 'everything else'. What would it be to fail to separate the form of the good from everything else? One way would be to treat the good as having no special status, for instance by failing to realize that it is an instrument for interrogating the claims of other forms to be true forms of justice, etc. This would be the ignorance of someone uncritical about values. Another way would be to equate the form of the good with something other than itself, and assign the interrogative job to this other thing. Thus, one might go about deciding whether EFG is justice by seeing whether EFG is pleasant, or lucrative, or in accordance with tradition, or likely to make one's family or class more powerful, etc. This would be like looking at things by a bad light – moonlight or firelight rather than sunlight – while taking it to be the best light for vision. These possible failures to separate the form of the good show how the guardians' dialectical success presupposes both their passion for truth and their fidelity to the values of their moral upbringing.

The passage shows the dialectician subjecting her- or himself to a series of intensely thorough and strenuous criticisms of candidate-definitions. The expertly trained analytic vigilance against error is unsparing; it leaves no imaginably relevant stone unturned. Love of truth not only makes a person quick to notice falsehoods and fallacies, but also encourages recognition of techniques of reasoning that reduce the chances of error. The ruler who lives up to this pattern (reminiscent, of course, of the Socrates of several earlier dialogues) will be a detector as accurate and reliable as anything human could be of the normative truths which it is a ruler's business to know. It seems wilful to insist that such thinking is not rigorous, especially when the ground of this complaint is (as it almost certainly is) that dialectic lacks the deductively formalizable rigour of mathematics; for such a move simply takes it for granted that mathematics alone sets the standard for rigour.

From what our last passage suggests, running the gauntlet of dialectical criticism is not easy: the dialectician can easily put a foot wrong. Warding off the attacks will consist in *giving reasons* that would convince the severest critic that her objections are mistaken or fail to apply: for instance, perhaps an objection would be damaging for the current candidate-formula under a certain kind of circumstance C, but the kind of circumstance that the reasoning actually needs to take account of is different from C, although the difference may not be obvious or easy to explain. The task of satisfying a severe critic requires, not only experience and imagination, but skill in analysing actual or possible situations and in detecting and articulating non-obvious but relevant similarities and differences. There is plenty of scope for exactness and precision.

Also, although the philosopher-ruler's judgement of the truth about justice will be immune to certain kinds of deterioration, such as letting the criterion be the pleasantness or lucrativeness or material grandness of what is proposed, some causes of wavering may be more insidious. For instance, through upbringing he or she will be attached to the fine traditions of Callipolis, respectful of the wisdom of previous rulers, cautious about criticizing a measure that his or her peers are happy with – qualities that might on occasion blind one to the right decision. So, getting it right consistently will require not only excellence in analysis and so on, but also uncompromising open-mindedness in asking the G-question, along with a fixed second-order determination to insist on having full reasons for every move – in other words, a determination to trust in self-criticizing reason alone and not give up looking for the best answer until you have found it. Such an attitude will raise your standards for what counts as good reasoning, heighten your awareness of when you might be on the edge of falling below those standards, and strengthen your moral nerve when necessary. Reliably asking the G-question as it should be asked, namely from a mind-set that maximizes the chances of perceiving, on any occasion, the true answer, is not easy – both in the sense of being achievable only by a specially trained and tested few, and also perhaps in the sense of sometimes requiring even from them a deliberate effortful resolve to keep their heads.

Such a second-order determination to adhere to rationality is surely not needed so much for securing good mathematical performance. Mathematicians must have sufficient grounds for their moves; but they do not need to cultivate a mind-set that bangs on about this, because the subject-matter of mathematics is cocooned off from principle-bending emotions in a way that cannot be completely guaranteed in even the best practical and political thinking. So, in a certain sense the dialectician has to be a much more explicit aficionado of rationality than the mathematician.

If the talk at 534b–d about demarcating and separating is taken to be about *defining* the form of the good (rather than using it to help specify the virtues), then the image of the dialectician's strenuous series of battles will seem to show how difficult it is to pin down the intrinsic nature of that super-form, and this will suggest that this nature is extremely rich, complex, deep, and abstruse. But if my argument is correct, the form of the good that enters into dialectic has the thinnest, simplest, and most familiar of contents, and what may indeed be difficult and takes an extraordinary combination of excellences is the business of reliably putting it to correct use. The same can be said about 511b5–6 (the context is the Divided Line) where the dialectician is described as 'not stopping short of the non-hypothetical (*mechri tou anhupothetou*) on his way to the principle of everything'.[135] These words lightly suggest that he

---

[135] The language suggests that speaking of the non-hypothetical is not the same as speaking of the principle of everything, at least from the dialecticians' point of view. The thought may be that

has to strain to get to the non-hypothetical and to the principle of everything. Here too we could suppose that he is working arduously towards comprehending the true definition of the good conceived of as conceptually rich in content; but the text equally supports a different interpretation, one according to which it can indeed be hard – needing great firmness – to cancel the distance between oneself and actually *asking* the conceptually simple G-question regarding a candidate-formula for one of the virtues – why? Because it sometimes *is* hard really to press that question, to stand back and subject a possibly well-established existing answer to seriously critical examination. See 517b8–9 which says that the form of the good is grasped last of all and with difficulty, *mogis*. As we know from Plato's earlier Socrates, really asking a question means really taking on board the sometimes deeply unsettling realization that one is ignorant of the answer and that knowing the answer might turn out to be more unsettling still.

I have tried to argue against the idea that if, as I maintain, the rulers' reasoning is practical reasoning, it is not rigorous enough to deserve topmost ranking in terms of *sapheneia* or cognitive excellence. Evidently this argument assumes that deductive reasoning is not the paradigm of rigour, exactness, precision, or not the sole paradigm. It is worth making the further point that reasoning need not be inexact simply because the premises are not all explicitly laid out, as happens (perhaps is bound to happen) with practical reasoning. In mathematics, logic, and philosophy one is urged to make all the premises explicit, and I am not disputing the rightness of that. But it does not follow that a line of reasoning is *inexact* (rough, impressionistic, inaccurate, sloppy) if some of the relevant data remains unformulated. What follows is that it cannot be safely passed on (taught) to everyone, because not everyone will make all the same tacit assumptions. But being indemonstrable in this sense does not entail being inexact. If we think of science as committed to the norm of making all its findings, and their justifications and explanations, available in principle to everyone, then practical reasoning is not *scientific*. But it does not follow that it is inexact or is not knowledge (*epistēmē*) in the fullest sense of that word. If reasoners respond with fine-grained discernment to all the relevant data, spoken or unspoken, their reasoning is exactly attuned to the data; therefore, it is exact, just as an expert tennis-player's strokes are exactly adjusted to the ball's angle and speed, to the opponent's anticipated position, to the state of the court, direction of wind, and so on. The exactness of her game is independent of whether her explicit reasoning, such as it is, could justify or explain her moves to anyone besides those few who are in a position to enter into them as if they were their own.

they will not get hold of the principle of everything if they stop short at something merely hypothetical; i.e. being non-hypothetical is a (the?) criterion for being the principle.

2.17   Why Is Dialectic Cognitively Superior to Mathematics?

The features differentiating dialectic and mathematics were their respective attitudes to hypotheses, and their use or not of diagrams. It is hard to see why either generates a clear-cut difference in degree of cognitive excellence. On the matter of hypotheses: no doubt the mathematicians would be at fault if, as Plato seems to think that some of them do, they believe their starting points to be absolutely secure and irreplaceable rather than being the best and clearest starting points currently available. But any of them who make this mistake can accept the criticism, shift to a less heavy-handed, more detached, attitude towards their starting points, and still go on doing mathematics on the *supposition* that they are true. Would Plato be justified in thinking that dialectic does better than that? Let us grant that the sun-like form of the good as invoked in the G-question is part of the essential framework of the dialectical method, so that one would not be doing dialectic unless one were somehow governed by the form of the good. Let us also grant that if we were engaged in a new and perhaps currently inconceivable mathematics in which, say, there were more or fewer than the three kinds of angles currently recognized (510c4–5), we should still be pursuing the good as we understand it, just as we do in all our activities. Thus, when we engage in dialectic we are formally ruled by something that informally binds our rational engagement in any kind of activity. But none of this implies that the results of dialectic – the rulers' judgements on whether this or that is the right interpretation of some virtue-concept – are infallible. The inescapability of the form of the good does not protect the results of dialectical reasoning from the possibility of error. For the results (according to the interpretation given in previous sections) are determined, not only by which way the G-question is answered, but also by the rulers' assessments of the empirical facts constituting the context in which a conception of, e.g., justice would be implemented. And the best minds making the best epistemic efforts may make an empirical mistake. Plato hardly notices that his ideal rulers might make factual as opposed to evaluative mistakes; but the possibility of this means that the best rulers and their results are no more infallible and certain than the best mathematicians and theirs.[136]

So far in this section I have argued as if certainty is the cognitive value in terms of which one discipline deserves to be ranked as more *saphēs* than another. But as we have seen (Section 2.5), *saphēneia* is itself a highly unspecific concept: it fails to discriminate between what we distinguish as several quite different informational, semantic, and epistemic desiderata, and certainty is only one of these. Perhaps each corresponding kind of shortcoming

---

[136] See 546a–d where the rulers miscalculate the number for determining breeding times.

may be thought of as a sort of 'unsureness' in what someone presents or in the presentation; but the defect can consist in such very different properties as vagueness, imprecision, inaccuracy, ambiguity, indecisiveness, lack of rigour, untrustworthiness through insufficiency of evidence or justification, even unclarity as to whether someone is making a serious assertion as distinct from saying something ironically or just floating an idea. There seems to be no principle for demonizing one of these defects over the others and thus setting up a single standard of comparison. Even if mathematics were inferior to dialectic because dialectic's best results were, *per impossibile*, absolutely certain truths, mathematics might be superior in some other cognitive value such as precision or definiteness, and who is to say that the *saphēneia* of certainty trumps these?

A further possibility is that Plato ranks dialectic more highly because practising it well over time demands a level of sustained vigilance against error that mathematics does not. What I mean is this. In mathematics it would be the height of intellectual responsibility to make a genuine effort to doubt one's starting points and then, unable to see any reason to reject them, to base train after train of deduction on them without revisiting the question of their acceptability, the assumption being that they continue to remain as safe as they ever were. One would have acknowledged that they might, some of them, be one day superseded in ways not currently imaginable, but it would be absurd to keep checking them now just because of that possibility. They are not going to become discardable, just like that, in the middle of our operations. By contrast, the intellectually responsible dialectician-ruler must (according to my interpretation) not only vet any proposed account of, e.g., justice with an eye to the context of implementation, but even after finding nothing wrong with it *now* he or she must remain on the *qui vive* against its turning out wrong for another occasion or in case the current context changes. That is, the ruler must be ready to re-apply the G-question in face of new contexts. Similarly, an account which has been discarded with reference to one context might have to be revived in light of another. The ruler's on-going dialectic requires, in a way the mathematician's work does not, an unremittingly critical attitude towards its hypotheses.[137] (In any given round of reasoning they are either rejected or

---

[137] This recalls the open-mindedness of Socrates (knowing that he knows nothing). Socrates in earlier dialogues epitomizes the perpetual non-finality of general abstract inquiry about values, while the philosopher-rulers according to my argument represent the non-finality of any single practicable conclusion about, say, justice, in that the matter will have to be thought through again from scratch on the next occasion. For an extended comparison between Socrates and the philosopher-rulers as *not* full knowers, see Rowe 2007c, ch. 7. 'The kind of philosopher Socrates is recommending as helmsman of the good city is another version of himself, as it were', 225. 'Plato's notion of the philosopher remains firmly attached to a self-confessedly ignorant Socrates who, despite his ignorance, nevertheless – whether in the pre-*Republic* dialogues, or in the *Republic* itself and post-*Republic* – has more than enough in the way of

accepted – see Section 2.15 – but rejections and acceptances need not stay constant from one round to the next.) Perhaps this ever-fresh vigilance was what Plato had in mind when he awarded dialectic first prize for *saphēneia*. The award would be based not on an excellence such as certainty or precision that attaches to individual results, but on a property of the whole method as practised over time.

These attempts to pin down the elusive property of *saphēneia* assume that Plato has arrived at an independent conception of it (even if an amorphous conception) *before* he ranks the two disciplines. But perhaps it is a mistake to assume this. After all, his main and perhaps only reason for discussing dialectic in the *Republic* is in order to explain what sort of wisdom the truly suitable ruler should possess (see Part 1). Perhaps this preoccupation leads him to conflate the question of what sort of discipline is supreme in respect of *saphēneia* with the question of what sort of rational excellence is needed for the supreme task of government. And from this point of view, mathematical *saphēneia* is very far from filling the bill. But what is at stake here, although Plato fails to grasp it clearly, is a difference in kind between disciplines rather than a difference in degree of some single intellectual virtue. No mathematical sort of discipline, including a system of ethics laid out *more geometrico*, deserves the honour of being the discipline of rulers; yet this is not because no mathematical approach is *saphēs* enough but because any such approach is of the wrong kind.

This interpretation has Plato producing a foregone conclusion when he announces that dialectic, the method of rulers, is maximally *saphēs*. If being supreme in *saphēneia* just is excelling in whatever is needed for rational excellence in government, it is a tautology that the method proper for rulers is the maximally *saphēs* method. What, however, is not a foregone conclusion, but interesting news that may have come as quite a shock to his followers, is the position, delineated through the contrast with mathematics, that *the method of the best and most truly rational rulers is not mathematical* (see Section 2.3). Is this what lurks behind Plato's claim that mathematics has less *saphēneia* than dialectic?

Before trying to answer this question, let us ask further about diagrams. Is the use of them in mathematics part of Plato's reason for the lower ranking? Scholars often assume that it is, but there is no statement of this in the text. Some have suggested that Plato connects the use of diagrams with mathematicians' illusion that their starting points are completely clear and firm. The idea is that he thinks looking at drawings of triangles, etc. can give the impression

resources to want, and to try, to unsettle existing preconceptions, and replace them with others that he has understanding enough to recognize as better', Rowe 2007c, 228. See also Schofield 2006, 163–4.

that the existence and nature of the mathematical elements is self-evident. Or perhaps he thinks that the use of diagrams for the purpose of proof gives the illusion that the reasoning is tighter than it really is. Again, Plato does not say that the use of diagrams is misleading in these ways. In any case this kind of criticism only applies to mathematicians with an inflated image of their subject; but this is not a stance mathematicians have to adopt in order to do mathematics, as we saw in connection with the supposed illusion that their starting points are more than the best available assumptions. Mathematicians do not put themselves out of business by admitting that assumptions is all that they are, nor by admitting that proofs done through diagrams are only as secure as the most professional construction and reading of diagrams can ensure. Plato is surely aware of this given the major role he plans for mathematics as propaedeutic to dialectic in the education of the rulers. The mathematics waiting in the wings to enact this role is surely not encumbered with a mathematically unnecessary inflated sense of its own cognitive superiority.

Some traditional interpreters have thought that the mere presence of sense-perceptible objects in mathematical activity is enough to render it intellectually impure. This has the unfortunate consequence that dialectic, as the intellectually supreme, hence purest, discipline is devoid of empirical content. Going along with this means accepting that Plato in the *Republic* has succumbed to some sort of mad dream when he equates dialectic with the discipline of *human rulers*.

We have been trying to find out why for Plato the two distinguishing features of mathematics make it cognitively inferior to dialectic, and we have drawn a blank. We have really only discovered that if Plato's mathematicians consider their starting points to be absolutely non-negotiable for all time, or their diagrams to be absolute guarantors of meaning and truth, they would be misguided. If mathematics essentially included either of these false views, this would be a good reason not to assign mathematics the highest place in the hierarchy of cognition. It would also be a good reason not to give mathematics the role of preparing the trainees for the dialectical stage of the curriculum. If doing mathematics essentially involved embracing these false views, the subject would be in danger of regarding itself as the cognitively most perfect discipline; and then the trainees would come to dialectic as if to something intellectually inferior – easier and less demanding. This Plato would surely regard as a grossly mistaken attitude. But, as things are, he evidently assumes that holding those false views about mathematics is not essential to being a mathematician. So why does he think that mathematics as such is cognitively inferior to dialectic?

It seems that his ranking is empty, since it comes with no guidance on the nature of the cognitive excellence which dialectic has more of and mathematics less. And, anyway, why should it matter whether dialectic – the method of ideal rulers but also by the associations of the word the legacy in some sense of Socrates – is cognitively superior to mathematics? Isn't it enough to show that dialectic is in its own way intellectually very demanding and deserves to be taken very seriously as an intellectual achievement, regardless of how much ulterior practical good it does? But perhaps, after all, Plato does not separate the degree of cognitive excellence from the degree of importance to life as a whole, so that for him the latter helps determine the former. He may reason that cognitive excellence and love of truth necessarily go together in such a way that those whose love is for the most important truths are to that extent most cognitively excellent. But this argument assumes that there is more truth, or greater truth, in more important truths. To make sense of this one might maintain that there are degrees of truth, and that one theory has greater truth than another because its objects or truth-makers occupy an ontologically higher status than those of the other theory. Perhaps when writing the *Republic* Plato endorsed a two-level ontology of intelligible being in which the objects of dialectic are somehow ontically superior to those of mathematics; but if so, he keeps quiet about it. Or perhaps in an ontologically more modest way he reasons that the foolishness and wickedness of the human world shows its *ignorance* of how to live, and that this depth of ignorance about what matters to us most shows in turn that finding correct non-truistic answers to those all-important questions is *intellectually* extremely difficult (otherwise, why haven't we made more progress?): so that getting those things determinately right would be, not just a great achievement on the part of intellectual creatures, but an *intellectually* great achievement. But such 'Socratic intellectualism' does not square well with the fact that the *Republic* distinguishes moral and intellectual education and sets as much store on the former as on the latter. Hence the difficulty of getting the great values of life determinately right may not always be due to the fact that those questions are *intellectually* very challenging. So, we still have no satisfactory explanation for the cognitive ranking between the two intellectual sections of the Divided Line.

A better explanation would be a psychological one: the pursuit of *saphēneia* is driven by love of truth, and in right-minded people love of truth is strongest when the truth in question is about 'the most important things to learn', namely fundamental values, especially when it is a matter of putting them into practice. So, the rulers' dialectical thinking seeks to be, and consequently is, more *saphes* than any other kind. Presumably this is what Plato would *hope* to be true of any good ruler. But it leaves out of account any comparison based on intrinsic features of the methods being compared. Yet the Divided Line does suggest without actually telling us that dialectic is epistemically superior to mathematics *because* of the latter's way with hypotheses and its use of diagrams. Perhaps, however, Plato (1) simply mentions these features as differentiating mathematics and then (2) logically independently proclaims mathematics inferior. So mathematics ranks lower just because it is mathematics, dialectic higher because it is not mathematics, and that's Plato's whole story? This would be disappointing, to say the least.

On the whole, I conclude that what underlies his ranking is the unspoken true perception that, however cognitively excellent mathematics may be, it must not be allowed to set the standard for excellence in the rulers' kind of thinking, because if this were to conform itself to the mathematical pattern it would, as *rulers'* reasoning, be pointless or a disaster. It would be pointless if, like a self-aware mathematics, it disowned at its basis any element of the non-hypothetical; for then it would make no reference to the form of the good as starting point, and without this the reasoning would have no practical heft. It would be disastrous if it kept the practical heft but, again like mathematics, drew its conclusions monotonically, looking neither right nor left at varying conditions of implementation. No doubt it was a mistake on Plato's part to suppose that the best way of saying 'Mathematics cannot sanely set the standard of excellence in practical and political thinking' is to say, as in effect he does, 'The intellectual perfection of good practical and political thinking surpasses the intellectual perfection of good mathematical thinking, which is why the latter cannot set the standard for the former.' This was a mistake because mathematics is the wrong model whether or not it is intellectually less perfect.

If this interpretation is right, then Plato is not committed to holding that the rulers' method is somehow infallible whereas mathematics is not. As noted, he says nothing that excludes the possibility of factual mistakes in the reasoning of even the most intellectually conscientious ruler. The ideal ruler's reasoning about fundamental values has an obvious affinity to the Socratic critical discussions explored in earlier dialogues, and so Plato labels it 'dialectical'. What the *Republic* adds is the new-found recognition that if 'dialectic', or reasoning about fundamental values, is to issue in practical conclusions – if it is to *rule* – then its procedure cannot be mathematical. What mainly disqualifies the ruling method from being mathematical is not that mathematics is less 'clear', whatever that means, but that mathematics is deductive.

At any rate, in repudiating the mathematical paradigm Plato continues his defence of philosophy begun in Book V. That paradigm generates the disjunctive charge that philosopher-rulers would be either useless or dangerous. In the Divided Line Plato pushes back: he wards off 'useless' by anchoring the rulers' reasoning in a principle (the form of the good) that is of unconditional practical relevance; and in a less lucid effort he tries to ward off 'dangerous' by banning diagrams from dialectic. The motive for this ban, on a charitable diagnosis, is an inarticulate sense that if dialectic were to share the *mathematicians'* way of using diagrams, it would be monomaniacally committed to reasoning always from or about the same kind of case in the same way (see Section 2.14).

On this interpretation, the claim that dialectic is cognitively more excellent than mathematics is not mere agonistic fanfare for the Socratic–Platonic dialectical brainchild. Rather, the Divided Line with its proportions of *saphēneia* is a confused attempt to protect the ideal of philosophical rule from being misconceived in ways that would write it off as absurd. The real message is that the intellectual method of philosopher-rulers is other than mathematical: so much so that falling for the seductive mathematical model is a misconception on the scale of treating unreasoned impressions as our sole source of truth about the world[138] – a stance in turn as deluded as mistaking shadows for authoritative revelations of their originals or even for originals themselves. With these comparisons Plato rejects the mathematical model in the strongest terms available to him, and surely in this he was right.

2.18   Why Are We Shown So Little about Dialectic in the *Republic*?

We are told only that dialectic is an intellectual discipline or method concerned with intelligibles; that it outranks all other modes of cognition, including mathematics, in *saphēneia*; and that it differs from mathematics in having a non-hypothetical principle, in not using diagrams, and in 'dislodging' its initial hypotheses. Why so little? For instance, why are we not given a single example of a dialectical argument in the *Republic* VI–VII sense of 'dialect-ical'? Compare Plato's profusion of examples, in some cases stunningly lengthy, in the *Phaedrus, Sophist, Statesman,* and *Philebus* of what is there called 'dialectic', namely the technique of collecting, dividing, and defining *per genus et differentiam.* See also his didacticism in the *Euthyphro, Meno,* and *Theaetetus* on offering a single definition as opposed to a set of examples to the 'What is it?' question. And think of the gigantic exercise of the second part of the *Parmenides.* Plato is generally eager to give illustrations of correct method. So why is he so tight-lipped about what he is calling 'dialectic' in the *Republic*?

(1) Let us start with the negative observation that Socrates is not guiding his interlocutors through their own use of the dialectical method prescribed for the rulers. It is not as if his discussion with Glaucon and Adeimantus can only proceed correctly if the three of them make moves sanctioned by *that* method,

---

[138] The reason this is a misconception is that sense and unreasoned impressions are vastly inferior to intellect in certain matters, and the most important ones. Plato does not think that they never get things right. The analogy of the sun assumes that there is such a thing as accurate vision, and the point of the large/small finger example is that intellect is not needed for identifying the object as a finger (523b–d). And mathematicians are not hallucinating their diagrams.

the method of the rulers. In the dialogues where he or the Eleatic visitor gives ample illustrations of some methodological point, it is always in the interest of the discussion conducted or about to be conducted in the dialogue between Socrates or the visitor, and the interlocutors. In the *Republic*, by contrast, Socrates is only *describing* the rulers' dialectic to his companions. From the point of view of the overall objective, which is to make it convincing that the best rulers would be dialectical philosophers, Socrates is under no obligation to lead Glaucon and Adeimantus by the hand along the detailed pathways of dialectic even if he could, because *they* are not being educated as rulers; they are only being told *about* the rulers' method, and for this there is not the same need to give examples of correct and incorrect dialectical moves. It seems to me that this consideration, which should surely be obvious to interpreters, might be a sufficient answer to the question asked in the title of this section – except for the fact that many interpreters have not been happy to leave the matter there but have wanted a more positive explanation of Socrates' silence about the details of dialectic. In what follows I try to address the matter more positively.

(2) One possibility, I suppose, is that Plato has gone off into an empty perfectionist fantasy: the perfect city has perfect rulers, and perfect rulers have a perfect method – so perfect that it is even more perfect than mathematics; hence the perfect method has to possess some attributes differentiating it from mathematics. In addition, the perfect method somehow involves the good as its principle since otherwise it would not be perfect. And that is all there is to say. This is very disappointing if we came to this part of the *Republic* hoping to be shown something non-vacuous about the nature of the good ruler's wisdom. But it perfectly explains why, when after the Cave and the programme of mathematical education Glaucon presses Socrates for details about dialectic, he is told that on this topic he has gone as far as he can go (533a1–2). It is also as far as Socrates can go and Plato too, because the empty shell of a perfectionist fantasy is all Plato ever wanted to flourish at us.

(3) It has been suggested that Glaucon and Adeimantus are excluded from entering the 'longer way' that goes via dialectic because they are still too much wedded to sense experience, not having undergone the intensive mathematical education designed, as Plato says, to release the mind from imprisonment in sensory and sense-like cognition.[139] And the *Republic* is set up in such a way that what can be placed before the reader is restricted to what can be explained to Glaucon and Adeimantus. Note that Socrates is on a par with Glaucon and Adeimantus in not having undergone the intensive mathematical education, although he can describe it in some detail. While he somehow has a notion of

---

[139] Miller 2007, 315.

the longer way, he has it from the outside, so to speak; it is never suggested that he has trodden the way or could tread it himself.[140] Yet it would be surprising if *Socrates* is shut out from the longer way on account of being, in effect, a prisoner in the cave or a struggling released prisoner still half in love with cave-shadows. The anonymous figure in the cave who forces a few prisoners to turn their heads and start the journey away from bondage is often compared to the gadfly Socrates. And it would be surprising too, even if less so, if we were meant to think of Glaucon and Adeimantus as shackled by sense experience. Thanks to their association with Socrates, they are familiar with philosophical conversation and with the difference between the many sensibles and the one form (cf. 475e6–476a9; 507a7–b9). So they are by no means unconverted cave-prisoners. Yet they are not able to follow the longer way travelled by Plato's rulers. It seems, then, that even though they have not had the entire liberating mathematical education, this lack is not enough by itself to explain what seems to be their wholesale exclusion from the longer way of the rulers' dialectic.

(4) It has sometimes been suggested that Plato imagines the dialectical method as culminating in a mystical vision of the form of the good. Although 'mystical' and 'mysticism' are used of a diverse range of phenomena, they are real phenomena whatever their epistemic value, so this suggestion is preferable to the perfectionist one in at least appealing to something we know does occur. It explains why we are told so little about dialectical method because it understands that method as governed by a principle whose content or significance cannot be properly conveyed in words, unless possibly to those who have

---

[140] At 532d8–e1 Glaucon wants to be told about the 'method, divisions, and paths' of dialectic. Some translations of 533a1 misleadingly suggest that Socrates knows more than Glaucon can about these things, by having him say: 'Dear Glaucon, you will not be able to follow me further' (Jowett 1892; Shorey 1935, vol. II; Lindsay 1935; Cornford 1941 and cf. Cornford 1932b, 176; Chambry 1946, Grube rev. Reeve 1997; Griffith 2000; Dixsaut 2001, 61; Vegetti 2003; 2013c, 206; Leroux 2004; Lee 2007; Waterfield 2008; Emlyn-Jones and Preddy 2014). But 'me' is not in the text, and there is no special emphasis on 'you' to suggest that Glaucon is excluded from knowledge that Socrates has. Here 'follow' means 'stay on the track' ('follow the thread of a discourse', LSJ *akoloutheō* II. 2; cf. *Republic* 451d1; *Lysis* 218e2; *Hippias Minor* 373a3; *Gorgias* 465b8; *Meno* 76c5; *Phaedo* 107b7–8; *Theaetetus* 185d4; 201d7). In the next sentence, 533a2–4, Socrates seems to back off from committing himself to anything at all in this area; his words are very obscure (see Rowe 2007c, 254). Still, if his situation is that he is none the wiser than Glaucon, why doesn't he reply that the two of them are on a par? Perhaps he mentions Glaucon's, and not also his own, inability to follow further because of the latter's evident longing for *anapaula . . . kai telos tēs poreias* (532e3), the thought being, partly: 'Since you are *so weary* you won't be able to go on.' (Cf. 511c3 and 534b1–2, where Glaucon admits to struggling a bit.) If so, Socrates does not align himself with Glaucon because he is famously indefatigable (*pace* Glaucon at 435d8); but this is consistent with his not having an answer to Glaucon's questioning about dialectic. Perhaps, however, if Glaucon is being contrasted with anyone, it is not with Socrates but with the dialecticians who are to rule. *They* are able to follow every aspect of their method and would not be struggling with fatigue.

undergone the same experience.[141] It is impossible to imagine how a mystical vision of the good would issue in determinate practical conclusions useful to rulers or about-to-be rulers, but treating that as an objection presumably begs the question against the view. It is sometimes objected that the to and fro of intersubjective discussion implied by the word *dialegesthai*[142] rules out mysticism,[143] but the claim is not that the whole process of dialectic is a mystical experience, only that the part where it touches the good is. A stronger objection, I think, is that whereas elsewhere Plato is happy to use the vocabulary of the Eleusinian mysteries in connection with the grasp of forms (*Symposium* 210a; *Phaedrus* 249c6–d1; 250b6–c3; cf. *Phaedo* 69c3–d2), and is familiar with notions of divine inspiration and 'channelling' (*Phaedrus* 238c5–d2; 245a1–7; *Ion* 533d–535a), there is hardly a whisper of any of this in what we are told about dialectical method itself in the *Republic*.[144] The passage most amenable to a mystical interpretation is the one describing how, at the very end of their entire training, the philosophers lift their gaze to the form of the good (540a5–b1); but, although this is expressed with poetic intensity, it carries none of the special vocabulary of 'initiation' and 'mystical viewing'. I have argued in Section 2.10 that the strange temporal positioning of this episode calls for a meta-dialectical interpretation; but the suggestion that the form of the good is grasped in a mystical vision is a suggestion about a moment in first-order dialectic. There is also 521c2–3, which introduces the whole topic of being led up out of the cave, comparing this to the passage of certain mythical heroes from Hades to the presence of the gods.[145] But this refers to the whole journey, including the mathematical part, from darkness to seeing the sun; it is not a statement about apprehending the form of the good as an element *within* the dialectical method as such. Then there is the over-translation of 533a1–2 (discussed in note 140), where Glaucon has just begged Socrates for a detailed account of dialectic, and Socrates replies: ' My dear Glaucon, ... you'll not be able to follow any further – although that wouldn't be for any lack of eagerness on my part.' There is a striking echo here of *Symposium* 210a2–4, where Diotima speaks of the erotic *telea* and *epoptika* as matters which she is about to explain although she is not sure whether Socrates will be able to follow.[146] If at 533a1–2 Plato deliberately recalls the

---

[141] There are different possibilities: either the content of the vision is ineffable or it is too sacred to be spoken of to the uninitiated.

[142] References in note 76.   [143] E.g. Vegetti 2005, 33–4; cf. 36

[144] *Pace* Cornford 1932b, 184, 187.

[145] Szlezák 2001, 371, sees here an allusion to the mysteries.

[146] If one reads too much into the intertextuality, it is easy to slip into assuming that Socrates in the *Republic* has insider's knowledge of dialectic just as Diotima in the *Symposium* has insider's knowledge of the higher erotic mysteries – whereas Socrates in the *Republic* disavows knowledge of the form of the good.

Symposium passage and then refrains from using the language of the mysteries, he may even be meaning to convey that the mysteries are *not* the right model for what is being talked about here in the *Republic*.[147] (We should also keep in mind that it would be one thing for Plato to view the philosopher-ruler's cognition of the form of the good as literally a mystical vision, and another for him to use – as in the *Republic* he rather noticeably does not – the familiar vocabulary of the mysteries to convey metaphorically that correct apprehension of the form of the good presupposes its own kind of intense and difficult preparation just as viewing the mysteries at Eleusis presupposes initiation-exercises.[148])

Still, it may be thought that the religiosity of Plato's tone in passages about reason and the form of the good is evidence for the mystical-vision interpretation. But one can explain that tone without invoking mysticism in the sense of a turn to the supra-rational and ineffable. Plato reveres intellect, including discursive intellect (and does he in fact recognize any other?). Thus he may well regard wicked or perversely frivolous uses of reason as a sort of desecration.[149] Reason even in human beings is divine or potentially divine (500d1–3; 501b; 589c8–d1; cf. 611d8–e2). He sometimes calls forms 'divine', which implies amongst other things the importance of not giving them a wrong title, i.e. a wrong account or definition. This solemnity is plainly compatible with treating the objects and operations of intellect as discursively rational.

(5) I turn next to the theory of the Tübingen interpreters (K. Gaiser, H. J. Krämer, and most recently T. A. Szlezák) that the reason we are told so little about dialectic is that knowledge of the form of the good is esoteric not because mystical but because abstruse science is involved. The science is the meta-mathematical metaphysics of the One and the Indefinite Dyad, which Plato worked on at some point in his career, and which Aristotle calls 'the unwritten tenets', *ta agrapha dogmata*. These include the theory that the One and the Dyad, which are the first principles of everything, jointly generate the numbers or the forms of the numbers. The One, by transforming the Dyad into a plurality of determinates, is the source of the being and knowability of the other intelligibles. Many scholars tend to think that this dualistic ontology was a late development for Plato (the *Republic* belongs to the middle of his career),

---

[147] This assumes that the *Symposium* is the earlier dialogue. If (as has been argued by Frede 1993) the chronology is the other way round, *Republic* 533a1–2 does not particularly suggest that the mysteries are in the offing.

[148] See Sattler 2013 for the proposal that in the *Symposium* Plato uses the vocabulary of the Eleusinian mysteries, which is familiar to his audience, as a metaphor for cognition of hard-to-grasp Platonic abstractions.

[149] This is not very different from Kant's attitude to pure practical reason, yet no one has ever accused Kant of introducing mysticism into the process of deciding what to do.

but we have no firm evidence that it was not already on the go when he was composing the *Republic*. There is also evidence that at some point Plato identified the good with the One. The non-mystical esoteric interpretation finds these theories beneath the surface of the *Republic*, concluding that the form of the good in Books VI–VII is nothing other than the One of the unwritten ontology. The reason, then, why Plato has so little to say there about dialectic is that he has framed the dialogue mostly as a conversation between Socrates and the brothers Glaucon and Adeimantus, and the brothers are not advanced enough in philosophy to be able to grasp the meta-mathematical theory of the One. Whether the Socrates-character should be thought of as grasping it is unclear, but the main point is that Plato is writing for an exoteric readership on the same level as Glaucon and Adeimantus.

It is surely correct that the *Republic* like most of the other dialogues was aimed at a general audience of educated people rather than solely at Plato's in-house associates, a group of advanced researchers; but even so it is strange, if this interpretation is right, that the dialogue carries virtually no trace of positive evidence for the meta-mathematical metaphysics.[150] One would think that the Socrates-character might here and there have given a passing glimpse of some specific feature of the doctrine, sidestepping Glaucon's or Adeimantus' inevitable demand for more explanation with 'That would take too long,' or 'You aren't ready to understand it properly,' or 'I don't myself know where I got this from or what it really means.' There was surely no harm in letting people get a whiff of what was going on in the seminars of the Academy. If as a result some outsiders went round mouthing a few technical notions beyond their comprehension ('E = mc^2' on a T-shirt), why would that matter?[151] To imagine such phrases as sacred, not to be 'taken in vain', is more appropriate for the mysticism hypothesis.

If the form of the good in the *Republic* is the same as the One of the unwritten tenets, it is strange that nothing corresponding to the Indefinite Dyad is presented in the *Republic*. From all the evidence, the unwritten theory of the One pairs it with the Dyad, like male with female parent, even though the One is superior ('more honourable').

---

[150] On 511d2, which to many has seemed a positive trace, see the discussion in Section 4.3.

[151] The Tübingen approach assumes that Plato regarded it as something of a disaster if the 'unsuitable and unprepared' were exposed to the theory of the One and the Dyad: so it had to be protected from them or they from it. 'The reason for esoteric reserve . . . lay not in the fact that the theory of first principles was impossible to formulate orally or on paper, but that unprepared persons who were confronted with it would inevitably be confused and misled', Gaiser 1980, 14. But much in the dialogues suggests that Plato can be fairly ruthless about confronting 'the unprepared' with initially baffling ideas. See e.g. the three waves of *Republic* V, the second part of the *Parmenides*, the being of non-being in the *Sophist*, and the one–many puzzles of the *Philebus*. What was it about the theory of first principles that always led Plato in the dialogues to sidestep preparing the unprepared to understand it?

In the *Philebus* Socrates puts forward something close to the doctrine of the One and the Indefinite Dyad. The main interlocutor, Protarchus, does not appear to be a deeply technically trained philosopher, any more than Glaucon and Adeimantus. It is true that Protarchus is often in genuine dispute with Socrates, which is almost never the case with the brothers in the *Republic*, but even so Protarchus is something of an amateur. For example, he needs to have the idea of taxonomical division explained to him (16c–18d; see esp. 17a6–7). The *Philebus* hardly seems to be tailored just for an esoteric audience, yet it contains what might fairly be called a version or analogue of the One–Indefinite Dyad doctrine. And from what we otherwise know of that doctrine, it seems not to be extraordinarily hard to grasp, at least in outline.

(6) The reader has probably anticipated my own answer to the question in the title of this section. According to this answer, Plato's sketch of dialectic in the *Republic* is an attempt to delineate an idealized version of something not only real but totally familiar, namely ethical reasoning in light of changeable circumstances. His version is idealized only insofar as it presupposes reason*ers* who are as intellectually and morally flawless as human beings can be. The idealization does not include making out the type of reasoning itself to be simpler and less beholden to circumstances than such reasoning actually is. Given this faithfulness to the logical reality of what he is presenting (trying to present), Plato's exposition labours under two kinds of impediment. First, there is the almost pitiful poverty of his logical vocabulary.[152] As well as not having terms for 'premiss' or 'deductive' – nor therefore 'non-deductive' as in 'non-deductive reasoning' – or 'defeasible', or any stock phrase for '*ceteris paribus*', he has no dedicated word or phrase for the notion of a normative reason for acting or believing. (It is not impossible that when he wrote the *Republic* he even lacked a reflective grasp of the difference between a fact or state of affairs as represented by a proposition, and a complex object.) It seems incredible that the culture into which he was born had so little impetus for developing a basic logical terminology, given its longstanding intense, self-conscious, rivalrous passion for skill in argument; but we have to accept that this was the situation, since otherwise Plato would have had more tools for presenting dialectic in the *Republic*. Apparently his elders had been too busy brilliantly doing what they did to have time to fashion much vocabulary for talking about it.

The second impediment to exposition is endemic to the topic he has chosen to write about, namely the intellectual method of rulers, which is a method of ethically loaded decision-making. He cannot point to existing stock examples of how ideal rulers reason about, e.g., justice, since the ideal rulers do not as yet exist.

---

[152] See note 11.

But even if some did, one outsider would scarcely be able to explain the rulers' thinking to another by giving examples, because it would be difficult, perhaps not feasible, for outsiders to understand how the reasoning would have been rationally compelling for the reasoner. For this, they would have had not only to share the ruler's values but also to know what circumstances the ruler faced so as to know what the problem was and what a good solution had to take into account. When discussing the irrelevance of gender to the question of whether someone is suited for leadership in Callipolis, Socrates spoke as if treating the irrelevant as relevant is bad dialectic, a fallacy of reasoning (Section 2.8 with note 65). This suggests that a clear example of the rulers' excellent reasoning *qua* reasoning should lay out all relevant considerations beyond what everyone can simply take for granted: not an easy task when what is relevant varies with circumstances.

And even if one knew all the circumstances and shared the rulers' values, and so could appreciate the example, this could not function as a reliable template for reasoning about justice, etc. in other cases. The same difficulty arises if we ask for an example of the practical reasoning of a wise and virtuous private individual, say Socrates himself. An example cannot, for the same reasons as with the good ruler, serve as a template of good reasoning for other agents and other cases. Thus, Socrates in the *Republic* can only give the most schematic account of how ethical wisdom operates through dialectic, but this in no way impugns any claim that he himself has ethical wisdom.

I have argued that because the dialectic wielded by Plato's ideal rulers is ethical reasoning, its force in any given instance is not accessible to everyone. This is not at all to imply that *contact with the form of the good* is available only to those ideal rulers. On the contrary, at 517c3–4 Socrates says: 'It also seems to me that anyone who is to act sensibly (*emphronōs praxein*), in private or in public life, must have had a sight of it [i.e. the form of the good].' So wise private individuals, no less than ideal rulers, invoke in their deliberations the very same form of the good. This strongly suggests that 'sighting the form of the good' is possible for some even though they have not been through the entire formal training of the ideal rulers. So (1) perhaps in Callipolis there is room for members of the two lower classes to have and exercise genuine wisdom over options that concern only private life (although members of the auxiliary class don't have much private life). Some non-rulers might be ruled by reason not merely in the sense of willingly obeying their philosophical rulers but also, over certain matters, in the sense of reaching and acting on their own reasoned decisions.[153] And (2) Plato surely allows that even in non-ideal environments there can be a few genuinely wise individuals who have not

---

[153] Admittedly, this is in tension with 474c1–3 where Socrates envisages for Callipolis an apparently exhaustive division between those who are fit for both philosophy and leadership, and those who are unfit for philosophy and fit only to be led.

studied mathematics and dialectic for fifteen years. Wherever wisdom is exercised (however acquired), the form of the good and *de facto* dialectic come into play. Indeed, this is what we should expect given the ordinariness of the G-question. Not everyone who asks it gets true answers, but this is not because the term 'good' has an esoteric meaning accessible to only a few. What sets the Callipolitan rulers apart is the moral and intellectual excellence that makes their answers reliably true, and also their culture of reflectiveness about their method and the G-question.

What bars us from fully entering into another's ethical reasoning is the fact that such reasoning necessarily depends on context. Contextual detail guides even the wisest judgement without necessarily surfacing into an articulate and thus transmissible complete description. Even if all the detail did surface, it would, I think, be impossible to demonstrate that it had. So, any course of ethical reasoning endemically possesses a measure of opacity to those who did not share its context, even if they would have shared the reasoner's values. But any wise person's reasoning about what would be genuinely fair or courageous in such and such a situation involves Plato's form of the good. This is because it involves the G-question, which, when asked by a truly wise questioner, captures and brings to bear the authentic sun-like form. So our and Glaucon's exclusion from the longer way of Plato's idealized rulers is not because the rest of us in principle lack access to the form of the good: it is because their ethical reasonings and ours are coloured by different contexts.

When Glaucon asks for details about dialectic and Socrates replies 'You'll not be able to follow any further' (533a1–2), we all, I think rightly, understand the path which Glaucon is unable to pursue further to be that of the Callipolitan ruler's dialectic. We need not infer that the qualification Glaucon lacks is a depth of wisdom unique to that ruler. Even if Glaucon were equally wise (not that anyone is claiming he is), he would still be unable to follow further unless he was also in the ruler's shoes. In principle no one not in those shoes can walk the ruler's path – not because there is a mystery about some special *content* of the ruler's wisdom, but because this wisdom by its practical-ethical nature operates from a perspective which is not universally accessible.[154]

To return to the title of this section: if Plato had tried to explain the ruler's reasoning by means of examples, he would have risked causing serious misunderstanding. If, on the one hand, he emphasized that the conclusion in some example has categorical practical force but only in relation to a certain

---

[154] It is true that on first mentioning the longer way at 435c9–d7, and then at 504b2, Socrates did rather give the impression that taking it was an option for him and his interlocutors, so that it was their *choice* to stay on the less exact level that had served so far. Still, nothing was *said* there about choosing. If we had the impression that there was a choice, it was *we* who formed it. In retrospect, Socrates may have been disingenuous at those earlier moments, but he was not positively misleading.

context which is not always present, and that what, e.g., justice demands here would elsewhere be unjust, he would seem to imply that the same thing is both just and unjust. But wasn't this the implication of the sight-lovers, those paradigms of non-knowledge whom Socrates so carefully distinguished from the real philosophers back at the beginning of this whole discussion of philosopher-rulers?[155] This is a funny sort of output from the method that was supposed to surpass even mathematics in cognitive excellence! If, on the other hand, Plato gave an example without emphasizing the mutable context, he would risk seeming to endorse it as proclaiming an exceptionless norm of justice, never needing to be re-visited. If, as a matter of fact, it did 'stay true', this could only be by the unpredictable accident of nothing coming along that made it false: so it would be epistemically irresponsible to claim to *know* it to be true.[156]

In conclusion to this section: if my argument is correct, then the meagreness of Plato's account of the ruler's dialectic is not to be blamed on mysticism, nor on the abstruseness of meta-mathematical ontology, but on the nature of practical-ethical reasoning. What Plato can say he does, and it amounts to four points. The first three are the now familiar differentiations between mathematics and dialectic in terms of the retention or not of provisional starting points, the presence or not of a non-hypothetical principle, and the use or not of diagram-like aids for reaching conclusions. The fourth point is rather cryptic: it is that the dialectician is 'synoptic': he or she sees things together (537c7). This, in my view, means (minimally) that he or she weighs up a proposed explication of some norm not in isolation but *together with* the context in which it would have to be implemented if it were implemented.[157] Excellent

---

[155] The sight-lovers are discussed in the next section.

[156] But surely with sufficient historical knowledge one could explain all the considerations that determined some revered figure's wise decision, while warning that because of the difference in circumstances, etc., it cannot serve as a model for wise decisions in general? It is not clear, I think, that in the *Republic* Plato would have seen this is as a live option. It is true that such explanations seem to be part of what the Socrates-character in the *Timaeus* longs to be shown when he asks the others for a story showing his ideal city (recognizably the Callipolis of the *Republic*, many scholars think) in action, rising to some major crisis with deeds and speeches 'worthy of its education and nurture'. But Socrates asks the others because he himself lacks the ability to produce such a story (19b–d; 20b–c). Socrates doesn't 'do' reconstruction of other people's practical reasoning. (It is Timaeus, not he, who expounds cosmology by reconstructing the reasoning of the divine craftsman.) If, in the *Republic*, Socrates, ever didactic and in his own person the exemplary psychagogue, were to give imaginary illustrations of the rulers' method of wise decisions, he could be construed as presenting models for everyone. After all, if Callipolis itself is meant as a corrective model by which to measure the deficiency of real city-states, the same might be taken to apply to any examples of good reasoning set out within it. This whole theme connects with Plato's misgivings about the idea of putting things down in writing for good and all, on which see *Phaedrus* 274c–278b.

[157] See Cornford 1932b, 182, for a similar interpretation of synopsis in dialectic, except that he does not speak of implementation.

practical reasoning is essentially in this sense 'synoptic' by contrast with excellent deductive reasoning, which proceeds with eyes dutifully closed to anything outside the area staked out for good and all by its starting points.[158]

2.19 True Philosophers versus Sight-Lovers

The sight-lovers entered the discussion at the point where Socrates began to characterize the philosopher. The first pass there was that the philosopher, the wisdom-lover, loves every kind of learning without picking and choosing, just as those we call 'boy-lovers' or 'wine-lovers' or 'honour-lovers' want to engage with every kind of thing that falls within the scope of their passion (474c–475c). Glaucon objects that this description covers people whom it would be strange to count as philosophers: these are the lovers of sights and sounds ('sight-lovers' for short), who omnivorously go to watch every spectacle, see every play, attend every concert, and so on. Their delight in these experiences is also a sort of delight in learning, but it would be very strange to call them philosophers, Glaucon says, because *they never engage in reasoning or discussion if they can help it* (475d4–6). We might think that this alone is enough to distinguish them from philosophers, but Socrates responds by laying out the classic tenets of Platonic metaphysics and epistemology. Focusing on values such as the beautiful, the good, the just, and their opposites, Socrates says that the mark of philosophers is to recognize and engage with these each as one and 'itself by itself', whereas from the sight-lovers' perspective no such separate unitary entities exist: all there is to beauty or the beautiful are the many beautiful sights and sounds which they go here and there to enjoy, and they cannot get their minds round anything else (476b4–c3; 479a3–4).[159] Socrates says, and Glaucon agrees, that far from being in touch with the truth, the sight-lovers live in a dream, and their cognition of beauties of sight and sound – which to them are the ultimate reality of beauty – is opinion (*doxa*), not knowledge (*gignōskontos gnōmēn*, 476d4). By contrast, the philosophers are wide awake in distinguishing the beautiful itself – the non-perceptible reality that in some sense 'makes' the many perceptible beautiful things beautiful – and they thereby exercise knowledge, not mere opinion

---

[158] The mathematician is also encouraged to be 'synoptic', but what this amounts to is different: it is a matter of looking for parallels and analogies between the five mathematical sciences (537b8–c3; cf. 531c9–d3). For more on synopsis see towards the end of Section 4.3.

[159] 'The many beautifuls' here refers to types, not particulars. By hearing a particular performance of a sonata, I hear that sonata, a multiply instantiable type. See Gosling 1960 and Irwin 1977 for grounds for taking the reference to be to types or kinds. It is natural to take the finger example at 523c3–d6 as referring to an individual finger, but this is not necessary. 'The middle finger is longer than the little finger but shorter than the hand' could be a general statement. On types rather than particulars as the 'other' of metaphysically separate forms, see Harte 2008.

(475e–476d). How do these Platonic tenets connect with Glaucon's observation that the sight-lovers don't go in for discussion and argument? The answer, I think, is that Plato assumes that to engage in discussion, even about the perceptible beautifuls, is, whether one knows it or not, to invoke the single form of the beautiful itself by itself; but more on this shortly.

The sight-lovers are imagined as piqued at being excluded from the top cognitive rank, so Socrates decides that he must convince them that a lower rung is where they belong.[160] He gets Glaucon, answering on their behalf, to agree that there are three fields: the field of what is, the field of what is not, and between these the field of what is and is not; also that there are three attitudes, namely knowledge which is lined up with what is, ignorance which is lined up with what is not (i.e. completely is not)[161], and opinion which is lined up with what is and is not; also that knowledge is a different capacity from opinion because knowledge is error-free whereas opinion may be mistaken: opinion is 'brighter than ignorance and darker than knowledge'. Socrates then asks these deniers of the reality of the beautiful itself by itself whose nature remains always the same – and so on with the just and the other cases – whether there is any of the many beautifuls that will not present itself as ugly, and similarly with the many just things and the many pious things: is there any that will not also present itself as the opposite? Glaucon, speaking for them, says that any of the many beautifuls 'must appear in a way as both beautiful and ugly', and similarly for the other cases (479a). They then admit, on the basis of what they have already agreed, that since the many beautifuls, etc. are in the field of what is and also is not, their beauty-judgements about those things manifest opinion,

---

[160] Why is he concerned to convince them, given Glaucon's observation, undisputed by Socrates, that they are allergic to arguments? (a) Perhaps this passage prefigures the suggestion at 499e–500e that rather than being hostile to ordinary people who disparage (real) philosophers as worthless or worse, one should persuade them of the opposite. (b) More likely, the notion of winning the sight-lovers round is a pretext for defending the linkage of knowledge with intelligibles in terms suitable for people who are not already convinced but ready to listen to an argument. (See Gosling 1960 and Fine 1978, 1999 on how this dialectical requirement rules out certain interpretations of steps of the argument.) Since Glaucon and Adeimantus are already sympathetic (cf. 475e4–7; 507a7–b10), it would be out of place to have Socrates aim such an argument at them; so Plato conjures up a target-group outside the Glaucon–Adeimantus–Socrates circle. The aim is to convince a sceptical or non-partisan reader. Plato assumes that this reader will accept such assertions as 'The very same thing is both just and unjust': strange to us, but a cliché when Plato wrote, if we accept the standard dating of the *Dissoi Logoi* (late fifth to early fourth century according to Burnyeat 1998; but see Bailey 2008 for cautious scepticism; also Molinelli 2018, arguing for a date between 355 and 338 and seeing Platonic influence in the work.)

[161] Thus, it seems that ignorance is not false belief about something and with something as its content, but the state of complete blankness about, or complete failure to focus on, some subject-matter S, a state to which nothing of S is present.

not knowledge.[162] Socrates suggests that it is also like this with double and half, large and small, light and heavy, and Glaucon, speaking for the sight-lovers, agrees (476d–480a).[163]

Later, when expounding the beginnings of liberation from the cave, Socrates speaks of how, for some minds, seeing something, say a finger, to be large and also small sparks puzzlement over whether large is the same as small since to perception they are mixed up together: the puzzlement provokes the soul into disentangling and separating each from the other, spurring it to ask 'So what exactly *is* largeness and what *is* smallness anyway?' *Intellect* has done the separation and asked the abstract question. The soul has been jerked into recognizing (and into awareness that it recognizes) the reality, unity, and self-identity of those forms (523a–524d).[164]

By contrast, the sight-lovers, from the picture we are given, are unpuzzled and acquiescent at the compresence of beautiful with ugly. We know that they feel no urge to look for the difference in respect or context that *explains* how the same thing (type of thing) has both these opposite attributes because Glaucon started out describing them as allergic to reasoning (*logous kai toiautēn diatribēn*, 475d4–6). They are therefore not the kind of connoisseurs who love to analyse or explain why a certain artistic effect is beautiful in one context but not in another.[165] The sight-lovers just get pleasure from

---

[162] They are assumed to accept that where G is the contrary of F, being G entails being not F.

[163] This summary bypasses some important interpretative debates. I am assuming that 'is' and 'is not' here are (almost always) predicative, i.e. amount to 'is F' and 'is not F', although it is tempting to read them as veridical at 479d. (See Fine 1978. Fine 1999, 89–93, argues that Plato is justified in moving from the predicative to the veridical.) I do not take a line on whether the argument can be formulated so as to come out valid, nor on whether an interpretation yielding validity is necessarily to be preferred. Even if a precise meaning does lurk in the argument's every stage, any interpretation will always be controversial. For a very clear discussion see Annas 1981, ch. 8.

[164] It is unnecessary to suppose that it is thereby also jerked into endorsing Platonic metaphysics considered as a general theory of what is real.

[165] In Christopher Rowe's word, they are 'limp' (Rowe 2007c, 205, 207). This interpretation differs markedly from that of Gosling 1960, who understands the sight-lovers' aversion to *logoi* as aversion to *dialectical* discussion, which presumably means, minimally, abstract argument. In particular, he thinks that they are impatient with philosophical efforts to give a definition or explanation of beauty that holds for all beautiful things. (One certainly sympathizes with this.) But in Gosling's view they are intensely interested in analysing what does or does not make a work of art beautiful: 'they become authorities in criticism, people who could set up to teach the principles of composition and so forth' (121). Gosling rests this on the description of them at 476a11 as *philotechnoi kai praktikoi*, which he takes to mean 'they think in terms of skill, art, technique, of finding out how things are done'. *Philotechnoi* may mean just that they love dazzling effects that can only be achieved by artistry. *Praktikoi*, which bears the weight of Gosling's interpretation, may, and I think does, mean something like: 'they engage with the concrete objects themselves in all their sense-perceived materiality'. They would be uninterested in a lecture about far-off statues at Delphi, or in a musical score. Cf. *Statesman* 258d–e and 259c–d, where *praktikos* divides off workers who use their hands from those who operate through *logoi* and calculation; NB *sōmata* at 258e2 and *sōmati* at 259c6–7. On the passivity of the sight-lovers see Irwin 1995, 270–1. Their position needs a Glaucon to

experiencing beautiful effects, and they may get a different sort of pleasure from registering points of ugliness, since this too is a kind of 'learning', an exercise of a cognitive capacity (cf. 475d3; 9). They may also be pretty reliable discriminators of what is beautiful and what is ugly. But they have no urge to justify or explain either their individual judgements or their application of opposite predicates to the same kind of thing.[166] We need not see them as acquiescent in self-contradiction. Possibly they take their perceptions to be inducing contradictory judgements and simply do not care. But they may feel, correctly, that the judgements are not inconsistent even if they would not care if they were. As we know, the actual situation is that the same object, or very same sort of object, is beautiful in one specifiable way and ugly in another, or beautiful in one specifiable context and ugly in another, or something specifiable about it has changed so that the previously beautiful thing is now ugly. But the sight-lovers are not interested in trying to identify the factor whose presence in the one case and absence in the other explains how each of the opposite predications is true.

When the predicates are 'beautiful' and 'ugly', Plato's main example in the passage about the sight-lovers, we may well think there is nothing *wrong* about applying both to the same thing without feeling any call to explain how both can apply. These sight-lovers are not training to be art-docents. They might concede that *something* must explain why the thing here is beautiful while the same thing over there is ugly, but they feel no obligation to track down that 'something', any more than one feels under an epistemic obligation to identify the scientific basis whereby these hairs on someone's head are grey and these otherwise apparently identical ones are dark. People can reliably assign the colours correctly without having any curiosity or even inkling about the underlying chemistry.[167] So, when beautiful/ugly is the example we may think that the sight-lovers' first-order judgements are unreasoned but not irrational any more than perceptual acts are irrational, even though we may also think that Socrates is right to maintain, and the sight-lovers to admit in the end, that those first-order judgements express not knowledge but opinion (at best, reliable opinion formed by use of a 'reliable mechanism' consisting in the practised eye of an experienced aesthete).

---

follow Socrates' argument against them and answer on their behalf, like Protarchus for effete Philebus in the eponymous dialogue.

[166] Their ability to judge correctly is a knack rather than an expertise according to the distinction at *Gorgias* 465a. They are lovers of *doxa*, opinion (479e–480a), and in the *Republic doxa* is 'atheoretical thought' in Jessica Moss's excellent phrase (Moss 2021, ch. 8).

[167] Perhaps in fundamental physics one may insist that the same sort of thing is both F and not-F without there being an explanation, but in most areas of life we solidly assume a factor that accounts for the difference, even when it is permissible not to care what that factor may be.

So, the sight-lovers are those who are not exercised by the compresence of beautiful and ugly into separating the two attributes: they do *not* recognize each as one and possessed of precisely its own identity, and wonder 'Just what *is* beauty anyway?' Perhaps their lack of this particular kind of puzzlement and curiosity shows that they are not philosophers or on the way to becoming philosophers; but in this they are surely not *culpable* if what matters to them is simply the experiencing of (in our phrase) aesthetically beautiful objects. But it is different when we move to the examples of just and unjust, pious and impious, or in general to *moral* beauty and ugliness. Reacting to this action as just and to another apparently identical one as unjust, and simply leaving it at that, is not innocently insouciant but grossly irrational. This is (at least) because being just or unjust has practical implications: we aim to put in place just arrangements and encourage just behaviour, and to get rid of the opposite. To register that the same kind of thing K is just and also unjust, and take the matter no further, is to give up on choosing whether or when to be for or against K things, and on guiding the choices of anyone else. It is because of the practical force of the terms that 'leaving it at that' is an irrational response to mixed-message cases of just and unjust, and the same holds for the other ethical predicates, and also for 'useful' and 'useless', 'healthy' and 'unhealthy', and many others. If you have the impression that the same K is unjust here although it is just over there, your only legitimate choice is: either withdraw one or both predications as based on a false impression, or be ready to identify and articulate the relevant difference between the two cases so that it is apparent that the just K has a specific feature that makes it just, while the unjust K lacks this feature. What is not an option is to stand by both predications and deny that you need to be able to explain the difference.[168] If you do this, it could be that your responses are all the same correct; but if you literally have no idea why one case of K morally stinks while another does not, and you still calmly stand by your judgements, then even if your responses did not feel like guesses – you felt the one case as *palpably* fair, the other one *palpably* not – still, arguably you are as epistemically feckless as if you had blindly guessed. Or one might say that you have not grasped the rules for making categorical ethical predications, so your acts of predication are in a certain way meaningless. Also, you are unteachable in this area, and incapable of teaching anyone else. Perhaps this does not matter so much with aesthetic responses, but

---

[168] It may be thought that when it comes to ethical predications no one could behave in such an irrational way across the board, so that the ethical equivalent of sight-lovers is a straw man. In reply: perhaps Plato is focusing not on an imaginary type of *person* but on a real type of ethical *response*, logically on a par with the unreasoned aesthetic responses typical of certain real people. 'It's OK for us to do it and it's not OK for them to do it, and that's all there is to say': people can be like this about some things and not others. Line 479d4 comes close to identifying the sight-lovers with 'the many'.

with ethical ones demanding practical co-operation the unreasoned stance means that if there is disagreement it can only be met with force, brainwashing, or mutual isolation.

Philosopher-rulers want to know what justice and its opposite are because they seek to implement the one and eradicate the other. Since implementation for human beings is necessarily implementation in a context, and the specific type of context can make a difference to whether an arrangement conforming to a proposed formula for justice would in fact *be* just in that context, the philosopher-ruler's question should be of the form 'What counts as justice given such and such a context?', not 'What counts as justice *simpliciter*?' This suggestion may seem at odds with Plato's insistence that philosophers have their sights on the form F itself by itself and always the same. But 'itself by itself' in the canonical occurrences refers to separation from the opposite of F, or from the many F things, or from sensible particulars, or all these. It is not at all obvious that the phrase forbids taking the nature of the context into account when working out how justice, the form, could be translated (even if only approximately) into a concrete this-worldly arrangement. If it does forbid this, then Plato has set up the philosopher-ruler as both a ruler and hopelessly impractical.

So if one is a practical agent, approaching the form of justice as a practicable form, one cannot be intelligent about it in abstraction from kinds of possible contexts. But the practical agent naturally at times modulates into something a step removed from the concretely practical, although closely related: this is the *devotee* of justice and the other virtues. The statue with the blindfold and evenly balanced scales symbolizes justice-as-object-of-devotion, invoked in the phrase 'in the name of justice'. The relation to practicability is close because for humans the consistent *doing* of justice depends on there being *devotion* to justice. When we determine what justice is so as to *do* it, we necessarily come up with different answers for different contexts. When asked why we care about the doing, and about getting the practical determinations right, and about getting better at getting them right, we make obeisance to the object of devotion which 'presides', one and the same and context-free, over the diverse reasonings and implementations that constitute our practice.[169] This ideal of justice isolated on a pedestal as it were, or enthroned as a goddess,[170] haunts our practical thinking but cannot itself dictate specific correct conclusions.[171] It could only do that if its content were an

---

[169] Cf. Annas 2011, 17–25 on virtue as involving the drive to aspire.

[170] Cf. *Phaedrus* 254b6–7. *Republic* 500c–d shows something like the devotional attitude modulating into the practical. The devotional one is a sort of meta-attitude; see Section 2.10.

[171] 'The commitment to morality – to do whatever it commands – does not by itself tell us what we must do. A pledge of allegiance does not set the commands or the limits of allegiance' (Rorty 2012).

unmanageably vast complete conjunction of gerundives or imperatives, each indexed to one or more types of situation. Only if we were to get, and then *per impossibile* knew that we had got, complete knowledge of this form and could hold it all in mind, would it direct us entirely from within itself without reference to context of implementation (since every such reference is already taken care of within the form). We would need superhuman mental power to get adequate knowledge of this form, and then, oddly enough, no thoughtfulness at all to apply it since we can crib exactly what we have to do each time from the mega-rule-book in Platonic heaven.[172] Also, to get the right answer for a given context, there would be no need for us to understand *why* that answer is right for that context, since the book tells us *that* it is. By contrast, Plato's philosopher-rulers find out *that* such and such an answer is right for such and such a context only by working out *why* one answer would be better, another one worse.

Fortunately, we do not have to read Plato as holding that philosopher-rulers respond to the questions facing them by getting the answers from a hyper-uranian complete rule-book. Instead, when the philosopher-rulers ask what justice demands in a given sort of context, they mentally test proposed action-types or different types of arrangement by asking the G-question about each in relation to the actual context of implementation. Their answer to this determines whether, say, EFG does or does not constitute justice, and the answer will be backed by a reason why justice consists in EFG in this context but not in that one. We have said (Section 2.16) that their moral, intellectual, and practical training have made them, in this ethical area, as accurate detectors of the truth as any human beings could be. We could equally have said that their training has nurtured minds of outstanding practical intelligence. It is by *intelligence* that they put things together (the specific context with this or that specific proposal), and their educated but still necessarily indefinite sense of what the goodness of justice demands takes them to the right answer along with the reason why it is right.

It is not enough for philosopher-rulers to say, following Socrates at *Phaedo* 100b–101c, that this case of EFG is just because of the presence in it of the form justice and this other one unjust because of the presence in it of the form injustice, and to *leave the matter at that*. They must have a reason or reasons for the difference. Otherwise they would simply be intuiting in a manner

---

[172] Cf. Rowett 2018, 162 (although her example, 'equality', is to one side of our present concerns): 'The grasp of "equality as such" ... is an inexhaustible source of explanation, which enables us to form an indefinite range of true propositions about equal things, no finite set of which would ever give a complete account of it. Our ability to offer some indefinite number of true propositions based on our grasp of "equality" gives evidence of a rich grasp of *what equality is* that outstrips any list of propositions or propositional science.' See Price 2011, 174–80 for an illuminating discussion of this and related matters.

analogous to sense-perception that the form of justice is present in this instance of K but not that one. They would be behaving like the sight-lovers. Of course, their appeal to the presence of eternal non-physical forms separates them from the sight-lovers, who appeal only to objects right there in front of them; but this is only a difference of *ontology*. So far as this goes, the philosophers' stance could be the same *epistemically* as that of the sight-lovers: it could be unreasoned *intellectual* perception involving no bodily organ. But this would not be real understanding of 'what justice demands'. It would still be blind. Real understanding (intelligence as distinct from the operation of a supposed special faculty of intellectual intuition) of the presence of justice is mediated by reason/explanation-generating principles such as beneficence, fidelity to promises, repayment of debts.

Asking the G-question with respect to a specific context and a specific proposal is what activates intelligence. I suggest that, for Plato, it is in the nature of intelligence to be activated by the G-question, and in the nature of the G-question to be an intelligence-activator. So, since the sun-like form of the good is what is brought to bear by the G-question, the sun-like form would be out of a job in Callipolis if philosopher-rulers ever came to be possessed of a concept of, e.g., justice that already contained within itself a self-announcingly complete set of situation-indexed gerundives. Each of the totality of gerundive-situation pairs must have been identified through someone's applying the G-question to possible combinations at an earlier stage, and ruling them out or ruling them in: but completing this whole operation, if not logically absurd, is beyond human capacity. It could only have been completed by a god who then by divine revelation gave a few human beings the exhaustive run of the divine rule-book with all its small print. This would not be a god who wanted men to use their intelligence in implementing justice, because in this situation human intelligence would be idle, having been replaced by obedient facility in looking things up.[173]

There may, however, be a worry that Plato's insistence on the uniqueness of each intelligible form commits him to that model of the divine rule-book. For allowing the nature of the context of implementation to determine, occasion by occasion, whether a given descriptive formula captures justice seems to imply a plurality of Platonic forms of justice, one for each type of context. Perhaps it even implies a *mutable* form of justice! Is it the case that the unique and changeless Platonic form of justice is either the absurd complete rule-book or the context-aloof entity that focuses our generalized love of justice but cannot dispense specific guidance? Ought Plato to surrender Platonism and accept a plurality of practicable justices? The answer is no: justice itself, the Platonic

---

[173] This is not a caricature of real religions of the book because none claims such a precise revelation as to leave no room for interpretation.

form, is not pluralized simply because it cashes out as different types of empirical arrangement in different types of situation, any more than it is pluralized by being instantiated in or by different sensible particulars of the same narrow type.[174] The form of justice as practicable is like a function in the logico-mathematical sense, yielding different outputs (specifications of what would be just) for different contextual inputs. No one thinks that what '4(x)' conveys or signifies is ambiguous or fragmented or mutable simply because for input 5 the output is 20 while for input 8 the output is 32. When philosopher-rulers focus on justice itself (the form) for the sake of putting it into practice, they treat justice itself as a single function ready to be applied over a range of different contextual inputs; and in applying it on different occasions to a variety of inputs with a variety of results they understand themselves to have been applying the identical function, and they see the results as having it in common that each is what justice consists in, given the respective context. Also, in the actual acts of application they presumably apprehend the function as having a constant content that determines the result in each case by preventing certain things from counting as results (as when we see that applying '(4x)' to 5 does *not* yield 12).[175] The *form* of justice invoked in the question 'What counts as just in *this* context?'[176] is (like a logico-mathematical function) the same in every context to which it relates: it is what it is from every point of view.[177] Throughout, what the acts of applying it seek to determine is one and the same, namely what-counts-as justice-given-the-context – even as their object of devotion, justice on the pedestal, is one and the same throughout.

---

[174] E.g. many qualitatively identical acts of paying taxes where there is no relevant difference between agents and circumstances in each case.

[175] I am not suggesting that they would have a special insight absolutely guaranteeing that the content of the function remains the same; they have the same right to assume this when there is no specific reason for doubting it as the rest of us have to assume that when we aim to multiply by 2 again and again we do just that each time.

[176] Here, '*this*' is a variable ranging over contexts, the demonstrative indicating that each is one to which the respective questioner relates.

[177] In Plato's phrase, it is *pantelōs on*, 477a3. He says there that *to pantelōs on* is *pantelōs gnōston*. That is: from no point of view should it be ranked as proper object of anything less than knowledge. This is by contrast with things that count as knowable from one point of view but not another. See 527a2, then 533d2–e4, for how the honorific title *epistēmē* shifts depending on what comparison is being made. At 527a2 it applies to geometry, the contrast being between physical construction of a diagram and its mathematical meaning, but at 533e4 Plato restricts it to dialectic, having just said that through habit we call the mathematical disciplines *epistēmai*, although they need a different label to mark their status as 'clearer (*enargesterou*) than opinion but dimmer than *epistēmē*' (533d5–6), words recalling the refutation of the sight-lovers (cf. 478c11–13). If my argument in this section is correct, *pantelōs gnōston* cannot mean that the philosopher has or could have exhaustive knowledge of what I am calling the applications of the form.

The comparison of the form of justice to a logico-mathematical function is not, of course, meant to suggest that the dialecticians arrive at correct answers about justice by literal computation. If this were so, their correctness would be due entirely to a sort of *mathematical* ability, and the fact that they have been brought up in the right moral values would play no part in grasping the right answers and the reasons why they are right. These virtues, or some distinctively moral discernment arising from them, would not be being exercised in grasping the right answers. For we do not need to be courageous, just, and temperate to be good at literal computation. What constrains the dialecticians' move from input to output is the G-questioning by which they check and sift possible outputs. This activity of G-questioning by a virtuous inquirer might be compared to the rules of computation by which an arithmetically competent person decides between different answers to the problem of finding, for a given input, the output from $4(x)$.

Let us return briefly to those attitudes, application of the form of justice and devotion to the form of justice. They are logically distinct even if they necessarily co-exist. In appealing to justice as an ideal commanding allegiance, the philosophers do *not* treat it as a function manifesting itself only in contextually dependent determinations, but as an isolate beyond or above context. One might ask: when they treat justice as a function, and when they treat it as an isolate beyond context, are they dealing with different 'sides' of one and the same form or with different forms of justice? This, if a genuine question, could only be answered in a more highly developed metaphysical framework than we find in Plato. Some would say that it is not a genuine question because it results from plucking the term 'justice' out of each of two ethically necessary human activities to which it is central – the activity of trying to put justice into mundane practice, and the activity of embracing justice as its lover or loyal adherent – while naïvely assuming, for each plucking-out, that the captured term is the name of something: and then asking whether the two captives name the same thing.[178] But in any event the two activities are intimately related because (1), as we have observed, the first depends on the second for support or strengthening, and also because (2) the second without the first makes a mockery of itself. It might be better to think of the two activities, each centred on the notion 'justice', as related somewhat as different moods, say imperative and optative, of the same verb.

To return finally to the sight-lovers, who triggered this section: the worry was that if we interpret the thinking of philosopher-rulers as able to yield the

---

[178] In the Fregean perspective, 'justice' in the logical-function sense indicates something unsaturated, hence is not its *name*, whereas justice as object of devotion seems more like a nameable substantial personified being – a goddess whom one should rise to defend when she is vilified (cf. 368b3–c3).

result that the very same (kind of) thing is both just and unjust, then we put them on a par with sight-lovers. That would be a *reductio ad absurdum* of the interpretation. In this section I hope to have shown that what distinguishes the sight-lovers is their lack of curiosity on finding that the same thing (type of thing) that is P is also O, the opposite of P. This distinguishes them from those for whom this kind of experience jump-starts a journey out of the cave, making the soul separate the opposites, recognize each as one, and begin to wonder what each is. These cognitive acts bring intellect and intelligence into play so that P and O, instead of being accessed only through unreasoned perception, have become present as intelligibles as distinct from mere sensibles. I have assumed (it is not clearly in the text) that once the soul has disentangled P and O and begun to ask what each one is, it cannot be satisfied with simply accepting that the same kind of thing is both (whereas the sight-lovers' attitude would be something like: 'That's just the way it is with P and O: they are wont to belong to the same kind of thing'). Faced with this the intelligent soul is irritated into asking: 'So K over here is P, and K over there is O: *what is the reason* why K here is P and K there is O?' And it is not satisfied until it can differentiate in terms of different contexts or occasions or aspects of K or positions of the subject, etc. It also realizes (I think) the illegitimacy (at least in the practice-relevant cases) of even in the first place judging both that K is P and that it is O unless one can point to something whose presence allows K to be P and whose absence makes it not-P or O. In other words, the intelligent soul is aware that whereas in many cases (the most obvious example is sense-perception) simply having a definite impression that something is so, even without the slightest idea of why it is so (what makes it so), can justify affirming *that* it is so, there are other cases, which it has learnt to recognize, where the right to affirm *that* something is so depends on being able to explain *why*, especially when the opposite holds as well.

I have argued that the practical slant of the philosopher-rulers' thinking requires skill or intelligence in judging how the nature of a potential context of implementation bears on whether some arrangement would be or not be just. This skill entails (if it is not the same as) skill in judging how a different context would have had the opposite bearing on the same arrangement, making it unjust rather than just or vice versa. Looking at things *ex parte post*, this skill is identical with the ability to explain why some actual arrangement is just here and unjust over there. This ability lies undeveloped if one feels no pressure to find and give an explanation. It is lacking in the ethical equivalent of sight-lovers because they are incurious where one ought to be curious. In this way, ethical sight-lovers are utterly different from philosophers.[179] If someone

---

[179] Their objects tumble about between being and non-being, whereas things known *are*, simply and unmixedly (479d–e). That is: the sight-lovers register the conjunction 'K is P and K is O'

confronts them with the question why, e.g., justice consists in this sort of arrangement in this sort of context and an opposite sort of arrangement in a different context, their lack of explanatory muscle has them falling back on 'Well, there are simply *different justices*, justice in this situation and justice in that situation; there is no such thing as one single justice . . .'[180] Or they might say, 'OK, let it be that there is one thing justice: but this one thing justice simply has a habit of appearing in this guise here and in that opposite guise there, nothing more to be said – like the gods in the stories' (cf. 380d–381e). *Per contra*, the philosophers show their commitment to the idea that justice is unique, immutable, and non-arbitrary by insisting that whoever detects variety in its modes of manifestation must be ready to explain those differences by reference to the contexts of manifestation, rather than by assuming the mutability or plurality or waywardness of what is manifested. Relatedly, when they meet a new context in which to carry out their permanent task of determining what it would be just to enact, they do not simply imagine alternative scenarios, one where they decide on A, one where they decide on B, etc., and simply wait to see which imagined decision given the context *strikes* them as just and which not (this is to behave like sight-lovers); instead,

where P and O imply each other's negation: end of story. So in judging 'K is P and K is O' they imply that K is P and not-P, and O and not-O. The positive predicates stand for modes of being, the negative ones for modes of not-being. Then, according to the schema at 477a–b their judgement is opinion not knowledge, because it equally predicates modes of being and the corresponding ones of not-being. Plato does not mark the sight-lovers down because they contradict themselves (it is unclear that they do, and he does not accuse them of it), nor because they both affirm and deny P of K. (I think it is fairly clear that they implicitly affirm negative as well as the corresponding positive predicates rather than both affirming and denying the positive ones. If they did the latter they would end up not having asserted anything at all.) Their defect in his eyes is that they are satisfied to take in, concerning K, a dapple or entanglement of modes of being and corresponding modes of not-being. By contrast, the curious-minded philosophers end up with 'K is P-because-of (or: *qua*) -being-in-context-C (or: -viewed-from-angle-C, etc.) and K is O because-of (*qua*) -being-in-context-D' (where C ≠ D). Let us, in each of these conjuncts, treat everything that follows the copula as the predicate (it is the original predicate qualified). Then the philosophers do not co-apply predicates that imply each other's negation. So each predicate stands for something which K simply *is* (as distinct from something it both is and is not). But why should the sight-lovers agree that the dappled nature of their judgements (predicates unqualified) makes those judgements less than knowledge? Why shouldn't they claim that some things (such as K) simply are a dapple of both P and not-P, and their judgements accurately track this and are therefore knowledge? Does Plato assume too easily that knowledge is only ever of something pure and unmixed with its opposite, instead of allowing that, as well as perfectly unambivalent knowledge of perfectly unambivalent things, there is also chiaroscuro knowledge of chiaroscuro things? Perhaps not, at least when something like justice is the example. He might say to the sight-lovers: 'If you were really interested in justice you would want to know why K here is just and K there is unjust,' and doubtless they will reply, 'We register justice and injustice in our own way, and as that's good enough for us, it's good enough.' This is fine – but only as long as they agree on particular cases. If not, they succumb to the relativism that makes joint action impossible unless some succeed in manipulating the others to fall in behind them.

180   See Irwin 1995, 265–6.

philosophers examine the context so as to discover in it reasons for preferring one option over others. That way, they do not simply *come across* or *encounter* the right option in its rightness; they track it down by their own efforts and in light of reasons they can share with others. This, I take it, is what Plato in the *Republic* means by coming to have knowledge (*epistēmē*) of the form of justice.[181]

There are different ways of showing commitment to the uniqueness and invariance of forms. One way is to insist, like Socrates in a number of Plato's dialogues, on being given a single answer to the 'What is F?' question rather than a bunch of examples. This, I suspect, cannot work happily when (a) F is an ethical form and (b) one asks the question seeking guidance on how to implement F in the world. An answer that is true irrespective of any context of implementation will, I suspect (and suspect that Plato came to suspect), be too abstract or truistic to give guidance in any direction rather than any other. Even so, giving on different occasions different practically useful, tailored-to-context, *reasoned* answers is also a stance that declares the invariance and uniqueness of the form: it does so by refusing to blame the diversity of answers on anything other than the diversity of contexts. It is worth noting that this approach to fundamental values is as open-ended as the range of possible contexts, including ones unimaginable to Plato. It insists on the eternal integrity of justice and the others while allowing for an infinite variety of interpretations matching countless differences of history and culture.

2.20   The Criteria and Scope of 'Good'

It is natural, given our interpretation, to wonder just *how* the rulers would ground their discriminations, by reference to the form of the good, of genuine specifications of the virtues or ultimate values of city and citizens. In other words: what are their reasons for those judgements? The fact that Plato says nothing, or nothing explicit, on this is not an objection to an interpretation that prompts this question. This silence is part and parcel with the abstract and schematic character of his account of dialectic in the *Republic*, discussed in Section 2.18. Still, it might strengthen the present interpretation if it could be shown to allow for a non-mysterious story about the basic reasons or principles or criteria guiding the rulers' judgements. But before turning to this, let us also ask about the scope of 'good', namely whether the good as invoked in dialectic takes shape as the good of or for or in relation to anyone in particular, or instead remains an absolute, unqualified, and (as is often said) impersonal good. The question about scope and the one about criteria or reasons are

---

[181] No doubt working out the correct 'justice' answers, with reasons, for various imagined or hypothetical contexts would be one of the trainee rulers' dialectical exercises.

similar in that both ask for a slightly more detailed determination of the rulers' dialectic.

On the scope-question, I tend to think that the good invoked in the dialectical G-question of dialectic is not as such determined by reference to a specific beneficiary. Asking whether implementing EFG would be good (and therefore, e.g., just) is not the same as asking whether implementing EFG would be good for you or me or the city. Even so, I assume that for Plato good decision-makers do what they do *for the sake of* those for whom they are responsible. For rulers this is the city (cf. 412d–e; 413c5–7; 428c11–d4);[182] for individuals as such, it is various others as well as themselves.[183]

By criteria for deciding what is good I mean criteria for deciding what is good or best to do or bring about. The reasoning of the rulers as I have interpreted it is consistent with more than one normative framework. It could be monistic in the sense of their looking to a single guiding value in all their practical reasoning, including conclusions such as that one case of EFG is a good arrangement, hence just and fair, and another not. If we prefer a monistic model, the most likely candidate for the role of the rulers' single guiding end is the healthy unity of the city (see 422e–423b; 462a–e2): healthy in that co-operation of the different sectors accords with what each is fitted to do, and is peaceful and wholehearted rather than imposed through force or threats of punishment.[184] This condition is, of course, what in Book IV Plato defined as the primary nature of justice in the city, giving an analogous account of justice in the soul of the just individual. And the presence of justice in this internal sense entails the presence of the other three cardinal virtues also understood as properties of the sectors composing the good city or the healthy soul.

However, a monistic model for rulers' decision-making is not mandatory. The important thing is that the good city is ruled by reason incarnate in the human rulers. And reason might recognize a number of different ultimate (but probably each defeasible) principles on the basis of which, with different ones to the fore on different occasions, the rulers reach their decisions. These would surely include a principle of fairness about distributing burdens, one of maintaining public order, one of preparedness against external threats, one safeguarding property rights and commercial fairness in the non-guardian class, one of looking after the city's material well-being, one of caring for children and the elderly, one of maintaining the cults of the gods, one of maintaining the retired rulers in their research activities. The rulers might hold that observing

[182] Cf. D. Morrison 2007, 243.
[183] 'For the sake of X (the city or a person)' does not quite mean 'for the benefit of X'. Roughly, the thought is that in doing something for the sake of X, one sees X as in some sense having a right to expect one to do it.
[184] Many interpreters emphasize the unity of the good city.

such principles conduces to the unity and integrity of the city, but this does not mean that they treat unity and integrity as a distinct overarching principle of decision that trumps all other principles.

If we think it important to maintain a close parallel between the rulers in the good city and reason in the individual soul, then a pluralistic model seems preferable. This is because it seems unrealistic to expect that decision-making reason in the healthy-souled individual will only ever be guided by conduciveness to the health and unity of that same soul. Socrates says that the individual whose soul-parts function together as they should will not appropriate deposits or commit acts of temple-robbery, theft, betrayal of individuals or the city, oath- and promise-breaking, adultery, neglect of parents, or disrespect to the gods (442d11–443a11).[185] We might think that a person thus described is guided by a number of different basic principles, and leave the matter at that. In that case, the city-soul analogy may suggest that the just city through its rulers is guided by a plurality of basic principles. But the analogy does not mandate such close parallelism. The city could be guided by one principle, the just individual by many.

Socrates says, concerning the individual, that in all those types of conduct (not temple-robbing, not oath-breaking, etc.), what explains the behaviour (*toutōn pantōn aition*, 443b1–2) is precisely the good condition of the agent's soul, the fact that 'each of the elements that he has in him is performing its own proper role in relation to ruling and being ruled'. (From this Socrates concludes that justice is nothing other than 'the power [i.e. the internal psychological arrangement] that gives rise to men and cities of this sort [i.e. of the sort to refrain from the kinds of actions just listed]'.)[186] Here it may seem that the mention of a variety of just action-types, whether the agent is individual or city, indicates the pluralist model of decision-making. But a slightly later speech by Socrates seems to favour the monistic model:

But the truth, it seems, was that justice . . . wasn't at all a matter of a person's external actions, but rather of what he did inside, in relation to his true self and what is truly his own, preventing each element in him from doing what belongs to others, and stopping them from meddling in one another's roles – in the true sense putting his own affairs in order, ruling over himself and setting himself straight, becoming a friend to himself as he fits together the three elements in him, just like three defining sounds of a musical attunement, highest, lowest, and middle, along with any others there are in between;

---

[185] Socrates clearly means that the internally ordered agent refrains from these actions just because they are these actions. They are given in pejorative terms; if neutral terms are substituted, no doubt some cases so described would not be unjust, e.g. turning temple treasures into money to meet a major crisis.

[186] Several of the acts listed can be committed by one city against another (cf. 428d1–3). The good city would normally refrain from, e.g., breaking an agreement with another city. We are not bound to think that it only refrains when its own healthy unity is at stake.

binding all these together, so becoming moderate and well-adjusted, completely one instead of many. Then and only then is it a matter of his acting, whether in relation to the getting of money, or looking after the body, or perhaps it'll be a matter relating to the city, or private contracts with individuals; and all the time he'll be thinking, and calling, 'just' and 'fine' whatever action preserves and helps to bring about this disposition of his, and 'wisdom' the knowledge that presides over such action; 'unjust' is what he'll think and call whatever action undoes his disposition, 'ignorance' the belief that presides over that. (443c–444a)

Here Plato seems to be saying that the just person's criterion for judging what is just and fine is effectiveness in producing and preserving within himself the psychic arrangement in which each part performs its proper role.[187] If Plato does mean this, he implies that just individuals will refrain from theft, perjury, betrayal, etc., on the single ground that these actions jeopardize their healthy psychic structure. Thus, he seems to endorse a monistic model of good individual decision-making whereby the single end aimed at is the healthy unity of that same individual's soul.[188]

In the case of the city, as I have said, such an internally focused monistic model has a chance of being plausible, but in the case of the individual it does not. In real life surely the best of us do not make every decision with an eye to whether it promotes and preserves the authority of our own reason, and the proper role of our spirited part in subordinating impulses; rather, good people often, if not always, decide on the basis of its simply being wrong (unjust) to cheat, steal, maraud, murder, break promises, desecrate holy places, and so forth. What is implausible, on the most obvious reading of the last quoted passage, is not merely the monism it implies for the just individual's reasoning but the claim, as it seems, that the single end envisaged is exclusively egocentric. Some monistic interpreters might hold that the just person pursues only the well-being of his own soul, yet interpret the soul's own well-being as necessarily bound up with a genuinely outward-looking concern for the good of others, or at least some others.[189] But Plato's language of 'setting himself straight', 'binding together the three elements within him', etc., seems to depict the just person as relentlessly self-absorbed. Given Plato's assumption that this person's soul is in healthy order, he or she is certainly in a condition that is valuable in itself. Hence, if, with Plato, we accept that this condition is the true referent of the phrase 'justice of the individual', we seem to be well on the way to meeting the brothers' original challenge to Socrates to show that my justice is better for me than anything gained through injustice would have been. But

---

[187] This is the interpretation of Brown 2007, 58–9.
[188] He also seems to imply that acting justly as an individual presupposes knowing the three-part theory of the soul.
[189] E.g. Penner 2007a, 102.

there is a difficulty. This is that we ordinarily think that an individual's justice is her or his steady disposition to (for instance) abhor the kinds of actions listed above simply because they are those kinds of actions. The topic of the brothers' challenge was justice as this is ordinarily understood, whereas the topic of Socrates' response seems to be something logically quite different: a state of soul in which reason stably maintains its own ascendancy over the other soul-parts. Socrates claims that this psychic arrangement is cause of the conduct by which we ordinarily characterize the just person, but he gives no reason why we should accept this claim.

Just now we have been discussing whether Plato, given his theory of justice as an internal condition, thinks that the just agent's conduct (as ordinarily understood) is governed by a single concern or by an irreducible plurality of concerns. But this has brought us to the classic question of whether Plato has any ground for asserting that the intra-psychic condition he identifies with individual justice explains and issues in conduct that respects property, oaths, parents, etc.[190] We seem to have been given no reason to believe that the harmonious state of the soul which Plato insists on calling 'a person's justice' simply *is* a steady disposition to refrain from those and other kinds of actions that overstep the boundaries of respect and decency towards others and towards the community as such. But what is the connection between this problem and the monadic-pluralistic question discussed so far? The connection lies in the passage just quoted, 443c–444a, which seems to describe the Platonically just agent as acting always with a view to his own psychic well-being, which would mean that he always acts on a single principle.

Plato's internalization of justice is problematic because it seems unable to explain why the relevant internal condition should issue in what he and we regard as just action in the world beyond the agent. What I think is the best response to this problem involves two moves: (1) interpreting his conception of reason (in the *Republic*, at least) in a certain way, and (2) accepting a non-obvious reading of 443c–444a. In combination, (1) and (2) enable us to make out an intelligible connection between being what Plato calls a just person and acting in the ways ordinarily regarded as just. The resulting picture is also one in which Plato's just person is naturally seen as embracing a plurality of ethical principles.

(1) We must think of reason as having a natural orientation towards, and affinity with, the beauty of what is *fitting* in whatever sphere. In any sphere the task of reason is to identify and explain fittingness when this is not obvious, i.e. when a well-trained sensibility does not automatically light upon it. When there is disagreement about what is fitting, there will be reasons on both sides

---

[190] The problem was formulated by Sachs 1963; for a recent treatment see Singpurwalla 2006.

and it is the task of reason to bring them out into the open, whether or not this ends in resolution.[191] In the sphere of human conduct the fitting consists in what is morally permissible and what is morally fine along with what is prudent within the bounds of morality. Thus, for reason, not bullied or clouded by one or another of the passions, to make a correct decision on how to act is for it to light on the action that is fitting for the situation the agent is in: this will be the right action. Then, if the other parts of the soul are operating as they should, the whole soul, with the body, acts accordingly. A soul whose reason either fails to identify the action to be done with the fitting action, or lacks the authority whereby the other parts obediently enact its decision, is a soul whose parts are not functioning as they should, and is therefore unhealthy and in fact miserable whether knowingly or not. The arrangement of the soul in which each part functions as it should is itself a fitting arrangement. This is because it is fitting that reason rules the others, in that reason alone can take the synoptic view and care for the interests of each part and of the whole (441e; 442c).[192] Connected with this is the fact that reason alone has the ability to appreciate the need for, and to give, explanations of why it restrains or allows free play to an emotion or appetite, depending on the occasion.

Now, the fact that reason alone can take care of every part of the soul does not imply that an individual's reason, insofar as it rules the soul and thereby functions well, is concerned *only* with maintaining fitting order in that same soul, or with looking after the interests of each part and the whole of that same soul. Reason's capacity for looking out for the whole soul is what qualifies it to rule the other parts, but this is compatible with its having concerns about matters outside the soul and caring about the fittingness of its external actions.[193] If, as suggested above, reason's affinity is with the fitting in every sphere, Plato is justified in saying at 442e–443b that the just person, whose soul is ruled by reason, will not steal, or neglect what is due to others, or act disloyally, or break promises, etc., and that this is *because* his soul is ruled by

---

[191] This approach is in keeping with Scott 2015, 33–40, who also brings Books VIII and IX into the argument. The nature of the just individual's upbringing can be read off from Plato's account of rearing the guardian class in Callipolis. The guardians' whole education from the earliest age is designed to cultivate, at the level of unreasoned responses, a comprehensive love of aesthetic and moral beauty, making the person morally 'fine and good' (*kalos te k'agathos*, 402a1). See Burnyeat 1997, ch. 1; Lear 2006. Lear emphasizes the role of *thumos* in responsiveness to beauty; the role I am assigning to reason does not conflict with this. In the practical sphere, once the well-conditioned reason discerns what is fitting to do, it does not hang around to enjoy the beauty of the decision, because the agent must set about enacting it before the opportunity disappears. Thus, the moral beauty of agency is for contemplative enjoyment only in an act (including motivation and reasons) as viewed by others or (if by the agent too) as already carried out.

[192] Cf. Irwin 1995, 245–8.   [193] Cf. Kraut 2003, 240–1.

reason. Such actions are paradigms of the unfitting;[194] hence the soul ruled by reason will find them hateful. So far, then, we are not driven to accept that what Plato calls the just person is wholly given over to cultivating her or his own internal garden.

(2) Yet this is what the passage last quoted (443c–444a) suggests at first sight. But we can avoid that conclusion if we read it in a certain way. (2a) We need not take the part about the just person 'in the true sense putting his own affairs in order, ruling over himself and setting himself straight', etc. as a description of something which he typically intends and experiences himself as carrying out within his own soul. Rather, we can take those words to be emphasizing two things: that the just person is internally harmonized, and that this is due solely to the just person himself. He may sometimes adjust himself introspectively, by consciously questioning or curbing an impulse or appetite, but he also maintains the order of his inner self simply by acting in such a way that each part does what it is supposed to when it is a matter of deciding on and carrying out externally fitting actions. What this amounts to becomes clearer at 444d, less than a Stephanus page further on. Here Socrates says, and Glaucon immediately agrees, that doing just or unjust actions is what makes the soul just or unjust, a commonplace (even if also Aristotelian) observation. Socrates at once interprets this in terms of the parts of the soul, and uses an analogy with health: even as healthy actions cause physical health in the agent by causing the right relationship of physical elements, so just actions cause justice in the agent (help make her or him just) by causing the right relationship of psychic elements. There is a non-vicious causal loop: the rule of reason in the person's soul explains why he or she acts fittingly, and therefore justly, in the outside world, and every action that expresses the inward rule of reason reinforces that internal arrangement by which reason rules and which Plato calls 'justice'. Reason itself is strengthened (in both its wisdom and its control) by its own exercise in effecting fitting action (external and internal); and this strengthening consists in a deepening of the internal psychic order whereby reason is in charge. Thus, fittingness propagates fittingness: the internally fitting hegemony of reason is expressed in the fittingness of the agent's external conduct, and fitting external conduct reinforces the internal rational hegemony. (This picture takes it for granted that not-murdering, not-robbing, not oath-breaking, *is* fitting external conduct, just as it takes for granted the fittingness of reason's ruling the rest of the soul.) The analogy with physical health is important, as we are about to see.

[194] I take it to be basic for Plato that this is not only straightforwardly true but expresses the conviction of any just person.

(2b) Let us turn to the declaration: 'and all the time [the just person] will be thinking, and calling, "just" and "fine" whatever action preserves and helps to bring about this disposition of his, and "wisdom" the knowledge that presides over such action; "unjust" is what he'll think and call whatever action undoes his disposition, "ignorance" the belief that presides over that' (443e2–444a2). Plato, I suggest, is not saying that the psychically well-ordered person identifies which actions are just or wise by seeing which actions conduce to his psychic order or the internal governance of reason; rather, Plato is speaking *de re* of the actions which the psychically ordered person calls 'just' (by ordinary external criteria) – which actions, Plato says, are the ones that reinforce the person's psychic order. On this reading, just as a physically healthy person instinctively chooses what is in fact health-reinforcing behaviour – eating moderately, exercising enough, sleeping regularly – without understanding the invisible physiology of health, so the just person in action may be ignorant about the anatomy of his own soul and the right order of its parts, and can always look outwards in determining what it would be just to do.[195] The fitting order within unconsciously gives rise to and is reinforced by the fitting external conduct.

If this is Plato's theory, it is quite a powerful defence of the value to the agent of justice in the ordinary sense – i.e. the value to the agent of being the sort of person who is disposed to act regularly and for its own sake in ways ordinarily considered just. There is a non-accidental identity between being such a person and having one's soul in healthy order. This position offers an incentive for embracing justice that could tip the balance in that direction for people confused between traditional values learnt at home and excitingly clever amoralist messages coming from sources in the surrounding culture (537e–539a; cf. 365a–c). In light of Plato's theory, or something like it, self-concern or self-respect may motivate an ethically undecided person to choose the hard work of becoming just, exactly as it may motivate someone to take more physical exercise for the sake of health; but it no more follows that every subsequent action expressing his internal justice is done from the intention of reinforcing that inner condition, or to satisfy his self-concern or uphold his self-respect, than it follows in the physical case that every healthy action engaged in is engaged in from the intention of maintaining health.

The amoralist thinker might counter Plato's argument in several ways. For instance, she could insist, with Hume, that although the successful unjust character cannot get ahead without reasoning, reason in the practical sphere is restricted to picking out not fittingness in general but only the fittingness of means to ends, and that it is not reason's function to endorse any end rather

---

[195] So, on this interpretation the just person need not be a philosopher.

2.20 Criteria and Scope of 'Good'

than any other. Hence the successful villain's soul is in fine order, with reason the servant of his passions. But if in the practical sphere reason's sole function is instrumental, the proponent of amoralism ought to explain why reason *seems* to be alive to so many non-instrumental kinds of fittingness, as in mathematics, dance, poetry, and music, in a well-turned piece of rhetoric, or a good joke, or a cogent philosophical argument – the kinds may be endless. Why uniquely in the practical area is there no such thing as non-instrumental fittingness? Or does the amoralist thinker insist that there is no such thing as non-instrumental fittingness in any area, thus seriously jeopardizing any reputation she herself might otherwise have for connoisseurship, taste, wit, and lively understanding in any sphere? Or will she say that there are many sorts of non-instrumental fittingness, but discerning them is the task not of reason but of some kind of sensibility – and (since she is defending amoralism) a truly well-tuned sensibility in the practical sphere is that of a person actively concerned only with her own advantage, and uncaring about the interests of others, except when heeding them leads to her own advancement? One could then ask whether this remarkably limited practical sensibility of the successful villain is really particularly admirable when compared with the wide-ranging practical discernment of the just person, who (being non-instrumentally concerned about other people too) is actively responsive to a much wider and richer field of fittingness-questions.[196] (Perhaps the amoralist of Plato's *Republic* does not deny outright that justice towards others demands things of us, or that killing the innocent or breaking oaths is unfitting: she merely regards those demands and fittingness-relations as unimportant to well-adjusted people like herself, like someone who is aware of a rule about removing outdoor shoes on entering a house but has no intention of inconveniencing herself by following it. The amoralist may be dimly aware of a much wider range of fittingness-relations than the range she sees fit to care about.) The defender of amoralism may have to decide whether it is still quite so obvious that the successful villain's success in terms of wealth, power, and pleasure unlimited by morality is worth his having turned himself into someone whose engagement with practical fittingness is non-existent outside the narrow area marked by egoistic instrumentalism, leaving him crassly unresponsive to whole swathes of the field. This thick-skinned condition is unbeautiful even if cleverly concealed by a cloak of deception.[197] The debate could develop in

---

[196] Here, drawing an analogy between mathematical and ethical structures does significant work. According to Hume, it is by sensibility, not reason, that we are alive to the morally significant, whereas reason can only discern mathematical and logical relationships and carry out inductive inference. The analogy calls into question the Humean opposition between reason and sensibility.

[197] 'Crassly' goes back to how Thrasymachus had to agree, to his own deep embarrassment, that his hero, the more-and-more-getter (*pleonektēs*), is a clumsy ignoramus (349b–350d). Thrasymachus began by admiring the *pleonektēs* as beautiful, leading a beautiful life, but is

many ways, as the subsequent history of philosophy has shown; my point is only that Plato's defence on behalf of previously defenceless justice (cf. 368b) moves the controversy to a place where amoralism may have to work harder than before to keep its thesis seeming attractive to anyone not already committed to the view.

This discussion (of whether Plato has a decent, even if not a knockdown, argument for the thesis that justice, and not injustice, is a great good for the individual herself) arose out of a discussion of the nature of the rulers' reasons for reaching their decisions. They can hardly be guided by the bare consideration of fittingness *per se* as this is too abstract to be a guide.[198] They could follow some type of consequentialism or Kantianism, embracing a single practical principle to show them what is fitting. But nothing in the text suggests that they do this. If we take closely the analogy between rulers in the good city and reason in the just individual, then we should probably think of the rulers as deciding what is fitting in terms of several distinct principles, as this is how Plato portrays the psychically ordered individual: he lists actions such a person would never do. It was open to Plato to try to integrate these prohibitions by claiming that they all follow from the single principle of producing the greatest good for the greatest number, or of maintaining maximal unity in the self or in the society, or from something like the categorical imperative; but he did not take that opportunity and perhaps never even noticed that it was there.

2.21   Main Positions of Parts 1 and 2

What follows is a resumé of the more or less controversial positions laid out and defended so far. They are summarized here without argument.

(1) The longer and more exact way spoken of at 504c–d consists in the ideal rulers' dialectical activity and their education for it (Section 1.2).

---

forced by Socrates to recognize the unrefined stupid crudeness (*amathia*) of the unbridled trait, betokening the opposite of anything resembling discrimination and good judgement. Also, one cannot be morally beautiful oneself if one has a false standard of the morally beautiful (physical beauty is not analogous in this). Presumably Thrasymachus, a sophisticated man, understands this general point; and presumably he, like everyone, wants to be or at least seem beautiful (worthy of being admired by the non-stupid). So, along with catching him out in an inconsistency Socrates makes him and the assembled company see that all the time he was extolling successful *pleonexia* he was displaying his own lack of moral beauty, i.e. his moral tastelessness. He does have something to blush for (cf. 350d2–3). Note that although he is refuted several times by Socrates (and doesn't like it), he *blushes* only at the refutation that turns on experts not outdoing experts.

[198] The same, I think, is true of 'maximiz[ing] the total amount of rational order in the world as a whole', proposed by Cooper 1977, 155–6, as the just person's 'criterion of choice' (although Cooper is discussing the just private individual, not the ruler).

(2) The aim of the dialectical part of the longer way is to determine in detail what the virtues demand in terms of specific actions and arrangements to be implemented in the life of the city. Getting this right is the fundamental task of the city's guardians. The definitions of the four cardinal virtues in Book IV were silent on this. It was clear from them that wisdom is the virtue of reason, the ruling part in an orderly soul, but this left it obscure how reason and wisdom would operate in reaching specific conclusions. The central books of the *Republic* contain Plato's attempt to fill this lacuna to the extent possible (Section 1.2).

(3) The rulers are assumed to know already that justice is good for the agent, hence the longer way does not include a defence of that position. Nor does it launch a new psychology improving on that of the three-part soul expounded in Book IV (Sections 1.3 and 1.4).

(4) Neither Socrates nor his interlocutors nor readers of the *Republic* have access to the longer way as trodden by the rulers (Section 2.7; see also (14) below), but this is not because the ideal rulers alone have access to the form of the good (Section 2.18).

(5) Dialectic (of both rulers and trainees) issues in the determinations outlined in (2) by critically examining proposed formulae for ethical virtues or norms of conduct. Dialectical inquiry vets the proposals for analytic or conceptual faults, and finally tests them by reference to the form of the good, the analogue of the sun. This test consists in asking whether actions and arrangements conforming to the vetted proposals would be good (or whether it would be good to carry them out) (Sections 1.4 and 2.8).

(6) We thus have a scheme involving the form of the good and 'the other forms'. The other forms in question are not the whole gamut of intelligibles but forms of virtues and forms corresponding to the proposals in (5). Hence the form of the good does not, in Plato's *Republic*, do the job of presiding over a comprehensive system of all forms (Section 2.7).

(7) The form of the good is the non-hypothetical principle of dialectic. It is non- hypothetical because whatever we do, we cannot not care about the good (Sections 2.2 and 2.6).

(8) Bringing the form of the good to bear on a given proposed account of a virtue or ethical norm is a matter of asking the G-question: would it be *good* if actions were taken, arrangements made, according to this account? The answer, whichever way it goes, must be backed by reasons. Only if the answer is positive is the account accepted as truly representing the virtue or norm (Section 2.8). The form of the good understood as brought to bear in the G-question is a principle of dialectic because it controls results of the method.

(9) The form of the good as imaged by the sun is therefore interrogative: it is what is brought to bear in the G-question. Being interrogative in this way is essential to this form, not an accident arising through contingent human interest (Section 2.9).

(10) The interrogative form of the good is a tool of dialectical inquiry, not an object studied by it. Hence the form of the good is not a premiss of dialectical reasoning or something to be defined by dialectic (Sections 2.7, 2.11, and 2.12).

(11) The form of the good is not a paradigm or template or pattern to which the ideal ruler looks for guidance on how specifically to order the empirical realities of the city (Section 2.10).

(12) We must take care to distinguish the dialecticians' use (first order) of the form of the good as a tool of dialectic from their methodological (second order) reflection about it (Section 2.10). We must also be wary of injecting the way the form of the good is presented to *us* (mainly via the sun-analogy) into the dialectician's first-order perspective on it (Section 2.7).

(13) The G-question (or: the form of the good brought to bear in the G-question) is sun-like, i.e. reliably brings to light *correct* answers about the virtues, only to the extent that dialecticians posing that question are wise (rigorously rational and imbued with the right values). Hence behind the rulers' wielding of the G-question lies their education, moral and intellectual (Section 2.1). Thus, it would be a mistake to identify the sun-like form with the *meaning* of the word 'good' used predicatively, since the meaning is equally available to those whose answers are mistaken.

(14) The rulers' dialectic differs from mathematics not only in its subject-matter but in its type of reasoning. Mathematics is deductive whereas the rulers' dialectic is non-monotonic: it is practical reasoning that takes account of the kind of context in which a proposed definition of a virtue or norm would be implemented (Sections 2.13, 2.14, 2.18, and 2.19). Whatever Plato may have thought in earlier dialogues, in the *Republic* it is clear to him that mathematics is the wrong model for dialectical reasoning. This is the most important lesson of the Divided Line.

(15) Dialectical reasoning draws on experience even though it does not and must not use diagrams or empirical models in the way they are used in mathematics (Section 2.13).

(16) Dialectic is not just part of the rulers' training; while in office they continue to engage in dialectic and to renew their contact with the form of the good (Section 2.15).

(17) There are no illustrations of dialectical reasoning in the *Republic* because here Plato is interested in dialectic considered as the method of rulers. Dialectic, so far as it concerns the rulers, is practical reasoning, and episodes of practical reasoning cannot be fully understood or appreciated except by those (probably few) who share the reasoner's circumstantial standpoint and values. This is what accounts for Socrates' reticence about the rulers' longer way. The explanation is not that grasp of the form of the good is the exclusive privilege of the ideal rulers, since Plato says that sighting it is the condition for any wise conduct whether of a public servant or a private individual (Section 2.18).

(18) The form of a virtue such as justice turns out to be indefinitely complex, but the ruler-dialecticians do not seek a complete grasp of it. They need to know only what it dictates in relation to the type of context in which they must act (Sections 2.15 and 2.19).

(19) Although their grasp of, e.g., justice is never complete or exhaustive, their conclusions are not provisional but unconditional and categorical (Section 2.15).

(20) Their grasp of the uniqueness and immutability of each form that concerns them amounts to a non-negotiable assumption that any variation in results of inquiries about, e.g. justice, is due entirely to the variety of contexts, never to change or fragmentation of the form. To embrace this assumption is also to be committed to the principle that the judgement-*that* something is, e.g., just must be backed by reasons-*why*. This is what basically distinguishes real philosophers from sight-lovers (Section 2.19).

(21) The circle of those for whose sake an agent takes decisions depends on which persons or institutions (e.g. the city) the agent is responsible for (Section 2.20).

(22) Does Plato think of the rulers in the city, and authoritative reason in the individual soul, as following one or many principles in their decision-making? He may be monistic about rulers considered as organs of the city, but with the individual, despite some textual appearances, he seems to lean towards pluralism (Section 2.20).

(23) The connection between justice as a psychic state of the individual and the individual's just conduct out in the world becomes intelligible if we assume that reason according to Plato is essentially attuned to *fittingness* in every sphere. This idea is the basis of a telling argument against Thrasymachean amoralism (Section 2.20).

(24) Although the above positions cohere with the text and with each other, the text itself shows the lineaments of dialectic only in glimpses. (Any interpretation of the material is bound to concede this much.) We are denied a fully joined-up, properly articulated, view largely because of Plato's lack of an even halfway developed logical vocabulary. For all his dazzling acuity and glorious eloquence, he was terminologically handicapped to a degree we can hardly begin to imagine what it would be like to live with. Nor can he communicate by giving examples of excellent ethical reasoning, because artificially concise examples would be misleading and complete ones impossible to articulate in full (see (17) above).

Part 3 The Form of the Good and Being

3.1 Preliminaries

> 'In the case of things that are seen, I think you'll say that the sun is cause not only (*mē monon*) of their being able to be seen, but also (*alla kai*) of their coming-into-being, their growth and their sustenance – even while not itself *being* coming-into-being.'
>
> 'Yes, of course.'
>
> 'Just so, in the case of things that are known, you need to say not only (*mē monon*) that being known belongs to (*pareinai*) them because of the good, but also (*alla kai*) that being and reality [or: essence] (*to einai te kai tēn ousian*) accrue to them (*autois proseinai*) because of it, even while the good itself is not reality [or: essence] (*ouk ousias ontos tou agathou*), but is even beyond reality [or: essence], superior to it in dignity and power.'
>
> (509b1–9)[1]

Suppose that, instead of offering this analogy with the sun, Plato had said simply: 'The things known (the forms) are known because of the form of the good, and they are real – or are really what they purport to be – because of the form of the good.' If he had just said that, it might have seemed attractive to try modelling an explanation of these claims on familiar Platonism: just as concrete or perceptible F things are F by participating in or imitating the form of F, so the ordinary forms – which are essentially good entities (so we insert) – are known and have their reality as forms by participating in or imitating the form of the good.[2] Some work would have to be done to explain and justify the assumption that the forms are good entities (since whatever participates in a form F is thereby itself F or an F). If we focus not on all forms but only on forms of good things such as virtues, then by self-predication it follows that these are good entities. If we focus on all forms, all intelligibles, the explanation for why, simply *qua* forms, they are good might have to rest on the idea of the ideality or perfection of forms as such. Then the thought

---

[1] This translation, to be defended below, departs from Rowe 2012, 236 at several points. Rowe gives the full meaning of *proseinai* in his translation in Rowe 2007a, 149 and 2007c, 247, but not in his 2012.

[2] See Section 3.5 for a version of this interpretation.

would be that the very being or reality of each ordinary form is nothing other than its goodness in the sense of perfection or ideality. And since Plato postulates a single form of the good on which the being of the other forms depends, he would then be saying that the other forms are known and have being because there is a single goodness in which they all participate or, to use the other great metaphor of familiar Platonic metaphysics, which they all imitate or take after. This would be an instance of the general relationship of One over Many, whereby the form corresponding to some predicate 'F' collects the many F-objects, whether these are concrete sensible particulars or forms.

There are two difficulties in taking this to be Plato's view in 509b1–9. One is that according to his actual words, 'the good is not reality' (509b7–8). This parallels his statement that the sun is not (the same thing as) coming-into-being (509b3). Although 'the good is not reality' has been interpreted in more than one way, a natural interpretation has it saying that the good or goodness of a thing is not the same as that thing's reality.[3] In other words, the form of the good is not the same as the form of reality (whatever exactly is meant by 'reality' here). If we assume that forms are real insofar as they participate in reality, it follows that since (as Plato says) the ordinary forms owe their reality to the form of the good, their owing of reality to the form of the good does not consist in their *participating* in the latter – as if the form of the good were identical with the form of reality. Instead, the situation seems to be that the form of the good, which is other than the form of reality, is responsible for their participation in the form of reality.

The second difficulty about holding that the ordinary forms get their being known and their being real by participating in the form of the good is this: since our actual passage does give the sun-analogy, we ought if possible to explain the relation between the form of the good and the other forms in a way that somehow reflects the relation between sun and ordinary visible objects. Now nowhere in the *Republic* is it said that ordinary objects of vision are, as such, 'suns' or 'sunny' or 'sun-like' entities,[4] or that they are as they are, and are visible as what they are, by participating in the sun or by being imitations of it. And if anything like this had been said, one would not have known what to make of it. This is because when we picture the actual sun on high above all the things down here which it nourishes and illuminates, we cannot get away from the fact that the latter are a multifarious bunch of mostly very un-sun-like entities. It is, of course, a matter of judgement which features of an analogy-base to take seriously, but it is hard to believe that Plato would have chosen the

[3] On another interpretation the phrase says that the good/form of the good is other than that reality which is the collective of the other forms. This requires taking 'reality' (*ousia*) at 509b7 in two senses in the same sentence only five words apart.
[4] In the vision-realm only the eye, light, and vision are said to be 'sun-like' (509a1). Similarly, only truth and knowledge (not the forms in general) are said to be 'good-like' or 'resembling the good' (508e5–509a5).

sun-analogy to convey the relation of the form of the good to the other forms if his doctrine were that it stands to them as participand to participants. If we try to explain the claims in 509b1–9 by leaning heavily on the assumption that the forms or their being are as such good, and then applying the familiar doctrine of participation, we seem to bypass and even make nonsense of the sun-analogy.[5] My point is not that the other forms do *not* participate in the form of the good, but that this notion does not help us to see any point in the sun-analogy. Hence it does not help us to understand how the other forms get their being and reality from the sun-like form of the good.

Let us start again.

The passage presents the sun and the good as each in its sphere a dual cause: for visible objects the sun is the cause whereby they (a) are seen and (b) come-to-be; and for intelligible objects the form of the good is the cause whereby they (a) are known and (b) have being and reality or essence. Now, the sun's contribution to visual cognition has been carefully laid out step by step at 507c–508c, but its contribution to the coming-to-be of objects seen is introduced all at once in the present passage. Even so, the point itself is not puzzling, because just as it is familiar that the sun by its light is responsible for seeing, so it is familiar that the sun by its warmth makes things come to birth and grow. As noted earlier in connection with sunlight and vision (Section 2.2), we do not need to understand how these physical processes work to be assured that they do really happen and that the sun is responsible. By contrast, we have nothing but Plato's assertion that the good is cause of the intelligibles' being and reality. Without some indication of *how* or *in what way* this is so, we might be forgiven for wondering whether the assertion is more than hot air.

Recall that the initially mysterious parallel declaration that the form of the good is the cause of the other forms' being known is followed by an indication of *how* this is so. For immediately after the sun-analogy we are given the Divided Line where Plato sketches the method he calls 'dialectic' in the *Republic*, and here, even without naming the form of the good, he presents a role for it in the dialectical reasoning whereby philosopher-rulers come to know certain other forms. So, we have at least a morsel of explanation of *how* the good causes other forms to be known, and thus some vindication of the claim *that* this is so (see Section 2.2). By contrast, the statement that the form of the good is cause of the being and reality of intelligibles is followed by no distinct parallel sketch of what the metaphysical or ontological relationship might be that makes that statement true. Are we then thrown back on Plato's say-so as our sole reason for accepting it? Could he not have given us at least

---

[5] Cf. Ferrari 2013, 167. The participand model of the sun-like good is discussed further in Section 3.5. On the relation between the form of the good as participand and as sun-like see Section 4.2 and Part 5, points (5) and (6).

another image or simile suggesting the nature of the good's ontological causation of the other intelligibles? Or is the relation too abstruse to be conveyed either in plain words or in images? Or could it be that calling the good the cause of being for other forms is a mechanical echo, in the key of true *being*, of the sun's well-known role as generator of things in the realm of *becoming*? Or is it not a mechanical echo but the considered conclusion of an inference: given (a) the analogy established between sun and form of the good on the *cognitive* side, plus (b) the sun's familiar role in making things come to be, it follows that (c) the good does some sort of corresponding thing on the *ontological* side? This is an unattractive reading, first because the relevant passage is not in the form of an inference, and secondly, because it seems fanciful to extend an analogy in this fashion without showing some independent reason to do so. One would hope for an interpretation that would lay to rest these questions about the role of the good as ontological cause.

It is perhaps natural to assume that in order to get a purchase on how the good is cause of the being and reality or essence of the other forms we need a distinct self-standing statement – even just one or two sentences – indicating the underlying metaphysics: an account comparable to the carefully framed (even though schematic) specification of dialectic in which the (unnamed) form of the good is shown contributing to knowledge by being the non-hypothetical principle. But on the ontological side, Plato provides no comparable explanation extending to even as little as one sentence. So, on the ontological side it seems we either face an explanatory brick wall or must ourselves piece together a theory without help from the one passage in the corpus where Plato says unequivocally that the form of the good is responsible for the reality of the other forms. Some commentators react by making up a model that has no direct textual basis and only awkwardly fits the text, while some seek clues by vigorously shaking the branches of other Platonic dialogues, testimony about Plato's unwritten doctrines, and theories of later Platonism. There is, however, an alternative approach. It consists in looking here, in this part of the *Republic* itself, for – if not a *statement* – then at least a hint or a glimpse of how he conceives of the good's ontological role *vis-à-vis* other forms. I shall argue that the text we have in front of us gives the glimpse we need. Sections 3.2 and 3.4 below spell out two proposals for interpreting it.

The focus of both proposals is Plato's use of the word *proseinai* at 509b7.[6] If Plato ever writes carelessly, I assume it will not be questioned that he writes carefully here. *Proseinai* balances while hinting at difference from *pareinai* at line b6. Syntactically, the clauses ending with, respectively, *pareinai* and *proseinai* are in close correspondence, bringing out the prepositional

---

[6] This has not received much attention from scholars. Sayre 1995, 186, 261 n. 42, is an exception.

difference between the prefixes. The repetition of *hupo* at b6–7 contributes to this effect. I do not think that *proseinai* here is mere elegant variation for the less surprising *pareinai*.[7]

It may be suggested that *proseinai*, which indicates some sort of being added or accrual of something to something, applies here to the framing of the assertion rather than belonging in the content of what is asserted[8] That is, at b5–7 Plato (thus the suggestion) says that as well as its being the case that known things are known because of the good, there is also the additional point that they have their being, etc. because of the good. That he does indeed here make a point, and then an additional point, is already amply clear from *mē monon ... alla kai* at b5–6. Hence *proseinai* must be telling us something else. And what it is telling us is surely that, because of the good, being and reality (or: essence) *are added or accrue to* those other forms – whatever this means. I have two interpretative proposals.

3.2   First Proposal

Suppose we take *autois* at 509b7 to refer to the forms which the philosopher-rulers are especially interested in identifying correctly, namely the forms of the virtues (see Section 2.7). It makes no sense to speak of essence being *added* to a form such as the form of justice, since a form just is an essence. Even if knowing the essence of a form F goes beyond merely referring to F (since one can ask what F is without knowing its definition and essence), we cannot think of the essence or nature itself of F as something added to F. Someone's understanding the essence of F may indeed be additional to her initial focus on the not yet understood F, but in seeking to pin down the essence one seeks to know not something additional, but what F *is*, its very own nature. So, let us translate *ousia* at 509b7 not as 'essence' but as 'reality' or something similar.

Now let us consider what the sun does to the visibles: as well as causing them to be able to be seen, it causes the living ones among them to come-into-being and gives them growth and nourishment. It is unclear whether giving them growth and nourishment is epexegetic of 'causes them to

---

[7] This despite the fact that at *Phaedo* 100d4–6 *prosgenomenou* is a variant on *parousia(i)*. Socrates there affects not to care about exact terminology. While both terms suggest the presence of X to Y from which it might have been absent, *prosgignesthai* emphasizes that X is additional to Y.

[8] The translation of Vegetti 2003, 91 seems to allow for both interpretations. But the assertion-framing way of taking *proseinai* spoils the syntactical balance with *pareinai* at 509b6. Many translations omit to render *proseinai* additively (Jowett 1892; Lindsay 1935; Cornford 1941; Chambry 1946; Bloom 1991; Grube rev. Reeve 1997; Griffith 2000; Lee 2007; Waterfield 2008; Rufener 2011; Rowe 2012). For *proseinai* with clear additive meaning in Plato: *Republic* 339b1; 373a2; 437d10; *Charmides* 154d8; *Hippias Major* 294d5–6; *Symposium* 189e1; *Cratylus* 394b3; *Parmenides* 144c7; 149e7; *Theaetetus* 150a9; b2.

come-into-being' or a further point. Either way, something everyone knows about the sun as cause of plant and animal birth is that the development starts with seeds, and the sun is not the cause of those seeds in the way it is the cause of the coming-to-be of recognizable animals and plants *from* seeds.[9] And even though the sun is indirectly the cause of the seeds through having brought to birth the seed-bearing parent, it remains the case that even at this remove the sun is not responsible for the natures of the various seeds – for the fact that these will sprout as wheat and those as thistles. The first proposal, then, is this: the forms or essences of justice, etc. are like seeds, natures that are there already: and the sun-like good adds to them a heightened level of reality, or one could even say 'substantiality'.[10] This happens via their getting to be reliably recognized in the way in which dialectic, wielding the G-question, enables the philosopher-rulers to recognize those natures. Then the natures will be implemented (even if somewhat roughly), and will thereby make a difference to, have an impact on, the world beyond the domain of intelligible forms. The point is not that the implementations, which are concrete empirical arrangements, have an impact on their earthly surroundings, although of course this is the case. The point, rather, is that the forms themselves, those pure eternal intelligibles, will have come into action as objects of human thought with the potential to affect society and people's lives. They are still there in the 'plain of truth' standing on their sacred pedestal (*Phaedrus* 248b6; 254b6–7), but they are no longer doing only that. They are no longer like a musical score which is indeed correctly called 'music' and 'symphony' or 'concerto' but is never played or chosen to be played, perhaps because no one can understand it. They are now like a score which even before it is played has been established as part of some working musician's repertoire. We might even suppose that it is of the essence of the virtue-forms to be lived up to as gerundives, paradigms, or standards: that this is their function. This is like saying that it is of the essence of food to nourish, even though, as we know, plenty of food goes to waste. But on the human plane, forms of the virtues cannot be lived up to, fulfil their function, unless someone in the community identifies them correctly. This is what the dialectician-ruler achieves by means of the light-shedding form of the good. In this way the form of the good ensures that the other forms take on their full stature in the scheme of things.[11] We have a transition from

---

[9] Cf. Mohr 2005, 256.
[10] This implies that Plato recognizes a non-predicative use of 'to be' and cognates. Cf. Mohr 2005, 253–6.
[11] How would this account fit forms of bad things such as injustice, recognized at 476a1–6? These are paradigms of what is to be destroyed or prevented (cf. *Theaetetus* 176e). Through use of the G-question they are not only discerned for what they are but become objects of practical concern, delineating what is to be acted *against*. The sun enables noxious plants too to sprout and be recognized, whereupon they make the difference such things should make – as objects of

forms' being mere intelligibles to their being something like plans, and then if all goes well, another transition from plan to implementation. The form of the good is involved in the first transition.

I have been talking about forms coming to be paradigms for action in a human community, and how this is a sort of enhancement of the forms' own being as forms. Obviously this enhancement (no less than concrete implementation) has to be mediated by human beings, the rulers. It cannot be that the bare forms, themselves by themselves through an intrinsic timeless metaphysical impulse, eternally 'overflow' into becoming guides of life beyond themselves, let alone into producing empirical implementations of themselves. An accentuated presence in the scheme of things, or in Aristotle's word 'actuality', is indeed added to them by the philosophical human ruler who by means of the interrogative good, in the context of dialectic as presented in Part 2 of this volume, finds out the true natures of justice, etc. so as to select these for practical implementation. In contrast to any 'eternal overflow' picture, the *contingency* of such dialectical interventions is very much present in the background in Books VI–VII of the *Republic*, and the *perishability* of the intellectual and social conditions permitting such interventions is the basis for the story of political deterioration recounted in Books VIII and IX.

So according to the first proposal, the forms of the genuine virtues become actual as opposed to merely potential standards because they come to be known through the form of the good. In becoming thus known they enter the human practical horizon, thereby *acquiring* a heightened level of being through having an impact, first on policy and then on lived civic life itself.[12] On this basis, what can Plato mean by the final statement of our main passage: 'the good itself is not reality (*ouk ousias ontos to agathou*), but is even beyond reality, superior to it in dignity (or: rank, *presbeia(i)*) and power' (509b7–9)? Perhaps it means that the form of the good does not possess the sort of reality it *confers*, since it is not only the conferrer but also the ultimate in this causal line: nothing confers reality on it. It is beyond the reality of things whose reality is conferred and superior to them in rank and power precisely because *it* is the conferrer.

We can develop this a little as follows: (a) the good as such, the form of the good pure and simple (as distinct from the form of, e.g., justice), is not *the same as* the reality (heightened actuality) that accrues to other forms insofar as they are selected for concrete implementation, because it is what confers such reality. And (b) the form of the good does not itself *have* this sort of reality

avoidance and detestation. See also the distinction between paradigm-forms and intelligibles in general, Part 4, note 74.

[12] This account is close to that of Patterson 1985, ch. 6. Unlike his, it does not lean on the idea that to be a form just is to be a formal cause and paradigm. See Part 4, note 74.

because this sort of reality can belong only to directly practicable forms. These are forms of specific good things, such as qualities of the soul, persons, laws, educational institutions, and so on. Good as such, by contrast, cannot be selected for concrete implementation, because good as such is not practicable. Good can only be concretely implemented *via* concrete implementation of forms that have acceded to the level of plans. That is: one can only bring about *good* by planning for specific good things. (And a thing can only masquerade as good by masquerading as some specific good thing, such as health or wisdom.) From the perspective of planning with a view to concrete implementation, the good is useless if taken all by itself, because a plan to bring about good, period, is no plan at all. But the form of the good is not therefore useless, because when it is taken all by itself, in the mode of a question dialectically applied to possible schemes of virtues and just institutions and so on, it is the intellect's great tool for sorting out true from false candidates: that is, those that should, from those that should not, be promoted to the additional reality of being actual plans or standards. The form of the good pure and simple is the dialectical controller of which forms receive that additional reality. But nothing else similarly controls *it*: it is a first principle.[13] Its status as such depends on its not being directly practicable; i.e. on its not belonging to the order of forms that *can* take on additional reality by being promoted from mere intelligibles to plans.

Now for objections to the first proposal. There are two which I shall not tangle with, the first easily imagined, the other once actually levelled. They are: 'The interpretation is too Aristotelian with its emphasis on rising to a new level of actuality', and 'If you are right, how come not a breath of your interpretation shows up anywhere in the almost thousand-year-long tradition of ancient Platonism?' On the first I say only that the use of Aristotelian language was purely for ease of exposition; no suggestion was intended of leaning on Aristotle's authority for the interpretation itself. Plato himself in the *Theaetetus* explicitly distinguishes something's being present but non-operational and its being operational (197b–d). To the second objection it seems enough to say that even twenty-four centuries of Plato-interpretation may not have noticed everything, and that in any case a few interpreters have come close to suggesting what I have labelled the first proposal.[14]

A more serious objection is the following. The proposal is in conflict with the parallel between the sun and the good. For, obviously, the visible things

---

[13] The quality of the questioner's character and intellect might be said to control his answering the G-question correctly, but this is not *dialectical* control, control by a principle of dialectic; character and intellect are the vehicle or sub-structure of dialectic.

[14] See Patterson 1985, ch. 6, although he is more concerned with the function of forms in cosmopoiesis; also Sayre 1995, ch. 6. More detail in Part 4, note 74.

have their equivalent of existence, namely they come-to-be or have come-to-be, *before* (metaphysical priority whether or not temporal) they are seen: so, given the parallel, the being and reality that belongs-in-addition to the objects known, the intelligibles, must (however we understand 'in addition') be prior to their being known. But according to first proposal, reality accrues to the forms as a result of their being known (recognized as true as distinct from illusory bearers of titles such as 'justice'). This gets things the wrong way round: the intelligibles do not acquire being through being known, but are known only insofar as the good has already given them being, just as the visibles are seen only because the sun has already brought them into the world so that they are there to be seen.

This objection depends on assuming that the analogy demands that what holds of visibles in relation to the sun's illumination, namely that they have their being from the sun independently of being illuminated by it, holds correspondingly of the intelligibles: they too must have their being from the form of the good independently of being known through it. First, let me stress that what is at issue is not the being *tout court* of the other intelligibles, but their being insofar as they owe it to the form of the good. The natures and basic existence of the seeds are independent of the sun and its presence. This corresponds to the fact that the correct answer to the question 'What is F?' asked of an intelligible, i.e. the content of what would be the correct answer even if no one existed to ask the question, is eternal and unchangeable. That content is what it is whether or not any mind actually understands it.[15] But what comes to those intelligibles through the form of the good is an additional level of being. The issue is whether this additional level comes to them independently of their being known through the form of the good. Now, it is a familiar fact that objects nurtured by the sun commonly exist even when the sun does not shine on them, and when no one can see them. The question is whether this fact is meant to be incorporated in the sun–good analogy, with the result that the analogy would be saying that any being that accrues to the intelligibles from the form of the good would be accruing to them whether or not they are also known through the latter.

The text is silent on this point. It is noteworthy that the sun-vision side of the presentation pays no attention to the visibles' being there already, visible but not yet actually seen, having been brought to birth by the sun independently of being seen in its light.[16] The corresponding point concerning the intelligibles,

---

[15] If it is right to claim (Part 5, point (6)) that for Plato the form of the good and intellect are co-eval, then for him the supposition that no intellect exists represents an impossibility. As far as I can see, this does not affect the present argument, since we allow counterfactuals with impossible antecedents to be non-trivially true.

[16] Note the indicatives (without modal auxiliary) *horasthai, horōmen, horōmena, akouomena* at 507b8–c2; 'the light of the sun brings about *seeing* and *being seen* [not merely *visibility*]' at

namely that their getting their being from the form of the good is prior to their being known through it, is not, I submit, so obvious that we can safely take it for granted as part of what Plato wants to convey. One can, however, see how it might be taken for granted, and also how doing so would generate a strong temptation to turn a blind eye to 'in addition' or else infer that it modifies the framing of the statement at 509b5–7, rather than being part of its content. For if the other forms' getting their being from the form of the good is prior to their being known through it, what can this being be which they 'get' from it if not their basic status as essences – as the intelligibles that would be known if anything knew them? But the being of an essence as such cannot be conceived of as even timelessly 'added' to the essence. The essence minus its being is not there to be added to. So one is constrained to ignore 'in addition' or to play it down in one way or another. But the word *proseinai* is still there in the text.

In any case, however, the objection that the being which the forms owe to the good is surely prior to their being known may be in conflict with this passage from the Cave allegory:

the way things appear to me is that in the sphere of the known what is seen last, and seen with difficulty, is the form of the good; and that given that it *is* seen (*ophtheisa*) one is bound to reason (*sullogistea*) that it, in fact, is cause for everything of everything right and beautiful, as both progenitor of light and of the source of light <i.e. the sun> in the sphere of the seen, and the source itself of truth and intelligence (*nous*)[17] in the intelligible sphere. It also seems to me that anyone who is to act sensibly (*emphronōs*), in private or in public life, must have had a sight of it. (517b7–c4; cf. 516b4–c2)

The first sentence can be taken in two ways. (1) One cannot get sight of the form of the good without reckoning that it is the cause for everything of everything right and beautiful.[18] (2) On finally sighting the form of the good, one is bound to reckon that it, *through* being sighted, is cause to everything of everything right and beautiful. Here, 'being sighted', *ophtheisa*, is taken twice

---

508a5–6; cf. *tois horōmenois* at 509b1. Then at 509d1 the sun–good analogy introduces the Divided Line, which is all about levels of *actual cognition*: see 509d8–10, *tou horōmenou...tou nooumenou ... tōi horōmenōi*. Socrates mentions the case where a potential observer is present and trying to use his sight but can't do so because light is absent (507d10–e1); he nowhere mentions the case where visible objects remain unseen because, although they are in sunlight, no one is there to see them. The story of escape from the cave, of course, implies that people emerge into a world of objects (a) previously unseen by them and (b) on which the sun has been shining in their absence (or, in the case of reflections and shadows, which it has already produced). It is noteworthy that while (a) is very important to Plato, he seems quite uninterested in (b).

[17] 'Intelligence', like 'truth', indicates intellect in success-mode.

[18] Whatever 'seeing' the form of the good amounts to here, the passage does have Socrates say *in propria persona*, even if only as a tentative impression, that the form of the good must be reckoned to be cause for everything of everything right and beautiful. Drawing this conclusion is not restricted to Plato's specially trained philosopher-rulers, just as, according to the final sentence of the passage, 'seeing' the form is not restricted to them.

over. The passage, with its reference to the sun as the 'offspring of the good' (cf. 506e2; 507a3), has cosmic scope,[19] but its reference to 'everything' means that it has human scope too: 'everything right and beautiful' includes those virtues and virtuous things that are the responsibility of human beings. So, according to interpretation 2, Plato is implying that *through being seen* (by the maker of the cosmos and by the good human ruler) the form of the good is cause of beautiful things. Its 'being seen' (in both the occurrences implied by interpretation 2) does not express a specific first-order asking of the G-question, but refers to general second-level contemplation of it (on the difference, see Section 2.10). In a second-level way the inquirer grasps the form of the good, conveyed in the G-question, as in general the cause of what is beautiful and right; and on interpretation 2 he or she also grasps it as exercising this causality through being grasped ('seen'). Here the grasping or seeing has itself as object, in part.

Let us stay with interpretation 2. According to it, the inquirer presumably sees that the form of the good as brought to bear in the G-question ('being seen') is somehow cause of such beautiful things as (*inter alia*) concretely existing human virtues (the goodness of certain particular persons, actions, institutions). But now if the virtue-*forms* are also included amongst 'beautiful things' (something which Plato might readily have assumed), then 517b7–c4 implies, on interpretation 2, that what the inquirer sees includes the fact that the form of the good, *through being seen*, is cause of the being (in some sense) of the virtue-forms. So the inquirer realizes that sighting the form of the good by an agent able to sight it (the inquirer himself, for example) is prior to, hence can result in, the being and reality, *in some sense*, of the forms themselves of justice, etc., these forms being in the class of beautiful things for which the form of the good is responsible. Thus, whatever the being and reality of these forms amounts to, the inquirer sees it to be an effect of the good's being sighted. It follows, given interpretation 2, that we must gloss this notion of the forms' being and reality in a way that fits this result. My first proposal delivers a suitable gloss. The first proposal is that the reality added to those forms is not their minimal being as possible objects of knowledge in the first place; rather, it is the acquired status of paradigms or templates for concrete instantiation by someone ready to work towards putting them into practice here in the empirical world. Even if this agent's purpose is insurmountably hindered, the forms in question are still more than bare intelligibles: they are the content of frustrated plans.

Running through the *Republic* is the motif of good things lying idle. In his conversation with Polemarchus, Socrates played with the idea that the just

---

[19] See Section 4.4.

person is useless compared with practitioners of the various *technai* (332d–333e). Polemarchus was nudged into suggesting that the just person is at least useful for safe-keeping valuables deposited with him when not in use by their owners: to which Socrates retorted: 'if justice is only of use for things not in use, it can't be worth very much!' Then there was the imagined scenario of the just man so profoundly misperceived that he is taken to be deeply unjust and suffers all kinds of punishment and restriction. Arguably, he would hardly be at liberty to act at all in the surrounding society since his characteristically just actions have been branded disgraceful or criminal. Nor would he be able to inspire others to justice by advice or example, since in the community he is a pariah and a repulsive example of *in*justice. His virtue precisely does *not* 'shine forth' or have any other external impact; its presence makes no difference except to his own soul. Then there was the theme of the uselessness of philosophers, remedied only in the unlikely event of philosophy becoming combined with political power in the same individuals. Finally, if the present interpretation is correct, there are the forms of the virtues, 'gems of purest ray serene', lying unrecognized and inert among the intelligibles until someone like Plato's dialectical ruler comes along.

3.3   Interim Discussion of 505a2–4

The occurrence of *proseinai* at 509b7 is reminiscent of a nearby earlier passage where tantalized Adeimantus finally gets to hear the identity of that 'most important thing to learn' which 'the guardian of the city and its laws' must make every effort to become proficient in (504c9–d3; e3–5):

> you've heard often enough that it's the form of the good (*hē tou agathou idea*) that is the most important thing to learn, <in that> just things and the rest become useful and beneficial by additionally taking on the use of it (*hēi kai dikaia kai t'alla proschrēsamena chrēsima kai ōphelima gignetai.* (505a2–4)[20]

A slightly less grinding translation would be: 'just things and the rest become useful and beneficial by additionally engaging with <the form of the good>', although this loses the consonance of *proschrēsamena chrēsima*. (To save the latter we might try: 'just things and the rest, by additionally engaging with <the form of the good>, become engaged and beneficial'.)

Whereas 509b6–7 says that because of the good, *being and reality* are added to the intelligible objects, the lines just quoted speak of *the good* being added to, additionally engaged by, 'the just things and the rest'. Here are some

---

[20] Cf. *proschrōntai* at 510d5: the mathematicians bring diagrams to bear in their reasonings. The diagram is essential to geometrical proof, but as a visible aid to intellectual activity it comes in from outside.

questions. (1) What are 'the just things and the rest' at 505a3? (2) What is the logical or metaphysical relationship between the above passage and 509b6–7? Both speak not only about adding something but also about the form of the good, which at 505a3 is said to be, itself, something additional, while at 509b6–7 it is said to be that whereby something other than itself, namely being and reality,[21] is added. How are we to put all this together?

Before turning to these questions, let us get a relatively easy point out of the way. In saying that just things and the rest, by relating in a certain way to the form of the good, become useful and beneficial, Plato is surely not iterating the great thesis of the whole dialogue, namely that justice in itself is supremely beneficial to the just person. The core of this thesis has already been established by the end of Book IV on the basis of the anatomy of the soul and the functions of its parts, including reason, whose function is to rule; whereas the context of the present passage is an exposition, stretching through much of the three central books, of what it means for reason to rule at *polis*-level. Moreover, the strange claim that just things, etc. become useful and beneficial by *additionally using* the form of the good is hardly a repetition or elucidation of the thesis that being just is beneficial for us. For that thesis surely claimed that justice is as such beneficial for us; i.e. it is (if we have it) beneficial simply because of what it is in itself, namely the equivalent of health on the psychic level. So the thesis was precisely *not* that being just is beneficial for us by engaging with something *additional* to its mere self (cf. 358d2–3; 366e5–6; 367b4–6; e2–3).

A further preliminary point: linguistically we can take *chrēsima kai ōphelima* in an instrumental sense, as pointing towards an independently specifiable good result caused by the just, etc. things when they – instead of simply being themselves – additionally engage with the form of the good (whatever that means). But this is not mandatory. *Chrēsimos* can simply mean 'operational' as distinct from 'idle'. Something is *chrēsimos* if it is doing what it is meant to do or what would be wasteful of it not to do, whatever that may be. This meaning fits with the first proposal, or at least it does if the phrase 'the just things and the rest' refers to forms of the virtues. As for 'beneficial', we need not understand it as referring to the production of a separate benefit. It could mean something more indeterminate and more metaphysically inflected: when just things, etc. (whatever exactly these are) fail to be connected in some way to the form of the good, they make no worthwhile difference to anything; they might just as well not be there at all.

The first main exegetical question about 505a2–4 was: what are 'the just things and the rest'? Are they straightforwardly the forms of the virtues – justice,

---

[21] Lines 509b7–8, *ouk ousias ontos tou agathou*.

courage, and the rest – which good guardians of a city need above all to have knowledge of (503e–504c)? Or are they relevant to the forms of the virtues without being those forms? One can ask the same question about the intelligible objects at 509b1–9, the entities to which being known *belongs* and to which being and reality *accrue*. The first proposal assumed that the intelligibles at 509b1–9 are forms of the virtues; the second proposal will assume that they are forms of something other than the virtues. More on this in the next section.

Either way, looking at the two passages together we can see that the verb-forms *proseinai* at 509b7 and *proschrēsamena* at 505a3 are more or less logical correlatives: at 509b7 something (being) is added to something else, and at 505a3 something adds to itself something (the form of the good). So far we have a dyadic relation and its converse. But, in fact, the later passage is better thought of as showing a triadic relation between the form of the good (the cause); being and reality (the effect); and the virtue-forms or forms somehow related to the virtues (recipients of the effect). And the earlier passage too shows a sort of triadic relation: between the form of the good (what is added or accrues); the 'just things and the rest' (things to which it accrues, its recipients); and the property of being useful and beneficial (what results in the latter by the former's being added to them).

The second main question was the logical and metaphysical relationship between the two passages. One way of putting them together would be this: as a result of acquiring a relationship with the form of the good, the recipients acquire being and reality, and become useful and beneficial. According to the first proposal, the recipients are the forms of the virtues, and acquiring being, etc. and becoming useful, etc. can be understood as amounting to more or less the same thing, namely making a tangibly worthwhile difference, first to policy, then to practice. We turn now to the second proposal.

3.4   Second Proposal

Our aim is still to interpret the famous statement:

Just so, in the case of things that are known, you need to say not only that their being known belongs to them (*pareinai tois gignōskomenois*) because of the good, but also that their being and reality [or: essence] (*to einai te kai tēn ousian*) accrue to them (*autois proseinai*) because of it, even while the good itself is not reality [or: essence] (*ousias*), but is even beyond reality [or: essence], superior to it in dignity and power. (509b5–9)

The second proposal is that being and *ousia* accrue not to the forms of the virtues proper, as in the first proposal, but to intelligibles such as *returning a loan, keeping a promise, telling the truth*. When the earlier passage which we have just examined (505a2–4) speaks of 'just things and the rest', it refers to actions that in themselves are ethically neutral although they tend to be regarded as epitomizing virtuous conduct (so also 'just and beautiful things' at 506a4).[22] For if Plato had meant to refer to the virtues themselves, he would have said '*to dikaion* and the rest' or '*hē dikaiosunē* and the rest'. The plural 'just things' suggests a plurality collected under the general label of justice. This must either be a plurality of particular instances of behaviour generally regarded as just, or a plurality of types of such behaviour. 'Types' is the right interpretation, because, as later passages insist, the form of the good, operating through dialectic, operates only in connection with intelligibles, and the types relevant here are intelligibles, things that demand our *rational* attention if we are to be right in judging about them.[23]

So according to the second proposal, the things which the form of the good causes to be known and to acquire being are *per se* evaluatively neutral forms, which yield or fail to yield prescriptions of true justice or true courage, etc., depending on the circumstances in which they might be implemented. The metaphysics here, as the reader may already surmise, corresponds with what we have already seen to be the epistemic task of the expert dialectician-rulers (see especially Section 2.19). The epistemic task is as follows. We, the dialectician-rulers, want to know whether *justice* would be enacted if we carry out EFG, the problem being that EFG (returning a loan, subsidizing farmers, or whatever it might be) is in some cases just and in others not, hence can appear to be just when it is not. We proceed by applying the G-question 'Would it be good?' to EFG, and the correct answer, now, depends on the kind of context present now. If the correct answer is that EFG *would* be good, then justice would be enacted by our carrying out EFG. Now, it is not difficult to recast the G-question as a matter of checking whether EFG, as well as being its mere self, also or additionally engages with the good or the form of the good, i.e. connects with it in such a way that what is contemplated is the complex

---

[22] Thus Adam 1907, 51. He refers back to 479d on 'the many norms recognised by ordinary people (*ta tōn pollōn polla nomima*) in connection with beauty and the rest, [which] tumble around somewhere between what purely and simply is not and what purely and simply is'.

[23] In case anyone finds it incredible that Plato should apply the evaluative word 'just' to types of behaviour conceived in purely descriptive terms, remember that his lack of technical vocabulary includes lack of the pair 'evaluative/descriptive', although he could surely make the distinction if we are to go by *Euthyphro* 7b–d. In any case the distinction does not always work uncontroversially. People disagree on whether lying is wrong. Is 'lying' descriptive or evaluative? If it is descriptive, meaning intentional untruthfulness, then many accept that lying is sometimes not wrong and sometimes even obligatory. Others think that calling an act a lie is already to condemn it ('liar' is an insult); and these split into those who hold that intentional untruthfulness is insufficient for an act to count as a lie and wrong, and those (like Kant in his famous essay on the 'so called right to lie') who hold that it is sufficient. Again, if one thinks that in some cases true justice demands mercy, one might express this by saying that here justice (i.e. what in other cases would be justice) would actually be unjust.

{EFG + good}, or in other words a case of EFG that's good.[24] If the answer turns out to be 'Yes', then we know that EFG does amount to justice in the present context.

I have just traced this out on the level of the expert dialectician's thought, leading to *knowledge* of what the virtue demands or allows for in this kind of situation. But it is reasonable to attribute to Plato a corresponding ontology. That is: what the excellent dialectician discovers by applying the G-question is whether, in the presence of a given type of context C, the form of evaluatively neutral EFG 'additionally engages with' the form of the good and thereby turns out to be, not merely apparently but really and truly, the form of justice as tailored to fit this type of context. If the answer is 'Yes', the excellent dialectician in a C-type context has identified EFG as a real or genuine facet of the great form of justice. Instead of merely purporting to be justice, EFG has acquired the status of *really being* justice or *being real* justice; and this acquisition of reality is due not to its being merely itself, EFG, but to the form of good with which, thanks to the context, it has additionally engaged, i.e. combined.[25]

---

[24] Note that in the context of this complex the form of the good is not interrogative. This is because the complex is the truth-maker for the declarative 'EFG is good'. For more on the two-sided nature of the good – interrogative and declarative – see Section 4.2. Also: Plato may choose the 'addition' phraseology in order to exclude the idea that EFG is good because it is a species of which the form of the good is genus, as this would imply the falsehood that every case of EFG is good. So there is a sort of contingency in, or underlying, the relation between EFG and the good. This sort of relation may be the meaning of *allēlōn koinōnia(i)* at 476a7 in the confrontation with the sight-lovers (on the phrase see Adam 1902, 362–4). Perhaps when a type-C circumstance combines with EFG then (if nothing else is relevant) it follows necessarily that this case of EFG is good; but the combination {C + EFG} is presumably contingent. The items combined are forms or types, not temporal particulars, but the combination at form-level is due to combination at particular-level. Contrast *Phaedo* 103c–105c which envisages only necessary relations between forms. Would Plato say that, given C, EFG *participates* in the form of the good? Yes, if the criterion for participation is that the participand is truly predicable of the subject. But perhaps 'No', since EFG is in some instances *not* good, e.g. when combined with circumstance D. Plato does not focus on the logical difference between 'this case' and 'all cases' of EFG.

[25] See also 506a4–7: 'if it's not known exactly how just things and beautiful things are good these won't have acquired (*kektēsthai*) a guard for themselves who's worth anything very much, that is, if he lacks that knowledge; and it's my guess that no one will properly know (*gnōsesthai hikanōs*) just and beautiful things before <he knows in what way they are good>'. This passage, discussed in Section 1.3, seems to waver deliberately between treating goodness as external to the objects referred to as 'just things and beautiful things', and treating it as essential to them so that to identify them at all ('properly know' them) involves recognizing their goodness. Here is a paraphrase of the clause governed by 'it's my guess that': 'No one will really know norms of justice – such as returning a loan and telling the truth – *as* norms of justice without knowing what it is about a specific case of returning a loan, etc. that makes that a good thing to do.' The norm-formula itself does not tell us what those features are whose presence or absence makes a given case a good or not-good thing to do. On real versus specious cases of the virtues see also 536a.

On this second proposal I think we might translate *ousia* as 'essence':

being and essence accrue to them because of it, even while the good itself is not essence, but is even beyond essence, superior to it in dignity and power.

That is: when EFG 'additionally engages with' the form of the good, 'EFG' is a truthful, even though partial and context-dependent, answer to the essence-seeking question: *'What is* justice?' This essence-of-justice status *accrues* to EFG through the latter's association with the good.

What about the second part of the sentence just quoted? Perhaps 'the good itself is not essence' means that the good as such is not the essence of EFG or any comparable form. We do not say *what* EFG is by saying that it is good. And perhaps '[it] is even beyond essence, superior to it in dignity and power' means that the good has no essence.[26] That is: the correct intellectual approach to the sun-like good is not to ask *'What is* the good, after all?' (as people did who defined it as wisdom or as pleasure), but to use it, pure and simple, as the prompt that triggers rational preference about other things, and to understand that things such as EFG depend on the compresence of the good for constituting justice, and indeed for constituting a good thing at all, whereas the good is what it is (namely, the signal for rational preference) without depending on any other form.

On this account, the statement at 505a2–4 that 'the just things and the rest, by additionally engaging with the form of the good, become useful and beneficial' may simply mean that they turn out to be trustworthy and therefore useful (safely usable) norms. The just things and the rest are *per se* neutral things: when they do *not* engage with the form of the good, they are sometimes bad and sometimes simply worthless. And when they do engage with it and are seen to do so by the dialectician-rulers, they get the credit they deserve instead of being mistakenly classed with cases of the same type that were worthless or worse. This may be suggested at 506a: 'if it's not known exactly how just things and beautiful things are good, these won't have acquired a guard for themselves who's worth anything very much'. There will be cases of EFG that *are* just and beautiful (because the good really is attached), but which need to be salvaged and protected by an expert because they are easily confused with oppositely valenced cases.

Let us compare the two proposals for interpreting 509b1–9. According to the first (Section 3.2), the being and reality that accrue through the form of the good accrue to the fully fledged forms of justice and the other virtues. The accrual depends on their having been discerned as forms of justice, etc., and the accrued reality consists in their consequent impact on policy, leading to

---

[26] It does not follow that it has no being. See Leroux 2004, 671 n. 140.

improvements in life on the ground. This reality is added to the fully fledged forms considered as pure intelligible entities. According to the second proposal, being and reality accrue to forms of neutral things which are good under some circumstances and not under others. The accrual of reality consists in the fact that when the good combines with forms of neutrals, the latter, thanks to the compresence of the good, are *really and truly* forms of justice, etc., as distinct from deceptive pretenders to the title. When that is so one delivers the truth if one specifies them, those forms of neutrals, when answering essence-seeking questions such as 'What is justice?' In sum, the second proposal envisages two additions or accruals, one arising from the other: (a) the form of the good is added to the form of the neutral thing (505a2–4), and (b) through this 'advent', the form of the neutral thing has added to it the status of being a real as opposed to merely apparent vehicle of justice. Because of this added 'reality-status', the form of the neutral thing functions as a contextually limited answer to the essence-seeking question 'What is justice?'

The two proposals seem to be exclusive alternatives. According to the first, the forms of essentially and invariantly good things such as the virtues acquire (because a suitable agent brings to bear the G-question) the additional reality of being plans or utilized standards. According to the second, the form of an essentially neutral thing sometimes takes on the nature of, e.g., true or real justice, and what makes the difference is the fact that, instead of being merely itself, it also engages with the good. In this proposal, unlike the first one, the reality that accrues because of the form of the good is prior to the rulers' knowledge, not mediated by it.[27]

It is not obvious which proposal is preferable, but in the end the second seems more satisfactory because of the way it connects 509b1–9 with 505a2–4 and 506a4–7, and thereby with the great Book V theme of things that both are and are not (478d–479d; cf. 523b–524b). But the choice is difficult because the first proposal provides a better fit with the sun-analogy. The first proposal says that the form of the good (by being brought to bear in the G-question) adds to the forms of the virtues the reality of making a difference beyond themselves, just as the sun adds development (*genesis*) to the seeds so that visible things result. The second proposal says that the form of the good, through being 'additionally engaged with' by certain neutral forms, adds to them the status of being not merely apparent but real forms of virtues (i.e. forms such that implementing them is implementing the virtues). But what is the parallel to

---

[27] This picture implies that intelligibles of neutrals such as EFG occur (so to speak) repeatedly, each time in combination with a different intelligible answering to a type of context. This should not pose any more of a metaphysical problem than the fact that the form of a triangle combines with the forms of the differentiae of the three kinds. In the *Republic* Plato does not seem puzzled by the one-in-many ontology of genus and species.

this in the realm of the sun? We have: the sun, through being additionally engaged with by the ???, adds to the ??? the status of being real visible things (meaning: real horses, real trees, etc., not horses and trees that are really visible). What is the right substitution for '????'? The natural answer is 'potential visibles' in the sense of 'potential horses, etc.', and so we are back with seeds or embryos. But strictly the second proposal requires that '???' stand for something analogous to the sort of morally indeterminate or neutral thing – like returning the weapon – that under some circumstances turns out to be just and right, and under others the opposite. The seed analogy fails to provide for that. Either an acorn develops into an oak tree or it fails to; there is no option of developing into some kind of anti-oak. A better analogue would be the gifted soul that can become a great force for good or for evil depending on its upbringing (491d–492a; 495a–b). But with souls we are no longer in the realm of visible things overseen by the sun.

The two proposals have quite a close connection through the notion of standards for action. According to the first, the virtue-forms (thanks to the G-question) come to life by becoming actually adopted standards. According to the second, *per se* neutral (or purely 'descriptive') intelligibles, often taken for granted as norms, achieve (thanks to their association with the form of the good) the status of *deserving* to be standards. Then if wisdom is in charge it will respect them as standards for as long as the context keeps them joined to the good.

At any rate, the key to both proposals lies in *proseinai* at 509b7. Hence it seems fair to say that they rest on the evidence of Plato's own final wording of the sun-analogy as given at 509b1–9. So the main clue to the cryptic doctrine that the good is cause of the being and reality of the other forms has always been under our noses in the crucial text itself. This is a point in favour of our two proposals as compared with the kinds of interpretation considered in the next two sections.[28]

Needless to say, the literature offers a huge array of attempts to expound the ontological relationship between the form of the good and the other forms. In the next two sections I examine two main types of approach on the assumption that each is fairly representative of a sizeable number of respected views. Since it is impossible to follow up and respond to everything, the discussion is sure to overlook findings that might have led me to modify it. But before leaving the present section let me briefly turn to the often suggested idea that according to the *Republic* the form of the good in some sense generates the other forms by a timeless sort of pluralizing diffusion of itself.[29] This is meant to explain

[28] *Proseinai* at 509b7 is in conflict with the perfectionist or ideality kind of account. It might be possible to integrate it into a system account, but, as far as I know, system-account interpreters have not paid attention to the word.
[29] See e.g. Adam 1907, 62; Gerson 1990, 61; 2002, 384, 387.

how the other forms derive being from the form of the good: they are
'virtually' present in it. But this diffusion-model, however potent in itself,
has to suppress or re-locate the meaning of *proseinai* at 509b7. For it would be
beyond weird to express the self-diffusion of the good by saying that the good
adds being *to* the intelligibles diffused. Perhaps self-diffusion is the model
Plato *ought* to have used! But he would have had to choose different language.
No one hoping to be understood would say: 'The fountainhead causes being to
be *added* to the distinct streamlets into which it divides itself.' One can also
worry that 'pluralizing diffusion' has no counterpart on the sun side of the
analogy. The visible objects which the sun nurtures are very obviously not
gestated by the sun; the sun is not virtually those objects; they are not
potentially present in the sun; they do not spring or stream forth from the
sun; and they are not determinate forms of the light it emits. The diffusion
model fails to interpret the form of the good as presented in Plato's own
analogical words.

I now turn to two other kinds of theories, perfectionist accounts and
system accounts.

3.5   Perfectionist Accounts

This family of interpretations arises from considering the attributive use of
'good' as in phrases such as 'a good horse', 'a good singer', 'a good pair of
lungs', 'a good electric kettle'. (Valid examples such as 'a good murderer', 'a
good thumbscrew', 'a good hiding', show that in general '*x* is a good F' does
not entail '*x* is good' or '*x* is a good thing' *simpliciter* or predicatively.)
Perfectionist theorists generally take a generous view on the range of forms
that Plato regards as ontologically dependent on the form of the good in
Republic VI. This is clear from their examples. For them the underlying point
is that when we say '*x* is a good F', we indicate by 'F' a *kind* of thing, and
assert that *x* is a good instance of it (defective ones also being possible); and
we typically learn what it is to be of that kind by studying good or perfect
instances. Coming to know what the kind is, its essence, depends on grasping
what it is to be a good member or instance of that kind; and the being or
essence itself of the kind just is what aspires to be good in accordance with
that kind.[30]

So far this is a neat approach, using a familiar fact about the way many kind-
terms operate in our thinking to draw a close metaphysical connection between
the essence of a thing and its goodness. In itself the connection might permit
the conclusion that there are as many kinds or forms of goodness or being good

---

[30] Cf. Hare 1965; Denyer 2007.

as there are kinds. But it is fallacious and ontologically gratuitous to infer to a single form of the good to explain how, for all the kind-forms, their being or essence is bound up with goodness. Even so, perfectionist interpreters assume that some such move is behind Plato's doctrine that the form of the good is cause, not only of the other forms' being known, but also of their being or essence.

However, something must be said to take account of the fact that Plato recognizes forms that are not forms of kinds of which there can be good and also defective members. For example, he recognizes forms of the virtues whereby human beings are good human beings: justice, courage, moderation, wisdom. Now, a defective knife is still a knife, but one that lacks virtues such as sharpness and ease of handling that make a knife a good one. If we were to allow for a good justice as opposed to a defective justice, we have to be able to identify, analogously to the knife example, the virtues of justice whose presence makes for a case of good justice and whose absence makes for a case of defective justice. And so we have virtues of virtues, perhaps *ad infinitum*. In order to avoid this difficulty and accommodate a wider range of forms, perfectionist interpreters speak in terms of perfection or ideality rather than goodness. In this perspective only a flawless knife is truly a knife, and what we used to call a defective knife simply fails to be a knife: it is only an approximation to one. Another reason for preferring the perfectionist approach is that whereas 'a good F' tends to suggest fitness for purpose or function, 'a perfect F' is less restrictive. A geometric line is perfectly a line (perfectly one-dimensional), whereas calling it 'a good line' is not felicitous.[31] If we add in the view, often attributed to Plato, that the form of F is itself the perfect example of F, we get the result that each (ordinary) form is, as such, a perfect instance of the associated kind or property. A perfect instance of F is understood to be one that is eternally, unchangeably, and absolutely F, as distinct from F at one time and not another, or in one respect and not another, or from one perspective and not another.[32] So: since each of these forms is a perfect instance of itself, they share or participate in the very abstract property of being a perfect instance of oneself. And this latter property of being a perfect instance as such, or of perfection or ideality as such, is the form of the good.[33] Thus the

[31] Sedley 2007, 268; cf. Denyer 2007, 288–9.
[32] See the form of the beautiful at *Symposium* 210e–211a.
[33] An ordinary form's ideal attributes are contrasted with its proper attributes. For a given form of F, its ideal or generic attributes are what constitute it a form as such, while its proper attributes are those which constitute it, and which follow from its being, the form of F specifically. See Aristotle, *Topics* 137b3–13. A classic perfectionist exposition of the form of the good is Santas 1980/1999, but see also Boyle 1974; Santas 2001. The view of Miller 1985, 182–3 is similar. Delcomminette 2006, ch. 16, proposes a highly developed version drawing on elements from the *Philebus*. For objections to the view see Sayre 1995, 182–4 and Karasmanis 2004, 38. Ferrari 2013, 165–7, gives a clear exposition of this type of interpretation, ending on a sceptical

form of the good helps constitute each ordinary form's nature or essence *as form* by being what is generic to forms as such. In this way 'the form of the good is truly *the form of forms*', i.e. the form whereby they are forms.[34]

(Evidently this theory will struggle somewhat to accommodate the fact that some sensible particulars are good. If their being good is their participation in the form of the good, and the form of the good is formal perfection as such, then those sensible particulars turn out to be forms! But perhaps this can be fixed by saying that in their case participation in the form of the good is a matter of aspiring to be the best possible sensible instances of their kinds.[35])

It is worth stressing that if the form of the good is the ideality as such that consists in being eternal, immutable, and perfect of a kind, then what we know of ordinary forms on the basis of their metaphysical relation to the form of the good is simply that they are entities having these ideal attributes. As far as I can see, this knowledge amounts to an understanding of how, because of their shared participation in the ideality as such that is the form of the good, they are totally other than particular objects of sense – particular objects of sense being perishable and changeable, and mere approximations. In other words, the knowledge of the forms afforded by their metaphysical relation to the form of the good is knowledge or understanding of what it is for them to be Platonic forms separate from sensible particulars. It is also an understanding of their knowability or intelligibility, since this is bound up with their ideality. But these impressive features do not yield knowledge of the specific natures of any of them.[36] Their connection with the form of the good, or inquirers' awareness of this connection, does not help the inquirer (whether a ruler or not) to answer such questions as 'What *is* F?', 'What *is* G?' where F and G are being considered not just as forms but as those specific forms. Insofar as 'dialectic' in the *Republic* still seems to mean something associated with the earlier Socrates, whose signature question was 'What is F?' for one or another specific F, it is hard to see, on the approach we are discussing, what the form of the good has to do with dialectic in the *Republic*.[37] If dialectic here is still (at least) a matter of investigation into specific forms such as the form of justice, the

---

note. Shields 2008 has a sympathetic discussion of both Santas 1980/1999 and system accounts without endorsing either.

[34] This sort of account is committed to the idea that the other forms are participants in what the account identifies as the form of the good. We have already (Section 3.1) seen reason to doubt that participation captures the ontological relationship of the ordinary forms with the sun-like good. See also Section 4.2 on the two forms of the good.

[35] See Santas 2001, 186.

[36] As Karasmanis 2004, 38 points out, the ideality theory explains how the form of the good makes them knowable, but not how it makes them *known*, which is what Plato says (508e10; 509b5; cf. 508d5). Presumably each one is known as being what it specifically is.

[37] See Rowe 2007a for a masterly discussion of Socratic continuity between the *Republic* and dialogues generally considered earlier. See also Sedley 2013.

ideality account sheds no light on how the form of the good could be the non-hypothetical starting point of *dialectic*.[38] We might, of course, postulate an un-Socratic way of conceiving of dialectic in the *Republic* that would bring it into line with the ideality account; on such a picture, dialectic's commerce with the form of the good achieves nothing beyond a clear grasp of why and how forms as such are different from sensibles as such, and why they must be accessed by intellection, not sense-perception.[39] On such a view the special dialectical method of the rulers certainly gives them a metaphysically skilled command of that general distinction; but what was promised was that it would make them the city's guardians of, specifically, *just things and beautiful things* (506a). We are told nothing, on the ideality account, that helps us see how this can be so.

Another ground for doubting the ideality or perfectionist interpretation is this. If the form of the good is ideality as such (if it is what it is to be eternal, immutable, perfect), then, I submit, Socrates could have formulated that theory to the brothers without all the fuss about not having knowledge – about not even having a presentable opinion – about only being able to give images – about at best offering the sun-image itself and the related Line and Cave...[40] And it is a puzzle why he did not. For although the theory is severely abstract, it is formulable. The form of the good, according to this theory, is not something wielded in dialectic to find out specific answers to questions about, e.g., justice – these answers being necessarily opaque to Socrates and to us because, as I argued in Section 2.18, the rulers' dialectic is practical reasoning, and we cannot follow practical reasoning properly unless we are in the reasoner's shoes (which are planted in shifting contexts), with the result that there is no generally available perspective from which we or Socrates can watch the form of the good in action for the rulers and so, from the outside, get a detailed picture of how it operates. By contrast, the ideality approach says nothing about the form of the good and its relation to other forms that could not have been stated in terms available to everyone (as it has been by its twentieth- and twenty-first-century exponents). It would surely not have been too difficult for Plato to have Socrates say to the brothers: 'Each of the familiar forms, the ones we are always talking about, is an ideal or perfect entity in its own way; so they share being perfect, and they share this by participating in the form of what it just *is* to be eternal, unchangeable, and perfect of one's kind: and precisely that is the form of the good, which is therefore at the core of what

---

[38] Thus Delcomminette 2006, 605–6 holds that the form of the good is ideality as such, and infers that it is not the non-hypothetical principle of dialectic.

[39] This implication is affirmed by Santas 1980/1999, 273. It seems to be one reason why Santas 2001 holds that the *Republic* features two distinct theories of the good; see esp. 187–93.

[40] On the ideality interpretation Socrates could have explained the form of the good by abstracting from what Diotima says, not at all tentatively or metaphorically, about the form of the beautiful at *Symposium* 211a–b.

they all are (like their common substance), and the *ne plus ultra* in the hierarchy of things perfect.'[41] (So those who identified the good with anything as full-blooded as pleasure or wisdom were not just wrong but hopelessly wrong.) If this explanation were to leave Glaucon and Adeimantus wondering how the form of the good assists the task of philosopher-*rulers* – well, they would be no worse off than we readers are when offered the above explanation.

3.6   System Accounts

Let us turn to system accounts. Here is a fairly simple statement of the general idea:

The good, then, may be understood not as something independent of the virtues and other specific goods, but as the appropriate combination and arrangement of them. This is why Plato believes the Good is not a 'being' in its own right, but beyond being; while the good is superior to the different specific goods that constitute it, it cannot be understood, defined, or achieved without reference to them ... We will begin to form an adequate conception of the good once we understand the virtues and other goods well enough to see how they fit together and how they should be combined with each other.[42]

It is reasonable to ascribe to Plato the view that all genuine intrinsic or final goods must harmonize so that none by its presence regularly clashes with the presence of the others: it cannot be that true courage depends on stupidity about danger, or that the right education for developing moderation is bound to make people soft so that they lack courage. Refusal to countenance regular mutual exclusion or even tension between the virtues is a way of asserting the unity of the virtues, a thesis which would have been familiar to the early audience of the *Republic* since Socrates defended a version of it in the *Protagoras*.[43] And more than once in the *Republic* itself Plato worries about the educational problem of combining in one personality such traits as gentleness and readiness to fight, intellectual quickness and emotional stability (375b–e; 503c–d). Insisting that both of each pair should be cultivated so as to co-exist harmoniously presupposes that neither is at its best or even truly itself at all when, in a single personality, it excludes or is in tension with the other. And if Plato even had a distinct category of aesthetic beauty, he would probably have insisted that if a work of art expresses immoral values this

---

[41] It seems some of us have got used to thinking of the characters Glaucon and Adeimantus as a bit stupid – anyway, stupider than ourselves. But the long speeches Plato assigns them in Book II are brilliant.

[42] Irwin 1995, 273; cf. Reeve 1988, 84–5, 92–3; Annas 1999, 108.

[43] The version defended in the *Protagoras* is stronger than any that surfaces in the *Republic*.

automatically makes it *aesthetically* ugly: true aesthetic beauty cannot co-exist with the morally vicious.[44] Thus it is a condition on the nature, and a criterion for the identification, of an intrinsic good that it fits harmoniously with all other intrinsic goods. So if *the* good is this harmonious arrangement, it is that by which other goods both are what they are supposed to be (namely goods) and are known as what they are. This interpretation accords with the swivelling of what is 'most important to learn' from plural to singular (503e3; 504d2–3). It also accords with the statement that the dialectician is one who takes account of everything together or of everything in the light of everything else (*sunoptikos*, 537c8).

However, if we flatly identify the whole system of forms of intrinsic goods with the form of the good itself, then we face the problem (which probably not all scholars take as seriously as I am inclined to) that the sun-analogy is a poor fit, since the objects brought into being by the sun are very definitely not members or parts of some kind of whole that is the sun. The sun's physical distance from the perceptible things it nurtures is matched by the form of the good's position 'beyond being [or: essence]' (*epekeina tēs ousias*, 509b8). But this problem can be avoided by identifying the form of the good not with the collective of systematically related forms, but with the principle whereby they relate to each other systematically.[45] This is ontologically prior to, because it explains, the system, and so is distinct from it like the sun from the things the sun nurtures. The principle surely is that they relate to each other harmoniously because it is *better* this way.

(To revert for a moment to my interpretation of the form of the good in terms of the G-question: the principle just mentioned would surely be one criterion, whether or not the only one, for answering the question affirmatively. To take the well-worn example of returning the borrowed weapon: returning it is not *justice* unless the action is controlled by the virtue of *practical wisdom* taking account of the circumstances. The same could be said for any other virtue: a type of action or policy or arrangement A does not instantiate or implement true courage or generosity, etc. unless A also expresses wisdom that gives due weight to the circumstances. Thus wisdom makes it *known* whether A would be courageous, etc., and (on the level of implementation) makes the difference between A's being a *real* as distinct from a pseudo- case of courage. It seems that the system account as represented above could easily develop into a theory that identifies the good with wisdom. But this conclusion runs up against the

---

[44] He might have held that even if the aesthetic beauty is in a sense intact, it counts for nothing compared with the immoral ugliness; but then since beauty is essentially lovable and valuable, it cannot be real beauty if it counts for nothing.

[45] On this sort of account, *ousia* at 509b8 may mean 'definable essence' (the mark of the ordinary forms), or it may refer collectively to the other forms.

fact that Plato refuses to identify the good with wisdom or knowledge: 505b8–c4; 508e2–509a5.

Returning to the sort of system account we were considering, according to which the form of the good is the principle of the 'betterness' of a harmony of intrinsic goods: one can raise the question whether 'better' applies primarily at the level of the relevant forms or to the concrete implementations or implementation-options corresponding to those forms. Is Plato more interested in having the forms, or in having the implementations, be as co-ordinated as they can be? The notion that it is better that the *form* of justice is harmoniously related to the *forms* of all the other intrinsic or final goods might seem to run up against the objection that betterness can only explain a fact that could have been otherwise; whereas to each form in the system it is essential, hence necessary, that it be in the system. However, think of betterness as the property of being more beautiful: it is not so clear that the superior *beauty* of even a necessary state of affairs is not the explanation or part of the explanation of its obtaining.[46] The alternative, that it simply happens to be the case that what we regularly have is more beautiful than alternatives, is uncongenial, or would have been so to both Plato and Aristotle. But, however that may be, I tend to think that Plato's concern in the *Republic* is primarily with implementations of the virtues, etc.: i.e. that the main point would be that these implemented values are better when their shapes are such that they work happily together. If so, then the corresponding forms – the standards for measuring whether those values have been implemented – must be forms of harmonious-when-implemented values. It takes a sort of self-predication – 'forms of the harmoniously interrelated are themselves harmoniously interrelated' – to get from that to the idea that the forms themselves constitute a harmonious system; but this is not an objection. Plato is not averse to self-predication, and he speaks of the forms themselves as harmonious when he writes:

as [the philosopher] turns his eyes towards an ordered array of things that forever remain the same, and observes these maintaining their harmony and rationality in everything, and neither behaving unjustly nor being treated unjustly by each other, he will imitate these and model himself after them as much as he can. (500c3–6)

Given Plato's overt interest in harmony, e.g. of parts of the soul and sectors of the city, the suggestion that he identifies the form of the good with the principle that intrinsic or final goods are essentially such as to co-exist happily (so that when this fails what we have are at best stunted versions of the goods)

---

[46] In Anaximander's 'The earth is stationary at the cosmic centre because there is no reason for it to move in one direction rather than another,' the earth's situation is presumably a necessary state of affairs, but not a brute necessity, since it is explained by the consideration that anything else would have been arbitrary, hence less beautiful.

does raise the question why his Socrates fails to state this. After all, it is not hard to explain in plain words that no person or action should be unqualifiedly praised under the heading of one specific virtue if he or it rates low under the heading of another, and that a comprehensive education for the virtues presupposes the (in some sense) unity of the virtues themselves. It is not necessary to be inside the minds of the *Republic*'s consummately educated rulers to understand and accept these things as true, and so it is not necessary for those outside those minds to speak of them only indirectly or through images.

According to a metaphysically more ambitious system account, the relevant system is the harmonious combination of all forms, the entire '*noētos kosmos*' itself,[47] or it is the system of all forms realized in the physical cosmos (we think of the intelligible paradigm of the Timaean cosmos). In one version, the form of the good itself is clearly distinguished from the system of forms: the system is that which is good, while the form of the good is the system's goodness. The goodness of the system is why the system is as it is and why the forms composing it are as they are; hence the goodness or excellence of the system, i.e. the form of the good, is the ultimate cause or ground of everything. Unlike the type of system account discussed above, this one includes forms outside the sphere of what humans themselves might implement. From here one can perhaps take different views of how ideal human rulers operate in relation to the form of the good. One idea is that they take the ordered goodness of the *noētos cosmos*, or of the formal structure of the physical cosmos, as an inspiration for producing beautiful order in human affairs. Another would be that they take the wider structure itself as their model for ruling. They might be scientists who come to identify arrangements of the natural universe by considering which arrangements are cosmically good, and then in some way seek to reproduce versions of those arrangements on the level of human society. An objection to this kind of interpretation is that little, if anything, in the actual text of the *Republic* suggests that the rulers' actions are guided by the intelligible paradigm of the natural universe, or by a cosmology based on assuming such a paradigm. In favour of the interpretation, however, is that it might help explain why the rulers need their massive mathematical education if we assume that in the *Republic* Plato already envisaged a deeply mathematical cosmology, as in the *Timaeus*.[48]

---

[47] Joseph 1948, 21; Gosling 1973, 67–8, 117–18. Patterson 1985, ch. 6, offers a sophisticated version of this view. According to it, the basis for intelligibles qualifying as Platonic *forms* in the strong metaphysical sense of templates and formal causes of phenomena (given an ideal agent such as the demiurge of the *Timaeus*) is that their combined implementation makes for the *best* result, whether cosmic or human.

[48] However, see Section 4.3, which argues that the mathematical education can be adequately explained on the basis of what is explicit in the *Republic*.

Part 4 Various Further Questions

4.1 Ambiguity of 'the Good' (I)

We recall that not long before the analogy of the sun Socrates briefly discussed two apparently familiar identifications of the good: that it is pleasure, and that it is wisdom. He dismissed both, the first on the ground that there are bad pleasures and the second on the ground that it leads to circularity: when its adherents are pressed to say which sort of wisdom the good is, they can only say that it is the wisdom about (literally: of) the good (505b–c).[1] Let us consider this charge of circularity.

The charge is fair only if, in the statement (W) 'The good is wisdom about the good,' both occurrences of 'the good' have the same meaning. In that case, W has the further fault of implying 'The good is wisdom about wisdom about the good,' threatening a regress. This is so if, for example, W means that the attribute of goodness is identical with the attribute of wisdom about the attribute of goodness. But W on this interpretation is not even universally true, since there are plenty of things that have the attribute of goodness (= are good) without having the attribute of wisdom about anything: e.g. bodily health is good but not itself wise. If, on the other hand, in W the two occurrences of 'the good' have different meanings, there is no reason to reject W as circular. But if W is taken in this way Plato has shown no reason to reject it, since his only objection was circularity.

The two occurrences would have different meanings on a hypothesis which I shall now discuss, namely that the first one refers not to the attribute of goodness, nor to whatever is good, but to the good in the sense of the *bonum supremum*, in the scholastic phrase, i.e. that specific good which is the principle whereby other good things are good. We may also call it the chief or sovereign good. It seems quite likely that the *bonum supremum* is what Glaucon and perhaps also at this point Socrates are talking about.[2] The notion

---

[1] Vegetti 2013c, 141 remarks that these *elenchoi* are 'too brief to be really persuasive'.

[2] As we shall see, the good-making good is not in a straightforward sense what Socrates is talking about when he presents the good as analogous to the sun. And Glaucon may not at any point have a clear theoretical role in mind when he uses and hears the phrase 'the good'. We also should allow for the possibility that the theoretical import of the phrase is one thing to Glaucon and another to Socrates

is that of a single specific kind of good thing (uniqueness always seems to be assumed) that is the unconditioned ground of the goodness of all other kinds of good thing, either because they are for the sake of it or because of how it deals with them, or both. For instance, it was something of a commonplace that the things we normally deem good to have, such as prosperity and social status, even health and physical beauty – things that human beings take endless trouble to secure for themselves and for those whom they care about – are truly good, worth desiring, genuine blessings, only if they are or will be pursued, managed, and enjoyed *wisely*: otherwise they may end up toxic to those affected by them,[3] with their possessors rightly regretting they had ever acquired or been given those things which everyone wants so much that it sometimes looks as if all human life is a matter of chasing after them or making sure they don't get away (505a6–b3).

Let the sovereign or supreme good in the sense of the scholastic phrase (whatever this good may be) be called 'the good-making good' since some kind of relation to it is what makes it the case that the other things commonly sought as good are actually or really good.[4] If the first occurrence of 'the good' in W refers to the good-making good, and the second refers to the many kinds of things commonly sought as good, then W says that the good-making good is wisdom about those things – the wisdom that selects, interprets, pursues, and manages them in ways such that they really are good for the wise agent or those whom she wants to benefit. Read in this way, W not only is not circular, but is a highly plausible view and one which it is hard to believe that Plato would not have held when writing the *Republic*.[5]

So are we to conclude that he did not notice the ambiguity of W and took it in a sense in which it can easily be faulted for circularity? This seems improbable. It is hard to believe that he was unaware of the ambiguity. It is also hard to believe that he was unaware that if W is taken as referring to the good-making good, W is non-circular and plausible. It is not circular because the goods discerned and managed *as* true goods by wisdom are not for the

---

(Plato), and also for the possibility of a change or development in its theoretical import as the conversation progresses.

[3] On blessings that turn into curses, see e.g. the myths of Arachne, Marsyas, Niobe, Tithonus.

[4] On this notion see Broadie 2007. This concept of the good-making good is not to be confused with the Platonic tenet that the form of the good is that whereby perceptible objects are good through their participation in or imitation of it. That tenet (recalled as familiar by Socrates at 507a–b) is simply an instance of the general Platonist theory of forms. From the point of view of that theory, a concrete instance of the good-making good in the sense used here (e.g. wisdom) would be metaphysically on a par with the goods it makes good (e.g. wealth, social position): it, like each of them, is one good among many, non-identical with the form of the good and participating in it. The form of the good considered as participated in by the many particular good things will be discussed in Section 4.2.

[5] The view is put forward at *Meno* 87d–88e and *Euthydemus* 280b–281e. See also *Laws* II, 661b–e, where the good-making good is 'justice and the whole of virtue'. Cf. Aristotle *Eudemian Ethics* VIII, 1248b26–34.

most part themselves wisdom, since they are the many kinds of things which it is normal to desire for oneself and for those whom one cares about. And W in this sense is plausible because it is hard to see how the good that manages the other goods well could be anything other than a kind of wisdom or intelligence, and indeed perhaps the most important kind and hence the one that most of all deserves to be called 'wisdom'. But if Plato was aware that W can be taken in a way that makes it non-circular and plausible, why does he not stop to tease out this sense of W and give it due credit?

The answer, as far as I can see, is that in this part of the *Republic* he is not seeking to settle the question of which of the many different kinds of goods (wisdom or pleasure or some third?) occupies that special status of the *good-making* good. I believe that for him this question is already settled in favour of wisdom. Here he is concerned with something which it apparently makes sense to speak of as 'the good' but also to explain as the analogue of the sun. I shall call this 'the *sun-like* good'. We know from the text that the sun-like good is not the same as wise knowledge: Socrates says this explicitly. Knowledge is not identical with the good in the sense of sun-like good: instead, it is the sun-like good's *effect* (508e–509a).

If, as I assume, Plato holds that wisdom is the good-making good, the *bonum supremum* in whose ambit alone the other so-called goods are worthwhile, then what is the point of postulating yet another 'the good', the sun-like good? Why is he not satisfied to assert or argue that wisdom is *the* good in the sense of the good-maker *vis-à-vis* the other goods, and to show – if he thinks it is necessary – that this assertion is not viciously circular?

He is not satisfied, I think, because here in the *Republic* he is trying to convey some idea of *how* wisdom, now understood as the philosopher-rulers' dialectical skill, gets its results.[6] There are two levels to this how-question. On one level it is asking 'What does wisdom do to get its results?' The answer to this is given only in outline. It is that wisdom gets its results (is able to act as a real good-maker) by the dialectical method, focusing first and foremost on the task of identifying genuinely virtuous things rather than look-alikes. (Once recognition of virtuous things is secured, it will not be difficult to determine when and to what extent, etc. non-moral goods such as health and wealth are truly good and to be pursued.) Identifying the genuinely virtuous things is a matter of applying the G-question to proposed accounts of the just, etc. in such

---

[6] Socrates in the *Republic* is no longer satisfied with what would be the *Phaedo*'s 'safe' answer: 'the wise are wise because they participate in the form of wisdom' (cf. *Phaedo* 100c–101c). He now wants to explain how wisdom operates and by what sort of education it is generated. This is all the more pressing given that he has committed himself to the position that the ideal ruler's wisdom involves *philosophy*. Not content to let this stand as an unexplained dogma, he must say something to show how such wisdom depends on philosophy for its operation and its development.

a way as to get correct results. *That* is how wisdom operates. But we can ask at a different level how wisdom achieves what it does. This is when we seek to know what it is that makes wisdom *wisdom*, i.e. what goes into the wise person's reliable correctness in answering the G-question and all the prior dialectical questions (see Section 2.8). To this, the answer lies in the entire moral and intellectual formation which the philosopher-rulers bring to their task. They bring to it impeccable moral integrity and strong, disciplined intelligence. This combination of qualities, the complex outcome of their education, is what ensures that the G-question really is like the sun that illuminates and brings into view what they are looking for. Their educational formation, which Plato describes not in outline but in lengthy detail, is what explains how human wisdom comes to exist so as to be able to get its results. For the form of the good, or the G-question, cannot get results all by itself (at least not in the human context): it depends for results on intelligent agents distinct from itself. Perhaps we are to think of the superbly qualified human inquirer as the servant or even instrument of the interrogative form of the good, channelling it and thereby enabling it to make a difference.[7]

Understood in this way the sun-like form of the good is what constitutes wisdom-in-action's cutting edge, so to speak. It is the cause whereby wisdom is wisdom. If wisdom is to be labelled '*the* good' on the ground that it alone ensures the true goodness of the other goods, then *that whereby* wisdom is wisdom is rightly also called '*the* good', although not in such a sense as to compete with wisdom's claim to that title. There is no competition because that whereby wisdom is wisdom is prior to wisdom, hence not on the same level.

Here is another way of looking at the situation. Wisdom, we have just said, is a disposition or plexus of dispositions built up through education, and one way of explaining wisdom is to go into detail, as Plato does in the *Republic*, about the nature of the education and its parts. 'Wisdom is the quality built up in such and such a way.' However, wisdom must also be viewed from the other end – not as the object of gradual development but as achieved wisdom in action. Wisdom in action is the inquiry-led attaining of non-accidentally correct value-judgements. This *activity* of wisdom is what brings to recognition true cases of justice and the other virtues. It generates, hence is not the same as, the wise knowledge (knowledge of *which* things are good, *that* so and so is good) which the rulers then implement in their policies. The activity of wisdom is metaphysically prior (a) to the states of new knowledge it generates through correctly answering the G-question, and (b) to the wise disposition of which it is an exercise; hence if either of these has a claim to be ranked as '*the* good', the activity deserves it more. Am I then saying that Plato's sun-like

---

[7] Cf. Vegetti, 2013c, 151: 'the philosophical government is somehow the historical representative of the Good'.

good is in fact identical with an activity, a mental activity exercised no doubt by God (see Section 4.4) and by human beings at their best? No, for that would be like saying that the literal sun is identical with successful vision; but this is something Plato expressly denies, saying that the sun is not vision (508a11; b9). The latter is such a truism at the literal level that Plato's reason for stating it (twice) can only be to underline the analogous non-truistic point that the ultimate good is *not* the activity of wisdom or intelligence.[8] And this, we are surely right to infer, is because the sun-like form of the good is the interrogatively inflected content or intentional object of actively good-seeking wisdom or intelligence.[9] As such the form of the good is the cause of wisdom's good-seeking activity in the sense of being its logical determinant.[10] The disposition that is wisdom lies idle (so does no good) unless and until wisdom actually asks the G-question about some given subject-matter, i.e. brings the form of the good into play. Interrogative wisdom thereby mobilizes its dispositional endowment, that plexus of pre-existing, pre-formed, moral and reason-enhancing virtues, to issue in an answer – which will be the right answer. The form of the good is *like the sun*, i.e. it is the reliable source of truthful illumination, because the G-question is being asked and then answered (with reference to a specific object) not by just anyone but by someone who has built up the habit of asking this question along with the plexus of qualities needed to answer it well each time. Thus we have the successful activity of wisdom. This activity is definitionally prior to dispositional wisdom, and the good interrogatively inflected is definitionally prior to the successful activity of wisdom. For the successful activity of wisdom just is the getting of correct answers to precisely that interrogation. Hence the interrogatively inflected content of the G-question is prior to the activity, being its logical determinant.

---

[8] I am grateful to Alex Long for pointing out that Plato might well have seen the *Phaedo* doctrine of forms as causes (100b–e) as a potential source of misunderstanding. According to the *Phaedo* it is *because of* the form of F that a sensible thing is F, and this 'because of' means 'because it participates in'. This pattern, transferred to the *Republic*, would imply that the form of the good makes things known, i.e. makes us wise about them, because we participate in the form of wisdom – which would only make sense if the form of the good were the same as the form of wisdom. In fact, in the *Republic* it is still true, of course, that we are wise about the forms because of, in the sense of by participating in, the form of wisdom; but we also, by a different type of causality, are wise about them because of the good, just as we see things because of (by participating in) the form of vision but also because of something else, namely the sun. Plato invokes the sun-like form of the good as part of a specific explanation of what it is to be wise. The purely metaphysical point that we are wise by participating in the form of wisdom goes no way towards this.

[9] Cf. *Parmenides* 132b3–c12: forms are not thinkings (*noēmata*) in souls because forms are objects of thought.

[10] My thanks to Barbara Sattler for pressing for a clearer formulation of the point expressed in this sentence.

But here the chain of dependence stops; nothing is prior to that determinant.[11] Combine this with the assumptions (1) that the good-making good is wisdom, and (2) that the good-making good is, in a sense, *the* good (the good among goods): it follows that the form of the good in its sun-like role has prior, and indeed the finally first, claim to being called '*the* good'.[12]

4.2   Ambiguity of 'the Good' (II)

I now turn to yet another sense of the ambiguous phrase 'the good'. This is the sense in which it refers to the Platonic form, the 'one over many', corresponding to the familiar term 'good' applied predicatively as distinct from attributively, which picks out the property that belongs to all good things as such. What is the relationship between the good that is one over many good things, and the sun-like form of the good which has been our main concern? We shall see that in a sense they are different and in a sense they are the same.

The philosopher-rulers' task is to determine which implementations of EFG would be good (and would therefore count as, say, just). Now, the term 'good' brought to bear in the G-question will also occur as predicate (affirmed or denied) in the rulers' reasoned and true declarative answers ranging over action-types, arrangement-types, etc.; and when they have put these answers into practice, 'good' will also occur in true declarative statements reporting that the resulting particular actions, arrangements, tendencies, etc. are good. The one form over the many participants (whether types or particulars) is called '*the* good'. According to the well-known Platonic doctrine, the goodness of ordinary good things (types or particulars) derives from their relation to this form – the relation known as 'participation'. This form of the good is a constituent of each of the many facts corresponding to true declarative sentences to the effect that this or that is good. Now, on the one hand, the predicate 'good' in these true declaratives is the same as the term that invokes the sun-like form. It has to be the same, since the content of the answer to a question must match the content of the question. On the other hand, the form

---

[11] There is a five-way distinction here: between (1) the activity of wisdom (or intelligence) in making correct value-judgements about what is just, etc.; (2) the logical determinant of the activity of wisdom; (3) the disposition or plexus of dispositions manifested in the activity; (4) the knowledge gained through the activity of wisdom; and (5) the activity of using this new knowledge in a practical way (or, for that matter, as a springboard for acquiring further knowledge).

[12] One implication of the above is that the form of the good *qua* sun-like is not the *meaning* of the predicate of the G-question since one might reasonably claim that the question means the same whether asked by the wise or the foolish about the same object, although asked by foolish it will fail to 'light the way' to the right answer. But there is presumably also room for a disjunctivist position on which the wise and the foolish do not ask the same question, even if each side thinks that they do.

corresponding to 'good' used in true assertions that this or that is good is not the *sun-like* good, given that the sun-like good is essentially interrogative. As such, the *sun-like* good cannot be what corresponds to the predicate in those true statements, i.e. it cannot be a constituent of the facts that make those statements true.

So are we to say that there are two forms of the good, an interrogative one and a declarative one, so to speak? Proclus in his commentary on the *Republic* was puzzled that Plato seems to recognize distinct forms of the good, the sun-like form *as well as* the form in which all good things participate insofar as they are good. (Let us call the latter 'the participand' form of the good.)[13] Proclus could not think of them as one form because he took the sun-analogy to entail that the sun-like form of the good is the cause of the being of all other forms including the participand form of good. One might question this argument on the grounds that where a primary entity is concerned self-causation may not be an incoherent notion. But in any case it seems pretty clear that the sun-like form of the good is not related to the other forms as participand to participants.[14] If one may lean on the sun-analogy (and there is not much else to lean on), the ordinary visible objects are not themselves bearers of the shared term 'sun'. They are not junior suns or images of the sun or called after the sun, and they do not have shares of the sun, whatever that would mean. Plato singles out just three things as 'sun-like', namely the eye, light, and vision, and these are not among the ordinary objects seen (508b3; 509a1).

---

[13] Proclus 1899, 269–87, discussed by Gerson 2015, 230–5; 2020, 164–73. Proclus distinguishes a co-ordinate and a superordinate form of the good. Gerson too *in propria persona* argues for such an account.

[14] Plato speaks of the participand good at 476a5–8 and 507b1–6. Then at 509b7–8 he says that the sun-like form of the good, through which reality accrues to the other forms, is not itself reality (or essence) (*ousia*). It is natural to take this as meaning that the sun-like form is not the form of *ousia*, although other interpretations have been proposed (cf. Rowe 2007c, 252–3). If the form of the good is other than the form of *ousia*, then participants in the form of the good are *thereby* (i.e. by this participation) given goodness but are not thereby given *ousia*. Yet Plato says that because of the sun-like form the other forms have (not goodness, but) *ousia*. All this has some important implications. (a) The form of the good *qua* participand is somehow different from the sun-like form whereby other forms have *ousia*. (b) It is not by participation in the form of the good that the other forms acquire *ousia* from it. (c)Two modes of being caused to have *ousia* are in play for the other forms. For (i) by standard doctrine they have *ousia* because they participate in the form of *ousia*, or, for short, they have *ousia* because of the form of *ousia* (cf. *Phaedo* 100b–e); and (ii) they also have *ousia* because of (*hupo* + genitive, 509b7) the sun-like form of the good, which 509b7–8 says is not the form of *ousia*. On the assumption, which admittedly cannot be taken for granted, that the meaning of *ousia* is constant, positions (i) and (ii) are consistent only if 'because of' conveys different modes of causality. For a similar point about the form of wisdom or knowledge, and the form of the good, as in different ways causes of wisdom, see Section 4.1, note 8.

I suggest that the plurality of forms of the good discussed by Proclus[15] comes down to the difference between interrogative and declarative, or more precisely between question and *true* answer. It is surely more economical to think in terms of two *roles* or *functions* of a single form than in terms of two forms, especially when the difference between the roles can be explained in terms of the anyway familiar contrast between declarative and interrogative uses of the same (underlying) indicative sentence. But against this: if when Plato brought in the sun-like form he was really bringing in one of two *roles* of the form of the good, why is there no indication of this in the text? If there is no indication because he was unaware of the distinction I have been drawing between the one form and its different roles or functions, then arguably this distinction cannot be the basis of an acceptable interpretation.

However, the argument that he was unaware of the distinction has to be made. A lot depends on how much or little we pack into 'aware'. The following chain of points is worth considering. (a) Plato obviously knew when he or someone else was asking a question[16] and when they were making an assertion, although we do not know whether he ever consciously reflected in a fully general way on the difference.[17] (b) He does, however, thematize it at a somewhat local level, namely when talking about the formal question-and-answer of dialectic.[18] (c) It is impossible to believe that if for some extraordinary reason he decided in this part of the *Republic* to countenance two distinct forms of the good, he would not have said so and said something, however brief, about the reason. (d) He registers no inconsistency between, in one place, talking about the form of the good as the one good over many goods, i.e. as the participand (507b), and in another (508d10–e5) talking about it as analogous to the sun. (e) These passages are not only spatially quite close but also connected in that the first is part of the lead-up to the second, as we shall see. (f) It is uncharitable to suppose that nevertheless there *is* an inconsistency (given the non-negotiable assumption of the uniqueness of forms) to which he

---

[15] Actually, Proclus recognizes a trio of entities designable as 'the good': (a) 'the good in us', i.e. the property possessed or possessable by the participants (see *Phaedo* 102d–e); (b) the separate-from-us participand; (c) the sun-like good. The present discussion ignores (a). Proclus notes the categorial disparity between the rejected candidates for the title '*the* good' (wisdom and pleasure), and the winner, namely the sun-like good (273, 6–16). Wisdom and pleasure correspond to the question 'What is the supreme possessable/practicable-by-us good?', but the sun-like good is not possessable or practicable according to Proclus, and also according to the present account (see the recapitulation at the end of this section, and see also in Section 3.2).

[16] Throughout this discussion 'question' means an open or 'genuine' as opposed to a rhetorical question or one framed to elicit a pre-determined answer.

[17] He, of course, has words for asking a question and giving an answer. This is not the same as focusing on the difference in the way Aristotle certainly did, perhaps responding to an already recognized distinction: *Rhetoric* III. 18; *Topics* I. 4.

[18] *Republic* 336c2–6; 487b3–5; 531e3–4; 534d9–10; *Protagoras* 336c; 338c–e; 348a; *Phaedo* 75d1–3; 78d1–2; *Cratylus* 390c5–7 (cf. 398d4–6).

was blind. (g) Yet, intuitively, *being participated in* and *being analogous to the sun* are two very different theoretical roles, so much so that to assign them both to one and the same form and just leave the matter at that seems a conceptually insensitive, even barbaric, thing to do. (h) Since we feel this, Plato would have felt it too. (Feeling it does not require reflecting on the matter; that is the point of 'intuitively'.) (i) But there is no lapse into barbarism if the single form is being considered in terms of two intrinsically correlated roles or functions: one of them – technically labelled 'participand' – whereby the form is a constituent of the fact that a thing is good, and the other without a technical label so far but illustrated by the sun-analogy. (j) Now, the sun-analogy is closely tied to the topic of dialectic, and dialectic consists in asking critical questions and receiving answers: those two are the principal actions of dialectic. (k) No one knew this better than Plato. (l) It seems pretty clear that of these two ingredients of dialectic it would be *answers* that represent things as *being* or *not being* good, i.e. as participating or not participating in the participand form of the good. (m) Hence, given that in the context of dialectic the form does occur in its sun-like persona, thus functioning in a way felt to be quite different from the being-participated-in way, it follows (given (j)) that in its sun-like persona the form is functioning not in the answer-way but in the question-way: not declaratively but interrogatively. This amounts to a proof that Plato's sun-like good is interrogative.

From the concatenation of (a)–(m) it is reasonable to conclude that Plato is operating in an at least implicit (unarticulated, unanalysed) awareness of the distinctions we label with terms such as 'interrogative', 'declarative', and 'roles or functions of a form', even though he does not mark them by special terminology and may not have scrutinized them reflectively. And by 'operating in awareness' I mean to imply 'operating sure-footedly' as distinct from happening along a coherent path by accident. Poets were using alliteration and assonance long before those terms were coined, and often, I should think, without carefully looking where to put their feet down before putting them down, but nonetheless putting them down in apt places skilfully and not accidentally.

So there is the form of the good in its sun-like, interrogative mode as distinct from its participated-in declarative mode. What, to fit in with this, should we say about the relevant other forms in the sun-analogy? (The relevant other forms, I have argued, are best thought of as virtue-relevant neutral types such as returning a borrowed item; see Section 3.4.) Well, in relation to the form of the good in *sun-like* or interrogative mode, these other forms cannot figure as participants. They participate neither in the form of the good nor in any contrary form. This corresponds to the fact that 'Is it good?', when asked of one of them, is a genuinely open question. Thus these other forms, too, have two different roles or functions: that of being subjects of the G-question, and that of helping to constitute the facts that make the true answers to it true.[19]

Even if all this is plausible, there is still room to ask why, given the distinction between modes or functions of the form of the good, Plato, by means of the sun-analogy, lavishes so much more attention on what I have called the interrogative mode. Why doesn't he, alongside the sun-analogy, say something about the form of the good in its other mode, that of being participated in by all good things? Well, let us recall that Socrates brings in the sun-analogy as his best shot in response to the brothers' demands that he tell them what the good, or the form of the good, *is* (506b–d). They are certainly not going to be satisfied with an answer that says, in whole or part, 'The form of the good is that whereby the many good things are good through participation in it.' This is because they are portrayed as having already, from many previous exchanges with Socrates, signed up in general to the one over many participation-doctrine, and as endorsing its application to 'good' along with other predicates. Socrates reminds them of this at 507a7–b7 (the backward reference, within the *Republic*, is to 476a1–8; cf. 596a5–9 and 597a4–9). So for them such an answer would be a truism, as Socrates knows. Now, Plato has Socrates remind them of the truism, and of their having already accepted it, just as he is about to set up the sun-analogy, which starts at 507c6 – the sun-analogy being the best response Socrates can make to the brothers' eagerness to be told what the form of the good is. Why does Plato have Socrates issue that reminder just here, at the moment of commencing the sun-analogy? Whatever the full reason, the positioning has an effect that can hardly not have been intended: it signals that the metaphysics of participation by many good things in the one participand form of the good will not be the gist of that best response. For if Anna knows that Bella is anxious to get from her the answer to question Q, then if Anna prefaces her answer with 'Let me first remind you of something you already know, namely P', it is unlikely that P itself is the answer which Anna is about to give to Bella's question Q.[20] It seems reasonable to expand this to: 'and it is unlikely that something *very obviously similar* to P is the answer which Anna is about to give'. I say this to take care of the fact that the familiar one–many contrast is often couched in terms of many sensible particulars versus one participand form, whereas within the sun-analogy any one–many contrast is going to be between many

---

[19] Trying to hold both functions together in a single perspective results in a Moore-style paradox: 'A is good but I am questioning whether A is good.'

[20] The default position is that if Bella already 'has' the answer in the sense of already knowing P, which constitutes the answer, then as soon as she wonders about Q she becomes aware of being able to fit P to Q *as* its answer; hence she does not need to consult Anna. I am leaving aside the issue of deeply buried knowledge that cannot be immediately called to mind by the sort of simple reminder that Socrates gives the brothers at 507a7–b7.

intelligibles and the one form of the good. It seems safe to discount this difference and infer that the familiar contrast, so far as it functions as a sort of foil to what Socrates is going to say via the sun-analogy, covers any participation of many in one form of the good, not merely the case where the many are sensible particulars.[21] So it seems safe to infer that the sun-analogy is not going to represent the 'other' forms as *participating* in the form of the good. And if metaphysical 'imitation' is equivalent to participation, the sun-analogy does not represent the other forms as imitating the form of the good either.[22] Furthermore, I believe, Plato relies on the good sense of the characters with whom Socrates converses (not to speak of the Socrates-character himself), and of the readers for whom he, Plato, is writing, not to start worrying that we've suddenly and without a word of explanation been dropped into a metaphysical *terra incognita* where two forms of the good both claim right of dominion. Yes, of course it is still true and could never not be true that the many things that *are* good are good by participating in the one and only form of the good; but now we are about to be shown something new and different about the same unique form of the good: namely, something of how this form functions in the context of *finding out which* things participate in it. As well as '*x* is good', there is 'Is *x* good?': one and the same form with two functions. The first is the participand, the second the sun-like function.

The immediate answer (conveyed by the sun-analogy) to the brothers' insistent question is that the form of the good is the tool for discerning which other things are good. But if by 'tool of inquiry' we mean 'effective' or 'successful' tool of inquiry, a tool that reliably gets at the truth about which other things are good, then the immediate answer has to be supplemented with most of what Plato covers in the long stretch between halfway through Book II to the end of Book VII of the *Republic*, where he scours from one angle after another, and in response to one after another objection, the nature, moral and intellectual, that has to be educationally developed in human beings if the tool as wielded by them is to lead reliably to true findings.

Finally: the interrogative function of the form of the good is arguably the primary one, i.e. prior to its non-interrogative function as the form participated in by the many good things. There are two grounds for this claim of priority. First, epistemologically the priority holds, since we can't properly grasp *that* something is good unless we have a reason for taking it to be so, and this mediation by reasons points backwards, so to speak, to the prior question

---

[21] In fact, back at 476a5–8 the many were types rather than sensible particulars (see Section 2.19 with the references in note 159).

[22] Thus the exchange at 507a7–b7 already rules out any account of the sun-like form of the good (such as the perfectionist one; see Section 3.5) that hinges on the idea that ordinary forms get their being by participation in the sun-like form. Cf. Ferrari 2013, 166–7.

whether the thing is good. Declaring 'X is good; here's why . . .' announces that one arrived at the judgement from a place where there was at least room to ask *whether* X is good, the space between question and answer where reasons for the answer grow.[23] So the wise judgement-that presupposes (logically, at least) the question-whether. Secondly, the sun-analogy is concerned with the relationship between the form of the good and forms of or connected with virtues and fundamental norms. But the relationship is ultimately for the sake of practice, i.e. the form of the good *qua* interrogative is brought to bear on those other forms in order that they be correctly identified so that true virtues and norms, not look-alikes, will be implemented on the empirical level. Such implementation will result in a host of new empirical good things, i.e. participants in the form of the good *qua* participand and non-interrogative. So, with respect to practicable kinds of good things, the form *qua* actually participated-in is in debt to the form *qua* interrogative. The participand form of the good generally owes its empirical participants to its interrogative sister. And if 'practicable kinds of good things' extends to the context of divine world-making (see Section 4.4), then it covers a huge range of natural kinds, so that ultimately the form of the good *qua* participated-in is massively in debt to its interrogative counterpart.[24]

The G-question with which we have been concerned so far, corresponding to the sun in the sun-analogy, is asked of forms, not empirical things, and with a view to practice. But as well as asking 'What sorts of things are good?' so as to put them into practice, one can also seek on the empirical level to understand the goodness of certain already existing things – 'In what way are they good?' – it being assumed that they *are* good. This teleological interest is the younger twin of the sun-like question. The younger twin is theoretical: it is the starting point for Platonic observers or scientists or historians who seek to explain

---

[23] Regardless of whether a temporally strung-out deliberation had to take place. There is more to be said, because some things, such as virtue, are essentially good, so that the 'reason' for their goodness is that they are what they are. Perhaps the overall point is that we should educate ourselves to know when we need reasons for judging that something is good. The educated would not (could not) stand back and *judge whether* virtue is good, *arriving at* the judgement that this is so (as if it might – epistemic modality – not have been) through weighing reasons why. Better to say that for the educated 'Virtue is good' is a presupposition, not a judgement, or that it is a judgement they always-already *have* made (aspect, not tense). (This is a formal consideration about 'virtue'; it allows for discussion of whether, e.g., justice *is* a human virtue; cf. 348c5–12.)

[24] So, in a way, Proclus was right to treat the participand form of the good as subordinate to its sun-like counterpart, although he was mistaken if he thought that the subordination consists in straightforward ontological dependence of the participand form *qua* form on the sun-like one. It consists, rather, in the fact that in general the sun-like form controls which empirical things, if any, come into being so as to participate in the participand. So in general the sun-like form controls whether the participand actually fulfils its nature and *is* participated in. See Section 4.4 for how this plays out in cosmopoiesis. I say 'in general' because presumably even for Plato good things can come into being by accident.

some existing phenomenon or even the existence of the cosmos itself. The younger twin presupposes a third-person benevolent intelligent originator, while the older twin is asked *by* a benevolent and hopefully intelligent about-to-be originator. If Plato's Callipolis were implemented on earth and its foundation-document, the *Republic*, were lost without trace, historians and political analysts coming upon the city entirely from the outside (as archaeologists so to speak) might explain its arrangements by asking the younger-twin question about them – provided they made the corresponding optimistic assumption about the city's founders and rulers (or if they simply asked themselves 'Why would I make a city like this?', since we assume ourselves to be well meaning and intelligent). Many scholars have sought to understand the *Republic*'s hints on the sun-like form of the good as somehow resonating with the teleological method of cosmic explanation which Socrates in the *Phaedo* so sorely missed in Anaxagoras and with which he is so generously compensated in the *Timaeus*. That sense of resonance is surely right, because the teleological question of Platonic cosmologists – and any Platonic historians of any actual Callipolis – is the sun-like G-question of *Republic* VI–VII turned inside out.

Let me recapitulate the different items discussed here and in the previous section under the ambiguous title '*the* good'. There is (a) the *bonum supremum*, the good that is one of many valued things such as health and power and pleasure, but is supreme among them because only in its ambit are the others truly worth getting and possessing. *The* good in this sense is on the same metaphysical level as the other goods, i.e. those rendered good by association with it. They are all 'practicables', things which can be pursued, obtained, possessed, wielded, at the physical and empirical level. I assume that for Plato in the *Republic* as elsewhere the *bonum supremum* is wisdom. Then, peculiar to the *Republic*, there is (b) the sun-like good, which in Section 4.1 I spoke of as 'what constitutes wisdom-in-action's cutting edge', and more laboriously as 'the interrogatively inflected content or intentional object of actively good-seeking wisdom or intelligence'. The sun-like good comes into the picture with the *use* of wisdom and is not itself in the category of practicable things. It bears the title '*the* good' because, given that wisdom is the *bonum supremum*, the sun-like good is wisdom-in-action's metaphysical determinant: it is in this sense supreme over the *bonum supremum*. And thirdly, there is (c) the participand form of the good, the familiarly Platonic 'one' in which 'many' things participate and are thereby good. It too is not a practicable, as Aristotle famously complained (*Nicomachean Ethics* 1096b32–34; *Eudemian Ethics* 1217b24–25). This is so in two senses. (1) As a form or intelligible it is not subject to coming-to-be. In this it is on a par with any form. (2) What the participand form of the good is the form *of* cannot be an immediate object of implementation. This is by contrast with, e.g., the forms of the virtues and forms of non-moral goods such as health and safety. That is to say: one cannot aim simply to produce or acquire *good* or *what is good* or *what participates in the form of the good* (and then devise means to that end); one can only aim to produce or acquire one or another good kind of thing (and devise means on that basis). Aiming to acquire or produce *good* without aiming to acquire or produce *some kind of thing or other* that's good is empty because it amounts to no more than aiming to produce something worth producing.[25] It is in non-empty aiming that every soul longs to be successful, and in this the soul can only succeed if it calls on the sun-like good to spotlight for it which (e.g.) virtue-candidates really are virtues by asking whether they are in fact good. Every soul pursues what it hopes will be genuine participants in the participand form of the good; but it cannot pursue them purely as such but only as this or that *sort* of good thing. So: to be successful a soul needs to be knowledgeable not only about the various sorts of valuable things in general but also about which objects or types of object really fall under such a sort as distinct from merely seeming to. Plato would, or anyway could, have agreed with Aristotle that the participand form of the good is not practicable. It becomes practicable only when parcelled out between the various categories, yielding *virtue* or *health* or *opportunity* or *due measure*, etc. But a story is still needed about how to distinguish real versions of these from spurious look-alikes, and this is where Plato's non-practicable sun-like good comes into play.

4.3   Why the Mathematical Education?

In the *Republic* the future rulers must undergo a long and intensive intellectual training to prepare them for dialectic. They must engage in a ten-year study of all the mathematical disciplines up to the most advanced level of Plato's time. The question of this section is: why is precisely this the suitable propaedeutic for dialectic? Actually, this question may seem a waste of time hermeneutically, because Plato many times gives the reason: it lies in the power of those disciplines, when undertaken in the right way (detached from empirical applications), to 'draw the soul towards truth' (521c1–8; 522e5–523a3; 524e4–525a14; 525b2–3; b9–c6; 526a8–b2; 527b4–10; 529b3–5; 533d1–4; cf. 526d7–e8). But how are we to understand 'drawing the soul towards truth'? Plato explains this as a matter of orientation. The imprisoned souls in the cave no doubt desire truth and think that they are getting it, but they are cut off from

---

[25] It is true that 'Will it do any good?' is a question we often ask when questioning the practical value of a project. (Thanks to the anonymous reader for pressing this.) But the answer is 'No' unless the project has a good chance of resulting in one or another specific kind of good such as health, security, moral betterment, promoting knowledge, etc. Of course, a positive answer in terms of one or more of these is only a necessary condition for moving into action; we are still short of the conclusion that doing so is best all things considered.

truth because they perceive only shadows and then images casting the shadows, and owe their vision in both cases to the light of the fire in the cave, not to the light of the sun. To begin the journey towards truth a soul has to turn or be turned away from its reliance on unexamined sensory and cultural inputs. The journey begins when it starts to puzzle over one and many, how the same thing shows up as both, and similarly with other opposites, and finds that the senses cannot settle the puzzlement (and unreasoned input from the culture cannot settle it either). It starts to ponder about one and two in the abstract, and an interest in abstract numbers has been born (523a–525c). The turn away from reliance on the senses, etc. has taken place, preparing the move into intensive mathematical training. The aim of the latter is to strengthen the new orientation, which is an orientation towards intelligible truth as such.[26]

A number of leading scholars hold that, according to the *Republic*, the future rulers must immerse themselves in mathematics in order to acquire a special kind of expertise – mathematical expertise – which they will need *in the very exercise of the dialectical reasoning* which lies ahead and is distinctive of rulers. It seems to me that the picture given us in the *Republic* does not support this view. There, Plato maintains that (1) a good dialectician and a good ruler needs an attitude towards truth that presupposes a deep mathematical education. He does not say that (2) the dialectician-ruler needs the deep mathematical education because dialectical thinking itself directly calls upon and employs professional mathematical expertise. Of course, (1) and (2) are compatible. Of course, too, it is completely obvious that Plato endorses (1). But (1) and (2) are different positions, and (1) does not entail (2). And it matters whether the *Republic* also incorporates (2) because this makes a very significant difference to how the dialogue conceives of dialectic and ultimately the form of the good. Consequently, the claim that position (2) is operative in the

---

[26] My treatment of the cave and the journey out of it is indebted to Schofield 2007. Schofield argues that the presentation is intentionally ambiguous between two incompatible perspectives. 'The Cave communicates not one philosophical vision but two' (216–17). The summary in this note follows Schofield in all essentials, differing in a few details and in the order of presentation. [A] Insofar as the exodus represents the mathematical curriculum of future rulers of Callipolis, the prisoners include youths reared in the guardian class (although some of them become auxiliaries, not rulers), as well as, presumably, everyone in the economic class. However, we are also told at the beginning (515a6) that [B] the prisoners are 'like us', which suggests that they are not merely rationally unawakened like the Callipolitan youths (see below in this section), but have grown up in a corrupt culture such as that of Athens. In [A] the shadows, etc. will by several removes be depthless and crude reflections of realities as they really are, while in [B] they will be reflections of distorted versions of those same realities, the distortion being due to the influence (confined to the cave) of demogogues, sophists, and uncensored poets. To add to the complexity, those who return to the cave are, according to [A], the Callipolitan philosopher-rulers whose return initiates their period in government, while according to [B] the returner is a Socrates-like character who goes down to face a mob who ridicule him, and would if they could kill anyone who tried to release them (517a). This section focuses on [A].

Republic needs good evidence. But the text itself furnishes virtually no evidence. Even so, some very distinguished and in general exemplary scholars do find (2) at work in this dialogue. I shall consider two approaches of this kind, although they often seem to be more or less combined.[27] One has it that for Plato the task of dialectic is or includes the task of giving mathematics what it cannot provide for itself, namely a foundation in an unconditional first principle. The other has it that the truly revealing ethical concepts are mathematical in nature.

On the first approach, Plato thinks that dialectic will provide mathematics with a basis whose non-hypothetical status is like that of the form of the good in dialectic.[28] Some indeed think that it is the job of dialectic to show how the form of the good itself is the ultimate principle of mathematics.[29] And, obviously, if it is the task of dialectic to give the ultimate foundation of mathematics, dialecticians will need expert knowledge of every field of mathematics. For they will need to be familiar with everything that is supposedly based on the ultimate foundation in order to be sure of formulating the correct theory of the foundation itself. However, the text itself, on a straightforward reading, almost entirely gives the impression that mathematics is perfectly fine as it is, starting from merely assumed or hypothetical starting points: that is its nature. It neither has nor needs a non-hypothetical starting point of its own, nor is it crying out to be anchored in some sort of pre-mathematical or meta-mathematical foundation.[30]

Almost entirely, for at 511c8–d2 we have:

because they [sc. the mathematicians] ... investigate ... only by using hypotheses,[31] they seem to you [Socrates] not to have an intelligent grasp of the things they study,

---

[27] As in, e.g., Burnyeat 2000, 46; Sedley 2007, 269–71.

[28] Cf. Cornford 1932b, 176–80; Gosling 1973, 102; Burnyeat 2000, 38, 41; Benson 2012, 192–3. *Pace* Burnyeat 2000, 38, 511b–c and 533c say only that mathematicians do not, not that the dialecticians do, account for the initial assumptions of mathematics.

[29] This approach understands the form of the good in the *Republic* as the One, which along with the Indefinite Dyad is the first principle of everything according to a theory current in the early Academy. The One featured in Plato's unsuccessful public lecture on the good (for a discussion of the evidence see Gaiser 1980). The One and the Dyad were held to generate the numbers. This may have been Plato's own theory at some point, but our question is whether it is necessary for explaining the *Republic*.

[30] Mathematicians and their admirers are at fault if they claim that mathematics is knowledge in the most demanding sense of the word, for that could only be true if the mathematicians' own starting points were more than mere assumptions. If they do claim this they are in a dream (533b5–c7), but the actual practice of mathematics does not depend on any such dogma. Even so, Plato's emphasis in the *Republic* on the fact that the starting points of mathematics are merely posited may have started, in him and others, a movement towards investigating the ultimate principles of number and dimension. But whether in the *Republic* itself he regards this as the, or even a, main task for the philosopher-rulers, or for dialectic, is a different question.

[31] In full, the 'because' clause says: 'because they don't investigate by rising up (*anelthontes*) to the true first principle <but> only by using hypotheses ...' On *anelthontes* at 511d1 (not part

although these are [or: would be] objects of intelligence when [or: if] <taken> together with a principle (*kaitoi noētōn ontōn meta archēs*).

The underlined words say that the objects of mathematics come or would come to be grasped at the highest cognitive level, here called 'intelligence', when or if they are grasped along with a foundational principle. Since the highest cognitive level is dialectic, the words suggest that dialectic raises the objects of mathematics to its own level by studying them in the light of a non-hypothetical principle.

I believe that S. R. Slings, the editor of the 2003 Oxford Classical Text of the *Republic*, was right to excise the crucial five-word phrase at d2 as an interpolation.[32] It had long been suspect because its use of *kaitoi* (modifying a participle) is almost unknown in the classical period. But to my mind the decisive point, discussed by Slings, is its location within a speech of Glaucon's (511c3–d5) with nothing equivalent ever being stated by Socrates. This speech as a whole is part of the finale to the Divided Line passage. Glaucon here repeats what Socrates has said to show he has understood: but the idea conveyed by the crucial phrase (and conveyed by it in a very clipped fashion) has not appeared before in the main exposition of the Line; nor does it appear in the immediately subsequent speech of Socrates summarizing and conclud-ing the Divided Line (511d6–e4), nor in his reprise of the Line at 533e3–534a8. So nothing like the crucial phrase occurs in the main exposition of the Line, and nothing like it is ever voiced by *Socrates*. The probability that Plato introduces a weighty and abstruse philosophical claim in this hit-and-run fashion is only just not zero.[33]

One is also bound to wonder how the supposedly dialectical ability to derive mathematics from meta-mathematical principles is relevant to helping the trainees become good *rulers*, even if one of these principles or the main one is identical with the form of the good. Even granted the identity one can

of the suspect passage), see Section 2.11. On whether there is tension between *noun ouk ischein peri auta* (d1–2) and the earlier classification of the objects of mathematics as *noēta* (511a4; cf. 534a2–3) see Adam 1907, 86–7.

[32] Slings 2003, xiv; 2005, 113–19.

[33] This is the philosopher who takes twenty-one lines to secure the point that seeing requires light (507c6–e3). The *Euthydemus*, whose chronological relation to the *Republic* is controversial, has a curious passage where Socrates speaks of mathematicians and astronomers handing their findings over to the dialectician to manage in some way that only the latter understands (*Euthydemus* 290c). This has been taken to mean that it is for the dialectician to discover the ultimate foundations of mathematics. However, as Rowe points out (2007b, 30), it may mean that the dialectician's job is to clarify that the visible heaven is not the true subject of the mathematical discipline of astronomy (cf. *Republic* 529a–530c). Or it may mean that only the dialectician can make sense of the ontology of mathematics; or that only the dialectician can identify the true value of mathematics, namely its power to draw souls out of the sleep of reason.

wonder why future rulers should need to care about the meta-mathematical implications of the supreme form when there will be so much for them to worry about in terms of some sort of practicable good. We, of course, cannot be sure that Plato did not imagine true ethical and political wisdom as essentially drawing on meta-mathematical expertise, but what it would be like in any sort of detail to imagine this is incomprehensible to us. Also, of course, what is incomprehensible to us might have been comprehensible to him; but acknowledging this does not help us if what we are trying to do is comprehend him.

One might ask too why the meta-mathematical programme is even *called* 'dialectic'. Is it simply to conjure up (what on this view would be) a transparently unreal link to the Socrates of earlier dialogues, who even if he sometimes engaged in a mathematical style of reasoning, surely never dreamed of meta-mathematics?

Even so, the meta-mathematical founding of mathematics might certainly be a suitable project for emeritus rulers. So could the idea be that when rulers-in-training reach the dialectical stage they are given a run of meta-mathematical theory just so as to acquire the burning interest in a post-retirement activity that will make them the best kind of rulers – the kind that does not love power and is only too glad to relinquish it (520d–521b; cf. 346e–347d)? If so, one may wonder why, if dialectic is understood as the meta-mathematical project, their training needs to include dialectic at all. Surely the intensive mathematics should be enough to rouse their curiosity about the meta-mathematical principles at the bottom of it all, making them eager to retire from government to find out more. One may certainly in that case wonder how a good preparation for *government* could consist in mathematics alone. But this question takes us to the second way of explaining why the future rulers have to learn so much mathematics.

According to the second approach, the form of the good, with which the dialectician rulers must cognitively engage, can be accessed only through the language of mathematics. Ethical reality is itself mathematical – mathematical in all its complex detail – just as physical reality as understood by scientists, including up to a point the Platonic scientist of the *Timaeus*,[34] is a wonder of mathematical structure.[35] That is why the future ruler must learn mathematics

---

[34] 'Up to a point' because while some major features of the Timaean cosmos are mathematically explained, not all are, in particular the anatomy of mortal animals, which is explained teleologically by reference to function.

[35] Cf. Gosling 1973, 102; Cooper 1977, 155; Burnyeat 1987; 2000; Sedley 2007, 269–71. For Burnyeat's Plato: 'mathematics is the route to knowledge of the Good because it is a constitutive part of ethical understanding', Burnyeat 2000, 73; cf. 45–6. Taylor 2008, 180, writes: 'the understanding of goodness is to be sought via the basic principles of mathematics' (but not everyone is as frank as Taylor in admitting that this interpretation is speculative, without 'direct

as fully as possible. One difficulty with this interpretation is that there is no direct evidence for it in the *Republic*.[36] Another is that it asks us to ascribe to Plato a view of ethical wisdom such that we cannot begin to imagine how this wisdom would frame the kinds of questions and derive the kinds of answers that human rulers, even ideally good ones, have to wrestle with. Granted, Plato can imagine things that we could never have imagined before he expressed them, but it does not follow that he can imagine just anything that we cannot. It is also surprising that Socrates never indicates to Glaucon and Adeimantus that the trainees need mathematics because the ethical reality that will concern them as rulers is at heart mathematical. This would have been easy to state in general terms, even if there is no hope of the brothers following the nitty-gritty of the rulers' handling of ethical concepts. It would not have been difficult to make Socrates say: 'It is beyond your technical competence to understand, and mine to explain to you, exactly how it is that the good and the virtues cannot be expertly grasped except through mathematics: but that it is so is what – even though I might be wrong – I am convinced one ought to believe.' Moreover, given that philosophers' apparent uselessness to society was a major discussion point near the beginning of the whole theme of philosopher-rulers (487d–489d), one might have expected one of the brothers to respond to the supposed counterfactual speech of Socrates by saying: 'Very well, Socrates; we, of course, accept your judgement that we are not expert enough to grasp exactly how true understanding of the good and the virtues is a sort of mathematical understanding. But please at least tell us whether, according to this idea, the rulers' mathematical wisdom leads them to better ethical and political decisions than could be made by an intelligent right-minded person using only ordinary terms, or whether it leads them to practical judgements that, although no doubt more *scientific*, are not necessarily more or more often *correct*; and if

textual confirmation', 182). Sedley 2016, 16: 'there is not much doubt that [these Platonic definitions of value terms] … would look, to our eyes, like fundamentally mathematical analyses, embodying high-level principles of complex proportionality'.

[36] The indirect evidence consists in the striking 'reticences' or 'deliberately left gaps' (the phrase of Szlezák 2015) in Books VI and VII, i.e. indications by Socrates that there is much more to say about the form of the good and the rulers' wisdom than is said in the dialogue itself; see 435d1–3; 503a7–9; 504b1–c4; 506d5–e4; 507a1–5; 517b6–8; 533a1–5. If this 'more' is the meta-mathematical ontology of the One and the Dyad, or the deeply mathematical nature of the good itself, Plato has an obvious reason for making his rulers mathematical experts. Cf. Burnyeat 1987, suggesting that the technical difficulty of the higher mathematics explains Socrates' reticence about the nature of 'the dialectical research programme', 231–2. But if the reticence can be accounted for, as I think it can (see Section 2.18), without reference to unwritten theories circulating in the early Academy, we have to identify a different reason for the mathematical education. (Burnyeat 1987, 238, admits the difficulty of believing 'that the goodness [i.e. the beauty of harmony and proportionality] which resides in mathematical relationships is one and the same with the goodness one needs to know to govern oneself and others', but he does not see this as telling against ascribing such a view to Plato.)

the latter, please give us some idea of why, if rulers' being philosophers means their being masters of mathematicized ethics, the philosophy makes them the slightest bit more useful as rulers?'[37] However the counterfactual conversation might continue, I hope that imagining it up to this point brings out legitimate doubts about the targeted view.[38]

Obviously, the theory that according to Plato mathematics is the language of ethics (human ethics) may take more and less extreme forms. In an extreme form, which surely no scholar would wish to endorse, Glaucon and Adeimantus would be entitled to ask Socrates (in the counterfactual conversation) whether the rulers' moral education – whether the moral virtues of justice, temperance, and courage in which they were brought up before they entered the intellectual curriculum – contributes *anything at all* to the wisdom they exercise as rulers. Of course, as citizens and as setters of examples the rulers must be morally virtuous, but Glaucon and Adeimantus might reasonably have wondered what this has to do with their special wisdom if the latter is mathematical in nature. For it is a fact of experience that expertise in mathematics does not necessarily go with being especially courageous, temperate, or just. If, on the other hand, we think that Plato's rulers' wisdom is, *qua* wisdom, necessarily infused with the moral virtues, then scholars who claim that it is also somehow mathematical owe us some suggestion on how one might coherently conceive of this infusion of moral virtue into, or its integration with, mathematical insight. If no more or less convincing suggestion is forthcoming, perhaps philosophical readers should conclude that Plato has marched off along a seriously cranky track.[39]

Perhaps help is to be found in a more relaxed approach, one that takes its cue from Plato's not exactly controversial view that a sense of balance, proportion, due measure, and harmony (what fits well with what) is essential for ethical wisdom (442c4–7; 486d; 500c; 531c). So ethical reality – the real formal structures that render our value-judgements objectively true when they *are* objectively true – is balanced, proportionate, and so on. This theme is common between the *Republic* and other dialogues (*Gorgias*, *Philebus*, *Statesman*) where interpreters generally do not take it to signal that Plato means that we

---

[37] Cf. *Meno* 97a–d: correct opinion is as good a practical guide as knowledge.

[38] Both this view and the one that tasks dialectic with uncovering the foundations of mathematics may even prompt the unpleasant thought that Plato is so inexplicit on such matters because he is aware that the question of usefulness might reasonably occur to a supposedly average mind such as that of Glaucon or the ordinary reader, and chooses not to stir it up because he has no good answer that they could understand or find acceptable.

[39] Some might think this anyway on the basis of Plato's nuptial number (546b–547a) and his calculation that the king's pleasure is seven hundred and twenty-nine times truer than the tyrant's (587b–d). But these numerological exuberances are curlicues on the main philosophy. A deeply mathematicized conception of human ethical wisdom (for which, let's not forget, there is no direct evidence in the *Republic*) would be right at the heart of the main philosophy.

must become advanced mathematicians in order to achieve ethical wisdom. Yes, social arrangements should be balanced, proportionate, harmonious, and rational (like geometry; cf. *Gorgias* 508a); but much more than this has to be said to persuade anyone that social balance and proportion would be so abstruse and technical that fully discerning such relationships can only be an exercise of professional mathematical expertise.[40] It is uncontroversial that in the *Republic* Plato holds that the excellence of the rulers' judgements *presupposes* such expertise. And no doubt he thinks that mathematical training enhances one's feel for balance and harmony in other areas; and perhaps this is true. What I am disputing is the different claim that in the *Republic* mathematical expertise is presupposed because it is directly brought to bear in the very making of the rulers' judgements.

It may be that fundamentally the same sensibility and feel for structure come into play both in apprehending the beauty of a geometrical proof and in appreciating the ingenious design of a settlement giving all parties what they justly deserve; but it does not follow that intellectual access to the structure of the just settlement is available only to those with advanced mathematical training, any more than it follows that access to the proof is available only to those with good ethical judgement. Nor does it follow that someone who understands the settlement solely in terms such as 'reparation that takes proper account of the rights and interests not only of victims but also of the perpetrator's innocent dependents' is missing a profounder layer of ethical reality hiding beneath the surface and graspable only by an intellect thoroughly trained in complex manipulations of mathematical concepts.[41]

---

[40] For scepticism about Plato's mathematicization of ethics see Shorey 1895, 218–23: 'mathematics was the dominant, the only definitely constituted, science of the day, and in every age ethical speculation has always borrowed its imagery, its analogies, and its terminology, from the leading contemporary science' (219). For an illuminating nuanced treatment of the question see Johansen 2013.

[41] Attributing the 'profounder layer' notion to Plato, Burnyeat 2000 quotes Reichenbach's telling statement of the difference between the real (physicalist) and manifest images of the world ('We see the iron stove before us as a model of rigidity, solidity, immovability; but we know that its particles perform a violent dance, and that it resembles a swarm of dancing gnats more than the picture of solidity we attribute to it', etc.) As Reichenbach's dancing particles are all that there objectively is in physical terms (he calls our manifest image a 'substitute world'), so Plato's mathematicized values are all there objectively is in ethical terms, as compared with the veil of ethical phenomenology generated by, in Burnyeat's words, our 'particular parochial perspective'. Burnyeat seems to overlook the possibility that postulating such a radical split between ethical reality as it is and as it appears to almost everyone would lead not merely to what he does envisage, namely the radical critique of most people's values, but also (as history shows did happen with the analogous split between appearance and reality of the physical world) to extreme scepticism about all ordinary values of all of us: it becomes untenable (or anyway inexplicable) that Solon any more than Plato's tyrannical man (unless Solon was a secret mathematician) *knew* – or even had reliably true belief about – 'the difference between right and wrong'. Do we want it to be Plato who opens the door to all this?

It appears that interpreters who explain the role of mathematics in the rulers' curriculum in ways such as these are loath to believe that Plato's own stated explanation is the whole explanation.[42] Plato's stated explanation is that intensive, comprehensive, training in abstract mathematics is needed to turn the soul away from immersion in sense experience and the like, so as to ally it firmly with reason. But evidently this is felt not to be an adequate explanation by itself. And I think that this feeling is understandable. What sort of non-rationality would it be that can only be decisively cured by ten or so years of comprehensive mathematics up to the most advanced level? Did Socrates himself have that depth of mathematical training?[43] Any interpretation needs to find a perspective from which the rulers' mathematical education drops into place as the solution to a problem for Plato. I have argued that the text of the *Republic* offers virtually no evidence that his problem lies either in meta-mathematical ambitions for dialectic or in the theory that ethical reality itself is mathematically structured. In addition, I see less relevance than some scholars do in the fact that major features of Plato's physical universe, as recounted in the later dialogue *Timaeus*, are mathematically structured because such structures help make the universe as good and beautiful as possible. Yes, it is certainly true that the god who constructed the Timaean universe had to be quite a formidable mathematician. But the human rulers of Plato's *Republic* do not have the task of organizing a physical cosmos from scratch.[44] Nor does

---

[42] The inference is explicit in M. White 2006, 233.

[43] The Socrates-character could not have been expert in stereometry, since at the *Republic*'s dramatic date this subject is in its infancy (528b–c).

[44] In general it seems unsafe to assume that since Plato found it possible and fertile to mathematicize central phenomena of physics and cosmology, he would therefore have found it possible and fertile to mathematicize human ethical values. In the *Timaeus* he thinks of the activity of both the cosmic soul and the human rational soul as mathematically structured circular motion. The human version gets out of kilter, but we can correct this by contemplating the regular motions of the heavens (90c–d). In this way we alleviate the malady underlying bad ethical judgement; but it does not follow that the *content* of good ethical judgements is or ever could be itself mathematical (any more than it follows that it is astronomical). The *Timaeus* theory is comparable to the contemporary view that human mental functioning is ultimately neuronal activity. But, as 'ultimately' hints, one can accept this part of the materialist picture while rejecting the possibility of conceptual reduction of the language of mind and value to the language of neuroscience; and this is a common, even mainstream, position in contemporary philosophy. Why should we assume that Plato simple-mindedly embraces conceptual reduction of ethical language to the language of mathematical structures? Note too that the most complexly mathematicized aspects of the Timaean cosmos, namely the rational soul and the structure of the elemental particles, are beyond reach of empirical verification, so Plato can let his mathematico-aesthetic imagination roam free. If one tried to make a practice of identifying, e.g., human justice with some particular kind of complex mathematical structure embracing (somehow) all three parts of the soul (the Timaean psychology is the same as that of the *Republic*), one of two things would follow for Callipolis. Either there would be some way of independently identifying the presence of this structure in individuals or their conduct, or not. If not, the mathematical aspect would contribute nothing towards shaping and upholding good

Plato ever say in the *Republic* that either their education or their activity as rulers must include mathematically informed contemplation of the physical world whether as inspiration or as example.

This negative result faces us with an explanatory gap which the reviewed suggestions have tried to fill. What do we put in their place? The answer I shall defend is that Plato identifies intensive abstract long-lasting mathematical work as the pre-dialectical cure for what he sees as human reason's extreme vulnerability, especially in the field of ethical judgement. But this is pretty much what we already know he says in the *Republic*: mathematical learning redeems us from bondage to the senses and the social environment. That this seems implausible as a complete explanation is, I suspect, because it is hard to believe that anyone could hold that *so much* mathematics is required for that. The amount of medicine Plato throws at the illness seems out of all proportion to the gravity of the illness itself, although no one doubts that for him the illness is very grave. The perceived disproportion between depth of problem and depth of cure naturally prompts the inference that a significant part of what we are calling his cure must really be designed for a different purpose, to solve an additional problem – the supposed additional problem being that the tasks awaiting the rulers are of a sort they will only be able to handle by bringing deep mathematical expertise into play in the very handling. After all, in our world those who study mathematics intensively for many years do so either just for its own sake or because they aim at a career that uses a lot of mathematics, say in software engineering or cryptography. Plato's Callipolitan students study mathematics not just for its own sake but for the sake of a career in government, so Plato must conceive of this career in government as involving a lot of on-the-job mathematical thinking.

The strategy of my response to this picture is to try to undermine that sense of disparity between the magnitude of the problem of reason's vulnerability, and the magnitude of Plato's solution, by bringing out the depth of the problem he finds himself facing. The aim is to show that it is so massive that ten whole years of mathematical study would not be an exaggerated solution. There are two aspects to consider: one concerned with universal limitations of the human being, and the other with the special context of Plato's Callipolis.

---

mores in the community: dialectician-rulers like everyone else would have to identify justice and its absence by the familiar criteria. If, alternatively, there were (by some method which no one has bothered to try to imagine) independent access to the presence of the mathematical justice-structure, then in principle the pattern of its occurrences in actual cases might diverge from the pattern of the presence of justice as judged by familiar criteria. (Cf. contemporary dreams in some quarters of identifying altruism with a chemical state of the brain.) Would mathematicizing interpreters respond to the possibility of divergence by insisting that mathematical justice without the familiar quality would be the true virtue, and the familiar quality without mathematical justice a 'false positive'?

We must set aside any idea that the basic cause undermining rationality and the right use of reason consists in unruly or misdirected passions. Obviously in the world in general unruliness or excessive focus on pleasure or power puts people on a collision course with reason; but these motives cannot be the locus of the primal fault. For Plato's 'cure' is designed for young people who, thanks to their very strict upbringing in the guardian class in Callipolis, followed by a selection process ensuring that only the best of their cohort go on to higher education (537a9–11; b7–8), are paragons of right values and good behaviour. Plato's cure is the correlate not of a contingent illness, something that could in principle be done away with under better social and educational conditions, but of a universal inborn human weakness like mortality itself. The vulnerability of reason is analogous to original sin, except that on Plato's view redemption is in our own hands.

The beginning of the problem is that human beings necessarily from birth grow up accepting sensory information from the physical environment and values from the social environment. On the sensory front we do not need to discover why something is the case in order to ascertain that it is the case: the 'craftsman of our senses' (507c6–7) has given us good sense faculties that mostly work well without our having to monitor them. On the social front we cannot get going in the world at all without simply accepting the say-so of others on a vast range of matters including historical matters and matters of value.[45] It can easily happen that by the time someone is approaching adult-hood, he or she has a deeply ingrained habit of uncritically accepting what senses and culture say, not asking or even knowing how to ask whether there is a deeper or more complex truth behind the wide, thick, swathes of what one is accepting. If everyone around us is like this too, there is also the ever-present pressure to conform. The ability to question and examine perspectives osmotically absorbed since birth and never challenged by those with whom we live does not develop automatically in the individual, even though it is a natural ability. Like the powers of sight and hearing it is innate in us, but unlike them is not automatically activated by ordinary commerce with our surroundings. It has to be aroused by something or someone that jerks us out of our comfort-zone, something we can't assimilate and can't get past, such as the finger which is both long and short (523a–524b), or a strange person throwing

---

[45] At 517b1–3 Socrates says that the visible world corresponds to the cave and the light of the fire in the cave corresponds to the power of the sun. In order to accommodate culturally conditioned reactions, we must take this to mean that imprisonment in the cave stands for that level where all our reactions are as rationally unmediated and confident as sensory impressions typically are; the shadows for which the fire is responsible include sense-impressions but also uncritical ethical impressions. Lumping these together may seem awkward, but after all for the prisoners their experience is all one network or barrage: it is not neatly divided into impressions of sensible objects and impressions of value.

questions at us from an abstract perspective we had no idea even existed until this moment (515c–d).[46] The strange person's questions are meant to get us, ourselves, to become questioners. And for that to happen we almost certainly need to be shown by example some first steps along the path of looking for answers (leave aside *finding* them: if we've never set foot on the path, we can't conceive what it would be like to be at the other end of it). For, arguably, when faced with a question that we can't answer just by looking around us or checking what the accepted view is, we also can't even enter into *asking* it if we are devoid of any sense of what it would be like to look for an answer. We get dizzy and the question slides away from us. Arguably, too, if the question slides away beyond the margin of our intellectual horizon, it is hard to get any purchase on believing that there really is a truth of the matter one way or the other, since for us the matter has been defined by a question we could not get inside the asking of.[47] Or in some cases, as with the real being and nature of the gods, one might have a sense that much more lies in that direction than the inkling we possess, but an equally strong sense that it is completely beyond human competence ever to get cognitive access to that 'much more'.

This is the early condition of everyone, including the young people of Callipolis who include the next generation of rulers. But in their case it is enormously intensified by special features of their culture: the authoritarianism of the regime; the eradication of individualism through communal parents, children, and living arrangements; and the banning of debate for young people. Plato is terrified that exposing the young to dialectical debate will infect them with nihilism about values and the objectivity of truth (537c–539d).[48] It seems that he wants them to enter higher education without ever having sat in on or taken part in an abstract discussion of how we should live. Yet some of them are going to be rulers and will themselves have to determine the truth about what is good and bad for the city often in complex situations with different factors pulling in different directions and potentially affecting many lives. Just as Plato wants his city to start from a blank slate (501a; cf. 541a), so he wants his twenty-year-old future rulers to enter the higher academy virginally untainted by the tussle of criticism and argument over ethical abstractions and principles. As children they will have learned how to do some calculations and geometrical exercises along with all the strictly controlled music, dance, and poetry (cf. 536d), but all this does not fit one out for raising and

---

[46] '... the fact that enlightenment is "natural" to us does not entail that we are born to it or find it easy to attain', Barney, 2008, 365.

[47] Logical positivism thus makes sense if relativized to some given level of intellectual literacy: if a level is such that those at it have no notion of how to answer question Q, question Q is meaningless at that level.

[48] At 515b4 the question is raised whether prisoners in the cave are in a position to *dialegesthai*, but this only means 'having conversations with each other'.

pursuing deeper questions.[49] They will be musically cultivated, imbued with impeccable values, including deep respect for the authorities over them, and outstandingly self-disciplined: but all that is a million miles away from having an intellect ready for the problems they will face when *they* are the ultimate authorities. They will be lovely young people, but for getting to the truth on matters of depth about ethics and human nature, they will be as nakedly unprepared as the lovers of sights and sounds. They do not know how to think about such things and are probably unaware that they even *can*. When faced with questions about the virtues and what is virtuous, the most they can do is echo the norms in which they have been reared.[50] Like many of us they have got used to being gracefully sure of themselves without any struggle of self-questioning, although in their case this has so far not led to disaster because their upbringing and limited environment have been perfectly healthy. But unlike us they have never been led to doubt any of their values by some perceived discrepancy between what they learnt at home and what seems to be approved by elements in the surrounding culture: for *their* upbringing and surrounding culture are perfectly co-ordinated parts of a single philosophically designed plan. If any surprising ethical idea were dropped into their midst, they would not know what to do with it. When faced with examples showing that the same kind of thing is both just and unjust, they will be paralysed as to how to proceed, or, worse, their sense of the objectivity of the indoctrinated norms will start to be whittled away.[51]

Immersion in mathematics is Plato's answer to this very real although partly self-inflicted problem of the future rulers' intellectual immaturity.[52]

---

[49] Lines 536d–e emphasize that the children should enjoy their lessons in calculation and geometry. I take it that this is about acquiring the skills, whereas only later comes the realization that exercising them presupposes a whole world of intelligible reality. This ontological realization develops through the ten-year total immersion in mathematics when they are not simultaneously learning dances, and music whose sensible patterns might grip them as supremely real. It is an exaggeration to think of the early education as non-rational or pre-rational *simpliciter* since it includes techniques of mathematical reasoning (needed, in any case, for various activities of the economic class). It is non-rational or pre-rational about fundamental values, not about everything. See Jenkins 2015. My thanks to Charles Brittain for making me get clearer on this.

[50] Cf. Benson forthcoming. Schofield 2007, 229–30, thinks that in the context of the ideal city, bondage in the cave means simply reliance on the senses. But it must also include unreflective reliance on cultural indoctrination, although these prisoners are lucky enough to have been brought up with morally healthy values.

[51] This problem of the inability of the twenty-year-olds to think for themselves was identified by Annas 1981, 87–8.

[52] But according to Rowett 2016 (a brilliant treatment of the 'Noble Lie' passage, 414d–415c), something of the utmost importance will happen to them just before they start the ten-year immersion in mathematics. Along with everyone in their age-cohort they will undergo a rite of passage to adulthood at which is instilled in them the self-understanding that up to now they have all, metaphorically, been embryo-humans dreamily gestating in the womb of the earth, so that only just now are they actually born into the world. (The earth-womb is a version of the

(We should probably see the ten years of mathematics as covering what for us is sixth-form level followed by undergraduate education followed by studies at master's and doctoral level, although it is not said that the trainees must carry out original research.) Through doing mathematics not in association with physical numbers or quantities, but as a way of getting to know the mathematical connections in themselves, they become aware of these as holding by themselves, or, as we say, in the abstract. Previously it would hardly have occurred to them, since there was no need for it to do so, that as well as twenty-four horsemen and their twenty-four mounts, there is also such a thing as the number twenty-four itself which has always in some sense been 'there' whether or not there are physical groups to be numbered by it. They become aware now (never having thought about it before) that it is *because* the abstract number twenty-four exceeds the abstract number twenty that a troop of twenty-four horses is bigger than a troop of twenty, not the other way round. They know such things now, although without having any particular metaphysical notion of how the abstract numbers exist and how they are related to physical things. They become sharply aware that although they reason by studying diagrams and models, they are reasoning about things which are inaccessible to the senses and whose nature never changes, since the diagrams may be in different perishable materials in different places, but what one returns to is unquestionably *the same* problem and *the same* proof (510d–511a). They begin to realize that the mathematical relationships have an inescapably systematic necessity that makes their own pre-mathematical sense-impressions of round things and square things seem now insecure, insubstantial, and even infantile. They realize that although they could tell which things were round and which were square, they hardly knew what they were talking about. They become aware that there is a great and interesting world 'out there' to be enjoyed only by reasoning. They start to swim under their own power in this new medium, and so learn to be at home in it. Through engagement they absorb the realization that the territory of pure mathematics is like an environment stretching beyond whatever place they have arrived at, and that the only way to travel it is by argument. So they learn how arguing leads towards serious discovery of truth – not just a game of verbal puzzles and eristic sparring where the inability to settle anything doesn't matter since the whole point is only to feel and show how clever we are and to outdo others. If they do discuss with each other and proceed by questions and answers, which seems

cave of unknowing in Book VII.) Hence they will now go forward to their different callings (depending on which metal has been developing in the soul of each, 415a–c) with the sense that *real* life starts for them only now and will be very different from what they experienced before. So those chosen for the rulers' curriculum will enter it in a highly positive spirit and ready to shed previous attitudes, even if they struggle at first to adapt to the new climate of thought.

highly likely,[53] they are aware all the time that a third party is present at the debate, namely the mathematical truth itself, and that the notion of outdoing or getting the better of *it* would make nonsense of their whole activity. They find that by following mathematical procedures one can discover surprising things and things which a pre-mathematical mind might have dismissed as ridiculous (e.g. that not all lines are commensurable). They learn that the proof is not a ladder to its conclusion, dispensable on arrival, since knowing *that* the result is true essentially involves understanding *why*. And they learn to be intelligent critics of their own and each other's arguments, looking for gaps and discrepancies. Given that the twenty-year-olds had never before been plunged into this or any similar world of co-ordinated non-sensory demands and standards, a decade spent acquiring, through mathematics, insiders' knowledge of what reason can do seems not excessive for forming in them what they will sorely need when they turn to ethical questions, namely an unshakeable trust in the objectivity and detailed complexity of the truth, and in rationality and their own ability to reason. What the total immersion in mathematics gives them is not a bit of 'mind-sharpening' or mental gymnastics to polish up their general intellectual effectiveness,[54] but induction into the whole world of intellect and practice of systematic rationality. Once domesticated or civilized into it they practise its exactness as unthinkingly as we all take for granted the subliminal fine-tuned protocols of our bodies' adjustment for getting around in the physical milieu. Unless mathematics has done its transformative work there is no hope of the trainees having success in what for Plato, it seems, is the most demanding kind of thinking of all, namely the exercise of ethical and political wisdom. But the text gives no reason for supposing that according to him the exercise of ethical and political wisdom is itself a mathematical kind of thinking.

(In view of the prevalence of a certain 'contemplative' picture of what Plato means by intellection, fostered by his own language at times, it is worth emphasizing that the purpose of the mathematical education is not train the students to get a fix on pure intelligible objects and then look at them very carefully. It is to teach them to trust their own power of reasoning to ask relevant questions and work towards answers. The truth that concerns them does not just open itself up to a pure intellectual gaze any more than to an impure sensory one; we discover it by actively conjecturing answers and looking for reasons why one is better than another. The answers are not just

---

[53] Cf. Netz 1998, section 6; Burnyeat 2000, 26–7; Netz 2003, 301–2 on oral presentation of mathematics. *Meno* 86e–87b imagines a conversation between geometers, and see *Republic* 525d6 and 526a2 on mathematicians 'holding discussions about (*dialegesthai peri*) numbers'.

[54] This is rightly dismissed by Burnyeat 2000, but he gives too little weight to the difference between mind-sharpening and acclimatization into the world of abstract thinking as such.

there waiting for us to come across them. If we are passive towards this kind of truth, this truth, and much of our intellectual capacity, might as well not exist.) In the *Meno* Socrates seeks to establish whether virtue can be taught by borrowing from geometry the move of identifying the condition on which the proposition being investigated would be true and examining whether the condition holds (86e–87d). This seems to be a case of the hypothetical method outlined at *Phaedo* 100a and 101c–e. Both dialogues assume that through 'recollection' (illustrated in the *Meno* by the episode with the slave) we can find our way not only to geometrical truth but also to philosophical truth about values. Such features suggest that Plato at one stage saw ethical reasoning and geometrical reasoning as similarly deductive. I have argued in Sections 2.3 and 2.17 that if at some point he held this view, the *Republic* shows him rejecting it, at any rate if ethical thinking is to have a hope of being practical. If that interpretation is correct, then when in Book VII he gets to the topic of mathematics as propaedeutic to dialectic, this is not because he treats both disciplines as resulting in deductive proofs and systems. Instead, what unites them is something more generic: namely that both are ways of discovering truth about things not accessible to the senses or to culturally conditioned sensibilities as expressed in unmediated judgement, and both demand and repay rigorous exactness.

The mathematician and the dialectician of the *Republic* share another characteristic: both must have cultivated the ability to 'see things synoptically'. In the case of mathematics this means, Plato tells us, looking at the five different branches of mathematics together as forming an ordered and unitary field and discerning the affinities and analogies between them (531c–d; 537b–c; cf. 510c5; 511b1; 530d on 'sister' notions and disciplines).[55] Achieving such a synoptic perspective in mathematics clearly goes beyond the exercise of deductive skill; it involves stepping outside any given one of the five branches, and it could lead to the discovery, through analogy and abstraction, of new branches of mathematics just as solid geometry had been a recent discovery according to Socrates.[56] Plato sees 'synopsis' in mathematics as an important bridge to dialectic, because 'if you're not capable of a synoptic view of things you can't be good at dialectic' (537c7, apparently the first occurrence

---

[55] Miller 1999 gives a detailed analysis of the interrelationships and pedagogical order of the five disciplines (arithmetic, plane geometry, solid geometry, the mathematics of solids in motion, and harmonics or the theory of ratios), showing how carefully Plato has arranged them so that they lead naturally to the threshold of the more abstract forms studied by dialectic. See also Burnyeat 2000, 67–70.

[56] Is Plato recommending this synoptic view of mathematics only to his imagined trainee rulers as answering to a special need of theirs, or also to real mathematicians? If the latter it seems he was opening up a new vista; see Reviel Netz's work showing that early Greek mathematics focused on solving individual or 'local' problems rather than on adding to the development of an all-encompassing system (Netz 2003, 315–17, referring to Netz 2004 for the full treatment).

of *sunoptikos*). But he does not explain what looking at things synoptically means in the case of dialectic. The idea, not surprisingly, has been interpreted in terms of a panorama of the whole of reality as hierarchically dependent on its first principle, whether this is the form of good or the form of unity, or a panorama of all the sciences including mathematics as somehow jointly springing from that same first principle. However, insofar as dialectic subserves government in the best city – and this is its primary task in the *Republic* and the basis on which dialectic was introduced into the discussion – it seems to me that 'synopsis' must at the very least refer to the good practical thinker's readiness to look beyond any course of step-by-step reasoning to take in the circumstances under which a conclusion might be implemented and to assess the relevance of features of the context.[57] From this synoptic perspective anything could be relevant, so dialecticians must be ready to take an intelligent interest in anything – to welcome any sort of consideration into their thinking. 'Sorry, that's not my field' is their anti-motto. (Cf. 474c–475c on the universality of the philosopher's interest.) In this they differ not only from mathematicians, whose inferences are constrained by their limited set of starting points, but also from practitioners of the productive *technai* (mentioned briefly at 533b2–5) who, insofar as their expertise is defined in terms of a certain type of result, are judged good or bad operators solely by the quality of the result as a thing of its kind regardless of circumstances of production or consumption. The philosopher-rulers' ability to think outside the box day by day would also give them the confidence and poise to take a periodic step back from the whole complex operation of the city to reflect on policy and priorities across the board. Such 'architectonic' thinking constitutes a more self-consciously holistic synoptic assessment, and it too is surely part of what Plato has in mind.[58] And philosopher-rulers in any generation must understand and be able to teach

---

[57] Cf. Cornford 1932b, 182. Plato recommends to mathematicians a synoptic grasp of the *mutual relevance* of the parts of their subject: *sunakteon eis sunopsin oikeiotētos allēlōn*, 537c2. I hazard the guess that he thinks of the dialectician-ruler in the same terms, i.e. as noting the *mutual relevance* of various considerations insofar as they bear on a practical solution. They 'belong to each other' because of their shared relevance for leading to the truth. Thus, at a high level of generality the good dialectician and the good mathematician *pick out exactly the same property* in exercising 'synopsis', although the criteria in each case are radically different. Plato may have been less struck than we are, following Aristotle (*Nicomachean Ethics* VI, 1139a5–14), by the fact that in mathematics mutual relevance is grounded in timeless and necessary features, whereas in the rulers' dialectic it belongs to contingently convergent factors which have different bearings in different contexts. Acuteness in seeing what is relevant to some fact or possibility S depends on readiness to try unfamiliar perspectives and comparisons that might turn out to be highly pertinent to S; and this holds in both mathematics and ethics. The topic of synopsis is not far removed from that of creativity in any sort of thinking.

[58] If or when dialectic is put to more purely theoretical work, one of its characteristics is still the synoptic stance: dialectic is not a special science, so no kind of consideration is as such outside its purview; cf. Aristotle, *Topics* 101a26–b4, on the use of dialectic to establish certain basics of specific sciences.

their successors to understand the rationale of the basic principles on which
their city was founded, since otherwise they and the successors will manage
their inherited institutions mechanically and unintelligently (cf. 497c8–d2).[59]
So dialectical training should develop the synoptic perspective of the political
philosopher. At the mathematical level, then, cultivating synopsis over all five
branches is valuable, not only because it may open doors to new mathematical
possibilities, but also as practice for dialectical reasoning, where tunnel-vision
is one of the worst dangers. Plato may even have feared that the principle that
each should do the task for which he or she is most suited might be taken as
implying that the ruler's proper business is to stay always in the same groove
of thinking.

This readiness to look outside the box, along with other intellectual habits of
utmost importance for rulers, is developed by studying *mathematics* because
mathematics is a field whose subject-matter is free from any propensity to
arouse emotions and feelings such as fear, jealousy, anger, hatred, partiality,
longing for material possessions or social prominence, and so on.
Mathematicians impress us with the precision of what they do, but what makes
it easy for them to insist on the utmost precision is the fact that their kind of
subject-matter generates no temptation to blur or twist meanings of terms and
steps in arguments, or to accept other people's blurred and twisted terms and
steps as good or good enough. They do not need *courage* in order to think
correctly, courage being defined as that whereby the spirited part of the soul
preserves against pleasures and pains the messages reason sends about what is
or is not fearsome (442b10–c2). Mathematics, because of the nature of its
subject-matter, is a safe space for acclimatizing – even addicting – human
minds to the objectivity and reality of facts and relationships that can only be
discovered by intellect.[60] Plato's future rulers will one day have to make
ethical judgements that will be implemented in policy and practice. Their
reasonings, however profound, will have to issue in answers to practical
problems that come up in the life of their city. But the vehicle of any practical
problem is an empirical situation in an empirical environment lived in by them
as well as by ordinary citizens. This is a fact about a ruler's subject-matter.
Hence rulers' reasoning cannot be shielded from the kinds of sensory and

---

[59] See A. G. Long 2013b, 21–2, 25.
[60] The distinctive remoteness of mathematical topics from life's fears and angers, etc. solves what
might otherwise be a puzzle: mathematics (whether its objects are forms or 'intermediates') is as
much about intelligible reality as dialectic, so why should it be easier to acclimatize the mind to
intelligible reality through mathematics than through dialectic? Why shouldn't the curriculum
go straight to dialectic, or work on both disciplines at once? The answer is not that mathematics
is more accessible because its use of diagrams provides a link with the world of the senses, since
we have argued that dialectic too has empirical content (Section 2.13). A better answer is that
reasoning about *practical* intelligibles is vulnerable to emotions that flourish in the field of
practice but have no purchase in the subject-matter of pure mathematics.

empirical and social stimuli that in most human beings easily trigger feelings of fear, anger, partiality, and so on. Such feelings and their objects tend to absorb all the attentional energy, destroying any chance of a synoptic view and issuing in practical impulses that feel authoritative and beyond criticism. The more this mind-set takes over, the more any reality discoverable only by the intellect fades out of sight. This weakness is due to human nature itself (cf. *Timaeus* 42a–b; 69d); not even the best upbringing can immunize against it.

So: the very context in which the need for reason is sharpest if we are to have a hope of living well in this world is one where the subject-matter of the reasoning renders reason extremely vulnerable. So there ought to be a place where reason can develop and learn its own strength out of reach of sensory and emotional bombardment; and for Plato this place is the world of mathematics. That's why his trainee rulers must become thoroughly at home there: not because the values that ought to guide humanity constitute an abstruse, arcane, intellectually super-difficult subject-matter, accessible like particle physics only through mathematics, but because most of us left to ourselves are deeply fickle and lazy about reason, given over to the mercy of other influences and unpractised in thinking carefully about difficult practical things. In the *Timaeus*, Plato's divine, context-free, purely rational world-maker is a mathematician because his task is to make the most beautiful universe, and the basic structures of such a universe can only be formulated mathematically. In the *Republic*, by contrast, human rulers need a basis in mathematics because their reasoning must issue from inside a pre-existing social and physical environment heavy with reason-threatening influences. Plato has finally succeeded in clarifying the relationship between mathematics and human ethical improvement: good ethical thinking does not imitate, still less is it a branch of, mathematics, but its lifeblood is the commitment to reason that mathematics (he thinks) is uniquely qualified to foster.

Finally: on the question of what leads scholars to interpret the rulers' work as itself intrinsically mathematical, I suspect that a main motive is perfectly understandable incredulity that so much mathematics is necessary for turning the young into reliably rational executives. We are incredulous because we know that many of *us* – which is to say interpreters of Plato, colleagues in the humanities across the university, friends in leading positions in law or administration or the civil service – are thoroughly committed to rationality but never got deeply into mathematics even by the standards of Plato's day; yet our lives have been lived in positions of responsibility, in some cases very heavy responsibility. If we sometimes lapse, no one immediately thinks it is because we did too little mathematics in college. How is this possible unless Plato is crazy to demand ten years of mathematics for the sole purpose of ensuring that his rulers will be thoughtful and rationally probing? But Plato is not crazy, so he must have an additional purpose in mind, namely to equip them to be rulers whose principal task *as rulers* is to decipher a mathematically structured reality, or work towards founding mathematics on the first principle of absolutely everything. (Before anyone cries 'QED!' note that defending Plato's sanity by attributing to him such notions of human ethical and political wisdom could be described as applying an antidote worse than the disease.)

Today, however, we enjoy resources, institutional and personal, that have made it possible for us and scores of previous generations to operate from deep confidence in reason even if we have not gone through a lengthy mathematical training. We have had lengthy formation in other highly developed difficult disciplines such as history, philology, law, legal theory, economics, or technical philosophy itself. They may not be exact sciences, but they demand and train us in almost endless exactness. In Plato's day these subjects were emergent at best, whereas mathematics was a uniquely well-established powerhouse of disciplined thinking. In short, the *Republic*'s cultural situation goes a long way towards explaining its assumption that deep training in mathematics is required for a rational approach to ethics and politics. If, instead, we hear that call for mathematically trained rulers as a historically unconditioned pronouncement of *philosophia perennis*, it may become tempting to suppose that, according to the *Republic*, the true profundities of humanly relevant ethics are mathematical profundities.[61]

4.4   Cosmology, Theology

This section has the limited aim of discussing the matters of cosmology and theology that show themselves in a few brief glimpses round themes of the central books of the *Republic*. From the paucity and brevity of these glimpses I think we should infer that Plato does not see his main arguments and presentations in these books as needing to be grounded in, or as pointing towards, a definite theological system. On the other hand, since the touches about divinity and the cosmos are obviously deliberate, they are somehow relevant to the main ideas and should not be ignored.

Socrates leads up to the sun-analogy by saying that he is unable to say directly what the good is, but instead will present something that is its 'offspring' (*ekgonos*) and 'bears a very close resemblance to it' (506e–507a; cf. 517c1–2). This turns out to be the sun:

So that's what you need to take me as calling the 'offspring' of the good – the sun, which the good fathered in proportion to itself (*egennēsen analogon heautōi*): as the

---

[61] I am not, of course, claiming that any philosopher in Plato's circumstances would have reached for advanced mathematics as necessary training for rulers. Aristotle did not, although his circumstances were not radically different. Nor am I claiming that Plato never engaged in some sort of pythagoreanizing of ethics. I have only aimed to show that there is tenuous reason, if any, to see this at work in the *Republic*.

good itself is, in the sphere of the intelligible, in relation to intellect and the things that are grasped by intellect, so the sun is in the visible sphere in relation to sight and the things that are seen. (508b12–c2)

So the analogy is not just an analogy: it is not just good luck that the familiar sun and what it does provides a way for us to grasp the mysterious form of the good and what *it* does. Rather, the form of the good 'begat' the sun to be 'in proportion to itself'. See also:

'... unless sight and colour are joined by a third kind of thing, by nature specific for exactly this (*idia(i) ep'auto touto pephukos*), you recognize that sight won't see anything and the colours will also be unseen.'
    'What *is* this third thing you're talking about?' he asked.
    'What you call light,' I said. (507d10–e3)

What the third thing's nature is specifically *for* is seeing and being seen. And this is presented not simply as an important fact about what we call 'light', but as the essence of what the word names.[62]

So the good generated the sun *as* analogue of itself and as source of light whose purpose is to enable seeing and being seen. The first of the passages above may be read in a weaker and a stronger sense. According to the weaker, the good generated the sun to cause, through its light, the visible sphere's analogue of what the good itself causes in the intelligible sphere. The stronger sense says the same but with the additional nuance that the good generated the sun to be recognized or understood as its own analogue in that way. That is: the sun is there not only in order to *be* the physical analogue of the form of the good, but also to be *grasped* as such, i.e. as a deliberate illustration of the latter. The first of these purposes benefits all creatures with vision, while the second benefits only those who are capable of wondering what the good is.

Either way, the offspring-sun is there on purpose, and, for all that we have seen, the purpose is in what is called its 'parent', the form of the good. We are also told that each is a king, one over the intelligible, the other over the visible realm (509d1–3). It is as if the good has appointed the sun as its viceroy in the visible domain, thereby ratifying its own sovereignty even over that domain. However exactly we understand the metaphysical relationship between the good and the sun (and between the good and the rest of the visible domain), the main message is clear: the power of the form of the good has cosmic scope.[63] We could not have gathered this from all that has led up to the sun-analogy in Book VI. So far the *Republic*'s horizon has been restricted to human values, human psychology, human institutions. Now we are shown that the backdrop

---

[62] By distinguishing the thing from its familiar name ('What you call light'), Plato throws emphasis on to the nature of the thing: cf. e.g. *Timaeus* 66a, 66b, 67c, 67d, 67e, 68a, 68b.
[63] Cf. Johansen 2013.

to all human affairs, the world of nature itself including our own congenital physique and psychology, is somehow a product of the good or the form of the good – the very same form that is the *megiston mathēma*, the most important thing to learn, for human rulers. The human ruler's task of making a good society of good human individuals is analogous to but also of a piece with a cosmos-wide project of governance by, or in light of, the good. Within the cosmos humans are like pockets not already filled up with natural arrangements: they are relatively indeterminate places which it is up to us to order through culture and human intelligence. To the extent that we order them well, both individual souls and communities, we carry forward the general work of governance by the good, extending it to those cosmologically unfinished areas where we can make a difference. This notion of carrying forward the work of ordering does not imply that we should order our affairs so as to reproduce in them (whatever this could amount to) the order of the cosmos itself, but only that if we order them well, we are doing the same sort of thing as the principle of the good has already done on a cosmic scale.

It should be noted that while this is a lesson for Socrates and his interlocutors, and for us readers, not much in the text suggests that it is a lesson or inspiration for the philosopher-rulers in Callipolis. Neither Plato's injunctions about what stories of gods can be safely included in children's education nor his plans for the rulers' intellectual curriculum mention a tale, or a philosophical argument, showing that a good principle 'created the heavens and the earth'. This will come later, in the *Timaeus*, and there it is presented not as a step on the educational ladder but as part of a private entertainment for sophisticated adults. The text of the *Republic* (unlike *Laws* X) is surprisingly silent on whether the rulers' intellectual equipment includes an account of the role of the good in the formation of the cosmos (although they will eventually get to this if cosmology is one of their retirement activities). They are said to rule in light of the forms of the virtues, not in light of how the principle of the good has ordered the cosmos.[64]

At one point, however, not only are we told that the good is the source of '*everything* right and beautiful', including cosmic order, but we glimpse Plato's philosophers grasping this too:

in any case, the way things appear to me is that in the sphere of the known the thing that is seen last, and seen only with difficulty (*mogis horasthai*), is the form of the good, and that given that it *is* seen one is bound to reason that it, in fact, is the cause for everything of everything right and beautiful, as both progenitor (*tekousa*) of light and of the source (*kurion*) of light in the sphere of the seen, and the source itself of truth and intelligibility

[64] Line 486a briefly glances at their interest in 'the whole of everything there is, divine and human' and at their contemplation 'of all of time and of all there is', but the form of the good is not mentioned here.

in the intelligible sphere. It also seems to me that anyone who is to act sensibly (*emphronōs*), in private or in public life, must have had a sight of it. (517b7–c4)

Socrates is surely not speaking only for himself and us when he speaks of realizing that the form of the good, as cause of everything right and beautiful, is the progenitor of visible light and of the sun. The link between grasping this conclusion and sighting the form of the good suggests that the same conclusion is drawn by those paradigmatic sighters of the form of the good, the philosophers of Callipolis at the end of their ascent from the cave. So they too enjoy the knowledge that the cosmos is governed by the same form of the good as that by which they will steer their *polis*.[65]

The image of the sun as the intended offspring of the form of the good is a sort of reassurance for us, and even for the ideal rulers too. The image ascribes cosmic relevance to that very same form of the good that makes all the difference to human happiness depending on whether we approach it intelligently or not. This cosmic relevance matters to humans because it spells the assurance that values are manifested in the world of nature too, and that these cosmic values are not alien to those that should govern human life. The law of nature and the law of man built up through culture and human contrivance are neither antagonists nor strangers to one another as in the sophistic contrast between *nomos* and *phusis*. Hence it makes sense for us to assume coherence between the value to us of goods given us by nature, and the value to us of goods that cannot be brought about unless *human* wisdom takes the initiative in identifying our need for them or their value for us, and works towards them through deliberate linguistically articulated organization of our lives. It is beyond doubt that nature has endowed us with goods. The literal power of vision is an example. Another is the bodily condition of basic physical health. (The great argument of the *Republic* that we are better off just than unjust, depends on its being self-evident that physical health is a blessing: see 445a–b with 357c2–4 on vision and health as valued both for their own sake and for what they give rise to.) So on the one hand, there are definitely goods that are both good for us and present to us through the workings of nature unless we are unlucky; and on the other hand, there are ethical and political goods which we can only acquire if we make deliberate efforts. The point is that if the very same form of the good in some sense presides over both classes of good, there

---

[65] This convergence between what we are told in the passage and what is grasped by the philosopher-rulers (and by wise non-rulers) does not, I think, justify assuming that the sun-*analogy* as such is shared knowledge between us and Plato's dialecticians. The analogy is an aid for Glaucon and co., and for us, to get an indirect sense of the form of the good's function as source of dialectical knowledge. Arguably, the dialecticians themselves do not depend on that analogy for understanding how they should operate with the form of the good. Things are the other way round: it is because they operate with it correctly that the form turns out to be the analogue of the sun, a source of cognition in the sphere of ethical values.

is hope that if on occasion the two kinds clash, we can find rational and principled ways of resolving or circumnavigating such conflicts instead of being torn by a brute dualism of values. The sun itself is a major factor in the physical health of humans and other animals,[66] and the form of the good, via its relation to the forms of the virtues, is the source of concrete ethical goods. So: since the sun is the offspring of the form of the good, the two kinds of goods have ultimately the same provenance; hence we may be reassured that they are fellows, not aliens.[67]

Let us turn to the question of *how* the form of the good may be supposed to 'generate' the sun. This hyper-form can hardly cause the being of the physical sun in the way it causes the being and reality of other *forms*. Books VI and VII refer twice to a 'craftsman' (*dēmiourgos*) of natural entities: once to the craftsman of our senses (507c6–7), once to the craftsman of the celestial system (529d9–530a7). The simplest answer is that a god or God constructed the world of nature, making some sort of essential reference to the form of the good. Thus the form of the good is central to the purposive origination of the natural world. But surely more than this is meant by calling that form the parent of the sun? Yes; the form of the good is involved in the origination of the whole of nature, but stands in a special relation of likeness to the sun because in their respective realms each is the source whereby the other inhabitants are cognized and have their being. Thus the sun is not merely dependent on the form of the good (this must ultimately be true of all natural kinds and their members), but 'portrays' it and may be said to have 'inherited' or to be the 'projection of' its sovereignty in a lower mode. It seems natural to tie all this up in the image of a son or daughter acting on the parent's behalf in a place where the parent cannot act directly itself. (By 'act directly' I mean: act as *a form*. When the form of the good acts, or contributes, as the *form* that it is, intelligence is also in the picture whether as beneficiary or also as enabling condition; see Sections 3.2 and 3.4.)

Whether or not Plato meant to identify the form of the good with the divine craftsman of the natural world – a doctrine which some interpreters have read into the *Timaeus* – he shows no sign in the *Republic* of being exercised by this question. The *Republic* keeps the two entities well apart, there being no immediate textual link between them. The craftsman of our senses is

---

[66] In line with common belief Plato speaks of the sun as a god (508a4). As Alex Long reminded me, according to Alcibiades (*Symposium* 220d) Socrates prayed to the sun at dawn. The sun-god Helios was closely connected – sometimes identified – with Apollo, who as Apollo Paean was the god of healing. The sun-analogy closes with Glaucon invoking Apollo (509c1).

[67] It is this affinity if not identity between our values and cosmic values that gives Plato his way into cosmological inquiry in the *Timaeus*. Knowing that the demiurge wanted everything to be as good as possible (29e–30a) cannot help us identify and explain cosmic arrangements if our use of 'good' and his are governed by radically different criteria.

mentioned at 507c6–7; then the focus is on light; then on the sun; and only then on the form of the good in the first clear statement of the sun-analogy at 508e–509a. (The *Timaeus*, by contrast, links the good immediately to the divine craftsman at 29e–30a.)

Let us assume that in the *Republic* at some level (not necessarily a studiously doctrinal one, as Plato is not doing systematic theology) we are meant to leave the divine craftsman of nature and the form of the good unidentified with each other. There is still an intimate connection between them because (although the point is not stated in the *Republic*) this divine craftsman surely invokes the good in crafting the world of nature. This raises the question of whether this divine good-ward orientation can be understood in a way that coheres with this book's earlier account of how the human ruler-dialectician, the expert on the structure and co-ordination of the ideal city, relates to the form of the good.[68] For instance, can the notion of the form of the good as interrogative be extended to the scenario in which a god crafts the natural world?

Let us start discussing this by noting differences between the good-oriented craftsman of nature and the good-oriented human dialectical ruler. First: the former, whether or not actually omniscient, automatically knows and understands everything relevant to his task. With the latter, perfection of knowledge and understanding can only be an ideal worked towards with education and effort. Secondly, the cosmic demiurge in a sense has a much simpler task, at least if the construction of the cosmos is as Plato presents it in the *Timaeus*. There, the only circumstance or context of world-making is the pre-existence of unfinished matter in disorderly motion, and the god used the entirety of physical matter to create the body of the universe; there is nothing physical beyond it (*Timaeus* 32d–33a). He 'adjusted' to this context of the about-to-be cosmos by making it all disappear *into* that same cosmos. Further, the construction of the whole was a one-off operation although depicted as occurring in stages; and the result is and will always remain perfect, so that there is no need of divine intervention for subsequent repair and maintenance. Moreover, time is a created feature internal to the cosmos, not an external pre-existing medium that might be thought to have, all by itself, the power of ageing the things that are 'in' time; the cosmos becomes older but is never senescent (38a; 33a).[69] All this means that the maker does not need to tailor his operation to

---

[68] In fact, Socrates is more like the craftsman of the natural world because he, not the rulers, crafts both city and rulers (in words) from scratch. But at no point does the Socrates-character *in propria persona* make formulaic reference to the form of the good as such when building his utopia – although obviously he argues that certain arrangements are better than others.

[69] The *Statesman* has the opposite story: there the cosmos has a tendency to run down through time towards chaos, and God, who is not represented as its demiurge, takes over periodically to halt the decline (269c –270b).

take account of a context that remains external to the product, or return for re-adjustments because changes in it or in his knowledge set up new demands. Furthermore, the entire intelligible paradigm from which he works is available to him all at once, so to speak. This is by contrast with the forms of justice and so on so far as they relate to human rulers; for (as was argued in Sections 2.14 and 2.18) even the best human rulers must re-interpret those forms again and again since justice and the others 'mean', or require, different things in different situations and cannot be exhaustively known once and for all.

Given these differences, we might think that the notion of the form of the good as interrogative is alien to the case of the world-maker, since 'interrogative' seems to imply the uncertainty and corrigibility that afflict intra-mundane rational agents. Still, it is worth recollecting that our discussion of the human rulers' commerce with the form of the good did test the interrogative interpretation through favourable comparison with alternatives such as the idea that this form occurs as a master-premiss or as a richly informative definition from which the dialecticians extract definitions of the virtues. Nothing in the *Timaeus* story suggests that the cosmic demiurge extracts his paradigm from a prior understanding of the form of the good functioning as master-premiss or definition. To this extent (although this is only a negative point) his stance conforms to the interrogative interpretation worked out for the case of human rulers.

More can be said. It is a truism that the judgement[70] that something is good should be backed up by reasons (except when it only means 'I like it'). An impression that X is good or a positive impulse towards X should be resisted until reasons for letting the impulse turn into a judgement become clear, or at least make themselves present for articulation whether or not they are articulated in full on the spot. This requirement of suspending judgement *that* X is good pending reasons can be seen as implying priority for the question *whether* it is good over the judgement *that* it is. This is because of the double fact that (a) reasons are needed for signing off on the judgement-*that*, and (b) the necessary reasons can only be netted if something determines what it is they are reasons *for*: and this determining factor is given in posing the question *whether* X is good. The determinant has to be a question since otherwise (so I assume) it would be the associated assertion, affirmative or negative – but then the judgement would have been made before any reasons weighed in! The upshot is that any responsible judgement *that* X is good, regardless of the agent's psychological state, rides on the back of the corresponding question *whether*, even if the agent's information is so complete and ready to hand that

---

[70] It would be useful to have different terms for (1) the initial unreasoned impression that this or that is good, (2) the reasoned verdict or judgement that it is, and (3) general value-assumptions based on no further reasons. All too often these types are all simply called 'beliefs'.

there is no room for hesitation, wondering, or seeking.[71] On this basis, going by the *Timaeus* story, we can say that even the cosmic craftsman's practical orientation towards the good (the form of the good) involves his having interrogated[72] possible cosmic arrangements for goodness in advance of implementing any; for the story is full of examples of his reasons for taking one creative route rather than another. Some are reasons of beauty and perfection, others concern the welfare of mortal creatures.[73]

Plato never suggests that the cosmic demiurge, like his human counterpart, is a dialectician. Perhaps this is because it is absurd to picture the cosmic demiurge as examining hypotheses (as to what is worth creating) for logical defects such as ambiguity and circularity, or as trying out hypotheses and discarding them. Still, the interrogativity underlying possession of a reasoned judgement that something is good puts the world-maker on a par with the Platonic ruler. And through the good or the form of the good other forms are known to the cosmic artisan and take on being or reality. As with the human ruler (called the demiurge or craftsman of civic virtue at 500d7–9) so with the cosmic demiurge: this metaphysical relation of the good to other forms holds of the forms that he regards as desirable to implement. The forms or intelligibles he finds desirable to implement are those that fit together as templates of the various kinds that compose a physical world as perfect and harmonious as possible. Wielded by him, the G-question singles out which these are and 'adds to' them the ontological status of being not merely objects of intellect but also formal causes or templates of the empirical phenomena (cf. Section 3.2). For example, the form of hemisphere is obviously an object of intellect, but quite possibly not the formal cause of any kind or kind-feature in the created world.[74] Presumably there are countless mathematical forms (intelligibles) that

---

[71] This analysis skips over the fact that it can be legitimate to accept that X is good on someone else's authority. But at some point there must be reasons behind the judgement. It is a striking difference between the Timaean account of world-making and the accounts in Genesis 1 and 2 that the latter include no reasons why what God made was good (except when it comes to the creation of woman, where we are told that it was because 'it is not good that the man should be alone', Gen. 2. 18, as if this case needs special theodicy). For the faithful, the fact that the creator has judged the contents of nature to be good, whatever the reasons, is sufficient for accepting that it is so.

[72] This need not imply that at some point he was ignorant of the answer: he has 'always already' interrogated.

[73] Examples include why he made a cosmos at all (30a); why he made it an intelligent, living being (30a–b); why it is spherical (33b); why he made the sun (39a–b); why he included mortal animals (41b); why we have limbs (44d–45a); why we have vision (47a–b); why the different parts of the soul are located where they are in the body (69d–70a); why we have the liver (71a–d); why the bone of the cranium is more fragile than other bones (75b–c); why we have hair (76c–d); why plants exist (77a).

[74] I am assuming that if physical hemispheres exist this is a spin-off from the fact that spheres do, so that the formal cause is the form of sphere. Richard Patterson has given a powerful explanation of Platonic forms as templates both for the natural kinds that make up a good and beautiful

do not make it to the level of formal causes of physical objects, just as there are many types of social set-ups lacking the good-making features that would render them eligible for implementation by the ideal human ruler. One could also say that only on condition that *isosceles* and *half-equilateral* each combine with the generic *triangle* (like specific favourable contexts combining with the generic rule of returning loans) do we get the '*virtuous*' types of triangle, i.e. those suitable as patterns for the basic physical triangles of the Timaean natural world (*Timaeus* 54a). In other words, when the divinity restricts the most basic triangles to isosceles and half-equilateral, *good* or *best* is added to (accrues to) *triangle* in that we now have the correct kinds of triangle for constructing the elementary particles (cf. Section 3.4). Similarly, through divine intelligence vague 'traces' of the four elements were circumscribed by number and measure and thereby had goodness added to them, i.e. they became suitable ingredients for building the cosmos (53b).

Finally in this section on cosmology and theology, there is the question whether, according to Plato, the form of the good is itself a god or the highest god, a view often ascribed to him.[75] (This is independent of whether the form of the good is to be identified with the demiurge of the cosmos.) Plato, in line with common belief, speaks of the sun as a god (*Republic* 508a4–8), and it has been argued on his behalf that the form of the good must therefore be a god too since it is anterior to and more exalted than the sun.[76] He also speaks of the form of the good as the *eudaimonestaton tou ontos*, the most blessed part of reality (526e4–5), 'blessed' being a traditional epithet of the gods. It is said to 'rule over' the intelligible realm as the sun rules over the visible (509d2–3). It is said to be 'more *timēteon*' ('more to be honoured or revered', 509a5) than the truth and knowledge it generates, where the verb *timaō* stands for an

---

cosmos, and for the institutions that constitute an excellent city-state. On his account, if I have understood correctly, the form of the good gives being to 'the things that are known' by making them be *as forms*. That is, it confers on them the status of paradigmatic and formal causes of phenomena. For only those intelligibles that jointly contribute to the *best* possible system deserve to be implemented, i.e. to be formal causes (Patterson 1985, ch. 6). Sayre 1995, 185–6, has a somewhat similar view according to which it is owing to the form of the good that the other forms acquire – not their basic being, but – their status as objective norms by which the excellence of other things is measured. See also Vegetti 2013c, 152. Patterson's understanding of what it is to be a form implies a distinction between forms and intelligibles in general (intelligibles as opposed to sensibles). Some of the intelligibles ('things known') are recognized as unfit to function as paradigmatic and formal causes of corresponding empirical phenomena: from the Platonic ruler's perspective an example would be *direct democracy*. (The distinction between intelligibles in general, and forms in Patterson's narrower causal sense, seems not to be reflected in Plato's choice of terms, at least in the *Republic*. E.g. when he says that dialectic descends to a conclusion 'without using anything perceptible at all, only forms (*eidesin*), themselves by themselves, to reach forms – and ends with forms' (*eidē*, 511b7–c2), this surely includes forms that are rationally discarded as unsuitable to qualify as formal causes of empirical effects.)

[75] For recent examples see Bordt 2006 and A. A. Long 2020.   [76] A. A. Long 2020.

attitude of deep respect or holding-precious whose pre-eminent objects are the gods, parents, and one's country.

This evidence is suggestive but leaves us short of the conclusion that for Plato the form of the good is a god. That the form is most blessed may mean only that it is the greatest source of blessings. That it rules over the intelligibles may simply summarize the cognitive and ontological functions which we already know it has. That it is more to be revered than knowledge and truth implies that knowledge and truth are to be revered: should we then think that they are gods too, albeit lesser gods?

It is unclear what is claimed in claiming that the form of the good is a god or God, or what hangs on the claim. What is it for X to count as a god, and what difference does it make? And if we hold that Y is a god and that X is in some way more exalted than Y, are we thereby bound to view X as a more exalted *god*? There seem to be no rules for deciding these questions. Let it be conceded that X counts as a god if it is object of cult or prayer.[77] This is too strong to be a necessary condition, because in the *Timaeus* the demiurge throughout is referred to as 'the god' or 'God', but he (unlike the divine cosmos itself, cf. *Critias* 106a–b) is never invoked in prayer.[78] The cosmos itself is briefly hymned as a god at *Timaeus* 92c, but never the demiurge. At *Republic* 540a6–b1 the form of the good (in the perspective of meta-dialectical reflection rather than dialectical 'use'[79]) occurs as an object of dedication to its service, even reverence, but not of worship (see Section 2.10). There will be, if the Delphic oracle permits, a cult of deceased rulers (540b7–c2), but the idea of a cult of the form of the good seems beyond the dialogue's horizon. It seems safe to suggest that for X to count as a god, X must at the very least be to some extent personified as an intelligent agent.[80] We need not discuss the meaning and criteria of personification, since the form of the good is obviously not personified, and in the *Republic* there is no vestige of the idea that it is itself an intelligence. In the *Phaedrus* myth the Olympian gods are shown as deeply dependent on the forms, 'feeding' on them (247a7–b1; d1–e2). Although some of the forms are at one point quasi-personified and treated as sacred beings (254b6–7), in general they are not deified and are assigned a different function from that of the gods who travel round heaven. They seem to represent the intelligible structure of the world, whereas those gods seem to have the function of transmitting this structure into the material and kinetic medium of a physical cosmos.[81] Of the forms it seems enough to say (*si fas est*, 'if

---

[77] The concession is too generous because there were cults of the seasons, nymphs, etc., but it is unclear whether to count them all as gods.

[78] Cf. Cornford 1937, 35.   [79] See Sections 2.7 and 2.10.   [80] Cf. McPherran 2006, 95.

[81] See van Riel 2013, 110–13, 116–17, 119, who puts forward the interesting idea that for Plato the forms, including the form of the good, stand to the gods rather as fate, *moira* or *heimarmenē*, stands to them in traditional mythology as a framework in which they must operate.

religion permits') that they *superare divos*, 'transcend the gods', and leave the matter at that. Thus the argument that since the offspring of the form of the good is a god, the form itself is a god, is not compelling.[82]

It seems that this debate can go from side to side indefinitely. Perhaps in the end the right solution is a sort of compromise according to which Plato's form of the good is correctly captured not as God or the ultimate god, but as *divinity*, whether this means the attribute of divinity or a supreme impersonal principle.[83] It is surely important, however, that Plato himself does not see his philosophical purposes in Books V–VII of the *Republic* as requiring endorsement or rejection of any of the options discussed in this section. It is unclear that we have reason to fill in the lacunae on his behalf, aside from our wish to see him as doctrinally more complete, and possibly this wish is fuelled by developments later than Plato.[84]

---

[82] At 597b–d a god is said to be maker of the unique form of couch. Possibly the thought is that some human individual was divinely inspired to inaugurate the couch and what it stands for, namely the symposium, a culturally central practice (Burnyeat 1997–8, 232–6). So by divine will it came about that the previously inert form of couch acceded to the ontological status of an actual template. (Thus we avoid thinking of the god as making the 'inert' form itself: see Section 3.2). No doubt this was for the good of human beneficiaries, but the god and the good had different causal roles. This god seems also to be the craftsman of the whole of nature (597d4–7).

[83] This is the conclusion of A. A. Long 2020.

[84] The beliefs about divinity of most people who have them are not doctrinally neat, I guess. I am not sure why we should expect it to be different with Plato just because he is a great philosopher. Arguably, a series of historical accidents has imposed on us the assumption that if great thinkers bring the divine into some of their arguments, they must have faced up to the responsibility of getting systematically clear about it and how it relates to other things of concern to them.

Part 5 Winding Up

This work has omitted discussing several exegetical problems in Books V–VII of the *Republic*.[1] It has focused on the sun-like form of the good, sticking to that theme and its ramifications so as not to lose momentum. Of course, in a work with many moving parts some corners may have been cut unwittingly. The most I can hope is to have proposed an account of Plato's sun-like form that is philosophically plausible and faithful to the text, although admittedly this hope is ambitious given the obscurity of the material.

(1) The seminal decision of the book was to think of the sun-like form of the good as interrogative. No doubt this idea is disconcertingly unorthodox – some might say wild. It seems to be unprecedented, and in the massive ancient and continuing tradition of Plato-interpretation anything unprecedented is surely rightly viewed, if not with suspicion or the now proverbial incredulous stare, then certainly as having to earn any consideration, let alone its keep, entirely from scratch without prior presumption of a sympathetic welcome. Even so, the decision has proved liberating. At one stroke it does away with the burden of explaining how, if (instead) the form of the good is given as a premiss of dialectical reasoning or as a sort of definitional starting point, the truth of this can be established. What is non-hypothetical cannot be derived, so it seems that (on such an account) knowers of the premiss or definition must have verified it by intuition or by elimination of alternatives. But once the candidates pleasure and wisdom have been eliminated, how is a more successful one to be found? We assume that there lurks a richly informational premiss or definition encapsulating the nature of the good; yet we are hopelessly in the dark as to what it might be. So Plato's dialectician-ruler, grasping things apparently beyond our grasp, comes to seem a superhuman figure – since our bafflement about this ruler's knowledge is not because we are stupid or

---

[1] For instance: correlating the stages of the Cave allegory with the sections of the Divided Line; determining, with reference to the Line, the epistemic status of Socrates' own discourse; the problem of how Callipolis is supposed to be got going; the interpretation of the verb 'to be' in the argument against the sight-lovers; whether the main thesis of the *Republic* is compatible with the philosophers' reluctant return to the cave.

inattentive. This is exegetically debilitating: we swing between casting Plato as quasi-superhuman insofar as he seems to have some sort of fix on the super-human knowledge of philosopher-kings, and wondering whether he has lost himself building empty word-castles. This second attitude shuts down exegesis while the former imposes no limit on what is admissible. By contrast, the interrogative interpretation postulates as form of the good nothing more obscure or complicated than what is conveyed by the familiar word 'good' used predicatively; and since this occurs in a question rather than an assertion, the problem of verification does not arise. The question operates as a *principle* of dialectical reasoning because, like a deductive premiss, it (according to the answer) imposes a control on what shall and shall not be accepted as a result of the inquiry. It is a *non-hypothetical* principle because concern about the good, or about what is good, cannot be suspended or laid aside.

(2) Although the interrogative interpretation of the form of the good can be shown to bring some exegetical advantages, it may still seem far-fetched and under-motivated. Towards counteracting this impression, I offer a conjectural reconstruction of how Plato may have arrived at the notion. First, if he ever thought of the form of the good as definable (whether analytically or synthetic-ally by means of a so-called real definition) in a way that could guide action (whether of rulers or of any practical agent), he abandoned this belief before coming to write the central books of the *Republic*. He abandoned it partly because he came to see that the properties of things that make it the case that those things are good are so multifarious that 'good' cannot be usefully (action-guidingly) defined in terms of any of these properties.[2] The word has, so to speak, no substantial meaning of its own, because that would block its application to some objects which are, nevertheless, *good*. (Compare what he says at *Timaeus* 50d–51a about the Receptacle having no qualities of its own.) Secondly, he came to see that the properties of things that make it the case that those things are correctly said to be good are not stable good-makers under all circumstances, because through changes in circumstances what was a good-maker may cease to be one, and may even become a bad-maker. So: given that wisdom is what delivers correctness on what is or is not good, it turns out to be impossible to define wisdom in terms of a single succinct non-circular account of what wisdom is correct about. In other words, wisdom cannot know in advance of any situation what the good choice would be like, what its nature would be. Plato, realizing this, would face two options. One is that there is no such thing as the good, i.e. no objective and real difference between things that are good and things that are not. This would entail that

---

[2] See Irwin 1995, 163–6, 200–201, 262–6, although his focus is not on putative definitions of good, but on the Socratic search for definitions of properties such as piety and courage.

there is no such thing as wisdom either, since wisdom is about what is good or not. It would follow too that there are no such things as justice and the other virtues since these in Book IV were defined, for both city and individual soul, by a set of definitions interlocking with the definition of wisdom. So, unless goodness is objective, these supposed virtues, and their contrary vices, are not even possible standards by which to judge empirical approximations as just or unjust and so on. Socrates has gained little by the proof in Book IV that justice intrinsically benefits the just person if it is going to turn out that there are no standards for predicating justice and injustice, whether of individual or city. It is no comfort that amoralist admiration for injustice is equally bankrupt. So much for the one option. The alternative is to keep the reality of the good and of wisdom and accept that wisdom's task is not to acquire a non-circular, non-vacuous, definition of the good and then examine each situation through that pre-established lens, but in face of each encountered situation to determine afresh what would be good to do or promote. For Plato the first option is not only impossible but perhaps even wicked or insane to contemplate. So he must accept the second. But note how natural it was just now to identify the task of wisdom by reference to what for us is an indirect question, but for the wise agent a direct one: in fact, our friend the G-question.

This account of wisdom as not working from a pre-established definition of the good does not mean that it reaches unprincipled or unreasoned conclusions about what is good and what is just, etc. Rather, it means that the relevant reasons or their force as reasons, and the relevant principles, become apparent only when wise intelligence studies a given situation with a view to finding out what (indirect question) it would be good to do in it or about it. Wise intelligence is *adespoton*, 'knows no master' (617e3), which includes not being shackled by a previously manufactured definition.[3]

(3) The G-question, or the requirement to ask it, is the non-hypothetical principle of dialectic. That the non-hypothetical principle is not a premiss from which to deduce consequences is suggested to us in the Divided Line, by Plato's ranking of mathematics below dialectic. Mathematics is the paragon of deductive control by a set of primary premisses. The core mathematical concept of proportion is Plato's ironically chosen tool for putting mathematics in its place, and his message is that in relation to dialectic, mathematics is as inferior as sense to intellect and as shadow to substance. The best way, it seems, of making sense of this staggering pronouncement is to see it as warning that if dialectic, whatever it is, is the distinctive method of the ideal ruler (or of any good practical agent), then modelling dialectic on mathematics is profoundly mistaken, because (as we would put it) the ruler's method must

---

[3] What the judgement of goodness in each case is based on is not *aporrhēton* (unsayable) but *aprorrhēton* (unsayable in advance, uncodifiable); *Laws* XII, 968e.

be a sort of practical reasoning and practical reasoning essentially involves non-deductive elements.

(4) The form of the good, according to the interrogative interpretation, is no more than the simple little unit conveyed by ordinary predicative 'good'. This approach makes possible a fruitful explanation of the strangeness of *proseinai* at 509b7 and *proschrēsamena* at 505a3, details so often ignored or smoothed over in translation. We now see that the form of the good functions as good-maker – and also as reality-conferrer in relation to forms that purport to be forms of the virtues – by being a logical or ontological 'addition' to evaluatively neutral things: things which, in the language that revealed the sight-lovers' stance to be mere opinion, 'tumble about between being good and being not good'. The special wisdom of the dialectician-rulers is skill in discerning which cases of neutrals are {neutral + good}, hence *really* count as virtuous. They discriminate these cases not by 'feel' but in accordance with articulate, discussable, reasons.

(5) The interrogative interpretation of the sun-like form receives indirect confirmation from Proclus' puzzlement (unknown to me until I was in the midst of this project) over the two forms of the good which he thought he detected in Book VI of the *Republic*: the sun-like form, and the participand one-over-many-goods. Now (i) Plato clearly recognizes the participand good as well as the sun-like good, and (ii) it seems clear that these are not to be flatly equated since the sun-like good is not participated in by the forms in relation to which it is sun-like, i.e. cause of their being known and being real (see Section 4.2). But (iii) it is a principle of Platonism that there is only one form for any predicate corresponding to a form. *Pace* Proclus, (iv) the best solution is surely to think of them as different modes or aspects or inflections of a single form of the good. Since (v) the participand form is obviously a metaphysical constituent of every fact corresponding to a true declarative to the effect that something or other is good, and since (vi) in the context of dialectic interrogative and declarative versions of the identical sentence are surely the only relevant items, corresponding as they do to dialectical question and answer, it follows that (vii) the sun-like form of the good can be nothing other than the *interrogative* inflection of the very same metaphysical entity that under its other aspect of participand helps constitute the facts that render true any true affirmative *answers* to the G-question.[4]

(6) In Section 2.8 I defended the idea that the form of the good is essentially interrogative – that interrogativity is not just an adventitious feature that attaches to it passingly when someone happens to pick it up to ask: 'Is so and so good?', 'Which things are good?', etc. But then there is also the

---

[4] Here this includes answers in response to the question when asked about particulars.

participand form of the good, which the last paragraph has just argued is the very same form as the sun-like one only under a different aspect or inflection. Yet surely it is essential to the participand form to be the participand, i.e. the kind of thing that is at least able to be participated in by empirical items if and when there are good ones. It seems, then, that the identical thing, in this case the form of the good, is being said to possess two essences. How is this not intolerable?

I think an answer can be developed from the assumption that for Plato mind or intelligence is co-eval and correlative with the form of the good itself. On 'co-eval': since his forms are eternal, he must hold that intelligence too is eternal. This condition would be satisfied if there were always intelligent beings in the universe: they need not be individually immortal, and each could have its own individual and mortal intelligence – they need not all be channelling a single eternal mind. However, Plato in fact holds that we as souls and intelligences are individually immortal and have existed from the beginning. (It may, however, be possible to hold that intelligence and the good are co-eval even if one is an expressivist and believes that intelligence has evolved; but I leave that aside for now.) On 'correlative' see the words: 'The good is what every soul pursues, the very thing for the sake of which it does what it does – divining that there is such a thing, but puzzled and unable to get an adequate grasp on what exactly it is . . .' (501e). What every soul pursues is the form of the good as actually expressed through actual participants, i.e. every soul pursues or strives to realize good things. Think of being pursued as essential to good things *qua* good. Thus participants in the form of the good are, as such, things fit or of a nature to be pursued, whether or not they are in fact pursued.[5] The property of being fit to be pursued – being the potential object of discriminating possessive interest – is correlative to the property of being the potential subject taking such an interest, and a pursuing subject looks to see which things are good, thus bringing to bear the interrogative form. The good as actually participated in is for being pursued by soul or intelligence, and soul or intelligence is for interrogatively pursuing that good. So the two aspects of the form of the good are correlatives, and the single essence of the one form essentially looks in both these directions.[6]

---

[5] Perhaps we may construe 'pursued' broadly so that it applies to such things as beautiful mathematical relationships: 'pursuing' them would consist in getting to understand them better, using them in further theorizing, clearing them of pointless accretions, these all being ways of making them one's own.

[6] If, as I believe, for Plato there is nothing strange in treating as primary the interrogative aspect of the form of the good, whereas for us, philosophically, this seems artificial and eccentric, the reason may lie in the difference between a primarily heuristic interest (his) in (at least some) linguistic terms and a primarily semantic one (ours). If one thinks of a term 'R' as characteristically used for discovering which things are R, whether there are R things, etc., 'R' comes across

(7) But in the human sphere pursuit of the good may fail to be pursuit of the actual good, just as someone who teaches may sadly fail to bring it about that anyone learns. So these are not correlated as tightly as master and servant or convex and concave. What restores the two aspects of the good to something approximating the snug embrace of convex and concave is method and education. The Sun needs the Divided Line with its account of the rulers' dialectical method, and the account of dialectic needs the Cave with its account of their education. For the interrogative form of the good to *be* truly sun-like, in other words an actual source for accurately tracking the natures of other intelligibles – the ones that have to be recognized in order for the good to be empirically brought about and possessed – the interrogation must be conducted by an intelligence in the right condition, and this condition is a love of truth trained to be at home in the world of intellect and undergirded by unshakeable moral excellence. In other words, in the human context the sun-analogy holds true of the one and only form of the good if and only if there exist human beings who have absorbed something like the rulers' entire education, moral and intellectual, described and defended from Book II to Book VII of the *Republic*. Plato's short sharp schematic sun-analogy, and his long and detailed exploration of the ideal education, are in a sense for him two sides of the same coin.

(8) I say 'for him', because it may be worth noting that any philosopher who eschews Plato's realism about values but still holds that ethical judgements are in some sense objectively correct or incorrect (as in some forms of contemporary expressivism) could in principle sign up to Plato's ideal of education. But without realism the ontology of the sun-analogy would not make sense, at least on this book's preferred second proposal for interpreting it (Section 3.4). According to that, a case of the *per se* ethically neutral EFG is a case of real justice because this case (on account of its context) is not merely EFG but {EFG + the good}. In this model the terms denote metaphysical counters that can occur separately from each other or in combination. Both counters are equally real, however different their individual characters. Let us suppose an expressivist who is a realist about properties. She accepts that EFG is a real property or combination of properties; this is because the designation 'EFG' is purely descriptive. But as an expressivist she holds that 'the good' or 'good', being non-descriptive, stand for no sort of real property; to apply them to

---

as intrinsically charged with interrogation. If one thinks of 'R' as characteristically introducing a property (for Plato, a participand form) that helps constitute facts picked out by true declaratives of the form 'R(x)', then 'R' appears as having no intrinsic interrogative spin. In a natural language some terms might be linked primarily to one of these uses and some to the other. (We may think that *being interrogative* is primarily a property of sentences or uses of sentences, not of terms; but it is quite plausible that Plato only arrived at a clear notion of *sentence* in his late dialogue, the *Sophist*.)

something is simply to express approval of that thing as distinct from proclaiming that one real item is joined to another. So the model of the counters gets no purchase. If that model is behind the ontology of the sun-analogy, expressivism is bound to regard that analogy as a waste of time. But this need not extend to the Platonic educational programme. It is interesting to speculate whether for Plato himself the value of that programme would inevitably stand and fall with the metaphysics of the sun-analogy.

(9) Not only for Plato is it fundamental that 'the good is what every soul pursues', but arguably this is the sole reason for being concerned with the form of the good at all. So: if we want a definition of the good or the form of the good it should only be so that we may pursue truly good things more effectively. The definition of the good as wisdom, which inevitably expands into 'the good is wisdom about what is good', is frustrating not so much because it is logically circular, if indeed it even is (see Section 4.1), but because it does not help for pursuing truly good things more effectively. The problem is that since wisdom is itself one of the things that are truly good, we cannot identify this wisdom so as to pursue it if we are in the dark over what the truly good things are that this wisdom would reveal; and we *are* in the dark about that or we would not be looking for a definition of the good in the first place. However, the failure to find an adequate definition of the good that would guide us in all our practice doesn't in the least matter if human beings have access to another source of reliable tracking of truly good things as good, and reliable rejection of things that are only seemingly good. And there is such a source, at least for Plato in the *Republic*: it consists in the combination in the soul of moral virtue and dialectically trained intelligence that characterizes his philosopher-rulers. Such a combination comes into existence in individuals through right upbringing and education, which consists not in grasping and following pre-established comprehensive definitions of the good or the virtues, but in lengthy practice (with correction and encouragement from elders and betters) in trying to recognize and enact responses suitable to kinds of situations encountered, and (after a certain age) in grasping, making explicit, and criticizing purported reasons why such and such a response fits such and such a situation.[7] So this sort of nurture and education, and presumably nothing else, is what builds the ethical competence we might initially have hoped to acquire, miraculously, all at once by being fed some divinely attained, comprehensively guiding, definition of the good. The good is truly sun-like, enabling us to see the values that are really there; but it does this not by being a rich-in-meaning definitional matrix requiring esoteric dexterity to fathom, but by being brought to bear in the thin, colourless, and familiar to everyone predicate of the

---

[7] See the very helpful discussion by Annas 2011, ch. 3.

G-question when this is asked in rigorous seriousness by someone who combines good character with love of truth and exactness.

(10) Throughout I have been guided in part by a sense that an adequate account of the sun-like good should allow for something analogous to the gap or mutual externality between the literal sun and the objects it illuminates. No law dictates which parts of an analogy-base to take seriously, but one might expect a philosopher of Plato's mental and expressive agility to craft analogies in which the format of the base as it presents itself to the empirical imagination is not seriously out of kilter with the structure of the intended abstract message.[8] In other words, if some of the prevailing interpretations are right then Plato has done a poor job in choosing the sun-analogy. I am referring to views that identify the form of the good with some sort of system of the other forms, or with the metaphysical attribute of ideality or perfect intelligibility that runs through all other forms, or with the unitary source that virtually contains them. Such views make irrelevant the 'beyondness' of the literal sun in relation to the objects which it nourishes and illuminates. It may be that Plato wants us to ignore this literal beyondness of the sun, but, if so, wasn't it for him to devise a more suitable image? Indeed, many interpreters seem to want to bask in the sun-analogy while pursuing explanations that make it not so great to bask in and dubiously illuminating.

(11) Perhaps such explanations stem from assuming that the form of the good yields knowledge of the other forms (even if only of their formal or generic nature) through being itself an object of study and contemplation. This ruins the analogy because although we can see the unclouded midday sun, we do not see other visible objects by or through looking at *it*. If we look straight at it we are blinded to them. Again, one might be moved to join various Platonic thinkers in contemplating, revering, and even glorifying the form of the good *as* cause, somehow, of the being known and being real of other forms. But to think of reverence towards the form of the good as the basic attitude of *the dialectician-rulers* is again to destroy the analogy, because it is not by honouring the sun as source of visibility and generation that one looks and by its light sees specific other things; and looking and seeing specific other things by the light of the sun is the analogical equivalent of what the dialectician-rulers primarily do. What they primarily do, if the argument of this book has been on the right lines, is devise and test conceptions of what is

---

[8] Smith 2019, 96, 114, writing about the difficulties of finding a consistent interpretation of the Divided Line, has suggested that Plato sanctions these difficulties in order to warn us that images of the truth are only images, not the reality itself; this view might be extended to include the claim that an image out of kilter with its original has been chosen so as to send that same message. But if it *is* possible to give a self-consistent or apt image of the original, why not do so? It is not as if a consistent and apt image, especially if we are anyway told it is only an image, is likely to be confused by us with its original.

virtuous, above all by asking and answering the G-question (looking and seeing) so as to distinguish real from specious versions, with a view to enacting them in human life. The sun-like form of the good invites and enables this intellectual looking and seeing but is not its focus. And of ethically neutral claimants to the titles of 'justice', etc. the form of the good turns some (depending on context) into real, authentic, bearers of the name by accruing to them as an item logically adventitious or external, and so in a sense retaining its separate or even transcendent status, like the sun. By contrast, a system of ordinary forms, let alone their shared ideality, is not exactly separate from those forms themselves.

(12) According to the account offered here the rulers' dialectic is something we classify as practical reasoning (whatever else Plato supposed it might also develop or branch off into). An important advantage of this sort of interpretation is that it directly integrates the form of the good, and the rulers' commerce with it, into the *Republic*'s overall concerns, which are the questions of how we should live and how a community should be governed. I can imagine, however, that the suggested account will strike some critics as too banal to capture whatever Plato had in mind when he framed the majestic analogy of the sun. 'That's all? The mountains go into labour … and out comes this drab little mouse?' To this I think the right reply is that the sublimity of the sun-analogy and the pathos of the cave-allegory are our measure of the importance Plato attaches to getting it right about living and being governed well. *Nothing* matters more or as much. More is at stake if our souls are immortal, but even if not, there is nothing whose value could outweigh or equal the value of living well.

'…the contest matters, my dear Glaucon', I said, 'more than we think, this contest of ours to become good or bad – too much for it to be worth our being lured by honour, or money, or any sort of power, or indeed poetry, into a neglect of justice and the other parts of excellence.'
  'I agree with you,' he said, 'given everything we've talked about, and I think anyone else would too.' (608b4–c1)

Socrates' 'more than we think' may refer forward to the topic of immortality which he is about to broach; but Glaucon, who as yet has no belief in immortality (see 608d2–5), is already anyway convinced of the supreme importance of virtue.

(13) All the same one might still wonder at the intensity of Plato's emphasis on the *expertise* of his rulers, on his positioning of dialectic as a *discipline* to be mentioned alongside mathematics even though having a different logical structure. That is: one might wonder how this makes sense if the rulers' dialectic, the dialectic they operate *as* rulers, is nothing much more than a virtuous person's ordinary-language practical reasoning. Surely dialectic is

more exotic than that? I believe that the situation here is similar to what we find in those dialogues where 'dialectic' has come to be particularly identified with the method of collection and division. Plato is tremendously excited about this method: in the *Philebus* it is 'a gift of the gods thrown down from the gods together with a most brilliant kind of fire by mediation of some Prometheus' (16c5–7); in the *Phaedrus* Socrates professes to being in love with divisions and collections and ready to follow behind an expert therein 'as if tracking the footsteps of a god' (*Phaedrus* 266b4–7). Collection-division is a universal and basic tool of human intelligence; because it is universal and basic there is nothing in the least esoteric about it from a general point of view, although using it skilfully so as to get at truth about things takes perspicacity that not everyone has. (For instance, not everyone, to put it mildly, sees that gender or sex is a false basis for dividing the fit to rule from the fit to be ruled: 453e–456b.) The gods gave us this tool, just as Prometheus gave us fire, but Plato does not say that the gods or Prometheus gave us the determination and discernment to use their gifts intelligently so as to reap the benefit fully.[9] So not everyone is expert in collection and division. I think it is the same with the rulers' dialectic in the *Republic*: context-attentive practical reasoning is there for everyone, and always has been, and is not in itself in the least esoteric. But use of it is at the mercy of human emotions and prejudices. The rulers of Plato's *Republic* are its dedicated experts in that they can be trusted always to use it discerningly, even in the midst of the most confusing and demoralizing practical problems. Their awareness of this as their special responsibility, one which they must pass on to their successors, induces reflectiveness about what they do: what they do takes on the status of a 'method', and they see themselves as professionals defined by their skill with the method and by their unswerving devotion in applying it to the mundane problems of managing a city. The rest of us use reason in fits and starts when nothing distracts and often almost casually, but Plato's rulers are consciously devoted athletes of reason. In this they are special, although what we have called their 'method' is a universal human possession. Hence they are to be honoured; after death they are to be publicly commemorated as blessed and godlike (540b7–c2).

If this whole syndrome seems pretentious, the opposite attitude – namely, good old complacent muddling along – is something which, anyway to Plato, the human race just cannot afford in its ruling element, whether this is internal to the individual or embodied in political leadership. Where the most important matters are at stake there is only one basis for reliably reaching right answers,

---

[9] In the traditional story Prometheus stole fire and fire-using skill from the gods to give to humans, and was punished by Zeus (*Protagoras* 321c7–322a2). For Plato the method of collection and division, channelled *via* some Promethean genius, is the gods' spontaneous gift to us.

and this is the carefully cultivated, carefully transmitted habit of reasoning one's way towards them. Even if the *content* of dialectic in the *Republic* is 'nothing much more than a virtuous person's ordinary-language ethical reasoning', Plato frames the *practice* of it as a precious thing meriting the most elaborate concern and even reverence, because to him this 'nothing much more' is immensely hard to practise consistently, particularly for those in positions of great worldly power. He is not dumbing dialectic down (for this worry see Section 2.16) so much as trying to invest the practice of ordinary-language virtuous reasoning with the authority to play a consistently sovereign role at every level of human life. The structure of Callipolis, along with its rulers' special education, which includes education to educate their successors (540b5–6), is designed to raise ordinary practical wisdom to the status of a grand and pervasive institution.

(14) According to the reading argued for here, the dialectical work of the rulers could be described as 'discovering what to enact by bringing limit to the unlimited'. They take the intelligible form of a neutral thing which is sometimes good and sometimes bad, or in itself neither, and apply the G-question with an eye to the circumstances of implementation. To something indeterminate or 'unlimited' they apply a circumstantial condition or limit such that the combination of this with the initial unlimited elicits their unequivocal approval or disapproval: 'It is good provided that the owner is of sound mind,' 'It is bad given that the borrowed thing is a dangerous weapon', etc.

This model of intelligently limiting an unlimited so as to make or bring about something good is a central theme of the later dialogue *Philebus*, whereas in the *Republic* Plato does not use the motif of limit and unlimited. In the *Philebus*, where the theme is mainly applied to cosmology, he casts it in terms of real metaphysical principles of the universe, with cosmic Intelligence applying Limit to the Unlimited, two fundamental entities underlying and pervading everything in the intelligible as well as the sensible sphere. Limit and Unlimited are conceptual kindred of the One and the Indefinite Dyad, which were the basis of Plato's unwritten views on the fundamental principles of all things, as reported by Aristotle.[10] The fact that the polarity Limit and Unlimited does not figure in the *Republic*, even though the dialectician-rulers' reasoning could easily be described in such terms, rather suggests that this pair, and therefore the kindred One and Dyad, were not salient to Plato in composing this dialogue. The point I am leading up to is that if, as the Tübingen interpreters hold, in *Republic* VI and VII Plato had the metaphysics of the One

---

[10] Cf. Kahn 2012, 172. In the *Philebus* cosmic Intelligence is a distinct third principle, whereas in the doctrine of principles reported by Aristotle the One seems to combine the functions of both Intelligence and Limit, and to operate in the first place at the level of numbers and forms.

and the Dyad in mind as somehow especially pertinent to the thinking of his dialecticians, there ought to be more sign of it in the text. He could easily, I submit, have had Socrates say a few words invoking the theory; Glaucon and Adeimantus might have struggled a bit to understand, but in the text as we have it, Socrates does sometimes say things they find difficult (see 510b9; 511c3; 517c5; 532d2–4).[11]

(15) All the same it is right, as I see it, to be puzzled by Socrates' ostentatious 'reticence' – his insistence on speaking through images and with the utmost tentativeness about what goes on in the dialectical part of the 'longer way'. This contrasts with his generally confident tone up until the introduction of the longer way in Book VI.[12] And why does Plato refuse, or fail, to produce any specific illustrations of dialectical reasoning, given that he is generally only too ready with examples of a method he is enthusiastic about? It would be good to have an explanation based on something about dialectic in the *Republic* that is not too far from being obvious. The Tübingen hypothesis offers to fill the need for explanation – this is its strength – but is rooted in assumptions that are a long way from obvious: first, that the philosopher-rulers' dialectic is somehow focused on the metaphysical theory of the One and the Indefinite Dyad; and secondly, that this theory is so far above the heads of Glaucon and Adeimantus and the general reader that Plato, despite his huge repertoire of styles and levels of expression, found it impolitic or impossible to put together for Socrates even a short speech dashing off, in a few swift sketchy words geared to an amateur audience, a rough profile of the theory that would gesture, even if no more than gesture, in the relevant direction.

The 'something not too far from being obvious' that seems to me to provide an economical explanation of the Socratic reticence is the consideration that the philosopher-rulers' reasoning is geared to specific ethical problems. This follows directly from the reasoners' position as rulers, and is credibly true of them unless we have somehow persuaded ourselves that their primary occupation is inquiry into theoretical metaphysics or the foundations of mathematics, or some sort of mystical contemplation. The relevant features of basic human practical-ethical reasoning are that it has to take account of the circumstances or context of the reasoner's own position as agent responsible for putting the conclusion into practice, and that it is shaped by the reasoner's ethical values. This means that, by contrast with mathematical reasoning or any purely

---

[11] See the excellent discussion by Mann 2006, esp. 373–4.
[12] But note the diffidence with which he takes up the brothers' challenge at 368b. Possibly everything that follows is meant to be coloured by that. If so, in the central books his heavily marked reluctance to say much about the longer way and the form of the good manifests diffidence on diffidence piled.

theoretical reasoning, it is not feasibly explained by giving a paradigm that could be usefully or even safely adopted by all reasoners any when anywhere. If such a template abstracts from circumstances it is useless or gives the disastrous impression of being applicable in all circumstances; if it refers to the circumstances of its original use it is useless for other kinds of context. In principle, the Socrates-character could explain the dialectician's study of the One and the Dyad but is not allowed to do so because it would be too difficult for Glaucon and Adeimantus. By contrast, the interpretation I am suggesting means that Socrates himself has no more access than his interlocutors to illustrations of the reasoning of the *Republic*'s dialecticians. He, they, and we are all necessarily on the outside: not because that reasoning has an especially abstruse subject-matter but because we are outside the perspective of the agents whose reasoning it is. My hypothesis is that Plato was alive to the infeasibility of our sharing the reasoning but lacked the apparatus for explaining it. His logical vocabulary was too scanty (for instance, as far as I know he lacked a word for 'perspective' in the sense just used) to enable him to explain in abstract terms why in principle everyone can share the mathematician's reasonings whereas this is not so for the reasonings of human practical agents, even of policy-makers at the highest level. In addition, an adequate explanation would surely involve confronting and then dismantling the erroneous view that the wise agent's conclusion, which Plato would undoubtedly have wanted to describe as 'true', is only *true for* that agent and anyone sharing her/his perspective, and possibly false for others for whom a contrary conclusion (concerning the identical situation) is true, so that we are plunged into the relativism of Protagoras in the *Theaetetus*.[13] The epistemological claim that the reasons supporting a true conclusion C are visible only from a certain perspective does not entail the semantic claim that C is only *true for* whoever occupies the perspective (or is only *true from* that perspective) as distinct from true *simpliciter*: but explaining this in limited vocabulary to not very technical philosophers like Glaucon and Adeimantus would have been a major challenge, requiring a long and strenuous excursus from the main argument.

(16) If practical reasoning's opacity to those outside the reasoner's concrete perspective is a problem, it is a general one. That is to say: it is not the result of some extraordinary nature of the rulers in Plato's *Republic*. For the text indicates (517b7–c4; cf. 536a5) that access to the sun-like form of the good via the G-question is not exclusive to those rulers: any person of wisdom accesses it perhaps several times a day in her or his practical reasoning. Hence

[13] There may be a hinted reference to this at *Republic* 538d6–e4, where Socrates describes the danger of too early exposure to dialectic; *katabalēi* at e1 may allude to Protagoras' book *Truth*, also known as *Kataballontes* [sc. *Logoi*], a term from wrestling which means 'throwing down'.

it is not because the ideal rulers alone are qualified to apprehend the form of the good that Socrates' approach to it is so indirect and tentative. As several scholars have emphasized, Plato shows what the good *is* by showing in a general way what it *does*: it is what makes it the case that other forms are known and are real. Because the unadorned statement of this is exceedingly abstract, he chooses to give it body through the sun-analogy. A further reason for using the analogy may have been that he has already decided on the allegory of the cave to portray the human condition, and the sun-analogy fits with that. Light and darkness, vision and blindness, are natural metaphors for insight versus ignorance, and Plato has already tapped into this imagery in the argument against the sight-lovers in Book V. Yet another reason is the opportunity to present sun and good not merely as analogues but as standing in the more intimate relation of child to parent, this being a way of affirming that the natural world ultimately owes its nature to the very same principle of value as that which should rule human life (see Section 4.4). These reasons together and perhaps even separately are enough to explain Plato's decision to use the sun as image of the good. What we should resist is the idea, conveyed by some interpreters, that Plato resorts to the image rather than speaking directly because the form of the good encompasses a fascinatingly profound nature surpassing the comprehension perhaps of Plato himself. We are not given the analogy as a substitute for perhaps unattainable insight into that fascinating nature, for the sun-like form of the good has no such nature: it is only what is brought to bear in the simple G-question wielded by a wise intelligence. Wisdom is not the ability to encapsulate that form in a definition, either in the mode of conceptual analysis or in the synthetic mode of scientific analysis; it is the good judgement that comes from moral virtue backed by the highest standards for seeking out truth.

(17) Throughout I have been considering dialectic as the intellectual art or skill immediately implicated in *rule* by philosophers. It is in this context that the sketchiness of Socrates' account of it is explained as due to the practical nature of rulers' dialectic. Still, it is rather incredible that for Plato when he wrote the *Republic* there is nothing more to what he means by 'dialectic': that dialectic now is only a method for improving the practical thinking about basic values that ought to be the task of rulers. Surely dialectic in relation to the author of the *Republic* is, like the dialectic discussed in later dialogues, more comprehensively theoretical than that, more fertile in deep philosophical questions? The feeling that this is so has understandably informed some central interpretative approaches criticized in this book; and even if the arguments supporting those criticisms are sound, the feeling is not going to go away easily.

To examine this question is not really part of the present project, but a few points can be raised. First, there is the fact that Plato does not draw the

Aristotelian boundary and contrast between practical and theoretical think-ing.[14] Secondly, there is the possibility that this stems not from lack of sophistication but from a deliberately non-compartmentalizing mind-set according to which the practice-oriented dialectic of rulers might somehow be nourished from discoveries and speculations of a more widely ranging philosophy. Thus in the *Phaedrus* Socrates insists that the true art of rhetoric entails mastery of an exact and comprehensive psychology which in turn rests on an understanding of the natural world as a whole, and that no sensible person would go to the trouble of attaining all this knowledge just 'in order to speak and act among human beings, but so as to be able to speak and act in a way that pleases the gods as much as possible', even if 'being pleasant to his fellow slaves ... may happen as a side-effect' (*Phaedrus* 270a–272b; 273d–274a, trans. Nehemas and Woodruff 1997). The education needed for true expertise in rhetoric would necessarily take one far beyond rhetoric's familiar purposes, so that a truly sufficient rhetorical education is necessarily over-education for persuasion in law courts and assembly. Did Plato, in parallel fashion, think that his ideal rulers need, when approaching the form of the good and the virtue-forms, an intellectual depth and breadth gained only through theoretical study of fundamentals such as being, non-being, sameness, and difference, Limit, Unlimited, and cosmopoieic Intelligence – even the One and the Indefinite Dyad – so that they too cannot be properly educated for their primary role without becoming over-educated for it?[15]

(18) The answer is not straightforward.[16] On the one hand, the philosophers' primary role once fully trained is to rule the state for a period. If the argument of this book is correct, then performance of this role does not include absorp-tion in theoretical metaphysics and cosmology, any more than it includes thinking in the language of mathematics or meta-mathematics (Section 4.3). Insofar as dialectic in the *Republic* is the method by which the ruler rules, dialectic is practical reasoning conducted in familiar terms. This position is all that is needed to make sense of what the text says about dialectic and its place in the Divided Line, and about the form of the good as non-hypothetical principle. The project of Books VI and VII was to show, even if only in a sketchy way, what 'philosophy' would contribute to the work of running a state. According to the argument of this book, its contribution consists in analytical and critical intelligence and unwavering commitment to rationality in reaching ethical judgements. There is no reason to think that it would include much, or any, self-consciously technical philosophy. *Philosophia* for Plato is basically the uncompromising methodical search for principled truth

---

[14] Cf. Delcomminette 2006, 4.   [15] Cf. Annas 1999, 104–6.
[16] I am grateful to Alex Long for comments that made me clearer about the issues in (18) and (19).

on matters of fundamental importance, whether or not that truth lies in some technical place.

(19) On the other hand, the question of what Plato himself would have counted as coming under 'dialectic' at the time of writing the *Republic* is different from the question of how he depicts the reasoning that guides his rulers *in* that dialogue.[17] There is no reason to assume that what Plato chooses to show about the reasoning of rulers *qua* rulers coincides with how he himself envisaged philosophy when writing the work. This unnecessary assumption has surely contributed to the urge to go behind the text and imagine Callipolitan leaders as governing with minds actively at work on abstract theories of metaphysics. Instead, more economically, we should think of them as epitomizing just what difference philosophy would make to the daily business of *ruling* if the two were joined. The difference would not consist in absorption in fundamental metaphysics and so on, because that would be irrelevant to the task at hand. However, philosophy does bring to ruling the sense or knowledge that there are grander things in life. One great virtue of truly philosophical rulers is reluctance to cling to power. They are consumed by a passion for truth, and presumably they somehow know that truth is not restricted to mathematics and policy-making. Presumably the passion for truth includes boundless curiosity. We are fleetingly shown how their first educational encounter with the form of the good sparks the realization that the good is the source of *everything* right and beautiful in both sensible and intelligible domains (517b7–c4). We may conjecture that this *aperçu* is not left to depend on private intuition but becomes a topic in the curriculum. Instruction would thus touch on the good in relation to cosmology and perhaps to the foundations of mathematics and universal metaphysics. When philosophy spreads in these directions there will be no shortage of technicality.

But Plato in the *Republic* does not go into any of this. His silence, I suggest, is because he does not think acquaintance with any of those recondite subjects is expressed directly in the thinking relevant to leadership. Yes, his best leaders will know the excitement of such theoretical questions; but this is in the way we today might think leaders should have some experience of personal love and affection, although not for a moment do we suppose that leadership itself consists in the activities of romantic love, family closeness, and so on. Furthermore, Plato's own ideas about those theoretical questions may have been little more than programmatic when he was writing the *Republic*. The very fact that here he constructs philosopher-rulers who look forward to retiring to a more enjoyable and beautiful kind of intellectual activity may be

---

[17] The separation of these questions is a fruit of my interaction with Christopher Rowe's work on Plato; he is of course innocent of any faults in the present argument.

what tipped him into carving out areas for non-ethical philosophy such as we find in the *Cratylus*, the *Parmenides*, the *Theaetetus*, the *Sophist*, parts of the *Philebus*, and the *Timaeus*. For the philosopher-ruler of Callipolis is not a *possible* entity unless some less constrained, more intrinsically satisfying, intellectual activities are available and identifiable; and Plato may have thought that this is true of rational rule in general aside from the specific setting of Callipolis. Finding the right kind of statesman depends, he now sees, on finding appropriate intellectual interests for the future ex-statesman.[18] But an agenda adequate to fill this bill is not provided by the already existing theories of reality, any more than traditional mythology is adequate for shaping moral development. Already existing theories were mostly materialistic, in some cases godless, and in the case of Parmenides seemed to call into doubt the very reality – certainly the importance for deep thinkers – of the practical, social, ethical world. Thus Plato may have seen the *Republic*'s own conception of fitness for rule as setting him a post-*Republic* task of creating new non-ethical paths for philosophy by initiating some himself and encouraging others.[19] If so, his later, more theoretical, work too would help substantiate the motivating belief of the *Republic* that reliable, consistent, rule of humans by human reason is possible after all. It is possible only if the right sort of ruler is possible, and the right sort of ruler is possible only if theoretical fields can be opened up that will cater for the unlimited passion for truth that shapes the right sort of ruler – one whose fulfilment lies not in ruling but somewhere beyond it.

(20) I have given a minimalist account of dialectic as wielded by Plato's philosopher-rulers. This dialectic does not, for its practitioners, include or rest on an elaborately theorized metaphysics of the intelligible world and its relation to the sensible world. But it does depend on what we might call naïve realism about forms. The dialecticians absolutely assume that there is such a thing as justice and so on for the other forms that concern them, and that posing the G-question is posing a question with an objective answer, one based on the real natures of the intelligibles they are trying to find out about. They experience no more resistance to this assumption than any of us normally experience in accepting the reality of our physical environment. Their realism about the intelligible comes not from arguments to that effect but from their previous immersion in mathematics. This is what has proofed them against scepticism about the intelligible, just as their moral upbringing has proofed them against moral corruption, and just as nature has proofed us all against

[18] In the *Timaeus*, which refers back to the *Republic*, the main character is a philosopher-scientist who has held the highest offices in his 'superlatively well governed' city (20a1–5).
[19] 'Non-ethical' should not be exaggerated. There is obvious meta-ethical relevance in the attack on relativism in the *Theaetetus* and the demonstration that falsehood is possible in the *Sophist*.

thoroughgoing scepticism about the independent being of the things we see and touch. By second nature they accept that the form, e.g., of justice is unique and changeless. This is because by second nature they are committed to rationality about such matters: they insist on having *reasons* for holding that EFG answers to justice here, when what answers to it over there is something contrary to EFG. This attitude embodies the assumption (see Section 2.19) that justice is *unique* – there are not different justices or different natures of justice scattered about. Likewise, their insistence on having reasons for holding that this case of EFG is just, this other one not, embodies the assumption that justice is *unalterably* whatever it is – not the sort of thing that sometimes does and sometimes doesn't occur in EFG just like that, perhaps because the weather has changed. The 'unique and unalterable' assumption amounts to the axiom that differences in the interpretation of justice, and any virtue-form, can only come from differences of changeable context or perspective. So the dialecticians are indeed animated by an underlying recognition[20] of unique and immutable justice 'standing there on a sacred pedestal', as at *Phaedrus* 254b6–7 (although the reference there is to the forms of beauty and moderation). The image captures the axiom's inviolability. At any rate, that uniqueness and immutability are a presupposition, not a theorem, of dialectical practice in the *Republic*. The question of justifying or explaining it does not arise for the practitioners. They and other such reasoners (including ourselves?) are probably sure that they will go on reasoning about justice and the like whether or not anyone ever produces a meta-philosophical justification of their right to do so, or a demonstration that the presupposed ontology is possible.

---

[20] Might Plato have said 'recollection'? The notion hardly surfaces in the *Republic* (there is a brief allusion at 498d3–5). According to Kahn 2012, 166–7, this is for rhetorical and artistic reasons rather than philosophical ones. In fact, there are several philosophical difficulties about adapting the notion of *anamnēsis* to explain dialectical reasoning in the *Republic*. (a) The first audiences of the *Republic*, especially if the *Phaedrus* is later as some scholars think, would have associated recollection with mathematical reasoning (*Meno* 82b–85e; *Phaedo* 73a–b); but since Plato now holds that dialectical reasoning is not mathematical in style he must avoid giving any impression to the contrary. (b) He would have had to explain why, if the rulers' dialectic is guided by anamnesis, it presupposes elaborate mathematical and moral education, given that the slave in the *Meno* lacked those advantages (cf. 85d3; e1–6). (c) In the *Meno* the demonstration of recollection depends on the fact that the slave's audience, Socrates and Meno (and most readers), know independently that the slave's final reasoning is correct (cf. *Phaedo* 73a–b); but a comparable scenario is impossible with practical reasoning; the rulers cannot be shown engaged in a specimen which Socrates, Glaucon, Adeimantus, and we ourselves already know is correct (see (15) above and Section 2.18). (d) If we simply assume the rulers' correctness, the most reasonable explanation is their massive education, including the fifteen years of practical experience, whereas with Meno's slave Platonic recollection fills an explanatory gap. Likewise the *Phaedrus* invokes recollection of the form of beauty to explain the lover's mind-blowing rapture, a phenomenon seemingly inexplicable by mundane causes. Difficulties (a) and (c) depend on controversial positions argued for in this book, but (b) and (d) do not.

(21) This naïve realism about intelligibles passes muster in the *Republic* because it is shared by the main interlocutors. Elsewhere Plato shows the notion of forms under attack, with sympathizers speaking up for it. Timaeus offers a defence (*Timaeus* 51b–e), and Plato's Parmenides-character ends his barrage of objections to forms with the assertion that rejecting them means destroying the power of rational discourse (*tou dialegesthai dunamin*, *Parmenides*135b–c; cf. *Republic* 511b3). The dialectical training that fills the rest of the *Parmenides* is an extreme display of the power of rational discourse. It may *inter alia* be meant to block scepticism about intelligible reality by plunging us into exercise about intelligibles (*gumnasthēnai, gumnasia*, 135c–e).[21] The punishingly hard work of *Parmenides* Part 2 not only makes us cleverer at abstract thinking but commits us, while we are at it, to the reality of its objects. (And Plato might well think it irrational, post-exercise, to shed the ontological commitment yet nonetheless pride ourselves on now being cleverer than before. If we emerge from the commitment, as from a dream or voluntary fiction, to face a world – for us, the only world – of empirical opinion which our new-found dialectical cleverness is profoundly unfitted to cope with, in what way are we now cleverer? We have emerged with a beautifully sharpened knife into a place where there is nothing for it to cut.) So *Parmenides* Part 2 is comparable to the mathematical training in the *Republic*.[22] Whether or not Part 2 in any way refutes the objections in Part 1, it provides a space such that to move about in it is to have taken intelligible reality on board. Precisely this is the point of the mathematical curriculum in Callipolis.[23]

Even so, the *Parmenides* and the *Republic* contexts are profoundly different. The former envisages a purely intellectual assault on self-conscious realism about the intelligible – an attack that could affect only a tiny band of the highly educated. The *Republic*, by contrast, is a sustained reflection on how to respond to something universally human: our readiness to loosen our non-theorized grip on the reality of things such as justice whenever a fit of anger, greed, passionate love, jealousy, fear, or self-importance starts to take possession. The only self-defence is to strengthen reason by cultivating habits and skills for using it in steady appreciation of its unique value for the whole of

---

[21] Engaging with the Part 1 arguments themselves would have the same benefit, but presumably Plato wants to provide an antidote whose logical content is not at odds with its therapeutic effect.

[22] Thanks to Tamsin de Waal for the suggestion that Plato recognizes non-mathematical ways of training for dialectic.

[23] The realism about intelligbles and trust in reason generated by the mathematical training will extend to any intelligible subject-matter, even though for the rulers as such its focus is limited to intelligibles relating to the human virtues.

life. This is the main message of *Republic* V–VII. It is not at all an intellectually surprising message. What is endlessly surprising, because so hard to face about ourselves, is our failure to hold fast to our most powerful asset when it comes to putting it into practice. Getting us to work towards correcting this is one great aim of the *Republic*.

References

Adam, J. (1902). *The* Republic *of Plato, Books I–V*, Cambridge: Cambridge University Press.

(1907). *The* Republic *of Plato, Books VI–X*, Cambridge: Cambridge University Press.

Annas, J. (1981). *An Introduction to Plato's* Republic, Oxford: Clarendon Press.

(1999). *Platonic Ethics Old and New*, Ithaca: Cornell University Press.

(2011). *Intelligent Virtue*, Oxford: Oxford University Press.

(2017). *Virtue and Law in Plato and Beyond*, Oxford: Oxford University Press.

Arneson, R. (2010). Good, Period. *Analysis* 70, 731–44.

Austin, J. L. (1979). 'The Line and the Cave in Plato's *Republic*'. In J. L. Austin, *Philosophical Papers*, edited by J. O. Urmson and G. J. Warnock, Oxford: Oxford University Press, pp. 189–303.

Bailey, D. T. J. (2006). Plato and Aristotle on the Unhypothetical. *Oxford Studies in Ancient Philosophy* 30, 102–26.

(2008). Excavating *Dissoi Logoi* 4. *Oxford Studies in Ancient Philosophy* 35, 249–64.

Baltzly, D. (1996). To an Unhypothetical First Principle in Plato's 'Republic'. *History of Philosophy Quarterly* 13, 149–65.

Barnes, J. (1991). Le soleil de Platon vu avec des lunettes analytiques. *Rue Descartes* 1/2, 81–92.

Barney, R. (2008). *Eros* and Necessity in the Ascent from the Cave. *Ancient Philosophy* 28, 357–72.

Bedu-Addo, J. T. (1978). Mathematics, Dialectic and the Good in the *Republic* VI–VII. *Platon* 30, 111–27.

Benson, H. (2012). The Problem is not Mathematics but Mathematicians: Plato and the Mathematicians Again. *Philosophia Mathematica* 20, 170–99.

(2015). *Clitophon's Challenge: Dialectic in Plato's* Meno, Phaedo, *and* Republic, Oxford: Oxford University Press.

(forthcoming). Dialectic in the Cave. In M. M. McCabe and S. Trépanier, eds., *Re-Reading Plato's* Republic, Edinburgh: Edinburgh University Press.

Berti, E. (2002). l'idea del bene in relazione alla dialettica. In G. Reale and S. Scolnicov, eds., *New Images of Plato: Dialogues on the Idea of the Good*, Sankt Augustin: Academia, pp. 307–17.

Bloom, A. (1991). *The Republic of Plato*, New York: Basic Books.

Blössner, N. (2007). The City-Soul Analogy (translated from the German by G. R. F. Ferrari). In G. R. F. Ferrari, ed., *The Cambridge Companion to Plato's* Republic, Cambridge: Cambridge University Press, pp. 345–85.

Bordt, M. (2006). *Platons Theologie*. Freiburg-Munich: Karl Alber.

Boyle, A. J. (1974). Plato's Divided Line: Essay II: Mathematics and Dialectic. *Apeiron* 8, 7–18.

Broadie, S. (2005). On the Idea of the *summum bonum*. In C. Gill, ed., *Virtue, Norms, and Objectivity: Issues in Ancient and Modern Ethics*, Oxford: Oxford University Press, pp. 41–58; repr. in S. Broadie (2007), *Aristotle and Beyond: Essays on Metaphysics and Ethics*, Cambridge: Cambridge University Press, 135–52.

(2007). Why No Platonistic Ideas of Artefacts? In D. Scott, ed., *Maieusis: Essays in Ancient Philosophy in Honour of Myles Burnyeat*, Oxford: Oxford University Press, pp. 232–53.

(2011). *Nature and Divinity in Plato's* Timaeus, Cambridge: Cambridge University Press.

Brown, L. (2007). Glaucon's Challenge, Rational Egoism and Ordinary Morality. In D. Cairns, F.-H. Herrmann, and T. Penner, eds., *Pursuing the Good: Ethics and Metaphysics in Plato's* Republic, Edinburgh: Edinburgh University Press, pp. 42–60.

Burnyeat, M. F. (1987). Platonism and Mathematics: a Prelude to Discussion. In A. Graeser, ed., *Mathematics and Metaphysics in Aristotle: Acts of the Xth Symposium Aristotelicum*, Bern: Haupt, pp. 213–40; repr. in Burnyeat (2012), vol. II, pp. 145–72.

Burnyeat, M. F. (1992). Utopia and Fantasy: the Practicability of Plato's Ideally Just City. In J. Hopkins and A. Savile, eds., *Psychoanalysis, Mind, and Art*, Oxford: Oxford University Press; repr. in G. Fine, ed., *Plato 2*, Oxford: University Press, pp. 279–308.

(1997–8). Culture and Society in Plato's Republic, The Tanner Lectures on Human Values delivered at Harvard University, https://tannerlectures.utah.edu/.

(1998). *Dissoi Logoi*. In E. Craig, ed., *The Routledge Encyclopedia of Philosophy*, London: Routledge; repr. in Burnyeat (2012), vol. II, pp. 346–8.

(2000). Plato on Why Mathematics Is Good for the Soul. In T. J. Smiley, ed., *Mathematics and Necessity: Essays in the History of Philosophy*, Oxford: Oxford University Press, pp. 1–82.

(2012). *Explorations in Ancient and Modern Philosophy*, 2 vols., Cambridge: Cambridge University Press.

Chambry, E. (1946). *Platon, Oeuvres complètes, tome 7:* La République *IV–X* , Paris: Belles Lettres.

Cherniss, H. (1947). Some War-Time Publications Concerning Plato,1. *American Journal of Philology* 68, 113–46.

Cooper, J. (1977). The Psychology of Justice in Plato. *American Philosophical Quarterly* 14, 151–7; repr. in J. Cooper (1999), *Reason and Emotion: Essays on Ancient Moral Psychology and Ethical Theory*, Princeton: Princeton University Press, pp. 138–50.

Cornford, F. M. (1932a). Mathematics and Dialectic in the Republic VI—VII (I). *Mind* 41, 37–52.

(1932b). Mathematics and Dialectic in the Republic VI–VII (II). *Mind* 41, 173–90.

(1937). *Plato's Cosmology*, London: Kegan Paul.

(1941). *The Republic of Plato, Translated with Introduction and Notes*, London: Oxford University Press.

Crisp, R. (2013). In Defence of Absolute Goodness. *Philosophy and Phenomenological Research* 87, 476–82.

Crombie, I. M. (1962). *An Examination of Plato's Doctrines*, vol. I, London: Routledge and Kegan Paul.

(1963). *An Examination of Plato's Doctrines*, vol. II, London: Routledge and Kegan Paul.

Cross, R. C., and Woozley, A. D. (1964). *Plato's Republic: a Philosophical Commentary*, London: Macmillan.

Delcomminette, S. (2006). *Le Philèbe de Platon: introduction à l'agathologie platonicienne*. Leiden: Brill.

Denyer, N. (2007). Sun and Line: the Role of the Good. In G. R. F. Ferrari, ed., *The Cambridge Companion to Plato's* Republic, Cambridge: Cambridge University Press, pp. 284–309.

Dixsaut, M. (2001). *Métamorphoses de la dialectique dans les dialogues de Platon*, Paris: Vrin.

(2005). Encore une fois le bien. In M. Dixsaut, ed., *Études sur la* République *de Platon*, vol. II, Paris: Vrin, pp. 225–55.

El Murr, D. (2014). Why the Good? Appearance, Reality and the Desire for the Good in *Republic* VI, 504B–06D. *Méthexis* 27, 47–60.

Emlyn-Jones, C., and Preddy, W. (2014). *Plato, Republic, Volume 2, Books 6–10*, Loeb Classical Library 276, Cambridge, MA: Harvard University Press.

Ferber, R. (2013). ho de diôkei men hapasa psuchê kai toutou heneka panta prattei. In N. Notomi and L. Brisson, eds., *Dialogues on Plato's* Politeia, Sankt Agustin: Academia, pp. 233–41.

Ferrari, F. (2007). Il problema dell' esistenza di idee di artefacta. In M. Vegetti (2007), pp. 151–71.

(2013). The Idea of the Good as Cause. In M. Vegetti, F. Ferrari, and T. Lynch, eds., *The Painter of Constitutions: Selected Essays on Plato's* Republic, Sankt Augustin: Academia, pp. 155–72 = Essay E in Vegetti (2003), pp. 287–326.

Fine, G. (1978). Knowledge and Belief in Republic V. *Archiv für Geschichte der Philosophie* 60, 121–39.

(1999). Knowledge and Belief in *Republic* 5–7. In G. Fine, ed., *Plato 1: Metaphysics and Epistemology*, Oxford: Oxford University Press, pp. 215–46.

Fink, J. (2012). Introduction. In J. Fink, ed., *The Development of Dialectic from Plato to Aristotle*, Cambridge: Cambridge University Press, pp. 1–23.

Foley, R. (2008). Plato's Undividable Line: Contradiction and Method in *Republic* VI. *Journal of the History of Philosophy* 46, 1–23.

Franklin, L. (2013). Commentary on Nails. *Proceedings of the Boston Area Colloquium in Ancient Philosophy* 28, 102–9.

Frede, D. (1993). Out of the Cave: What Socrates Learned from Diotima. In R. Rosen and R. Farrell, eds., *Nomodeiktes: Greek Studies in Honor of Martin Ostwald*, Ann Arbor: University of Michigan Press, pp. 397–422.

Gaiser, K. (1980). Plato's Enigmatic Lecture 'On the Good'. *Phronesis* 25, 5–37.

Gentzler, J. (2005). How to Know the Good: the Moral Epistemology of Plato's *Republic*. *Philosophical Review* 114, 469–96.

Gerson, L. (1990). *God and Greek Philosophy*, London: Routledge.

(2002). The Development of the Doctrine of the Good and Plato's Development. In G. Reale and S. Scolnikov, eds., *New Images of Plato*, Sankt Augustin: Academia, pp. 379–91.

(2015). Ideas of Good? In D. Nails and H. Tarrant, eds., *Second Sailing: Alternative Perspectives on Plato*, Helsinki: Societas Scientiarum Fennica, pp. 225–42.

(2018). What are the Objects of Dianoia? *Plato Journal* 18, 45–53.

(2020). *Platonism and Naturalism: the Possibility of Philosophy*, Ithaca: Cornell University Press.

Gertken, J., and Kiesewetter, B. (2017). The Right and the Wrong Kind of Reasons. *Philosophy Compass* 12, no. 5.

Gosling, J. C. B. (1960). Republic 5: ta polla kala. *Phronesis* 5, 116–28.

(1973). *Plato*, London: Routledge and Kegan Paul.

Griffith, T. (2000). *Plato: The Republic*, ed. G. R. F. Ferrari, Cambridge: Cambridge University Press.

Grube, G., revised by C. Reeve (1997). *Republic*. In *Plato, Complete Works*, ed. J. Cooper, Indianapolis: Hackett.

Hare, R. M. (1965). Plato and the Mathematicians. In R. Bambrough, ed., *New Essays on Plato and Aristotle*, London: Routledge and Kegan Paul, pp. 21–38.

Harte, V. (2008). Plato's Metaphysics. In G. Fine, ed., *The Oxford Handbook of Plato*, Oxford: Oxford University Press, pp. 191–220.

Hobbs, A. (2007). Plato on War. In D. Scott, ed., *Maieusis: Essays in Ancient Philosophy in Honour of Myles Burnyeat*, Oxford: Oxford University Press, pp. 176–95.

Irwin, T. H. (1977). Plato's Heracliteanism. *Philosophical Quarterly* 27, 1–13.

(1995). *Plato's Ethics*, Oxford: Oxford University Press.

Jenkins, M. (2015). Early Education in Plato's *Republic*. *British Journal for the History of Philosophy* 23, 843–63.

Johansen, T. K. (2013). Timaeus in the Cave. In G. Boys-Stones, D. El Murr, and C. Gill, eds., *The Platonic Art of Philosophy*, Cambridge: Cambridge University Press, pp. 90–109.

Joseph, H. W. B. (1948). *Knowledge and the Good in Plato's Republic*, London: Oxford University Press.

Jowett, B. (1892). *The Dialogues of Plato*, Oxford: Clarendon Press.

Kahn, C. (2012). The Philosophical Importance of the Dialogue Form for Plato. In J. Fink, ed., *The Development of Dialectic from Plato to Aristotle*, Cambridge: Cambridge University Press, pp. 158–73.

Karasmanis, V. (1988). Plato's *Republic*: the Line and the Cave. *Apeiron* 21, 147–21.

(2004). Dialectic and the Good in Plato's *Republic*. In J. Tsimbidaros, ed., *Platon et Aristote: dialectique et métaphysique*, Cahiers de Philosophie Ancienne 19, Brussels: Ousia, pp. 31–50.

Krämer, H.-J. (1990). *Plato and the Foundations of Metaphysics*, ed. and tr. J. Catan, Binghamton: SUNY Press.

Kraut, R. (2003). Penner's Anti-Paradeigmatism. *Modern Schoolman* 80, 235–43.

(2011). *Against Absolute Goodness*. Oxford: Oxford University Press.

Lafrance, Y. (1980). Platon et la géometrie: la méthode dialectique en *République* 509d–511e. *Dialogue* 19, 46–93.

Lear, G. R. (2006). Plato on Learning to Love Beauty. In G. Santas, ed., *The Blackwell Guide to Plato's Republic*, Oxford: Blackwell, pp. 104–24.

Lee, D. (2007). *Plato: Republic* (revised edition), London: Penguin.

Leroux, G. (2004). *Platon, La République: traduction, introduction et notes*. Paris: Flammarion.

Lesher, J. (2010). The Meaning of '*Saphēneia*' in Plato's Divided Line. In M. McPherran, ed., *Plato's* Republic: *a Critical Guide*, Cambridge: Cambridge University Press, pp. 171–87.

Lesses, G. (1987). Weakness, Reason, and the Divided Soul in Plato's *Republic*. *History of Philosophy Quarterly* 4, 147–61.

Lindsay, A. D. (1935). *Plato's* Republic, London: Dent.

Lloyd, G. E. R. (1990). *Demystifying Mentalities*, Cambridge: Cambridge University Press.

Long, A. A. (2020). Politics and Divinity in Plato's *Republic*: the Form of the Good. In F. Leigh, ed., *Forms, Language, and Education: S. V. Keeling Memorial Lectures in Ancient Philosophy, 2011–2018*, BICS Supplement 141, London: Wiley, pp. 69–87.

Long, A. G. (2013a). *Conversation and Self-Sufficiency in Plato*. Oxford: Oxford University Press.

(2013b). The Political Art in Plato's *Republic*. In V. Harte and M. Lane, eds., *Politeia in Greek and Roman Philosophy*, Cambridge: Cambridge University Press, pp. 15–31.

McCabe, M. M. (2006). Is Dialectic as Dialectic Does? The Virtue of Philosophical Conversation. In B. Reis, ed., *The Virtuous Life in Greek Ethics*, Cambridge: Cambridge University Press, pp. 70–99; repr. in McCabe (2015), *Platonic Conversations*, Oxford: Oxford University Press, pp. 100–24.

McPherran, M. (2006). The Gods and Piety of Plato's *Republic*. In G. Santas, ed., *The Blackwell Guide to Plato's* Republic, Oxford: Blackwell, pp. 84–103.

Mann, W.-R. (2006). Plato in Tübingen: a Discussion of Konrad Gaiser, *Gesammelte Schriften*. *Oxford Studies in Ancient Philosophy* 31, 349–400.

Miller, M. (1985). Platonic Provocations: Reflections on the Soul and the Good in the *Republic*. In D. O'Meara, ed., *Platonic Investigations*, Washington, DC: Catholic University of America Press, pp. 163–90.

(1999). Figure, Ratio, Form: Plato's Five Mathematical Studies. *Apeiron* 32, 73–88.

(2007). Beginning the 'Longer Way'. In G. R. F. Ferrari, ed., *The Cambridge Companion to Plato's* Republic, Cambridge: Cambridge University Press, pp. 310–44.

Mohr, R. (2005). *God and Forms in Plato*. Las Vegas: Parmenides.

Molinelli, S. (2018). Dissoi Logoi: a New Commented Edition, doctoral thesis, Durham University. Available at http://etheses.dur.ac.uk/12451/.

Morrison, D. (2007). The Utopian Character of Plato's Ideal City. In G. R. F. Ferrari, ed., *The Cambridge Companion to Plato's* Republic, Cambridge: Cambridge University Press, pp. 232–55.

Morrison, J. M. (1977). Two Unresolved Difficulties in the Line and Cave. *Phronesis* 22, 212–31.

Moss, J. (2008). Appearances and Calculations: Plato's Division of the Soul. *Oxford Studies in Ancient Philosophy* 34, 35–68

(2021). *Plato's Epistemology: Being and Seeming*, Oxford: Oxford University Press.

Mueller, I. (1992). Mathematical Method and Philosophical Truth. In R. Kraut, ed., *The Cambridge Companion to Plato*, Cambridge: Cambridge University Press, pp. 170–99.

Nails, D. (2013). Colloquium 3: Two Dogmas of Platonism. *Proceedings of the Boston Area Colloquium in Ancient Philosophy* 28, 77–101.

Nehamas, A., and Woodruff, P. (1997). Translation of the *Phaedrus*. In J. Cooper, ed., *Complete Works of Plato*, Indianapolis: Hackett.

Netz, R. (1998). Greek Mathematical Diagrams: Their Use and Their Meaning. *For the Learning of Mathematics* 18, 33–9.

(2003). How Propositions Begin: Towards an Interpretation of ὑπόθεσις in Plato's Divided Line. *Hyperboreus* 9, 295–318.

(2004). *The Transformation of Mathematics in the Early Mediterranean World: From Problems to Equations*, Cambridge: Cambridge University Press.

Patterson, R. (1985). *Image and Reality in Plato's Metaphysics*, Indianapolis: Hackett.

(2007). Diagrams, Dialectic, and Mathematical Foundations in Plato. *Apeiron* 40, 1–33.

Penner, T. (1987). *The Ascent from Nominalism*, Dordrecht: Reidel.

(2007a). The Good, Advantage, Happiness and the Form of the Good: How Continuous with Socratic Ethics Is Platonic Ethics? In D. Cairns, F.-H. Herrmann, and T. Penner, eds., *Pursuing the Good: Ethics and Metaphysics in Plato's Republic*, Edinburgh: Edinburgh University Press. pp. 93–121.

(2007b). What Is the Form of the Good the Form of? A Question about the Plot of the *Republic*. In D. Cairns, F.-H. Herrmann, and T. Penner, eds., *Pursuing the Good: Ethics and Metaphysics in Plato's Republic*, Edinburgh: Edinburgh University Press, pp. 15–41.

(2008). The Forms in the *Republic*. In G. Santas, ed., *The Blackwell Guide to Plato's Republic*, Oxford: Blackwell, pp. 234–62.

Peterson, S. (2011). *Socrates and Philosophy in the Dialogues of Plato*, Cambridge: Cambridge University Press.

Philoponus J. (2004). *Against Proclus on the Eternity of the World 1–5*, trans. I. Kupreeva and M. Share, London: Duckworth.

Press, G. (2002). Sun and Good from the Perspective of the History of Philosophy. In G. Reale and S. Scolnicov, eds., *New Images of Plato: Dialogues on the Idea of the Good*, Sankt Augustin: Academia, pp. 237–49.

Price, A. W. (2011). *Virtue and Reason in Plato and Aristotle*, Oxford: Oxford University Press.

Proclus (1899). *In Platonis Rem Publicam commentaria*, vol. I, ed. G. Kroll, Leipzig: Teubner.

Reeve, C. (1988). *Philosopher-Kings: the Argument of Plato's* Republic, Princeton: Princeton University Press.

(2012). *Blindness and Reorientation: Problems in Plato's* Republic, Oxford: Oxford University Press.

Repellini, F. (2013). The Line and the Cave. In M. Vegetti, F. Ferrari, and T. Lynch, eds., *The Painter of Constitutions: Selected Essays on Plato's* Republic, Sankt Augustin: Academia, pp. 173–98 = Essay G in Vegetti (2003), pp. 355–404.

Riel, G. van (2013) *Plato's Gods*, Farnham: Ashgate.

Robinson, R. (1953). *Plato's Earlier Dialectic*, 2nd ed., Oxford: Clarendon Press.

Rorty, A. (2012). The Use and Abuse of Morality. *Journal of Ethics* 16, 1–13.

Rose, L. (1966). Plato's Unhypothetical Principle. *Journal of the History of Philosophy* 4, 169–98.

Rosen, S. (2005). The Good, the Divided Line, and the Cave. In Rosen, *Plato's Republic: a Study*, New Haven: Yale University Press, pp. 255–302.

Ross, W. D. (1953). *Plato's Theory of Ideas*, Oxford: Clarendon Press.
Rowe, C. (2005). What Difference Do Forms make for Platonic Epistemology? In C. Gill, ed., *Virtue, Norms, and Objectivity*, Oxford: Oxford University Press, pp. 215–32.
   (2007a). The Form of the Good and the Good in Plato's *Republic*. In D. Cairns, F.-H. Herrmann, and T. Penner, eds., *Pursuing the Good: Ethics and Metaphysics in Plato's Republic*. Edinburgh: Edinburgh University Press, pp. 125–53.
   (2007b). The Place of the *Republic* in Plato's Political Thought'. In G. R. F. Ferrari, ed., *The Cambridge Companion to Plato's* Republic, Cambridge: Cambridge University Press, pp. 27–34.
   (2007c). *Plato and the Art of Philosophical Writing*, Cambridge: Cambridge University Press.
   (2012). *Plato, Republic*, trans. with an Introduction and Notes, London: Penguin.
Rowett, C (2016). Why the Philosopher Kings Will Believe the Noble Lie. *Oxford Studies in Ancient Philosophy* 50, 67–100.
   (2018). *Knowledge and Truth in Plato: Stepping Past the Shadow of Socrates*, Oxford: Oxford University Press.
Rufener, R. (2011). *Der Staat/Politeia: Griechisch – Deutsch, Platon*, Berlin: Deutscher Taschenbuch Verlag.
Sachs, D. (1963). A Fallacy in Plato's *Republic*. *Philosophical Review* 72, 141–58.
Santas, G (1980/1999). The Form of the Good in Plato's Republic. *Philosophical Inquiry* (Winter 1980), 374–403; repr. in G. Fine, ed. (1999), *Plato I: Metaphysics and Epistemology*, Oxford: Oxford University Press, pp. 247–74. Page references are to the reprint.
   (2001). *Goodness and Justice*, Oxford: Oxford University Press.
Sattler, B. (2013). The Eleusinian Mysteries in Pre-Platonic Thought: Metaphor, Practice and Imagery for Plato's Symposium. In V. Adluri, ed., *Philosophy and Salvation in Greek Religion*, Berlin: de Gruyter, pp. 151–90.
Sayre, K. (1995). *Plato's Literary Garden: How to Read a Platonic Dialogue*, South Bend: University of Notre Dame Press.
Schofield, M. (1997). ΑΡΧΗ. *Hyperboreus*, 219–35.
   (2006). *Plato, Political Philosophy*, Oxford: Oxford University Press.
   (2007). Metaspeleology. In D. Scott, ed., *Maieusis: Essays in Ancient Philosophy in Honour of Myles Burnyeat*, Oxford: Oxford University Press, pp. 216–31.
Scott, D. (2015). *Levels of Argument: a Comparative Study of Plato's* Republic *and Aristotle's* Nicomachean Ethics, Oxford: Oxford University Press.
Sedley, D. (2007). Philosophy, the Forms, and the Art of Ruling. In G. R. F. Ferrari, ed., *The Cambridge Companion to Plato's Republic*, Cambridge: Cambridge University press, pp. 256–83.
   (2013). Socratic Intellectualism in the *Republic*'s Central Digression. In G. Boys-Stones, D. El Murr, and C. Gill, eds., *The Platonic Art of Philosophy*, Cambridge: Cambridge University Press, pp. 70–89.
   (2016). An Introduction to Plato's Theory of Forms. *Royal Institute of Philosophy Supplement* 78, 3–22.
Shields, C. (2007). Forcing Goodness in Plato's *Republic*. *Social Philosophy and Policy* 24, 21–39.
   (2008). Surpassing in Dignity and Power: the Metaphysics of Goodness in Plato's *Republic*. *Philosophical Inquiry* 30, 1–17.

Shorey, P. (1895). The Idea of the Good in Plato's *Republic*. *Classical Philology* 1, 188–239.

(1935). *The Republic*, with English translation, Loeb Classical Library, 2 vols., London: Heinemann.

Singpurwalla, R. (2006). Plato's Defense of Justice in the *Republic*. In G. Santas, ed., *Blackwell Guide to Plato's* Republic, Oxford: Blackwell, pp. 263–82.

Slings, S. (2003). *Platonis* Rempublicam *recognovit brevique adnotatione critica instruxit*. Oxford: Oxford University Press.

(2005). *Critical Notes on Plato's* Politeia, ed. G. Boter and J. van Ophuisen, Leiden: Brill.

Smith, N. (2018). Unclarity and the Intermediates in Plato's Discussions of Clarity in the *Republic*. *Plato Journal* 18, 97–110.

(2019). *Summoning Knowledge in Plato's* Republic, Oxford: Oxford University Press.

Stocks, J. L. (1911). The Divided Line of Plato *Rep*. VI. *Classical Quarterly* 5, 73–88.

Stroud, S. (2013). 'Good For' supra 'Good'. *Philosophy and Phenomenological Research* 87, 459–66.

Szlezák, T. A. (2001). L'idée du bien en tant qu'*archē* dans la *République* de Platon. In M. Fattal, ed., *La philosophie de Platon*, vol. I, Paris: L'Harmattan, pp. 345–72.

(2003). *Die Idee des Guten in Platons Politeia*, Sankt Augustin: Academic Verlag.

(2015). Are There Deliberately Left Gaps in Plato's Dialogues? In D. Nails and H. Tarrant, eds., *Second Sailing: Alternative Perspectives on Plato*. Helsinki: Societas Scientiarum Fennica, pp. 243–56.

Taylor, C. C. W. (2008). Plato's Epistemology. In G. Fine, ed., *The Oxford Handbook of Plato*. Oxford: Oxford University Press, pp. 165–94.

Thomson, J. (2008). *Normativity*, Chicago: Open Court.

Vegetti, M (2000). *Platone, Repubblica: traduzione a commento*, vol. IV, Naples: Bibliopolis.

(2001). Le règne philosophique. In M. Fattal, ed., *La philosophie de Platon*, vol. I, Paris: L'Harmattan, pp. 265–98.

(2003) ed. *La Repubblica: traduzione e commento*, vol. V, Naples: Bibliopolis.

(2005). Glaucon et les mystères de la dialectique. In M. Dixsaut and F. Teisseranc, eds., *Études sur la* République *de Platon* 2. Paris: Vrin, pp. 25–38.

(2007) ed. *La Repubblica: traduzione e commento*, vol. VII, Naples: Bibliopolis.

(2013a). *Beltista eiper dunata*: the Status of Utopia in the *Republic*. In M. Vegetti, F. Ferrari, and T. Lynch, eds., *The Painter of Constitutions: Selected Essays on Plato's* Republic, Sankt Augustin: Academia, pp. 105–22 = Essay A in Vegetti (2000), pp. 107–49.

(2013b). Dialectics: Configurations and Functions. In M. Vegetti, F. Ferrari, and T. Lynch, eds., *The Painter of Constitutions: Selected Essays on Plato's* Republic, Sankt Augustin: Academia, pp. 199–214 = Essay H in Vegetti (2003), pp. 405–34.

(2013c), *Megiston mathema*: the Idea of the Good and its Functions. In M. Vegetti, F. Ferrari, and T. Lynch eds., *The Painter of Constitutions: Selected Essays on Plato's* Republic, Sankt Augustin: Academia, pp. 137–54 = Essay D in Vegetti (2003), pp. 253–86.

Vlastos, G. (1973). The Individual as Object of Love in Plato. In G. Vlastos, ed., *Platonic Studies*, Princeton: Princeton University Press, pp. 3–42.

(1988). Elenchus and Mathematics: a Turning-Point in Plato's Philosophical Development. *American Journal of Philology* 109, 362–96.

Waterfield, R. (2008). *Plato: Republic, a New Translation*, Oxford: Oxford University Press.

Weiss, R. (2012). *Philosophers in the* Republic, Ithaca: Cornell University Press.

White, M. (2006). Plato and Mathematics. In H. Benson, ed., *A Companion to Plato*, Oxford: Blackwell, pp. 228–43.

White, N. (1976). *Plato on Knowledge and Reality*, Indianapolis: Hackett.

(2006). Plato's Concept of Goodness. In H. Benson, ed., *A Companion to Plato*, Oxford: Blackwell, pp. 356–72.

Wiggins, D. (2009). What Is the Order among the Varieties of Goodness? A Question Posed by Von Wright; and a Conjecture Made by Aristotle. *Philosophy* 84, 175–200.

Wolfsdorf, D. (2008). The Method ἐξ ὑποθεσέως at *Meno* 86e1–87d8. *Phronesis* 53, 35–64.

Yang, M.-H. (2005). The Relationship between Hypotheses and Images in the Mathematical Subsection of the Divided Line of Plato's *Republic*. *Dialogue* 44, 285–312.

Index of Passages

General Index

For EU product safety concerns, contact us at Calle de José Abascal, 56–1°, 28003 Madrid, Spain or eugpsr@cambridge.org.

www.ingramcontent.com/pod-product-compliance
Ingram Content Group UK Ltd.
Pitfield, Milton Keynes, MK11 3LW, UK
UKHW020354140625

459647UK00020B/2460